OUR ROOTS GROW DEEP

The Story of Rodale

Notice

Mention of specific companies, organizations, or authorities in this book does not imply endorsement by the publisher, nor does mention of specific companies, organizations, or authorities imply that they endorse this book.

Internet addresses and telephone numbers given in this book were accurate at the time it went to press.

Printed at Offset Impressions Inc. in Reading, Pennsylvania.
Bound at Hoster Bindery Inc. in Ivyland, Pennsylvania.

Rodale Inc. makes every effort to use acid-free ♾, recycled paper ♻.

Written by Daniel Gross

Book design by Eric Baker Design Associates

Cover design by Andy Carpenter

Cover photo © Dennis Chalkin. Please see page 272 for complete photography credits.

Illustrations © John Burgoyne

Library of Congress Cataloging-in-Publication Data

Our roots grow deep : the story of Rodale.
p. cm.
Includes index.
ISBN-13 978-1-59486-154-3 hardcover
ISBN-10 1-59486-154-4 hardcover
1. Rodale (Firm)–History. 2. Rodale, J. I. (Jerome Irving), 1898–1971. 3. Organic gardening–United States–History. 4. Physical fitness–United States–History.
SB453.5.O97 2008
338.7'6107050973–dc22 2008005152

2 4 6 8 10 9 7 5 3 1 hardcover

We inspire and enable people to improve their lives and the world around them

For more of our products visit **rodalestore.com** or call 800-848-4735

To all those who have helped Rodale grow
and who are working to make the world a greener, healthier place.

"We're interested in helping people to see their ability to achieve self-reliance. We keep the bottom line in perspective. It is important but so are many other things. American business could make money and still look out for the interest of all people, including future generations. Someone has to. We have to."

Robert Rodale, 1982

CONTENTS

THE ROOT OF IT ALL

THIS BOOK IS THE STORY of our family and business and is centered around the man who created Rodale Inc.—my grandfather, J. I. Rodale.

One of my earliest memories of my grandfather was a day when I was 4. I helped him unveil an organic maiden statue for a gathering of major supporters of the arts in Pennsylvania. Together we proudly pulled a red cloth from the standing nude bronze statue in front of friends and family.

As I write this, I am in my grandfather's library on the original organic farm. I can't help but be inspired as I sit at the same table where he wrote the articles, the plays, the magazines, and the books that are the foundation of our company. We've recently renovated my grandparents' home in hopes of keeping their spirit alive. Although we sit on new chairs at meetings here, their collections of books and art still surround us.

My parents, Robert and Ardath Rodale, built a house less than 200 yards from here on the farm for their growing family, and we (my sister Heather, brother David, and I) moved here in 1956. My parents were in their mid to late 20s. Located at the corner of Cedar Crest Boulevard and Minesite Road, the place was still farmland. We walked the fields; played in the gardens; ate fresh, sun-warmed strawberries and tomatoes in summer; painted fences; collected eggs; picked weeds, weeds, and more weeds. I learned to cook and paint from my energetically productive and creative grandmother.

I raised my own family half mile from here in an area known as the minehole where iron was excavated for steel more than 100 years ago. My two sons and their cousins have their own special memories of this place.

This place has seen many parties, birthdays, company clambakes, art shows, and even the funeral of my father, Robert Rodale, on one very memorable, sunny, warm September day in 1990. Hundreds of people came and walked the fields that day.

My brother David started this project and passed the baton to me more than 20 years ago. Although the book has not been easy to produce, it was a challenge I wholeheartedly embraced. We have a good story that needs to be told now.

In writing this book, we've tried to get the facts straight, but some of that is relative. Many people have stories to tell of their experiences knowing my family or working for Rodale. I encourage you to send them to me please! We will keep them for our future generations to read and remember what happened here.

I hope you enjoy this book. Let the story begin!

Heidi Rodale
April 2008

Manhattan's Lower East Side, an eastern European Jewish shtetl transplanted to New York, where J. I. Rodale was born in 1898

CHAPTER I

1898 TO 1922

The Birth of an American Dream

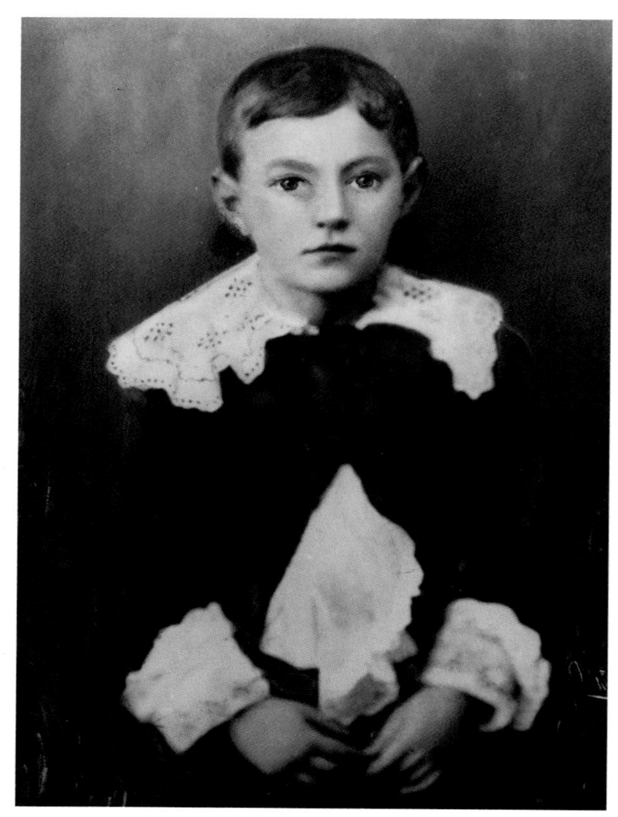

Yakov Cohen poses in finery for a formal picture.

JEROME IRVING COHEN was born on August 16, 1898, in the back of a tiny grocery store, in a Jewish shtetl that happened to be planted squarely in the crowded grid of Manhattan's Lower East Side. His parents, Michael and Becky Cohen, were among the millions of people from eastern and southern Europe who streamed into New York between 1880 and 1910. Just as immigrants had been doing for three centuries, they had crossed the Atlantic by ship to unknown shores to seek a new life. In his first 25 years, the child who spent a great deal of his youth in religious study would grow into a young American man. First known by the Hebrew name, Yakov, he then became Jerome Cohen, and finally J. I. Rodale–a professional accountant, occasional writer, budding entrepreneur, and ebullient soul.

Michael Cohen, J.I.'s father: Jerome and his siblings chafed at their father's strict orthodoxy.

Michael Cohen, born in Poland (most likely in Lodz) in 1864, fled as a teenager "to avoid military service in the Polish army" and joined his four sisters in London's Jewish Whitechapel section. Two years later they all came to New York, and Michael settled on the Lower East Side, a 2-mile-square district of tenements, sweatshops, noise, and commerce, densely populated with Yiddish-speaking Jewish immigrants.

Michael was a cap contractor by trade—he hired girls and women to sell caps for 20 cents each. One of his employees was Bertha Rouda, known as Becky, a Polish-Jewish immigrant with a "peaches and cream complexion." Born in 1871, she had arrived in New York at the age of 6 or 7 among the earlier waves of eastern European immigration. "It was the equivalent of coming over on the Jewish *Mayflower,*" J. I. Rodale recalled in his richly evocative unpublished autobiography, *The Promised Land.* "She graduated from elementary school and spoke a fine English with an uptown accent." They were married in the late 1880s. When a cap industry strike crippled his business, Michael opened a grocery. The rapidly growing family took up residence behind the store, at 47 Norfolk Street. The Cohens had a child roughly every two years, starting in 1890. First came two sons, Aaron (Archie) and Solomon; then a daughter, Tina; then another son, Joseph; and then Jerome Irving in 1898, followed by another son, Rubin, and two daughters, Sally and Estelle.

The grocery, about 10 feet by 40 feet, stood on the same block as the Beth Hamidrash Hagadol—literally, "the large synagogue"—a former Baptist church that became home to a large Jewish congregation in 1885. "The store was a boy's heaven, with its shelves bulging with nuts, cookies . . ." J.I. recalled. In the crowded apartment, the parents spoke Yiddish to one another and English to the children. "Father never lost that tiny tinge of English accent he acquired in the few years he spent in the London ghetto," observed J.I. Since Becky worked in the store, "we boasted the unheard of luxury of a servant, a girl who was just off the boat."

Bertha Rouda Cohen was an immigrant, a working mother, and an inspiration to her eight children.

For young Jerome Cohen—he was called by the diminutive Yiddish Yeinkeleh—childhood was a mixture of happy discovery and frequently grinding duty. "For the most part of my

1898
New York annexes land from surrounding counties, creating the City of Greater New York. The city is geographically divided into five boroughs: Manhattan, Brooklyn, Queens, the Bronx, and Staten Island.

February 15: The USS *Maine* explodes and sinks in Havana Harbor, Cuba, killing more than 260. This event helps lead the United States to declare war on Spain. Contaminated meat kills more U.S. troops than do bullets during the Spanish-American War. The public demands government regulation of meatpacking industry.

August 16: Jerome Irving Cohen is born on Manhattan's Lower East Side.

Cancer Lab is established at New York State Pathological Laboratory in Buffalo.

The Cohen family, early 1900s. ***From left, standing:*** **Joseph, Tina, Aaron, and Solomon;** ***sitting:*** **Michael, Jerome, Sally, and Bertha, with Estelle on her lap**

1899

February 12: International six-day, two-man team bicycle race takes place in New York City.

Pure-food bill is defeated in the U.S. Senate.

Cholera epidemic begins and spreads throughout much of the world, continuing until 1924.

March 2: Mount Rainier National Park is established in Washington State.

July 18: Rags-to-riches author Horatio Alger Jr. dies.

Horatio Alger Jr.

Agreement made this 27th day of July, 1912, by and between the Rzerzower Verbruderungs Verein, a religious corporation of the State of New York, party of the first part and Jacob Cohen of the same place, party of the second part:

Whereas the party of the second part is by profession an Alto Singer, and the party of the first part is a religious corporation conducting religious services at its synogogue at No. 68-70 Willett Street, City, the parties hereto agree as follows:-

That the party of the second part agree to render services as an Alto Singer in the Choir at the said services to be conducted by the party of the first part, on all the Jewish Holidays hereinafter mentioned in the year 1912, as follows: Sleuceeth Night, Rosh Hashonah two days, Yom Kippur Eve and Yom Kippur Suxxuth first two days, and last three days, and Simcath Torah Eve; that is the party of the second part is to render said services at said times in conjunction and together with the choir.

That doe said services the party of the second part is to receive the sum of $50. to be paid to him as follows : $ 40 00/100 on Yom Kipper night and the balance on Sucketh night

That the said party of the second part agrees not to render similar services during said times aforementioned in behalf of any other person or persons, other than the party of the first part.

In Witness Whereof the parties hereto have hereunto set their hands and seals the day and year first above written.

In presence of:

Michael Cohen

Rzeszower Verbruderungs Verein

by H. Schiff

President.

Jacob I. Cohen

childhood, I was under the knuckles of my father, who picked me for higher things." That meant becoming a learned Jew and an accomplished performer of Jewish rituals. When Jerome was 6, "my father thought he detected singing qualities in my voice so he turned me over to the choir leader of our congregation." At 11, Jerome essentially turned professional singer, becoming the alto soloist at Beth Hamidrash Hagadol. He was also a member of a choir that sang at weddings and funerals, which gave him a rare glimpse of bucolic surroundings. "The cemeteries were located in the wilds of Long Island, Jamaica, Cypress Hills, Ridgewood, and even Staten Island," he recalled. "It was my first exciting glimpse of country life, where I saw cows, green fields, barns and hay-stacks." A contract from July 1912 shows that Jacob (Yakov in Yiddish) Cohen–"by profession an Alto Singer"–was to be paid $50 for singing the High Holidays at the Rzerzower Verbruderun Verein, a nearby synagogue. Tickets printed in Yiddish from the same year invited listeners to come hear "the 14 year old boy-chazan, Yakov Cohen" at Beit Hagadol. The price of admission: 15 cents.

5)

Michael Cohen, who couldn't read English, was of medium height, with "black hair, a commanding nose, and one eye half brown and half grey," according to J.I. He was rigid and uncompromising, a man of austere tastes. "On extremely rare occasions when Caruso sang, he went to the opera with my uncle Barnet Rouda and sat in the seventh gallery." And he was not to be defied. "He was a man of iron and as a parent, relentless as a tidal wave." While Jerome inherited many of his father's physical features, his gentle temperament was more akin to that of his mother. He was closest to his brother Joseph, who was two years older.

A talented alto singer, Yakov Cohen began singing professionally in Jewish choirs as a young boy, performing at High Holiday services, as this contract stipulates.

1900
American car companies make 1,681 steam, 1,575 electric, and 936 gasoline cars.

Joseph Pernet-Ducher develops the yellow hybrid rose, "Soleil d'Or."

Illiteracy falls to a record low: 10.7 percent of the U.S. population.

Ferdinand von Zeppelin builds the first successful airship.

Kodak introduces the first Brownie camera.

The Zeppelin airship

Tickets, written in Yiddish, for a performance by the "boy singer" Yakov Cohen at a synagogue on the Lower East Side. The price of admission: 15 cents

After school, Jerome would spend afternoons at a Dickensian Hebrew school. Housed in a building that also contained a vest-making enterprise and a dry cleaner and reeked of benzene, the school was run by a tyrannical red-bearded teacher whom Jerome and his friends called Red Donkey. "Red Donkey cruelly pounded the Bible into our unregenerated minds," he wrote. The teacher may have been filled with fury because his effort to cultivate a centuries-old lifestyle in the alien soil of America was a losing battle. "Most of the boys were beginning to take to the ways of America: to baseball, trips to the menagerie, picture cards, shooting dice and smoking," J. I. Rodale wrote. "The old Bible didn't stand a chance."

The acculturation took place in New York City's public schools. First Jerome attended nearby P.S. 62, later known as Seward Park Middle School. But it also took place on Norfolk Street. "Inside the houses it was Europe. In the street it was America." At first, Jerome's universe was largely confined to the grocery and nearby blocks: "Our block was a village within a village." In the jewelry store next door was Mr. Gold, a "free thinker" who clashed with the "militantly religious" Michael Cohen. Also next door lived the Axelrod family, neighbors for 20 years. The neighborhood drunk, Jim, performed Shabbat tasks. Across the street, at 56 Norfolk, lived a family that ran a small umbrella store. "We called the father Umbrella-Shteken [umbrella stick] and their dog, Umbrella-Shteken's dog." In 58 Norfolk lived Big Jack Zelig, a well-known gangster. The building was also home to Louis Ludwig, Jerome's best friend from the age of 8, and Tanta (Aunt) Zelda Brown, Becky Cohen's oldest sister, who helped watch the Cohen children.

To young Jerome, the known universe expanded only slightly beyond the confines of Norfolk Street. Two blocks away, on Essex Street between Grand and Hester, was the delicatessen Isaac Gellis, where kids could buy frankfurters for a penny. And the warren of narrow streets of the Lower East Side hosted a "variegated kaleidoscope of street corner activities which sometimes took

1901
February 25: J. P. Morgan incorporates the U.S. Steel Corporation.

March: Group of New York conservationists proposes the Hudson River Palisades be a park. The Rockefeller family, which owns most of the land, supports and adds a parkway to the proposal.

September 6: Anarchist Leon Czolgosz shoots and fatally wounds President William McKinley in Buffalo.

December 12: Guglielmo Marconi receives the first transatlantic radio signal in Newfoundland, Canada.

1902
January 28: The Carnegie Institution is founded in Washington, D.C., with a $10 million gift from Andrew Carnegie.

April 2: Electric Theatre, the first movie theater in the United States, opens in Los Angeles.

Biologist Jacques Loeb pioneers bioengineering.

Andrew Carnegie

Michael Cohen, a stern and devoutly religious man, operated a grocery store on the Lower East Side.

on the air of an untented circus." Pushcarts everywhere sold hot knishes, sweet potatoes, and cantaloupes. Jerome's paternal grandfather "had a pushcart on which he sold only caps" and lived alone in a small apartment on Attorney Street, about three blocks away.

Like many immigrants, the family struggled financially in the early part of the 20th century. "Father couldn't keep the grocery store running without the generosity and open hand of Uncle Abe Lipman." Alfred (Abe) Lipman, who had married Michael's younger sister, Rose, was a successful furrier and lived uptown on Riverside Drive. Twice a year, Michael would take his books to Lipman, who would sign notes enabling Michael Cohen to draw funds from the Corn Exchange Bank. "Lankevitzky, the money-lender, was called in only in desperate situations." Michael Cohen started a men's furnishings store on Grand Street, but it failed. And for a period, the family made toots—folded paper bags in which small quantities of loose items like pepper and sugar were sold. Michael took out many of his frustrations on the children. "He would rain frightful blows at one of us and then suffer unspeakable agony, breathing dangerously fast, as if he were going to pass out."

The boys in particular chafed at the occasionally harsh regime. Archie ran away from home and worked as a farmhand. Sol, "after he had received an unusually severe beating from father," hopped a freight train. He returned, but "ran away again later for good and did not return until father died." In 1915, Joseph joined the cavalry and served on the Mexican border. When he was about 14, Jerome ran away. "My curriculum was becoming so overcrowded and life such a monotonous grind that I decided to go away from it all." On a hot summer's day, he donned several layers of clothes and took a train to see his brother Archie, who was working at the Gulden's pickle factory in Deer Park, Long Island. "I took long walks in the fields and down country lanes. I listened to the music of the babbling brook, to the song of the birds and the rustle of the leaves." After a few days, he returned home.

The country offered a brief respite from the gray, clangorous mass of life in the city, from the busy routine of work, school, choir practice, and intensive Jewish study. For Jerome, the routine didn't end after his voice dropped and he had completed his Bar Mitzvah, as it did for most Jewish boys. His father prodded him to become a "lehner"—the person who sings the weekly Torah portion.

1903
Publisher Joseph Pulitzer gives $2 million to establish Columbia University School of Journalism, a portion of which is used to establish the Pulitzer Prizes.

Theodore Roosevelt makes Pelican Island off the Florida coast the first federal wildlife sanctuary.

July 1 to 19: First Tour de France bicycle race won by Maurice Garin.

Jack London's *The Call of the Wild* is serialized in the *Saturday Evening Post.*

Antoine-Henri Becquerel and Pierre and Marie Curie win Nobel Prize in Physics for discovering radioactivity.

1904
February 17: Puccini's *Madame Butterfly* debuts in Milan.

April 30: World's Fair opens in Saint Louis.

October 27: First New York City subway line opens.

First subway train

At the turn of the century, the Lower East Side, a crowded, vibrant neighborhood bursting with life, culture, and ambition, was the Yiddish-English crucible in which Jerome Cohen grew up.

DAIRY
RESTAURANT
LENA KARP
SERVANTS OFFICE
POLSKI BIURO
DAIRY RESTAURANT
182
DAIRY
RESTAURANT

Jerome's father tried his hand at several retail businesses, including a men's clothing store.

1905
Gifford Pinchot, chief forester of the USDA, is appointed to head the newly formed U.S. Forest Service.

National Audubon Society is formed.

Anna Andrews is born in Mahanoy City, Pennsylvania.

1906
President Roosevelt signs the Pure Food and Drug Act and the Meat Inspection Act.

April 18: Earthquake destroys much of San Francisco.

British biochemist Frederick Hopkins suggests the existence of vitamins.

1907
The number of new books published in one year rises to a record 9,620.

Ivan Pavlov demonstrates conditioned responses in salivating dogs.

Rudyard Kipling, best known for *The Jungle Book* and *Just So Stories*, is awarded Nobel Prize in Literature.

Rudyard Kipling

And once he had mastered the tropes, Michael Cohen "determined now to set me on the road to the rabbinate." As a teenager, Jerome would spend afternoons at a Talmudic seminary. "Did I cover myself with sack-cloth and ashes and bemoan the harsh jobs of an evil fate which set me apart from other boys and which robbed me of the golden childhood days which the poet sings about? Yes, I am afraid I did, and it made a man of me before my time. I recall that it gave me a demon-like urge to grow up so that I could be on my own; it made the fires of ambition burn savagely in my breast."

Jerome slowly ventured from the environment of the Lower East Side, which was simultaneously nurturing and stifling. In 1913 he entered DeWitt Clinton, a public high school at 59th Street and 10th Avenue on Manhattan's West Side. This would be "the first step in a metamorphosis in which I would finally turn into, not a frog, but a rounded-out citizen who could think like the average native American." Every morning, he would walk to Allen Street, take the Second Avenue elevated train downtown to the Battery, then switch to the el running up Ninth Avenue. "Five delicious miles spent in studying and dreaming.... This was the happy springtime of my life, when I made new friends, beheld new scenes, and came under the spell of warm-hearted and understanding teachers." At first, however, he did poorly. His first year, completed January 14, showed high marks in drawing (93) but lower marks in biology (78) and elocution (70). He failed several subjects, which he ascribed to poor eyesight.

Jerome may have been distracted that first year by his father's declining health. Chronically overweight, Michael Cohen suffered from kidney trouble and had a heart condition. Bedridden since late 1913, he died March 27, 1914, at the age of 50. "I never realized until his funeral what a well-thought-of man he was on the East Side," J. I. Rodale recalled. "The turnout was so terrific that the police reserves had to be called out to keep order." But for 15-year-old Jerome Cohen, it was liberating. "When father died, I immediately seceded from synagogic activities," he recalled. "My wonderful mother offered little opposition."

Freed of his Jewish learning responsibilities and equipped with glasses, Jerome devoted himself to schoolwork. "The plan I embarked upon entailed the doing of four years of schoolwork

Becky Cohen *(right)* and her sisters

1908
January 1: A ball signifying New Year's Day drops in New York City's Times Square.

Theodore Roosevelt holds the first Conservation Conference at the White House. Officials include state governors.

Henry Ford produces the first Model T.

1909
January 16: Ernest Shackleton's expedition finds the magnetic South Pole.

Harvard Classics book series is first published.

Ernest Shackleton

March 7: First Arbor Day in California held in honor of the botanist Luther Burbank.

September 27: President William Howard Taft establishes 3 million western acres for national park land.

U.S. Bureau of Soils calls soil "the one resource that cannot be exhausted."

in two and a half years." The grades improved dramatically in his second and third years, when he regularly scored 90 percent and above, and he graduated in 1916.

As he grew older, Jerome had more time to explore the city. On Sundays, he and Louis would go to Van Cortlandt Park, in the Bronx. At home, he tried to replicate the wondrous activities he saw in nature. "Dozens of times I planted flower seeds but never could get them to the flowering stage." Much to the chagrin of his mother, Jerome continually tried to raise pets in the cramped apartment. He also sent away for instructions on how to grow mushrooms. "I had a conference with mother explaining to her that I had chosen my life's work and had decided to become a mushroom grower." But she wouldn't let him grow mushrooms under the bed because they needed manure.

Jerome had always worked–in the grocery, delivering goods, and as a singer. But as a teenager with a widowed mother and several younger siblings, he was expected to make a more significant contribution. During summers in high school, he collected installments for Singer sewing machines, sold colored Christmas tree bulbs, and worked as a stock runner on Wall Street. This latter post "whetted my appetite to set sail in the dangerous shoals and rocky waters of Wall Street," J. I. Rodale later recalled. While still a high school student, he started trading stocks. "The upshot of my financial operations amounted to the crushing loss of all the money with which I was speculating, about 100 dollars over a period of a year." He also invested money on behalf of the family's "servant girl," who entrusted him with $1,000–which he promptly lost. Jerome and his mother agreed to pay her back, which forced him to take a loan. "It took a few years and taught me thrift." Responding to an advertisement for land on Staten Island, Jerome and Louis "purchased two lots jointly for 30 dollars." When a highway was built close to the lots several years later, values rose. "I sold my share for about 300 dollars. It was my first taste of easy money."

When he completed high school in 1916, Jerome was determined to make his way–even if he wasn't quite sure where his ambitions lay. First, he decided to become an accountant, in part because he had read a biography of John D. Rockefeller, "who said that the fact that he had been a bookkeeper had much to do with the accumulation of his riches." In the fall of 1916, Jerome started

1910
January 13: In the first live musical radio program, radio pioneer Lee De Forest broadcasts a performance of Enrico Caruso from the Metropolitan Opera.

May 6: George V becomes King of the United Kingdom upon the death of his father, Edward VII.

Social reformer Jane Addams publishes *Twenty Years at Hull House*.

1911
President Taft dedicates the New York Public Library.

March 25: Fire at the Triangle Shirt-waist Factory in New York City kills 146 sweatshop workers.

Jane Addams

May 2: IBM incorporates as Computing-Tabulating-Recording Company in New York.

German scientists isolate a bacterium, *Bacillus thuringiensis*, that later becomes a significant player in the organic control of insects.

After graduating from DeWitt Clinton High School in 1916, Jerome Cohen found work as an accountant. In 1919, he would move to Washington, D.C., to work for the Bureau of Internal Revenue.

Record at DeWitt Clinton High School 2.

Music	40 weeks;	1 per. per wk:	70%
Phys. Train	40 " ;	2 " " ";	75%

Third year completed in Jan. 1916

English	40 weeks;	3 per. per wk:	83%
French	40 " ;	5 " " ";	91%
History	40 " ;	3 " " ";	90%
Algebra	20 " ;	5 " " ";	70%
Phys. Tr.	20 " ;	2 " " ";	70%

Fourth year completed in June 1916

English	40 weeks;	3 per. per wk;	73%
History	40 " ;	3 " " ";	88%
Physics	40 " ;	6 " " ";	78%
Trigonometry	20 " ;	5 " " ";	65%
Elocution	20 " ;	1 " " ";	75%

* Jerome I. Rodale completed a 4 yr. course in 3½ years.

1912
March 7: Roald Amundsen announces discovery of the South Pole.

April 15: The *Titanic* sinks.

September 25: Columbia University Graduate School of Journalism founded. Vitamin A is discovered.

Titanic

1913
February 2: New York's Grand Central Station opens.

February 3: The 16th Amendment to the U.S. Constitution is ratified, authorizing a federal income tax.

May 14: Rockefeller Foundation's charter is approved.

May 29: Igor Stravinsky's ballet *The Rite of Spring* premieres in Paris.

Cancer is recognized as a leading cause of death. Educating people becomes a mainstay in helping to prevent the disease and to recognize its symptoms.

Jerome Cohen enters DeWitt Clinton High School.

NEW YORK UNIVERSITY 47 Norfolk St.
SCHOOL OF COMMERCE
ACCOUNTS AND FINANCE

REPORT OF GRADES

For Re-exam Term — September 1918. School Year 1917-18.

NAME Cohen, Jerome I.

The passing mark is 60%. A minimum final average of 70% in all subjects is required for graduation.

Name of Course	No.	Grade	Name of Course	No.	Grade
ACCOUNTING			JOURNALISM		
ADV. and M'R'K'T'G			LAW		
ENGLISH			MANAGEMENT		
ECONOMICS					
FINANCE	1	(87) 70	METHODS		
	2	70 (81)			
GEOGRAPHY			SOCIOLOGY		
GOVERNMENT			TRADE and TRANS.		
Failed * Repeat †			LANGUAGES		

While working full-time, Jerome Cohen took accounting and finance courses at Columbia University and New York University from 1916 through 1918. He didn't earn a degree.

taking evening courses at New York University—borrowing money from Uncle Abe Lipman. "I passed the year's work by the skin of my teeth," with scores mostly in the 70s. He performed best in political economy, receiving a 95 in his first term.

During the day, he had a series of short-term bookkeeping jobs: for a wholesale newspaper delivering agency, an auto fender works in Brooklyn, a secondhand mattress processor, a "petty banker," and a ladies' hat frame business owned by some cousins. At a ladies' hosiery company, "I learned more bookkeeping here in two months than I did at New York University in a year."

When the New York University academic year ended in the spring of 1917, he took courses for four months at Columbia University, moving to a "cubbyhole in Livingston Hall on the campus" to enjoy the college atmosphere. But in the fall of 1917 he received an appointment as a temporary bookkeeper in the New York City Department of Finance and was assigned to the Bureau of Municipal Investigation and Statistics in Queens. The pay: $4 a day. This post constituted another step out into the broader world. Although Queens was only a few miles from the Lower East Side, it was a world away from Norfolk Street and the other jobs he had known. At the age of 19, Jerome was "thrown in with Irishmen, Englishmen, Jews and Swedes, some old enough to be my grandfather." Here he made some of his first non-Jewish friends, chief among them Thomas Hanley.

Jerome's college coursework tended to focus on practical aspects of accounting and finance. But he possessed a wide-ranging, if undisciplined, sense of curiosity about the world. A keen observer of his own life and his surroundings, he soaked up information. And he continually pursued learning and information in the forms that were available to him. A habitual orderer of mail-order products and get-rich-quick schemes, he tended to read advertisements uncritically.

1914
January 5: Ford announces an eight-hour workday and a minimum wage of $5 for a day's labor.

March: Michael Cohen (Jerome's father) dies.

The pasteurization of milk begins in large cities.

September 26: The U.S. Federal Trade Commission (FTC) is established by the Federal Trade Commission Act.

November 7: The first issue of the *New Republic* magazine is published.

1915
January 12: Rocky Mountain National Park is established by an act of Congress.

February 8: D. W. Griffith's controversial film *The Birth of a Nation* premieres.

Albert Einstein publishes his general theory of relativity.

Congress creates the National Park Service in order to manage the swelling number of visitors to the nation's 13 national parks.

In *The Holy Earth*, Liberty Hyde Bailey writes of nature's intrinsic value and humans' responsibility to learn about and care for the earth.

Joseph Cohen joins the Army.

"My bible was the glowing advertising sections of the slick-papered magazines that spoke to me in dulcet accents, that advised me in a fatherly manner, that guided my feet in the path they should tread in the ups and downs of life."

Jerome Cohen seemed to be on a direct path—working as an accountant by day, studying accounting and finance by night. But it was an uncertain time. Once the United States entered World War I in April 1917, a draft was instituted. In 1918 the draft was expanded to include men between ages 18 and 45, which made Jerome potentially eligible. "I would have been among the first to go, as my serial number was drawn 496th," he wrote. His brother Joe, in early 1918, was training in Chickamauga, Georgia. "Say, Jerry, whatever you do, don't ever get a notion and enlist as war is hell. We are having no fun here; the chow (meaning *food*) we are getting now is just rotten." Joe emphasized the hardship that leaving would exert on their mother, who was running the grocery. A month later, Joe was packed up and prepared to leave for Europe. "Don't tell this to Ma ... I took out a $10,000 war policy so if I get killed in action Ma will get $5 a month for 20 years."

Jerome tracked the progress of the war closely—he had a big war map on the wall in his room at Columbia. And Joe gave him regular updates. "While at the front we supplied the artillery and infantry with ammo," he wrote from France in July 1918. "By the looks of things Germany must be all in. They are retreating so fast they have no time to bury their dead." Several weeks later he reported that "we have the Huns on the run." Joe and his company had shot down a low-flying German plane with their rifles, and in a captured German dugout, he found a prayer book that was "half German and half Jewish."

Jerome was intent on figuring out a way to continue with his studies and work, while avoiding the service. He tried to get a job with a company in a "war industry" to gain an exemption and applied for the Student Army Training Corps. (He was rejected in September 1918 due to poor eyesight.) Throughout the fall, he bounced between his job with the city and private sector jobs. He registered at New York University and canceled a week later. In October 1918 he applied for a position with the Office of the Alien Property Custodian, in Washington, D.C., where his friend Louis

An ambitious and intellectually curious young man, Jerome Cohen was eager to explore the world beyond the Lower East Side.

1916
January 28: Louis D. Brandeis becomes the first Jewish judge appointed to the U.S. Supreme Court.

May 20: *The Saturday Evening Post* publishes its first cover with a Norman Rockwell painting.

Monet paints *Water Lilies.*

Japanese beetles, having hitched a ride into the United States on the roots of shrubs from Japan, spread throughout eastern United States.

Water Lilies

Jerome Cohen takes courses at New York University.

November 7: Jeannette Rankin of Montana becomes the first woman elected to the U.S. House of Representatives.

was living. Jerome was intent on leaving New York to take a government job. "How cold does it get in Washington in the winter time and are there any ponds for ice-skating?"

But amid all the short-term planning, Jerome Cohen seemed to have developed a long-term plan—one that involved neither New York nor Washington. "I started thinking again about the farm and my mind was never as made up as it was last night," he wrote to Louis. He was concerned that "if I stay in the accounting game until I am 40—if I live so long—I will be as blind as a dormouse.... My intentions at present are to stick to accounting until a favorable opportunity presents itself for going into business (probably both of us will go into it) and then as soon as I or we can accumulate enough money, say at about the age of 30 or even sooner, to get out as much as we can to God's Land."

He continued, as well, to try to amass more capital by trading stocks, but it went poorly. "Well, this is absolutely the end of my career on the N.Y. Curb," he wrote to Louis, after detailing a $158 loss on Northwest Oil stock. Sounding a lament heard many times since, Jerome wrote: "The insiders are the only ones who make the dough."

In late November 1918, his job with the city ended. "I tried to get into the big accounting houses but it seems they don't employ Jews," he told Louis. "Since the draft and since two weeks ago when the socialists and Bolsheviki have been making some trouble in Madison Square Garden, they believe every Jew is a Socialist and a Bolshevik." He took the civil service test, did well, and awaited word from Washington. Intent on finding more regular work, Jerome placed an advertisement in the *New York Times.* Within a few days, he was hired by an accounting firm run by J. Kleinman, at $25 a week. On November 11, he was undergoing a draft board medical examination when he heard news of the armistice.

For the time being, he decided to stay in New York. But in early 1919, he was walking down Grand Street with Louis, heading toward the East River. When they reached Attorney Street, Louis wanted to turn and Jerome wanted to go straight. Louis won the argument. And it proved fateful. For they soon ran into Charlie Abramowitz, a friend from the neighborhood who told them that the government was hiring auditors in Washington at a salary of $36 a week. "A few days later I was

1917
April 6: The United States declares war on Germany.

June 4: First Pulitzer Prizes are awarded. Herbert Swope of the *New York World* receives the first Pulitzer Prize for Journalism.

Herbert Swope *(center)*

Jerome Cohen appointed temporary bookkeeper for the city of New York Department of Finance.

November 7: Bolshevik leader Vladimir Lenin leads a coup in Russia.

Vitamin D is isolated from cod liver oil.

Vladimir Lenin

CITY OF NEW YORK
DEPARTMENT OF FINANCE
CHARLES L. CRAIG, COMPTROLLER
CHARLES F. KERRIGAN, SECRETARY TO THE DEPARTMENT

LOUIS H. HAHLO, DEPUTY COMPTROLLER
JOSEPH JOHNSON, DEPUTY COMPTROLLER
ARTHUR J. PHILBIN, DEPUTY COMPTROLLER
FRANK J. PRIAL, ASSISTANT DEPUTY COMPTROLLER

IN REPLYING REFER TO

October. 26. 1918

To whom it may concern:

I take pleasure in recommending the bearer, Mr Jerome Cohen, as an industrious, capable, and conscientious worker. I have known him for about 12 months, and he has worked in this department under my supervision during that period. He is very rapid in his work and quick to learn. I believe him to be very patriotic — as he has invested his savings in Liberty Bonds + contributes monthly to the Red Cross through this department.

Yours very truly
Wm. H. Ivimey, Accountant

Jerome Cohen's first full-time job was as an accountant at the New York Department of Finance, where he impressed his boss as an "ambitious, capable, and conscientious worker."

1918
Victory Gardeners conserve resources and plant front-yard food crops to support the war effort.

May 15: The Post Office begins the first regular airmail service in the world (between New York City and Washington, D.C.).

Early airmail stamp

July 16: Bolsheviks execute Czar Nicholas II of Russia and his family.

August: Spanish flu epidemic starts, killing more than 21 million people in six months.

November 11: World War I ends as Germany signs an armistice agreement with the Allies.

Czar Nicholas II

down at the Custom House undergoing an oral examination. The need for men was so urgent that applicants were being rated only on their qualifications based on their actual experience."

The Bureau of Internal Revenue had a great need for accountants. The first individual income tax had been passed in 1913, with low rates, topping out at 7 percent. But as war preparations increased, rates rose rapidly. By 1917 the top rate was 67 percent. The first permanent corporate income tax had been enacted in 1909 and similarly rose during the war. With the government's wartime need for revenue, and with the growing complexity of the tax code and tax returns, accountants were in demand.

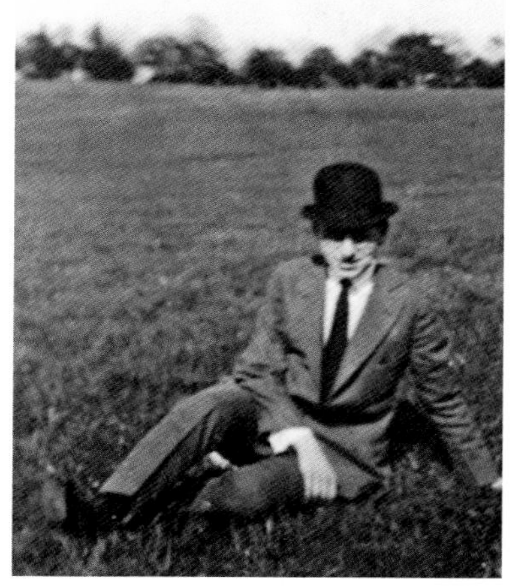

Jerome enjoyed exploring his new environment while working in Washington, D.C.

In February 1919, Jerome Cohen received an appointment to become an auditor in the Income Tax Unit of the Bureau of Internal Revenue at a salary of $1,600 per year, plus a bonus. Louis had taken a job in Washington previously, so Jerome got a room in the boardinghouse where he lived. Then Louis got a job in New York with a company that made silk-weaving machines, so Jerome moved into the same boardinghouse as Tom Hanley, who had also received an appointment. Jerome settled into the area northeast of Capitol Hill, at 630 Lexington Place NE. Although he was away from home, Jerome went to a temple on Eighth and I Street NW every Friday night for services and took his Passover meal at Freemans, a Jewish restaurant. But he continued to explore and experiment with his newfound freedom, living in a place where he wasn't necessarily constrained by geography or religion. He started smoking a pipe, joined the Elks Club, and took long walks on the Cabin John Canal. At nights he would go to the Congressional Library, "reading up on the higher points of corporate organization and finance."

At work, he started in the personal audit section–reviewing individual returns. After a month he transferred to the Miscellaneous Audit Division, which handled more sophisticated corporate projects. While the job was demanding, it left time for him to learn. "I must say that I have it all velvet down here. Any time of the day that I choose I can just lay off my work and read for hours at a time." By the end of the year, he was in the Consolidated Returns Section of the Technical Division. "I have some great news! I have been detailed together with another man to go

1919
January 16: The 18th Amendment to the U.S. Constitution, authorizing Prohibition, goes into effect.

February 5: Charlie Chaplin, Mary Pickford, Douglas Fairbanks Sr., and D. W. Griffith launch United Artists.

Prohibition arrest

February 26: An act of the U.S. Congress establishes most of the Grand Canyon as a U.S. National Park.

February: Jerome Cohen gets a job as an auditor with the Bureau of Internal Revenue in Washington, D.C.

Kellogg's starts marketing All-Bran breakfast cereal.

In 1919, after receiving an appointment to the newly formed Bureau of Internal Review, Jerome Cohen joined his childhood friend Louis Ludwig in Washington, D.C. He relished the freedom and possibilities to explore the world beyond New York.

OFFICE OF
COMMISSIONER OF INTERNAL REVENUE

ADDRESS REPLY TO
COMMISSIONER OF INTERNAL REVENUE
AND REFER TO

TREASURY DEPARTMENT

WASHINGTON

IT:HSP-St

February 19, 1919.

Mr. Jerome Cohen,
47 Norfolk St.,
New York, N. Y.

Dear Sir:

Recommendation for your appointment in an auditing capacity to the Income Tax Unit, Bureau of Internal Revenue, for service in Washington, D.C. at $1600, per annum, has just been made.

It is understood that this carries in addition the annual bonus granted by Congress.

You will, no doubt, receive official notification ... appointment within the next ... ch time it is suggested that ... touch with this office to ... date to take up the new duties, ... r inability to enter the ser-

Very truly yours,

Horner G. Pace

Acting Deputy Commissioner.

CLASS OF SERVICE	SYMBOL
Day Message	
Day Letter	Blue
Night Message	Nite
Night Letter	N L

If none of these three symbols appears after the check (number of words) this is a day message. Otherwise its character is indicated by the symbol appearing after the check.

WESTERN UNION TELEGRAM

NEWCOMB CARLTON, PRESIDENT — GEORGE W. E. ATKINS, FIRST VICE-PRESIDENT

CLASS OF SERVICE	SYMBOL
Day Message	
Day Letter	Blue
Night Message	Nite
Night Letter	N L

If none of these three symbols appears after the check (number of words) this is a day message. Otherwise its character is indicated by the symbol appearing after the check.

RECEIVED AT

GOVT RUSH

1918 NOV 26 PM 10 46

F273W 57 GOVT NITE

WA WASHINGTON DC 26

JEROME COHEN

47 NORFOLK ST NEW YORK CITY

IF NOT IN GOVERNMENT SERVICE AND WILL ACCEPT APPOINTMENT CLERK QUALIFIED IN ACCOUNTING GOVERNMENT MUNITION PLANT OUTSIDE OF WASHINGTON TWELVE HUNDRED DOLLARS PER ANNUM REPORT FOR DUTY EARLY AS POSSIBLE CIVILIAN PERSONNEL SECTION FOUR FIFTY ONE PENNSYLVANIA AVENUE WIRE WHEN WILL REPORT

GIBSON CIVILAIN PERSONNEL TWO SIX FIVE ARMY ORDNANCE.

to New York and examine the books and accounts of the *Standard Oil Company of N.Y.!* Some job!" His salary was boosted to $2,250 a year, plus a $240 bonus. Within a year, the young accountant, accustomed to dealing with largely marginal businesses, had become engaged with the world's largest and most powerful corporation.

Since there was a great demand for income tax expertise, Jerome was offered positions in the private sector. His boss wanted to move to San Francisco and open offices as income tax experts, and he received an offer from the *Merchants Trade Journal,* which evaluated income tax returns. But Jerome was homesick. "All I can see on my map now is lil ole New Yawk where I want to be with my family." All his siblings had remained in New York, and several of them had married and started their own families. "In the last three weeks Archie's wife gave birth to a girl, Sol's wife to a boy, and Tina to a girl," he wrote to Louis. "I am an uncle to five." Becky Cohen was still running the store on Norfolk Street, although she would later move to the Bronx.

Still, Jerome was highly ambitious. In one autobiography, he said he had a vague but insistent recollection of being chased. "All my life I have been on the running end. Something is always chasing me into doing something." And after a year in government service, in March 1920, he joined the accounting firm of Robertson, Furman, which had offices in New York and Pittsburgh, starting at a salary of $3,600 per year. He was immediately sent to Pittsburgh—another step into the larger world. "My first job is an Allegheny Steel return for 1919, while I am working on a claim for overpayment of tax in 1917," he told Louis. "The corporation paid a tax of $3,500,000 in 1917 and I will see if I can't have a measly million or so refunded to them."

This new post afforded him an opportunity to continue to expand his horizons. He spent a great deal of time in Pittsburgh and in smaller steel and coal towns in Pennsylvania and Ohio. "I attended a lecture delivered by William Jennings Bryan a few days ago at the Carnegie Music Hall," he reported to Louis from Pittsburgh. "The topic was Ingratitude." Restless, Jerome continually applied for jobs—burnishing his credentials on occasion. In October, applying for a tax job with a group of coal and coke companies, the 22-year-old accountant claimed to be 25. And he was

1920
January 3: Boston Red Sox owner Harry Frazee sells Babe Ruth to the New York Yankees.

March: Jerome Cohen joins accounting firm Robertson, Furman.

Babe Ruth

August 18: Women gain the right to vote with the passage of the 19th Amendment to the U.S. Constitution.

German entrepreneur Adi Dassler makes his first athletic shoes.

Proportion of U.S. population living on farms falls to about 30 percent.

Suffragettes

constantly making plans. Even though he didn't intend to get married any time soon, Jerome told Louis in 1920 that he planned to buy a diamond now "because I read the other day that the blue clay diamond deposits of South Africa are being rapidly exhausted."

Even so, while he had come a long way in a short time, Jerome still felt held back by the circumstances of his birth. And as part of an ongoing process of carving out his own place in the world, he decided to change his last name. In January 1920 he told Louis he was going to start legal efforts to "change my name to Jerome Rodale." In typical fashion, he planned to do so without a lawyer. In New York he had seen that anti-Semitism had retarded his career progression. And with his easily recognizable last name, his appearance, and his accent, Jerome Cohen perhaps feared that bias would continue to hamper his advancement in the steel towns in which he worked. His name change also marked another step of conscious self-invention, or maturation—a break with a past that he found constricting. As his sister Estelle recalled, "He was the *maverick* of our family—always doing or thinking something differently than the rest of us." It is unclear why he chose Rodale, although it was probably a variant on his mother's maiden name: Rouda.

EDWARD H. FLOOD, Attorney at Law, No. 1737 Oliver Bldg., Pittsburgh, Pa. In the Court of Common Pleas of Allegheny County, State of Pennsylvania, ss: No. 357 January Term, 1921. In re petition of Jerome I. Cohen for change of name to Jerome I. Rodale. Notice is hereby given that an order was made by the above Court at the number and term aforesaid, authorizing the filing of said petition on October 18, 1920, and that no objections having been filed, the decree prayed for was made on January 19, 1921. ED. H. FLOOD, Attorney for Petitioner.

Jerome Cohen formally changed his name to Jerome I. Rodale.

Eventually, Jerome did hire a lawyer in Pittsburgh, who submitted a petition in the Court of Common Pleas of Allegheny County in October 1920. It was granted on January 19, 1921. From that day on he would be known as Jerome I. Rodale.

While Jerome worked as an accountant, Joe Cohen and Louis went into business together. Joe had finally returned to New York after being discharged from the army in the summer of 1919. An extrovert and natural salesman, Joe didn't possess more than an elementary education. "But he didn't need formal schooling because he had a native intelligence which you don't acquire at college." First, Joe worked as a salesman for a dress and suit company, traveling to Kentucky, Tennessee,

Yale scientists Dr. Leo Frederick Rettger and Henry Cheplin devise acidophilus milk for people who can't digest whole milk.

F. Scott Fitzgerald's *This Side of Paradise* is published.

F. Scott Fitzgerald

Joe and Esther Rodale in 1939

and Ohio. When he went to Cincinnati, Joe would stay with his Aunt Minnie (Becky's sister). There he met his first cousin Esther Brooks. They would be married in Covington, Kentucky, because such a marriage was illegal in Ohio.

Joe and Louis formed a company to make silk winding machines, the Eagle Textile Manufacturing Company, with a factory in Brooklyn. It went poorly. "I am so sorry to hear that the Eagle Textile is not what you anticipated it to be," Esther wrote to Joe in July 1920. "I suppose you will have to work pretty hard in order to make it a success."

Soon after they formed the venture, the silk market crashed and there was little demand for their machines. Within months, they were seeking assistance. "I received a letter from Joe yesterday in regard to my purchasing stock in your company," Jerome Rodale wrote to Louis in July 1920. He agreed to invest $200, which he viewed as a first step. As the company struggled, Jerome and others continued to lend the partners money and to purchase stock. "Before I knew it, the boys were in my debt for close to $5,000, a big sum of money in 1922," J.I. recalled.

Rather than simply liquidate, they decided to shift gears. Sol Cohen was involved in distributing electrical products—with the spread of electricity and the advent of devices like radios, the market was booming. So with Sol's assistance, Joe and Louis started making electric plugs. They renamed the company the Eagle Electric and Manufacturing Company.

Jerome could afford to help. "By the way, my capital is increasing steadily week by week," he told Louis. He maintained a brokerage account and was actively trading stocks—many of those with which he was familiar, such as U.S. Steel and Bethlehem Steel. In 1922, Robertson, Furman gave him a 5 percent interest in the firm, and the following year his salary was $5,000. Jerome Rodale bought a Ford Model T, although he failed his driving exam three times.

J. I. Rodale's first car, a Ford Model T

1921
January 19: Jerome Cohen formally changes his name to Jerome I. Rodale.

July 27: Researchers at the University of Toronto announce the discovery of the hormone insulin.

September 7: First Miss America Pageant held in Atlantic City, New Jersey.

George Washington Carver testifies before Congress regarding the usefulness of the peanut.

The Sheik, starring Rudolph Valentino, premieres.

Rudolph Valentino

Jerome didn't simply focus on ledgers and balance sheets. He had slowly migrated to the fringes of the publishing business. With one of the partners at Robertson, "we published a pamphlet, *The Art of Conversation,* a modernization of an old text on the subject." And with his brother Joe, in 1922, he started a business called the District Publishing Company to sell the book through mail order. Advertisements placed in the *New York Times* and other outlets failed to draw much response. Ultimately, in October 1922, he sold it for $250 to a bookstore at a loss of about $50.

In his spare time, Jerome wrote an article on depreciation at steel plants and submitted it to an accounting trade group. In January 1923 he proudly reported to Louis: "I have just received a letter from the National Association of Cost Accountants that they have accepted my article entitled 'War-Time Depreciation in Open Hearth Steel Plants,' and that it will be published in the form of a pamphlet which is to be sent to practically every industrial accountant in the country." The booklet, published on March 15, 1923, was perhaps the first widely distributed publication to bear the name J. I. Rodale. It wouldn't be the last.

Throughout 1922 and early 1923, Jerome continually expressed a desire to "come with the Eagle." But the indications were that the Eagle's future was limited. "Somehow or other, I get the impression that everything is not all right," he wrote Louis in April 1923.

By the fall of 1923, his interest in income tax work was abating. J.I. wanted to return to New York and get involved with an entrepreneurial venture. He seemed eager to pursue the master plan he had outlined to Louis five years earlier: Start a business, do well, and acquire land. There was a slight twist, however. With the Eagle seemingly grounded, Jerome and Joe had resolved to form their own electrical business. So in September 1923, J.I. formally severed his connection with Robertson, Furman. The partners bought him out for $1,000, and he made plans to move back to New York for good. "The romance of developing a new business beckoned enticingly."

J. I. Rodale loved writing and was thrilled when a trade group published a pamphlet he wrote on a technical accounting issue in 1923.

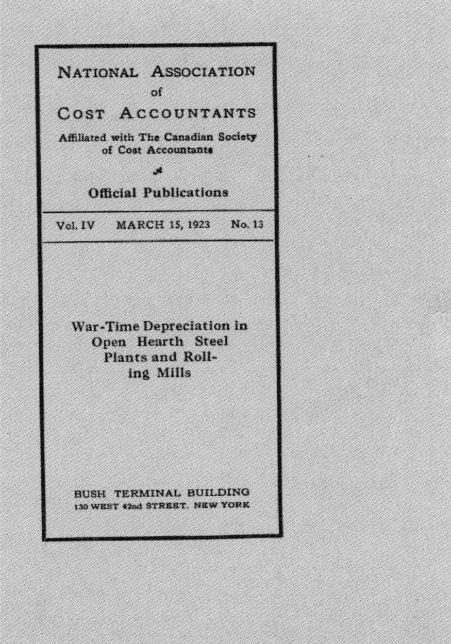
NATIONAL ASSOCIATION
of
COST ACCOUNTANTS
Affiliated with The Canadian Society of Cost Accountants

Official Publications

Vol. IV MARCH 15, 1923 No. 13

War-Time Depreciation in Open Hearth Steel Plants and Rolling Mills

BUSH TERMINAL BUILDING
130 WEST 42nd STREET, NEW YORK

1922
February 2: James Joyce's *Ulysses* is published in Paris.

May 30: The Lincoln Memorial in Washington, D.C., is dedicated.

Soybean processing plant is established by A. E. Staley in Decatur, Illinois.

James Joyce

Beatrix Farrand designs gardens at Dumbarton Oaks.

Reader's Digest is founded by Dewitt Wallace and his wife, LilaBell Acheson.

J. I. Rodale forms District Publishing Company to sell his first book, *The Art of Conversation*.

Anna and J.I. explored the countryside for a place to settle down.

CHAPTER 2

1923 TO 1939

They Came to Emmaus

J. I. Rodale in the 1920s

IN 1923, J. I. RODALE returned to New York full time to settle after an itinerant few years. Working for the government in Washington and for the accounting firm in Pittsburgh had expanded his horizons. But strong forces impelled him back to New York. He was eager to make more money and to be engaged in an entrepreneurial business, and he missed his family. The Cohen-Rodale family remained close-knit, even if it was no longer centered on the Lower East Side. After the grocery store closed, Becky Cohen moved uptown, to 57th Street and 10th Avenue. Many of her children lived in the area. At 25, J.I. had experienced a variety of enterprises. He had worked in a large government agency and in a small accounting partnership, and he was intimately familiar with the affairs of the nation's

The daughter of Lithuanian immigrants, Anna Andrews made her way to New York, where she met J. I. Rodale in 1924.

largest companies. But for J. I. Rodale, the natural form of business organization was the one he had known growing up: a family business.

When J. I. and Joe Rodale (who had changed his name as well) decided to get into the electrical manufacturing business, their older brother Sol, who had moved to Brooklyn and worked in electronic wholesaling, advised them. J.I. and Joe were able to scrape together funds—$6,000 or $7,000—including funds from their brother. Estelle, their youngest sister, worked as their "girl Friday." They set up shop in a loft on West Broadway, with three employees, and started making small electrical components—plugs, switches, and parts of appliances. "I didn't know an ohm from a kilowatt, but I got along," J.I. recalled. As electricity evolved from an unimaginable luxury to a staple, the Rodales, along with hundreds of other companies, large and small, aimed to provide the unglamorous and technologically unsophisticated guts of electric appliances. The first item produced by Rodale Manufacturing Co. was an electric flat-iron plug. This business partnership with Joe would last for 30 years.

A year after the formation of Rodale Manufacturing, at the Arcadia Ballroom, a dance hall on Broadway just north of the theater district, J.I. met the woman who would become his lifelong partner: Anna Andrews.

At first blush, J. I. Rodale and Anna Andrews seemed mismatched. Anna was a 19-year-old, relatively carefree country girl, the child of Catholic Lithuanian immigrants. She shared a small apartment with three other young women. J.I. was 26, a Jewish child of the Lower East Side, who had spent virtually his whole life in cities, was accustomed to living alone, and owned a business. And he was ready to settle down. "I felt he was really in search of a marriage partner when I first met him," Anna recalled.

Anna Andrews was born in 1905, the daughter of immigrants who had come to the rich coalfields of eastern Pennsylvania. Mahanoy City, the town of her birth, was located in the southern part of coal country. At the turn of the 20th century, the industrialized region was increasingly populated by immigrants from eastern Europe, Italy, and Ireland.

1923
March 2: *Time* magazine debuts.

March 15: J. I. Rodale's pamphlet on depreciation is published.

July 6: Union of Soviet Socialist Republics is formally established.

August 2: President Warren G. Harding dies in office and is succeeded by Calvin Coolidge.

J. I. and Joseph Rodale form Rodale Manufacturing.

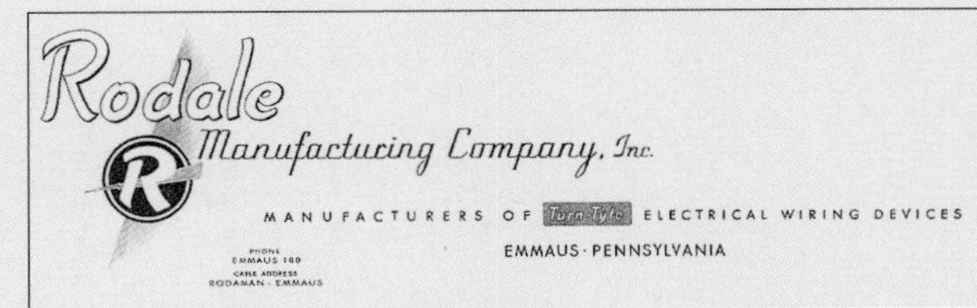

Rodale
Manufacturing Company, Inc.
MANUFACTURERS OF ELECTRICAL WIRING DEVICES
EMMAUS-PENNSYLVANIA

The Andrews family *(from left):* Anna, Anna, John, and John

Anna's parents had come to the United States as teenagers. Her mother, Anna (or Ona), arrived in 1893 at the age of 18. Her father, John Andrews (née Andrewofsky), was one of 13 children. He served in the Russian Army and came to the United States in the late 1880s or early 1890s.

The coal mines were a dangerous place to work. Anna's maternal grandfather was killed in the mines. But the steady work provided immigrants with a pastoral, hardscrabble version of the American dream. Anna's family raised pigs, geese, and chickens and smoked their own hams and sausages. In 1910, the Andrews family (Anna and her five siblings) moved 11 miles east from Mahanoy City to Tamaqua, near Collier 14 of the Lehigh Coal and Navigation Company. "Our new home was on Dutch Hill, with a long yard for gardening, a cherry tree to the side of it," she recalled. On Sundays, when he stayed home from church, John Andrews would cook stewed veal or lamb.

Schooling was a luxury—and one the Andrews family could barely afford. After completing sixth grade, Anna went to work at local hosiery mills. "I got a job when old enough as a looper," she recalled. Anna had to work, in part because her parents were both ill. Her mother died in childbirth at the age of 41 on May 9, 1916. The following year, John Andrews succumbed in the deadly influenza epidemic. After the death of her parents, Anna lived for several years with her grandmother (also named Anna), who worked as a midwife, took in boarders, and helped look after her family. Her work ethic would remain a lifelong inspiration to Anna.

Having grown up in the crowded warrens of lower Manhattan, J. I. Rodale romanticized the Pennsylvania coal and steel towns he visited as an accountant. Meanwhile, Anna Andrews was steadily making her way from rural Pennsylvania toward New York. In 1920, she moved to Edgewater, New Jersey, to work in a lunchroom run by a Lithuanian family. She worked there for three

1924
Rudolph Steiner advocates biodynamic method of agriculture.

May 10: J. Edgar Hoover is appointed the head of the Federal Bureau of Investigation.

November 27: First Macy's Thanksgiving Day parade is held.

December 1: Cole Porter's *Lady, Be Good!* debuts on Broadway.

J.I. meets Anna Andrews.

Cole Porter

Anna Andrews ***(left)***

years as a waitress and cook, mastering dishes ranging from pigs' knuckles to clam chowder. In 1923, she moved to New York and took a job at a Schrafft's lunch counter with her two sisters. In the spring of 1924, she became a hostess at the Arcadia—a legendary club that featured two bandstands for jazz bands. Men would buy tickets to dance with the hostesses for 10 cents a dance. And on her first Sunday at the Arcadia, she met J.I.

J.I. asked Anna to dinner, and for the next three years these two strong-willed, self-reliant people would enjoy an on-again, off-again courtship. Anna lived far uptown, on the ground floor of an old apartment building near Columbia University. J.I. lived on West 20th Street. At times, the distance between the two was far greater than the 5 miles that separated their homes. In the summers, J.I., who was primarily interested in Jewish girls, would go to the Catskills resort areas to try to meet a potential bride. In early 1927, the relationship appeared to be over. "Dear Little Spit-Fire," J.I. wrote to Anna in early 1927, "I cannot cater to you the way you demand and have respect for myself, nor do I think it interesting to be led around by the nose.... You are showing very good judgment in calling a halt to our friendship right here."

J.I. kept busy with Rodale Manufacturing, which was growing. In fiscal 1927, the company had sales of $387,165 and an operating profit of $13,000. J.I. and Joe were each able to take salaries of $10,000. (J.I.'s income for the year was lower, about $8,000, because he hadn't quite kicked the habit of losing money in the stock market.) In 1927, the company moved again, this time to the Green Terminal building at 200 Hudson Street, in the southwestern section of Manhattan.

J.I.'s mind was actively engaged in the world. In the spring of 1927, he decided to tackle a problem that had vexed great minds for decades: New York City traffic. He submitted a 10-page formal plan, complete with diagrams, to loosen congestion in midtown. "Take two avenues and

1925
February 21: *The New Yorker* publishes its first issue.

May 25: John T. Scopes is indicted in Tennessee for teaching Darwin's theory of evolution.

John T. Scopes

June 6: The Chrysler Corporation is founded by Walter Percy Chrysler.

F. Scott Fitzgerald's *The Great Gatsby* is published.

J. I. Rodale and Anna Andrews were married in a civil ceremony at New York's City Hall on December 1, 1927.

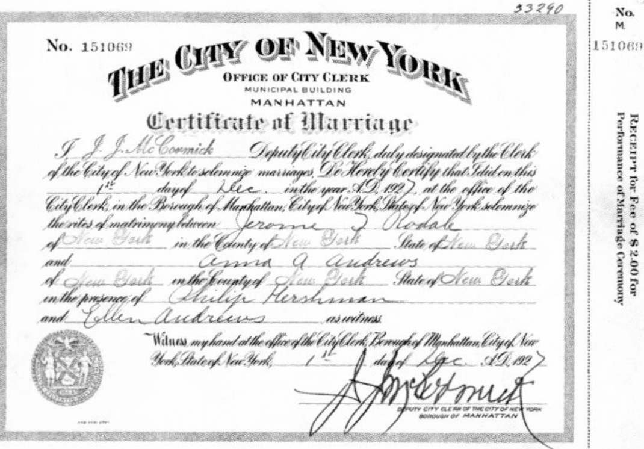

33290

No. 151069

THE CITY OF NEW YORK
OFFICE OF CITY CLERK
MUNICIPAL BUILDING
MANHATTAN

Certificate of Marriage

I, J. J. McCormick Deputy City Clerk, duly designated by the Clerk of the City of New York to solemnize marriages, Do Hereby Certify that I did on this 1st day of Dec. in the year A.D. 1927, at the office of the City Clerk, in the Borough of Manhattan, City of New York, State of New York solemnize the rites of matrimony between Jerome I. Rodale of New York in the County of New York State of New York and Anna A. Andrews of New York in the County of New York State of New York in the presence of Philip Hershman and Ellen Andrews as witness.

Witness my hand at the office of the City Clerk, Borough of Manhattan, City of New York, State of New York, 1st day of Dec. A.D. 1927

J. J. McCormick
DEPUTY CITY CLERK OF THE CITY OF NEW YORK
BOROUGH OF MANHATTAN

No. M 151069

RECEIPT for Fee of $2.00 for Performance of Marriage Ceremony

make 'one-way' streets out of them," he suggested. When the *New York Times* reported on the ambitious plan on June 19, 1927, it was the first mention of the name J. I. Rodale in the newspaper of record.

J.I. and Anna evidently had a rapprochement in fall 1927, and in October, they agreed to get married. On Thanksgiving, they drove to Pennsylvania to meet Anna's grandmother and passed through Allentown. "The main street was tree-lined; we were deeply impressed," Anna remembered. When she introduced J.I., who wore a black fedora, to her grandmother, who didn't speak English, she said: "He's all right; he looks like a priest."

The young couple spent their honeymoon in Atlantic City.

The difference in religion–and J.I.'s disillusionment with the strict Judaism of his upbringing–precluded a traditional wedding ceremony. In fact, the couple had apparently not discussed how the differences in their backgrounds would be worked out in their marriage. On December 1, 1927, when they were married at City Hall, the only member of J.I.'s family to attend was his youngest sister, Estelle. Already Anna could see that her husband was something of a contrarian. He responded "Yes, sir," to the judge instead of "I do." And he didn't want to go on a honeymoon "because everyone else did the same." But Anna prevailed. After a small reception, they went to the Charles Hotel in Atlantic City.

The newlyweds moved into J.I.'s bachelor apartment, a one-room kitchenette at 233 West 21st Street. Anna stopped working, while J.I. worked all day and brought his work home at night. "He worked evenings redesigning G.E. little plugs to get around patents," recalled Anna. For a woman accustomed to supporting herself, Anna found the apartment and her new role confining. What's more, relations with J.I.'s family were uncomfortable. "In the beginning, relatives of J.I.'s family were cold." Anna didn't meet Becky Cohen until several months after the wedding, when Anna was already pregnant. "Quietly and persistently I was pressured into the rites of becoming a Jewish mother," Anna wrote. And so, largely against her will, Anna underwent a conversion in the fall of 1928, which culminated in a trip to the ritual bath. In December 1928, a year after their civil

1926
Book of the Month Club begins.

April 21: Princess Elizabeth is born in London.

October 14: *Winnie-the-Pooh,* by A. A. Milne, is published.

November 15: The 24-station NBC radio network opens.

Dr. Harold Hain, an early advocate of health foods, starts selling all-natural carrot and celery juices, founding Hain Natural Foods Co.

The newlyweds spent their weekends touring the countryside around New York City.

1927

January 7: First transatlantic telephone call is placed from New York City to London.

May 20: Charles Lindbergh embarks upon the first successful solo, nonstop transatlantic flight.

Charles Lindbergh

May 27: Ford Motor Company stops making the Model T.

June 19: *The New York Times* discusses J. I.'s traffic-control plan.

Commercial manufacturer of synthetic vitamin D is started.

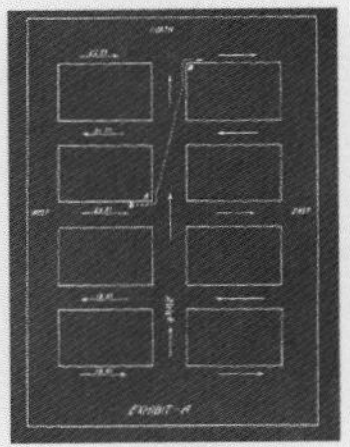

J.I.'s traffic-control plan

October 6: *The Jazz Singer*, starring Al Jolson, is the first movie with spoken dialogue.

December 1: J. I. Rodale and Anna Andrews are married.

J.I. and Anna with Ruth, their first child

marriage ceremony, the couple held a Jewish wedding ceremony with relatives holding up the traditional canopy. "I cried all thru the whole ritual like my heart would break," she later wrote. "It was a severing of my whole childhood from my dead parents and now into something so strange and foreign."

In December 1928, the Rodales' first child, Ruth, was born. Three weeks later, the young family moved to the Bronx, to a larger apartment on the 17th floor of an apartment building. "We went to the 5&10 store," Anna recalled. "I bought kitchen equipment; J.I. bought loose-leaf books." J.I. needed the books because he had started writing short stories. The budding author didn't have much luck getting them published, but J. I. Rodale had trained himself to think systematically whether it was accounting for large-scale corporations or designing tiny electrical components. And so he set out systematically to improve his writing by collecting words and phrases that had been used by published authors. Eventually, he began making envelopes for nouns and then filed verbs that went well with them inside. He did the same with adjectives. "After a while the envelopes began to bulge interestingly," he wrote.

At the time J.I. was too busy with Rodale Manufacturing, his family, and other pursuits to do much with this collection of words. The family soon moved from the Bronx to Greenwich Village in Manhattan to be closer to work. And increasingly, J.I. and Anna spent their weekends exploring the areas north and east of the city, driving through Westchester County and into Connecticut. On one such weekend drive, they got lost and found themselves in "a beautiful village lined with tall old trees and beautiful old homes set way back from the sidewalks." It was Ridgefield, Connecticut, the quintessence of New England, about 35 miles (and a world) away from the Bronx.

1928
March 4: Transcontinental foot race starts in Los Angeles and finishes in New York City on May 26.

May 15: Animated short *Plane Crazy* introduces Mickey Mouse.

Margaret Mead's *Coming of Age in Samoa* is published.

Winter Olympics takes place in St. Moritz, Switzerland.

December: Ruth Rodale is born.

Book on cornstalk paper is printed in New York City.

W. H. Park produces effective tuberculosis vaccine.

Smitten, the Rodales visited a real estate office and soon found a 27-acre farm with "a tiny house and broken down barn" that "seemed like a page from Dickens come to life." With help from Joe Rodale, they bought it in October 1928 for about $5,500 and fixed up the rustic house. J.I. had no interest in farming or gardening. "We just sat there and drank in the romance of the trees, breathed in the fragrance of the wild flowers, and watched the birds flying about."

In fall of 1929, J.I.'s two most significant partnerships—the one he and Anna had formed in 1927, and the one he and Joe had formed in 1923—were thriving. Anna had just become pregnant with the family's second child, and Rodale Manufacturing was on track for its best year. In 1928, the company had sales of $359,000 and a net profit of $37,332, and it was expanding. In 1929 the Rodales acquired a small rubber-molding plant in Doylestown, Pennsylvania, with annual sales of about $30,000. Since many electrical components were insulated or housed in rubber containers, this was a complementary business. And while Joe continued to head the sales efforts, J.I. traveled to Doylestown, about 30 miles southeast of Allentown, once a week to check on the operation.

In October 1929, the stock market crashed, signaling an end not just to the long-running bull market but to a long-running economic expansion. As businesses and banks failed and unemployment grew, Rodale Manufacturing's sales fell off a cliff. In the midst of this challenging period, in March 1930, Anna gave birth to the couple's second child, Robert, at a hospital in Brooklyn.

Rodale Manufacturing faced a problem common to many manufacturing businesses in New York. Its fixed costs—rent on the factory—and labor costs were high. And with business in a sharp slump, drastic change would be required if it was to survive. The salvation came in the form of a proposition from a friend from Emmaus, Pennsylvania, a town of about 6,400 (1930 census). Named after the biblical town where Jesus was seen by his disciples after his crucifixion and resurrection, Emmaus had been

The Connecticut farm in 1937. Young Ruth is out front.

1929
January 17: Comic strip *Popeye* debuts.

February 26: Grand Teton National Park is created.

August 19: Radio show *Amos 'n' Andy* debuts.

Charles Atlas creates company to sell health and fitness program by mail order.

October 29: On Black Tuesday, the stock market falls 12 percent, kicking off the Great Depression.

STAGE BROADWAY SCREEN

VARIETY 25¢

WALL ST. LAYS AN EGG

November 7: The Museum of Modern Art opens in New York City.

Nobel Prize goes to Christiaan Eijkman for discovering vitamin B and to Frederick Hopkins for discovering vitamin A.

J. I. and Joseph Rodale: brothers and business partners

Rodale Manufacturing Co., Inc.
EMMAUS, PA. • WOodring 5-9071

J. I. RODALE
President

Manufacturers of
ELECTRICAL WIRING DEVICES

As the Depression started, the Rodale Manufacturing Company found a new lease on life by moving to Emmaus, Pennsylvania.

founded by Moravians in 1759. The region's economy was primarily based on agriculture, coal, and steel. In the 19th century it had grown into a center of silk production as well. But that sector had fallen on hard times. Emmaus contained several empty factories, including a large two-story factory building at Sixth and Minor Streets, just southwest of the town center, which had previously housed the D. G. Dery and Amalgamated Silk Mill.

The building was offered to the Rodales essentially for free, along with tax breaks. Moving would mean leaving their home. But leaving New York offered the Rodales the ability to lower their rent and labor costs—since wages were lower in Emmaus—not to mention their own living costs. J.I. and Joe were familiar with the area, through their many trips to Doylestown and J.I.'s visits to Anna's family in nearby Tamaqua. Evidently, the Rodales moved quickly to occupy the factory. By July 1930, the first Emmaus-based employees had come aboard, among them Elmer Barto, William Ehrenfeld, Charles Haberstumpf, and Anthony F. Timar. In August 1930, J.I., Anna, Joe, Ruth, and five-month-old Bob drove to Allentown, checked into the Hotel Traylor, and quickly decided to rent a twin house on the south side of Allentown for $70 a month.

J.I. had also brought his stacks of envelopes. The impulse to write and publish, which he had expressed in several ways in the past 10 years—from *The Art of Conversation* to the New York traffic study—was plainly powerful. "Looking at the colorful array of magazines at a newsstand would do something to me," he recalled. And so within several months of moving to Emmaus, he started a magazine. "Allentown is the birthplace of a new magazine that made its bow to the national public during the past week," the Allentown *Morning Call* boasted on December 7, 1930.

With J. I. Rodale as the editor and H. P. Tuffy and A. A. Andrews (Anna) as associate editors, *The Humorous ScrapBook* debuted in January 1931. Truth be told, most of it wasn't humorous.

1930
February: *Fortune* magazine is founded.

February 18: Pluto is discovered by American astronomer Clyde Tombaugh.

March 27: Robert Rodale is born.

April 6: Hostess Twinkies are invented.

June 6: Frozen food arrives on the market.

November 5: Sinclair Lewis is awarded the Nobel Prize in Literature.

Sinclair Lewis

Vita Sackville-West and Harold Nicolson plant wildly at Sissinghurst Castle.

The average farm uses more than 2 tons of commercial fertilizer.

Soon after moving to Allentown in 1930, J.I. realized his long-standing ambition of publishing his own magazine: *The Humorous ScrapBook*.

New Magazine Makes Bow Here

'Humorous Scrap Book' to Be Circulated Nation-wide

Allentown is the birthplace of a new magazine that made its bow to the national public during the past week when the number for the first quarter of the new year was placed on news stands all over the nation. The periodical, "The Humorous Scrap Book," is being published at 840 Maple street, this city, by the Scrap Book Publishing company and bids well to succeed and in doing so bring the name of this city to the attention of readers in all parts of this country.

Not only is the distribution of this periodical of national scope but the advertising that appears in its columns is also of national nature. A plentiful supply of advertising matter, that is interestingly presented, will add to the prestige this new magazine is bound to enjoy.

The editor, J. I. Rodale, and associate editors, H. P. Tuffy and A. A. Andrews, have chosen a variety of subjects for the reading matter of the initial issue of the Humorous Scrap Book that will prove to be entertaining reading for people of all walks of life.

The article and cuts have been carefully chosen to carry out the policies of the editor of presenting some of the best humorous stories and pictures that appeared in publications generations ago. The cover design, a drawing by G. S. Reinhart that appeared in Harper's Weekly in 1878, "Archery Practice on Staten Islanr" clearly illustrates what may be expected by the readers inside the covers. All articles and stories were at one time prize writings of the best old-time writers of fiction and news stories.

The stories are all written in the most simple language so that young and old may read and understand with ease and appreciate the wit and humor presented by the pens of the writers.

The cover of the periodical is in colors and the printing throughout the book is clear and clean. The cuts are the work of the Morning Call engraving department.

The magazine is a quarterly publication with the first edition representing the January to March number.

The quarterly—offered for an annual subscription of $1—was stocked almost entirely with reprints from other magazines and books. The articles included an excerpt from a biography of Thomas Edison, a full-page sketch from 1845 of a telegraph wire strung over a river and held up by what looks like three blimps, and a short story about Da Vinci's designs for flying machines. It did contain a few ads—from Yale University Press and Columbia University's home study courses, for example. But *The Humorous ScrapBook* was a bust financially. J.I. lost $1,500 on a single issue—a large sum considering his income for 1931 was $6,200.

Such losses may have been particularly ill timed given the situation at Rodale Manufacturing. Even after the move, the company struggled for survival. "We were in terrible financial trouble and had to have outside assistance," J.I. recalled. Sales plummeted to about $200,000 in 1932. The payroll had shrunk, and J. I. and Joe Rodale cut their own salaries by about half to almost $3,200. In 1933, they closed down the Doylestown plant.

The brothers from New York made something of an odd couple in Emmaus. A natural salesman, Joe was the taller of the two, with broad shoulders. He could frequently be seen with a cigar. Rodale Manufacturing survived the worst of the Depression in part because of Joe's tenacious sales efforts, and in part because of its huge store of inventory—parts and finished goods. "Our peculiar type of business always required a large inventory, but in the excitement and turbulence of the prosperous days that led up to the Depression, we had accumulated what was for us a tremendous inventory," J.I. later wrote. "Just as a fat man, faced with a paucity of food, will actually live for certain length of time on his reserve fat, so did we live off our inventory." In the early 1930s, they sold far fewer goods than they had in the late 1920s, but they had essentially already paid for their supplies.

As the family adjusted to life in Emmaus, and as Rodale Manufacturing continued to struggle for survival, J.I. continued to dabble in publishing. One day he brought a mock-up for a 16-page catalog to an Emmaus printer to see how much it would cost. The price came back: $75 for 5,000 copies. "I figured that for $75 I could become a magazine publisher," J.I. later wrote. "And

1931
January: *The Humorous ScrapBook*, J.I.'s first magazine, is published.

May 1: Construction of the Empire State Building is completed.

August 23: Ford Motor Company orders employees to grow vegetables or give up their jobs.

Pearl S. Buck's *The Good Earth* is published.

October 18: Inventor Thomas Edison dies.

J.I. in the 1930s

that is exactly what happened." In the summer of 1932, he decided to start another magazine. Similar to *The Humorous ScrapBook*, this new periodical would deal with a range of humorous and intriguing subjects and include both original content and reprints. "The magazine is proceeding along very nicely," he wrote to Anna and the children in August 1932, when they were at the New Jersey shore. "I already told Joe all about it and after explaining the whole thing, he feels fairly good about it.... This was a big surprise to me. He is a pretty good skate."

The magazine in question was *The Clown*, advertised as "A Bit of Fun for Everyone," which came out in fall of 1932. The magazine included straightforward attempts at humor, including jokes written by J.I. "Someone recently said that the backbone of the Depression was busted," he wrote. "We never knew that the Depression had a backbone." Joe Rodale was listed as the business manager. *The Clown* was full of ethnic jokes–many of which would be deemed politically incorrect today. One page featured quotes and one-liners about Albert Einstein. "Einstein says space is limited. That is self-evident; editors have been returning our manuscripts for years." J.I. was plainly the animating spirit, and his voice was evident everywhere in the magazine. He created a comic character–a bungling fool named "Massa Finklestein."

In 1933, in part to save on rent, the Rodales moved to a house on a mountain outside of town for several months. At the end of the summer, however, they moved back to the city, to 119 South Madison Street. "It was extremely difficult sledding, because my complete income was about $70 a week, and about $45 of it had to go toward keeping the magazine alive," he wrote. To save, he would buy cartoons from a well-known cartoonist, Bill Hollman, eight or nine at a time on credit. Anna was steadfastly supportive of all his efforts. "I never questioned any of his projects,"

1932
April: Vitamin C is identified and isolated.

June 6: The Revenue Act of 1932 creates the first federal gas tax (1 cent per gallon).

July 28: President Herbert Hoover orders the army to evict 15,000 World War I veterans seeking benefits from Washington, D.C.

Fall: *The Clown* debuts.

November 8: Democrat Franklin D. Roosevelt beats incumbent Herbert Hoover in the presidential race.

William Faulkner's *Light in August* is published.

William Faulkner

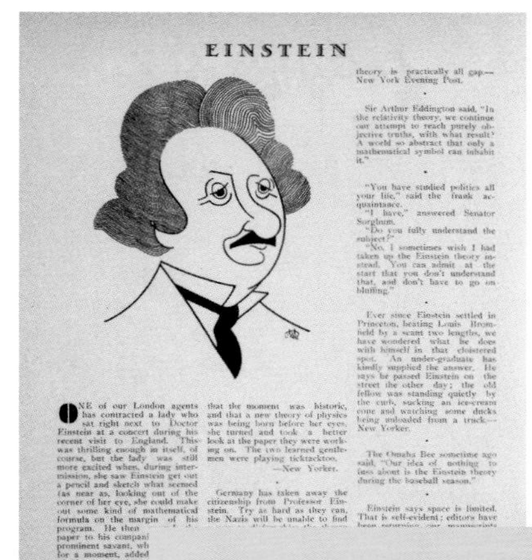

EINSTEIN

ONE of our London agents has contracted a lady who sat right next to Doctor Einstein at a concert during his recent visit to England. This was thrilling enough in itself, of course, but the lady was still more excited when, during intermission, she saw Einstein get out a pencil and sketch what seemed (as near as, looking out of the corner of her eye, she could make out some kind of mathematical formula on the margin of his program. He then [illegible] paper to his compani[illegible] prominent savant, wh[illegible] for a moment, added [illegible] of his own, and pa[illegible] again. This process [illegible] until at last the lady [illegible] got the better of her that the moment was historic, and that a new theory of physics was being born before her eyes. She turned and took a better look at the paper they were working on. The two learned gentlemen were playing ticktacktoe.
—New Yorker.

Germany has taken away the citizenship from Professor Einstein. Try as hard as they can, the Nazis will be unable to find [illegible]

theory is practically all gap.—New York Evening Post.

Sir Arthur Eddington said, "In the relativity theory, we continue our attempt to reach purely objective truths, with what result? A world so abstract that only a mathematical symbol can inhabit it."

"You have studied politics all your life," said the frank acquaintance.

"I have," answered Senator Sorghum.

"Do you fully understand the subject?"

"No. I sometimes wish I had taken up the Einstein theory instead. You can admit at the start that you don't understand that, and don't have to go on bluffing."

Ever since Einstein settled in Princeton, beating Louis Bromfield by a scant two lengths, we have wondered what he does with himself in that cloistered spot. An under-graduate has kindly supplied the answer. He says he passed Einstein on the street the other day; the old fellow was standing quietly by the curb, sucking an ice-cream cone and watching some ducks being unloaded from a truck.—New Yorker.

The Omaha Bee sometime ago said, "Our idea of nothing to fuss about is the Einstein theory during the baseball season."

Einstein says space is limited. That is self-evident; editors have [illegible]

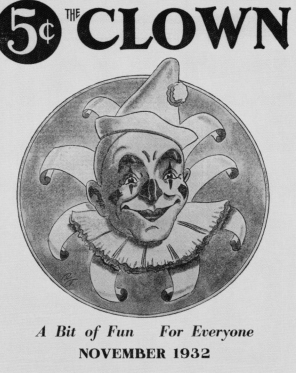

she recalled. Living expenses, fortunately, were very low. "I paid a girl $6 a week for domestic help," Anna recalled. The rent on the house was $70 per month. J.I. used the dining room as his study, working on a large desk strewn with papers, magazines, and books.

J.I. had a voracious appetite for knowledge and an equally voracious desire to disseminate information. Even as he lost money, he was learning about publishing and about direct marketing. Many of the companies that advertised in his magazine were direct-mail firms. "Some people went to colleges to study journalism and never learned. I went to life and I think I accumulated a great deal of interesting publishing know-how." He continually adjusted to keep losses low. "When my losses became too great, I changed into small digest-size magazines," he said. *The Clown* shrank in size and turned into *The American Humorist* in 1933.

Rodale Manufacturing began to recover as the economy did. Sales in 1935 rose to $275,000. The payroll swelled to about 100, with employees earning about $12 per week, a substantial wage during the Depression. In the 1930s, Joe increasingly took over the operations of Rodale. J.I. came to regard the factory as a venue for his publishing ventures, and his publishing activities as an escape from "my boring duties at the electrical plant in Emmaus." J.I.'s interest in magazines—and disinterest in electronics—was a bone of contention between the two brothers. Though the magazines didn't lose money, and they didn't make much either, Joe thought them a waste. J.I. wanted Joe to buy out his half interest in Rodale Manufacturing so he would have more resources to plow into his magazines. But Joe refused. "If I did that, the money would disappear even faster than it does now, and you'd still come back to me for more," he told J.I. "What's worse, I'd probably end up giving it to you!"

The Clown, started in November 1932, was J.I.'s second attempt at a humor magazine.

J.I. first printed *The Clown* locally and then sent it to Philadelphia. He continued to publish

1933

February 17: *Newsweek* magazine debuts.

March 4: In his inauguration speech, President Franklin Delano Roosevelt declares: "The only thing we have to fear is fear itself."

President Roosevelt

March 31: The Civilian Conservation Corps is established to relieve rampant unemployment.

November 4: Scientists report success in treating obesity by using the drug alphadinitrophenol to increase patients' metabolism.

November 11: In South Dakota, a dust storm strips topsoil from farmlands.

The U.S. government institutes the Agricultural Adjustment Act, which pays farmers not to produce abundant crops such as wheat, corn, and hogs.

In *100,000,000 Guinea Pigs,* Arthur Kallett and F. J. Schlink warn of the dangers of chemicals in cosmetics, food, and drugs.

the magazine, but he decided to become his own printer. "Actually, I think he liked the smell of ink," Anna recalled. With his assets largely tied up in Rodale Manufacturing, J.I. lacked the resources to buy an entire printing press operation at once. There were eight steps to the printing process—from setting type to folding to printing covers, stitching, and finally trimming. And each step required expensive machinery. So, with the advice of Emmaus printer Fred Bernhard, J.I. first bought a trimming machine—the one used in the final step of the process—and set it up in a corner of the factory in 1934. "I went into it backward because I was terribly afraid of being able to do it all in one shot," he recalled.

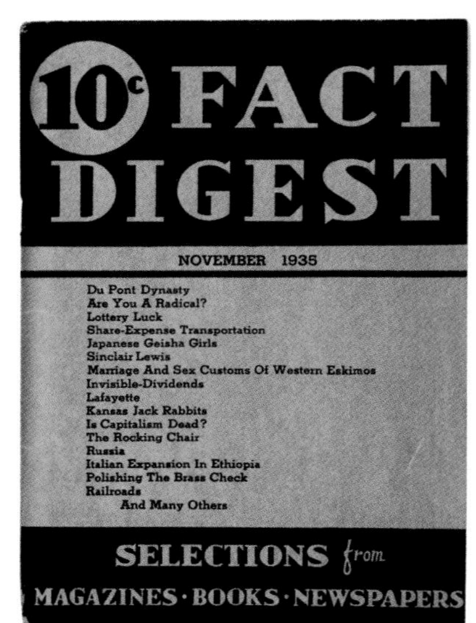

J. I. Rodale launched *Fact Digest* in the fall of 1935.

J.I.'s printing needs were growing. In 1935, he decided to launch a second magazine, to be modeled on the popular *Reader's Digest*. In the October 1935 edition of *The American Humorist*—by now reduced in size to 5 by 8 inches—he announced the publication of *Fact Digest*, a new magazine "which will consist of reprints of the best articles of the month gathered from hundreds of magazines, books, newspapers, etc." The first issue, which appeared in September 1935 (a subscription was available for $1 for 12 issues), featured an article on phobias by the satirist Robert Benchley, which first appeared in the *New York American*. ("Tell us your phobias and we will tell you what you are afraid of.") It also included, among other features, an article on the female mosquito from *Scientific American*; excerpts from Louisiana Senator Huey Long's 15½-hour filibuster speech of June 13, 1935; and lists of facts on subjects like Ethiopia. "When a debtor fails to meet his obligations in Ethiopia, both the borrower and the lender are chained together until the debt is paid."

In addition to paying for the printing machinery, J.I. had to pay people to work it. Al Moyer started in September 1934, working for $25 a week, alongside one pressman and a compositor. "We had a model 5 linotype TJ with a melting pot," he recalled. "The headings for articles were all set by hand from foundry type.... We had two flat-bed presses which were quite old and full of troubles." Over time, as Rodale Manufacturing continued to throw off larger dividends and salaries, "I gradually bought the equipment to do my own printing and binding," J.I. wrote. Eventually,

1934
January 26: The Apollo Theater opens in Harlem.

Apollo Theater

April 19: Five-year-old Shirley Temple debuts in *Stand Up and Cheer!*

Shirley Temple

May 23: Bank robbers Bonnie Parker and Clyde Barrow are killed by Texas Rangers in Louisiana.

June: Talking book for the blind issued in New York City.

J.I. and Anna worked together to build a home and a business.

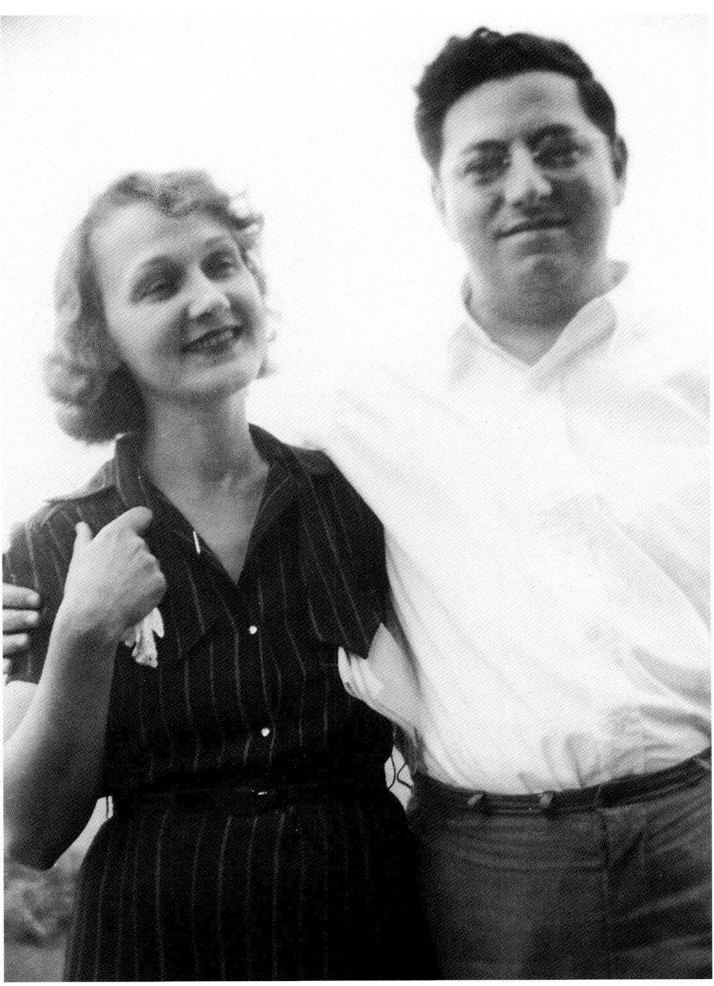

the printing equipment came to include a stitcher, a typesetting machine, a Mergenthaler linotype, a gang stitcher, a rotary magazine press, a mat rolling machine, and stereotyping equipment. In 1935, Rodale Manufacturing showed publishing and printing income of $4,645, the first indication that J.I.'s efforts were appearing on the books of the company.

In 1936, *The American Humorist* shut down. "I had lost about $12,000. But it was worth it." J.I. later wrote. "It was practical experience which stood me in great stead later on." That year, he began publishing another magazine, *New Biography*, which, like *Fact Digest,* featured reprints. To a degree, J.I.'s early magazines functioned much like today's Internet search engines do. They scanned the known publishing world for information and documents, some related to one another, and some obscure. Then he picked out data that interested him, acquired the rights to publish it gratis or for a minimal charge, and reformatted the information so that readers could access it cheaply.

Aside from magazines, the equipment J.I. acquired could also be used to publish books. Throughout his early years in Emmaus, J.I. had continued to collect words, and he began to think he had the makings of a comprehensive guide to pairing verbs with nouns. But his research eventually came to mimic the factory. He hired labor (high school and college students), purchased the raw material (books and magazines), and had them cut out phrases that went together. "In a few years I had dozens of boxes of these envelopes all around the house." He hired Professor

1935
May 29: Construction of Hoover Dam is completed.

August 14: President Franklin D. Roosevelt signs Social Security Act into law.

September: *Fact Digest* debuts.

October 10: George Gershwin's *Porgy and Bess* premieres on Broadway.

November 5: Parker Brothers releases the board game Monopoly.

First Penguin paperback books are published.

George Gershwin

Congress establishes the Soil Conservation Service to manage soil and water conservation throughout the United States.

Artificial heart is invented in New York City.

Kingsbury M. Badger of Muhlenberg College to edit the material. And when the *Verb-Finder* was rejected by New York publishers, J.I. decided to publish it himself.

The *Verb-Finder*, which was ready for distribution on July 1, 1937, was the first major book published under the Rodale Press logo. Substantial and heavy at 512 pages, with a green cover, "its purpose is rather to furnish the writer, whether journalist, advertiser, fiction writer, poet, lawyer, business man, or letter writer, with a storehouse of words." Among those who helped collect material were Ruth Adams, Harold Kahn, and Jim Miller. A typical entry read as follows: "ABDOMEN–develop, distend, enlarge, exercise, jut out (see stomach, intestine, paunch, belly)." Instead of selling the volume through bookstores, J.I. decided to pitch it through direct mail–and through advertisements in his magazines. "When we began to send out circulars, the orders came pouring in beautifully," J.I. recalled. "It seemed that the general writing public were starved for verbs."

The *Verb-Finder* (1937) was the first major book published by Rodale Press.

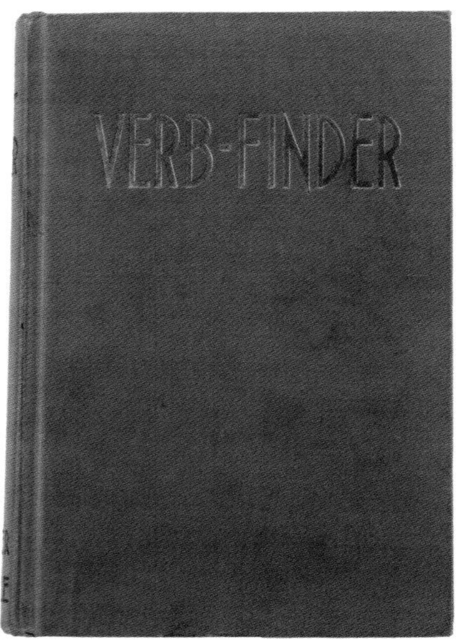

Figures on sales and expenses for Rodale Press and for the magazines in the early years are not available. But the brothers ran their operation on a shoestring and generally at a loss. When J.I. wanted to publish the *Verb-Finder*, he had no money to pay overtime. "I had no car then, had to use the bus which I took at 5:10 a.m. and returned at 10 p.m.," recalled Al Moyer. And J. I. Rodale had a hard time selling advertisements in his magazines on a cash basis, since they lacked large circulations. Many of the advertisers were companies selling items through the mail–items like the Sticker Circular, which offered 1,000 gummed stickers with the name and address printed for $1.

Unlike many other magazine publishers, who paid salaries to staff writers and maintained large overhead, J.I. could afford to pursue topics and areas that interested him–regardless of whether there was broad-based interest in them. And he didn't mind pulling the plug on a new publication if it failed to find an audience. The *Ad-Builders*, published in the summer of 1937, were 32-page word finders geared toward advertising copywriters on topics such as suits. Three issues were published before it was canceled. J.I. could afford to experiment because he owned the equipment and didn't pay much for the content. He wrote much of it, and he frequently asked and received permission to reprint material that was already published.

1936
July 11: The Triborough Bridge in New York City opens.

August 9: American sprinter Jesse Owens wins his fourth gold medal at the Summer Olympics in Berlin.

Jesse Owens

November 23: The first edition of *Life* magazine is published.

November 25: Germany and Japan sign the Anti-Comintern Pact.

Jack LaLanne opens a health club in Berkeley, California.

J.I. begins publishing *New Biography*.

The Rodale family on the Atlantic City Boardwalk. *From left:* Ruth, J.I., Nina, Anna, and Robert

Although it was a marginal business, J.I.'s publishing efforts occupied his life at the office and at home. Being a publisher opened him up to new worlds and gave him the ability and occasion to correspond with other men and women of letters—people whose paths he would never have crossed in running Rodale Manufacturing. In the late 1930s, he wrote to columnists like Walter Winchell and H. L. Mencken for permission to reprint articles, as well as to prominent public figures like Albert Einstein and New York City mayor Fiorello La Guardia (who granted permission to reprint an article he wrote in the *New York Times* about "Ten Misconceptions of New York"). The activities brought him a small measure of celebrity. "Lowell Thomas mentioned J.I.'s name in reference to *Fact Digest* on the 7 o'clock news," Anna wrote. And he enjoyed the prestige associated with being in the media business. When he took the family to the 1939 World's Fair in New York, he was able to use press passes to gain entrance to all the exhibits.

The Rodale family continued to put down roots in Allentown. In November 1936, Anna and J.I. moved to a house on North 30th Street. The following year, J.I. and Anna's third child,

1937
January 11: The first issue of *Look* magazine is published.

February 11: General Motors recognizes the United Automobile Workers union.

May 6: The German airship *Hindenburg* bursts into flames when mooring to a mast in Lakehurst, New Jersey.

The *Hindenburg*

July 1: The *Verb-Finder* is published.

Albert Szent-Györgyi wins Nobel Prize for discovery of vitamin C.

Nina Rodale is born.

A decade after leaving New York, J.I. and Anna had built a prosperous life for themselves in Allentown. As a result, the second generation of Rodales would grow up in a far different environment than J.I. had—a world of cars and bicycles, backyards and gardens, carousel rides and piano lessons, skiing and roller-skating.

Nina, Anna, Bob, J.I., Esther, and Joe

CARLS

Nina, was born. In many ways, it was a traditional home, with Anna primarily responsible for the children. But it was also an intellectually active home, filled with books and magazines and discussion. In 1940, the Allentown *Morning Call* covered a musical quiz that J.I. held in his home for neighborhood children.

By the late 1930s, Rodale Manufacturing had made up much of the ground it had lost in the early part of the decade. Electrical parts was a competitive but expanding business. There were many problems with patents, as companies, including Rodale, tried to mimic products on the market. "We honestly believed that many of these impressive looking and beribboned documents were not worth the paper upon which they were printed," J.I. wrote. In 1938, Joe and J.I.'s salaries rose to above $10,000. (J.I. continued to plow most of his salary into the publishing business.) A statement of assets from that year showed that J.I. had $350 in cash, a LaSalle automobile worth $500, and stakes in Rodale Press and Rodale Manufacturing worth $20,000 and $50,000, respectively.

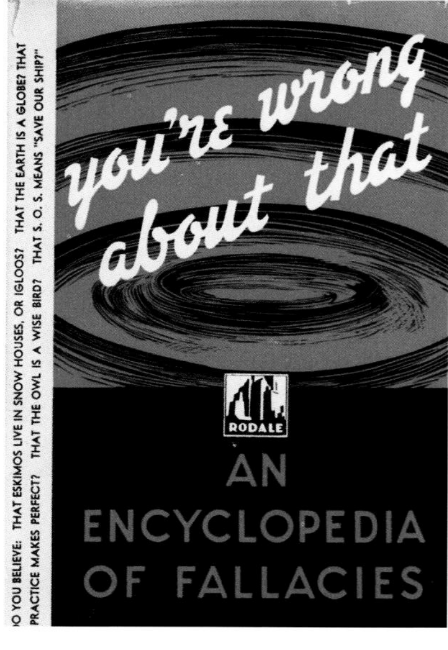

J.I. saw his magazines as an educational tool that could dispel common misconceptions.

J.I.'s skepticism about patents was indicative of his general outlook. J.I. was preternaturally leery about professional training and society's acceptance of established wisdom handed down from credentialed professionals. He seemed to have an active dislike of those who held information tightly. In his constant scanning of magazines, clipping of journals, and reviewing of books, J.I. relentlessly sought out wisdom and insight on matters relating to history, current events, and science. His counterintuitive impulse was given voice in a magazine entitled *You're Wrong about That*, which started in August 1938. On the cover, the digest magazine posed a series of questions. Do you believe "that freemasonry is a secret society? That Robin Hood actually lived? That eating between meals is bad for true health?

1938
January 16: Clarinetist Benny Goodman leads a jazz concert at Carnegie Hall.

March 12: German troops occupy Austria.

July 10: Howard Hughes sets a new record by completing a 91-hour airplane flight around the world.

Howard Hughes

August: ***You're Wrong about That* debuts.**

October 30: Orson Welles's radio broadcast of *The War of the Worlds* causes panic in the eastern United States.

John Dos Passos's *U.S.A. Trilogy* is published.

In his household,
J.I. cultivated a love
of reading, writing,
and learning.

The last day of school: Even as a child, Robert Rodale embraced an active life with exuberance.

Then you're wrong." Billed as "A Magazine That Corrects Common Errors of Thought," it consisted of excerpts from books and other publications on everything from whether Paul Revere really made that famous ride to whether the face is a guide to character. Many of the topics dealt with health and food. Lincoln Schuster, the head of Simon & Schuster, wrote to subscribe to *You're Wrong about That*. "On a recent trip through Pennsylvania I was particularly interested to note your little magazine," he wrote. "For many years I have been doing a great deal of research in the field of popular fallacies and have amassed a huge docket of material on this subject."

This interest in food and health informed a second digest magazine that started at about the same time: *You Can't Eat That*, first appeared in April 1939. Billed as "A Magazine of Nutrition and General Health Articles," it contained plenty of advice to individuals as to how they could improve their own health and ward off illnesses or alleviate chronic conditions. The October 1939 issue contained a review of a book, *Nearsightedness Is Preventable*, by Emanuel M. Josephson, M.D.; an article on how to "Make Spinach Popular" (boil it rapidly, leave the lid off, add salt); and "Should I Take Enemas?" an excerpt from the book *How to Conquer Constipation*, by J. F. Montague, M.D. *You Can't Eat That* also attracted a small but growing breed of advertisers—people and companies peddling products that could improve people's health and lives. The December 1939 issue, for example, contained ads for an Oscillatherm, a device intended to relieve prostate suffering; a natural foods store in Manhattan; Honey Brook Candy Bars of Honey Brook, Pennsylvania; a natural home treatment for colitis from W. H. Graves in Los Angeles; the K&K

You Can't Eat That reflected J.I.'s ongoing interest in food and health.

Publishing magazines and books afforded J. I. Rodale entrée to the world of ideas and letters. He relished the opportunity to exchange ideas and correspondence with writers, intellectuals, and celebrities.

Curious and self-taught, J.I. used his books and magazines to communicate valuable information about health.

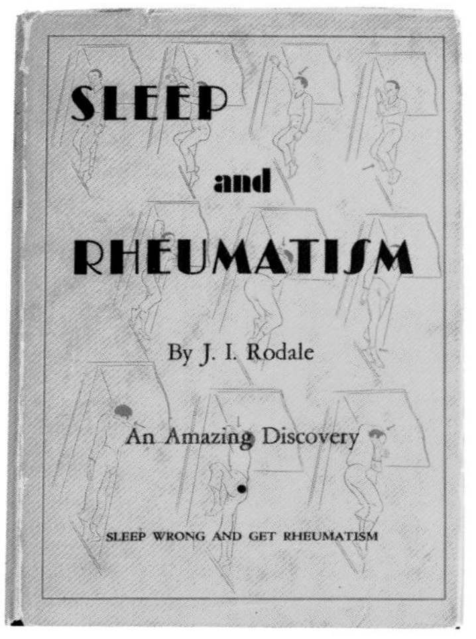

Vegetable Shredder; and a book on stopping tobacco cravings. In 1938 and 1939, J.I. started two other digest magazines: *Everybody's Digest* and *Science Facts.*

J. I. Rodale was always concerned—even obsessed—with his own health, in part because of the early death of his father and several other relatives. Throughout his 30s, J.I.'s weight had risen, from 138 pounds in 1927 to about 205 in 1938. He had a boundless curiosity about the human body in general and about his body in particular. In 1939, J.I. wrote and published a slim 130-page book, *Sleep and Rheumatism*, that neatly encapsulated his approach to publishing material about health. Written in a discursive, engaging style, it used a combination of personal experience, research, and intuition to dispel what he viewed as popular myth—all while profiting from the self-revelatory and revealing experience. "This book is the result of an experiment conducted by the writer upon himself in which he cleared up a stubborn case of neuritis," he wrote. Complete with diagrams of poor and proper sleeping positions, the book laid out the optimal sleeping position for avoiding pains and concluded with a series of instructions, such as "do not sit with knees crossed." (Pressure of one knee upon the other is bound to diminish the flow of the blood.) He proposed the production of an ergonomic mattress and wrote: "In conclusion, I want to advocate bigger and better beds for all."

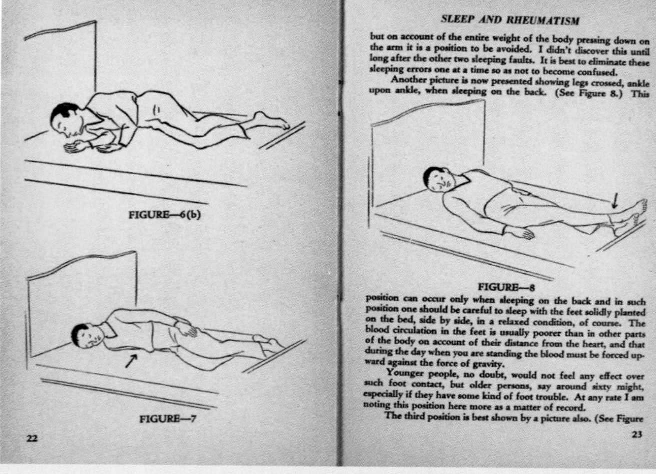

FIGURE—6(b)

FIGURE—7

22

SLEEP AND RHEUMATISM

but on account of the entire weight of the body pressing down on the arm it is a position to be avoided. I didn't discover this until long after the other two sleeping faults. It is best to eliminate these sleeping errors one at a time so as not to become confused.

Another picture is now presented showing legs crossed, ankle upon ankle, when sleeping on the back. (See Figure 8.) This

FIGURE—8

position can occur only when sleeping on the back and in such position one should be careful to sleep with the feet solidly planted on the bed, side by side, in a relaxed condition, of course. The blood circulation in the feet is usually poorer than in other parts of the body on account of their distance from the heart, and that during the day when you are standing the blood must be forced upward against the force of gravity.

Younger people, no doubt, would not feel any effect over such foot contact, but older persons, say around sixty might, especially if they have some kind of foot trouble. At any rate I am noting this position here more as a matter of record.

The third position is best shown by a picture also. (See Figure

23

Several books from Rodale Press were published in 1938 and 1939, with their subjects ranging from *Beating the Culbertsons: How the Austrians Won the World Contract Bridge Championship*, by Dr. Paul Stern, captain of the Austrian world-champion team; to a biography of columnist Irvin S. Cobb; to a memoir by Lee Ping Quan, one-time steward on the presidential yacht USS *Mayflower* (recipes included shrimp à la king in puff pastry—Mrs. Harding's preferred style) to *Around the World on $100 a Month.*

The subject matter and the authors were somewhat out of the mainstream of New York publishing. The authors J.I.

UPTON SINCLAIR
STATION A, PASADENA
CALIFORNIA

May 29, 1939.

Rodale Press,
Emmaus, Pa.

My dear Rodale:

Thanks for your very kind letter of May 25th, I will make inquiry about reproducing "Our Lady". I am sorry about the accident, but thank you for your courtesy.

I am amused by your suggestion that I should send you an anonymous novel. As it happens, I have an anomynous novel written by a friend of mine, called "Dear Janey". It was in the hands of Filteau for a while--- I wonder if he showed it to you. If not, I will be pleased to send you a copy of the manuscript. My name is not to be mentioned in connection with it.

I appreciate your courtesy in offering me the idea for a story. You will understand my position when I tell you that I am about one-third of the way through what is going to be the longest novel I have ever written. The scenes are laid in Europe during the past twenty-five years. Henle of the Vanguard Press has been giving me a lot of advice on it and is putting what I have so far into type so that I can submit galley proofs to various friends abroad.

I have never been able to use other person's ideas successfully, I have so many of my own that I cannot write them.

Sincerely,

published were either not particularly well-known—for example, he published a book called *My Cousin Mark Twain*, by Cyril Clemens—or well-known authors who were out of favor. One such author was Upton Sinclair, the novelist lionized early in the 20th century for his muckraking books like *The Jungle*, who had largely fallen out of favor due to his left-wing politics. Rodale agreed to publish a new edition of Sinclair's *The Flivver King* in 1937, and Sinclair freely offered advice on how to market it. "The only places I have found would pay with my books are liberal magazines—*The Nation, The New Republic, Common Sense*. . . . The readers of the Communist and Socialist papers are interested in my books but apparently have not the money to buy cloth-bound books."

J.I. was also busily preparing the two successor volumes to the *Verb-Finder*—the *Adjective Finder* and the *Adverb Finder*, which he planned to publish in 1940. But he found time for other efforts.

His interest in health and food, combined with his now-rural location, naturally translated into an interest in small-scale gardening. "Traveling from Allentown to Emmaus, every day I saw farmers tilling the soil," J.I. wrote. In 1939, he planted his own vegetables in the small garden behind his house. "The soil was extremely hard, and without knowing why, I used no fertilizer of any kind. I merely dug in a few seeds. The results were terrible!" he wrote. At roughly the same time, Joe Rodale had used an abundance of chemical fertilizers on his lawn, with nothing to show for it.

J.I.'s interest in growing plants for food—and the relation between the manner of raising crops and health—took on a new focus when he latched onto the work of Sir Albert Howard on organic farming. "Up to this time, in reading many books and articles on health, no one had ever questioned how a vegetable was raised as far as its nutritional quality was concerned." He first came across Howard's work in the British publication *Health for All*. Intrigued, he bought a copy of Howard's book *An Agricultural Testament*. "I obtained a copy and read it with great enthusiasm."

1939
April 30: President Roosevelt, appearing at the World's Fair in New York, becomes the first U.S. president to give a speech broadcast on television.

August 12: *The Wizard of Oz* premieres.

September 1: Germany attacks Poland, starting World War II.

Germany invades Poland

Swiss scientist Paul Müller uses DDT as an insecticide and later earns the Nobel Prize for his efforts.

The Grapes of Wrath, by John Steinbeck, is published.

John Steinbeck

In the late 1930s, J. I. Rodale published works by and about great American literary figures.

In the 1940s, J. I. Rodale found his calling as an organic farmer and an organic publisher.

CHAPTER 3

1940 TO 1950

An Organic Publisher Is Born

Sir Albert Howard's pioneering work on organic farming inspired J. I. Rodale to change his life—and his life's work.

BY 1940, J. I. RODALE had a remarkably full life. After a decade of difficult economic times, Rodale Manufacturing was growing and profitable again. He and his wife, Anna, had three young children. His publishing activities, although still unprofitable, included magazines like *Fact Digest* and a host of books. The grandly named Rodale Press was housed in and largely subsidized by Rodale Manufacturing. For more than a decade, J.I. had been intent on devising a system to improve writing. To the *Verb-Finder*, first published in 1937, J.I. added the 439-page *Adjective Finder,* authored with Theodore G. Ehrsam, a former instructor in English at Lehigh University, and the smaller *Adverb Finder* in 1940. Taken together, J.I. promised, "they form a comprehensive new system in word-finding."

In 1940, J.I. and Anna purchased a run-down farmhouse on a tired, 63-acre farm in Emmaus. It became their home and the birthplace of the organic movement.

But at age 42, J.I. had become consumed with developing a system for something more concrete, practical, and far-reaching: the organic production of food and crops. In the spring of 1940, J.I. had been struck by the force of British agriculturist Sir Albert Howard's arguments about soil and health.

Raised on a farm—his family raised cattle—Howard was a mycologist in the West Indies in 1899, specializing in diseases of sugarcane. He worked as a botanist at Wye College, and then in 1905 was named Imperial Economic Botanist to the government of India. He spent 19 years at the Pusa Agricultural Research Institute, where he was given 75 acres to experiment with crop production. His work, a combination of Western scientific method and Eastern mentality, led him to a new synthesis. "Agriculture has become unbalanced; the land is in revolt: disease of all kinds are on the increase." The horrific scene in the Dust Bowl in the United States was just one example.

The problems, Howard concluded, were caused by the rapid industrialization of agriculture. Nature is efficient—mixed vegetation protects the soil with lots of humus. In Asia, "balance between livestock and crops is always maintained" because people need oxen and buffalo for milk. Soil fertility has been preserved, and "the crops are able to withstand the inroads of insects and fungi without a thin film of protective poison." But in the West, and particularly in the United States, crops weren't rotated, livestock had been replaced by machines, and artificial fertilizers—nitrogen, phosphorus, and potassium—had replaced manures. This was all to the detriment of soil and crop health. "Can mankind regulate its affairs so that its chief possession—the fertility of the soil—is preserved?" he wondered. "On the answer to this question the future of civilization depends."

Between 1924 and 1931, Howard, working at the 300-acre Institute of Plant Industry in Indore, central India, had devised a process to make humus, the "complex residue of partly oxidized vegetable and animal matter together with the substances synthesized by the fungi and bacteria that

1940
February 29: Hattie McDaniel, who played Mammy in *Gone with the Wind*, becomes the first African American actress to win an Academy Award.

June 14: Paris is occupied by German troops.

November 5: President Roosevelt becomes the United States' first third-term president.

Lord Northbourne publishes his book *Look to the Land*, which is credited with having the first printed reference to "organic farming."

Sir Albert Howard's *An Agricultural Testament* is published.

Rodale Press publishes the *Adjective Finder* and the *Adverb Finder*.

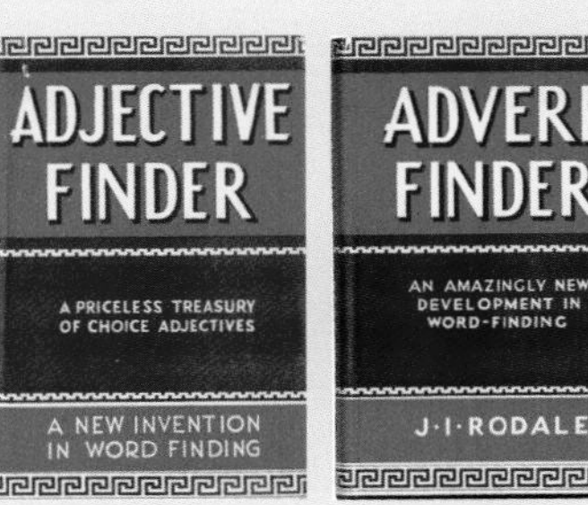

J.I. and family on farm tour

break down these wastes." Essentially, he practiced organic farming, a term first found in print in the book *Look to the Land*, by Lord Northbourne, in 1940. Howard's ideas gained currency through lectures and academic papers, but also in large-scale demonstration projects throughout the British Empire: at coffee estates in Kenya, sugarcane plantations in the West Indies, tea plantations in India and Ceylon, and vegetable farms in England. In all these trials, he reported, "the conversion of vegetable and animal wastes into humus has been followed by a definite improvement in the health of the crops and of the livestock." The book contained a passionate argument against the "slow poisoning of the life of the soil by artificial manures," which he dubbed "one of the greatest calamities which has befallen agriculture and mankind." He concluded with a plea for people to produce their own vegetables, fruits, cereals, and meats using the methods outlined in the book.

The book didn't just strike a chord with J. I. Rodale, who had been developing his own worldview on health and nutrition over the past several years, it touched off an entire symphony. "It fanned the fires!" he later wrote. "I decided that we must get a farm at once and raise as much of our family's food by the organic method as possible."

With his background as a publisher, the resources afforded to him by the success of Rodale Manufacturing, and the availability of cheap farmland nearby, J.I. believed he had the opportunity to put Howard's words into action in the United States. In April 1940, he and Anna went looking for farm property nearby. J.I. drove, and Anna knocked on doors at several farms to inquire whether one might be for sale. They finally found one a few miles northwest of Emmaus's town center, at Cedar Crest Boulevard and Minesite Road, in Lower Macungie Township. The 63-acre farm was known as the Reinhart Farm—owned by two sisters-in-law who shared the last name. Its chief selling points were its poor condition and low price. There were dead chickens in the corncrib. A tenant farmer lived in the rundown house, and a slaughtered steer hung in the stairway, ready to be cut up. "The windows were torn out, and the birds would fly in," Anna recalled. J.I. remembered that "a

1941
May 1: Orson Welles's *Citizen Kane* premieres.

Darkness at Noon, by Arthur Koestler, is published.

Orson Welles's *Citizen Kane*

First crops grown on J. I. Rodale's organic farm.

November 12: Heredity clinic opens at the University of Michigan.

December 7: Japan bombs Pearl Harbor, initiating U.S. involvement in World War II.

Japan bombs Pearl Harbor

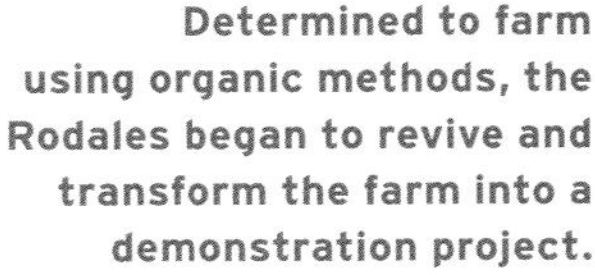
Determined to farm using organic methods, the Rodales began to revive and transform the farm into a demonstration project.

government farm agency told me later that they had turned down a request for a loan to this farmer because they couldn't see how he could make a living on this farm." But the Rodales believed the farm's decrepit condition would make it an excellent proving ground for Howard's methods. And to the child of the Lower East Side who had owned a farm in Connecticut nearly 20 years before and had long yearned to get to "God's Land," the price was right: $7,000. J.I. and Anna sold their Allentown home to Joe Rodale and packed up. They were, in Anna's words, "restless to get in and start living."

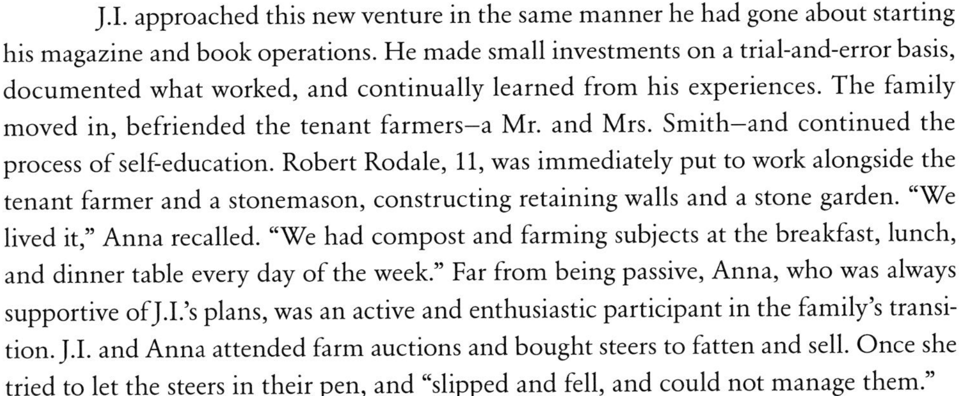
J.I. approached this new venture in the same manner he had gone about starting his magazine and book operations. He made small investments on a trial-and-error basis, documented what worked, and continually learned from his experiences. The family moved in, befriended the tenant farmers—a Mr. and Mrs. Smith—and continued the process of self-education. Robert Rodale, 11, was immediately put to work alongside the tenant farmer and a stonemason, constructing retaining walls and a stone garden. "We lived it," Anna recalled. "We had compost and farming subjects at the breakfast, lunch, and dinner table every day of the week." Far from being passive, Anna, who was always supportive of J.I.'s plans, was an active and enthusiastic participant in the family's transition. J.I. and Anna attended farm auctions and bought steers to fatten and sell. Once she tried to let the steers in their pen, and "slipped and fell, and could not manage them."

Finding help was hard, as the nation and the economy were mobilizing for a potential war. And, noted Anna, "The big problem was to hire someone who went along with the Organic Method." The couple grew tomatoes to sell to a canning company in Alburtis, and when they couldn't get help, J.I. and Anna picked the tomatoes themselves. "They were turned down because there was some green near the stems," Anna recalled. Ultimately, they hired an older Pennsylvania German man to help fertilize the crops by natural means. "The compost was made by piling up animal manures mixed with leaves, weeds, soiled hay, and other organic refuse we could lay our hands on," J.I. wrote.

Although the farm was run-down and worn out when they bought it, the Rodales gradually brought the farm and its soil back to good health.

Like his publishing ventures, the farm was at first a money-losing proposition. In 1941, J.I. earned a salary of $12,000 from Rodale Manufacturing but lost $1,220. The handwritten account of expenses included $659 for a farmhand, $164 for "tomatoes labor," and $134 for lime, which had to be added to the poor soil. That year, they also brought in $786.99 in revenues by selling wheat, tomatoes, and corn. But for J.I., the most important results weren't financial, they were physical. He noticed that after about a year on the farm, his health was improving. The family began to eat what they grew and focused on maintaining an organic diet. At that point, "I was not aware that I was gradually building a health system." The results from the field in that first year of farming were equally gratifying. "At harvesttime, wagonload upon wagonload of long, golden healthy corn came into our cribs," J.I. wrote. "When I saw this, I felt that I had to share this information with the rest of the country."

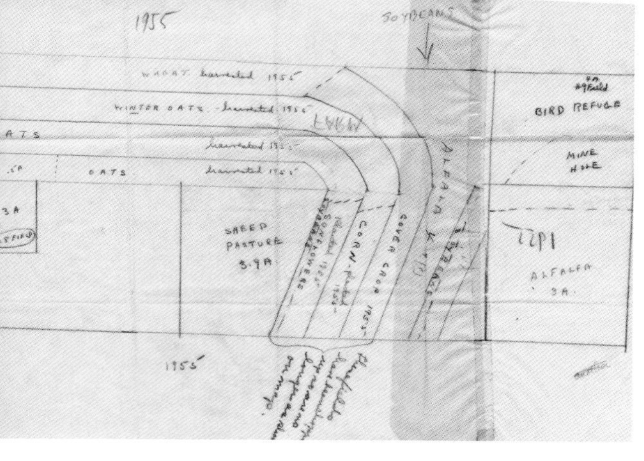

The Rodales' farm was a work in progress. This sketch, from the 1950s, shows one plan they experimented with.

The natural vehicle for doing this would be a magazine devoted to organic methods in agriculture. But as J.I. began to consider the prospect, the world interfered with his plans. Once Japan attacked Pearl Harbor on December 7, 1941, the United States was a nation at war. The war effort quickly staked a claim on the nation's human and natural resources—from the young men who might work on the farm to the paper on which the message of the organic method might be printed.

What's more, the war proved a massive spur to American industry generally and especially to companies that made items that could be used in the war effort, such as electrical components. And that meant J.I. would be needed to help manage Rodale Manufacturing's growing plant. The company's sales through November 1941 jumped 65 percent from the year before, to $528,000, as the nation began to mobilize. And once the United States entered World War II, the company was flooded with orders from military contractors and the military itself. Aside from its traditional plugs and wiring connectors, Rodale also began to make consumer items such as radios and doorbells out of the synthetic resin Bakelite.

The plant expanded in several directions. They dug a basement in the main building to

Eager to share experience and insights from his Emmaus farm with the public, J. I. Rodale in May 1942 started *Organic Farming and Gardening* magazine.

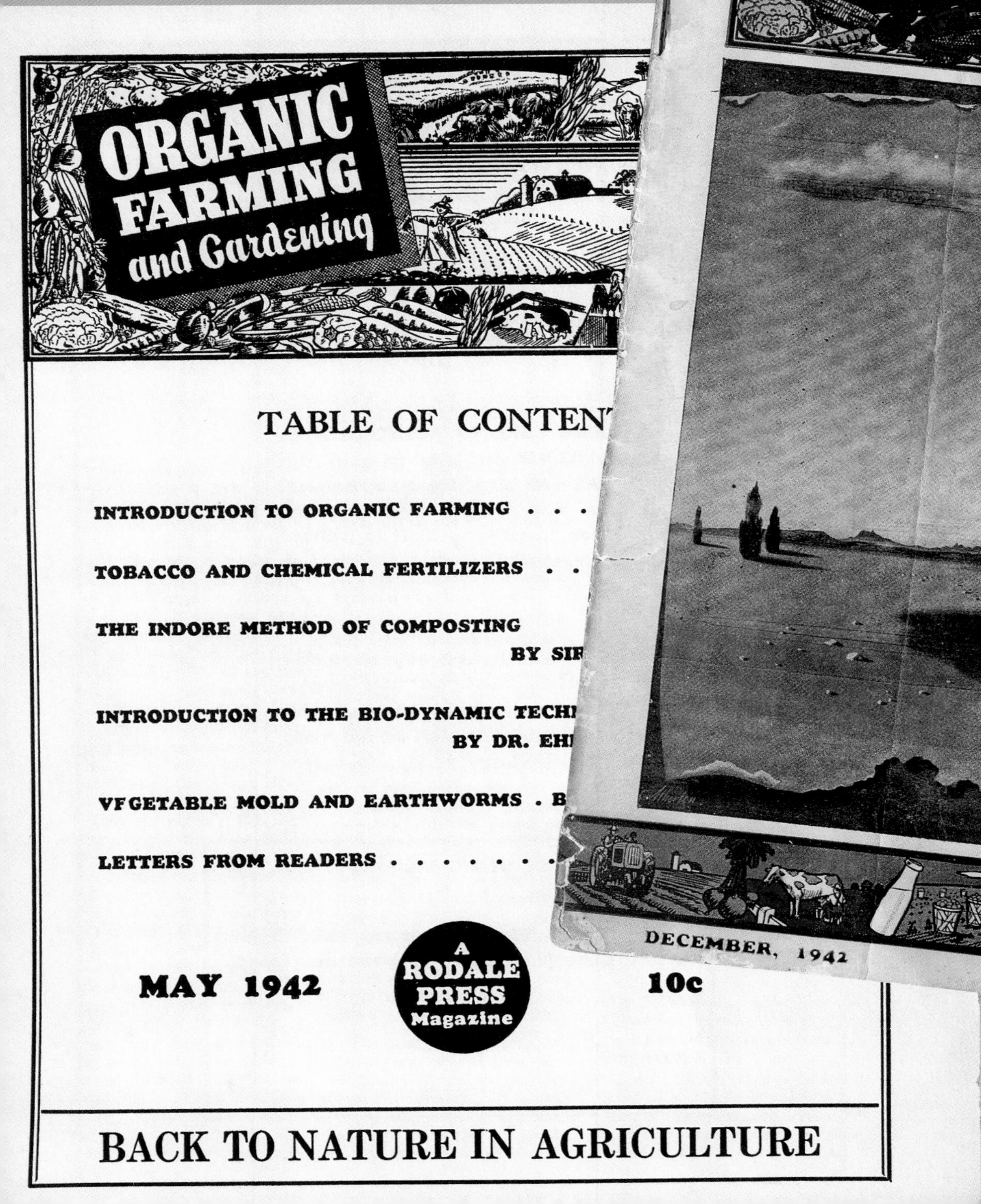

TABLE OF CONTENT

MAY 1942

10c

BACK TO NATURE IN AGRICULTURE

ORGANIC
Gardening
and FARMING

DECEMBER, 1942

25c

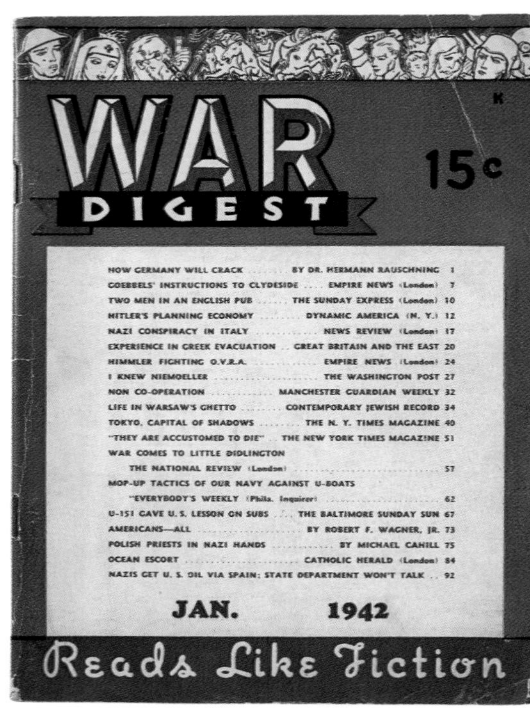

WAR DIGEST

15c

HOW GERMANY WILL CRACK .... BY DR. HERMANN RAUSCHNING 1
GOEBBELS' INSTRUCTIONS TO CLYDESIDE .... EMPIRE NEWS (London) 7
TWO MEN IN AN ENGLISH PUB ...... THE SUNDAY EXPRESS (London) 10
HITLER'S PLANNING ECONOMY .... DYNAMIC AMERICA (N. Y.) 12
NAZI CONSPIRACY IN ITALY .... NEWS REVIEW (London) 17
EXPERIENCE IN GREEK EVACUATION .. GREAT BRITAIN AND THE EAST 20
HIMMLER FIGHTING O.V.R.A. .... EMPIRE NEWS (London) 24
I KNEW NIEMOELLER .... THE WASHINGTON POST 27
NON CO-OPERATION .... MANCHESTER GUARDIAN WEEKLY 32
LIFE IN WARSAW'S GHETTO .... CONTEMPORARY JEWISH RECORD 34
TOKYO, CAPITAL OF SHADOWS .... THE N. Y. TIMES MAGAZINE 40
"THEY ARE ACCUSTOMED TO DIE" .. THE NEW YORK TIMES MAGAZINE 51
WAR COMES TO LITTLE DIDLINGTON
THE NATIONAL REVIEW (London) 57
MOP-UP TACTICS OF OUR NAVY AGAINST U-BOATS
"EVERYBODY'S WEEKLY (Phila. Inquirer) 62
U-151 GAVE U. S. LESSON ON SUBS ... THE BALTIMORE SUNDAY SUN 67
AMERICANS—ALL .... BY ROBERT F. WAGNER, JR. 73
POLISH PRIESTS IN NAZI HANDS .... BY MICHAEL CAHILL 75
OCEAN ESCORT .... CATHOLIC HERALD (London) 84
NAZIS GET U. S. OIL VIA SPAIN; STATE DEPARTMENT WON'T TALK .. 92

JAN. 1942

Reads Like Fiction

The outbreak of World War II provided a new subject for a Rodale magazine but also led to restrictions on paper supplies.

accommodate new Bakelite machinery, and production started at a smaller building on Sixth Street in Emmaus. The plant was primarily Joe Rodale's province, and he was assisted by Elmer Barto, the company's president. "[Joe] was always on the floor, giving us workers a pat on the back and thanking us for our good work when we finished a special job," recalled Marianne and Chalmers Kline, who met at Rodale Manufacturing in 1941. Over the course of the war, Rodale made items such as "recoil gun mount adapters for aircraft, submarine hatch gaskets, land mine plugs, and parachute hooks." By 1945, the company's sales nearly tripled from the 1941 total, to $1.44 million.

The paper quotas made it difficult to start new publishing ventures without canceling existing ones. In 1942, J.I. was publishing several magazines: *Fact Digest, Science Facts, War Digest*, and *You Can't Eat That.* His book-publishing operation, which produced several new volumes each year in the late 1930s, had essentially ground to a halt. In 1942, J.I. packaged the three word-finding books into a boxed set called *The Word Finder*, which he sold for $6.50.

But J.I. plowed ahead, and in May 1942 he published the first issue of *Organic Farming and Gardening* magazine. "What did I know about farming or gardening? Practically nothing." But J.I. had been reading and conducting his own small-scale experiments. "I went from book to book and from farm to farm trying to squeeze into days what should have gone into years." And J.I. had already learned a great deal–for example, how much natural fertilizer he could glean from his own farm by cutting weeds, or how to use corncobs for compost instead of burning them. He viewed the magazine as a cooperative venture among writers, practitioners, readers, and the publisher–"a wonderful means for farmers and gardeners to pool their cumulative experience."

The first issue featured an article by Sir Albert Howard on the Indore Method, the process of manufacturing humus from vegetable and animal wastes that he oversaw in the late 1920s in Indore, central India; an excerpt from Charles Darwin's writings on vegetable mold and earthworms; and advertisements for everything from cow breeders to J.I.'s book *Sleep and Rheumatism*. In the lead article, J.I. laid out his vision of how a growing appreciation for the organic method would change the economics of farming. "One of these fine days the public is going to wake up

1942
Casablanca, starring Humphrey Bogart and Ingrid Bergman, premieres.

May: First issue of *Organic Farming and Gardening* appears; in December, the name is changed to *Organic Gardening and Farming*.

Casablanca

Forty percent of vegetables consumed in the United States are grown in Victory Gardens.

November 7: The American Medical Association council on foods and nutrition suggests people limit consumption of sugar in candy and soft drinks.

December 2: A team led by physicist Enrico Fermi initiates the first self-sustaining nuclear chain reaction at the University of Chicago.

For *Organic Farming and Gardening*, Rodale drew inspiration and content from sources old and new.

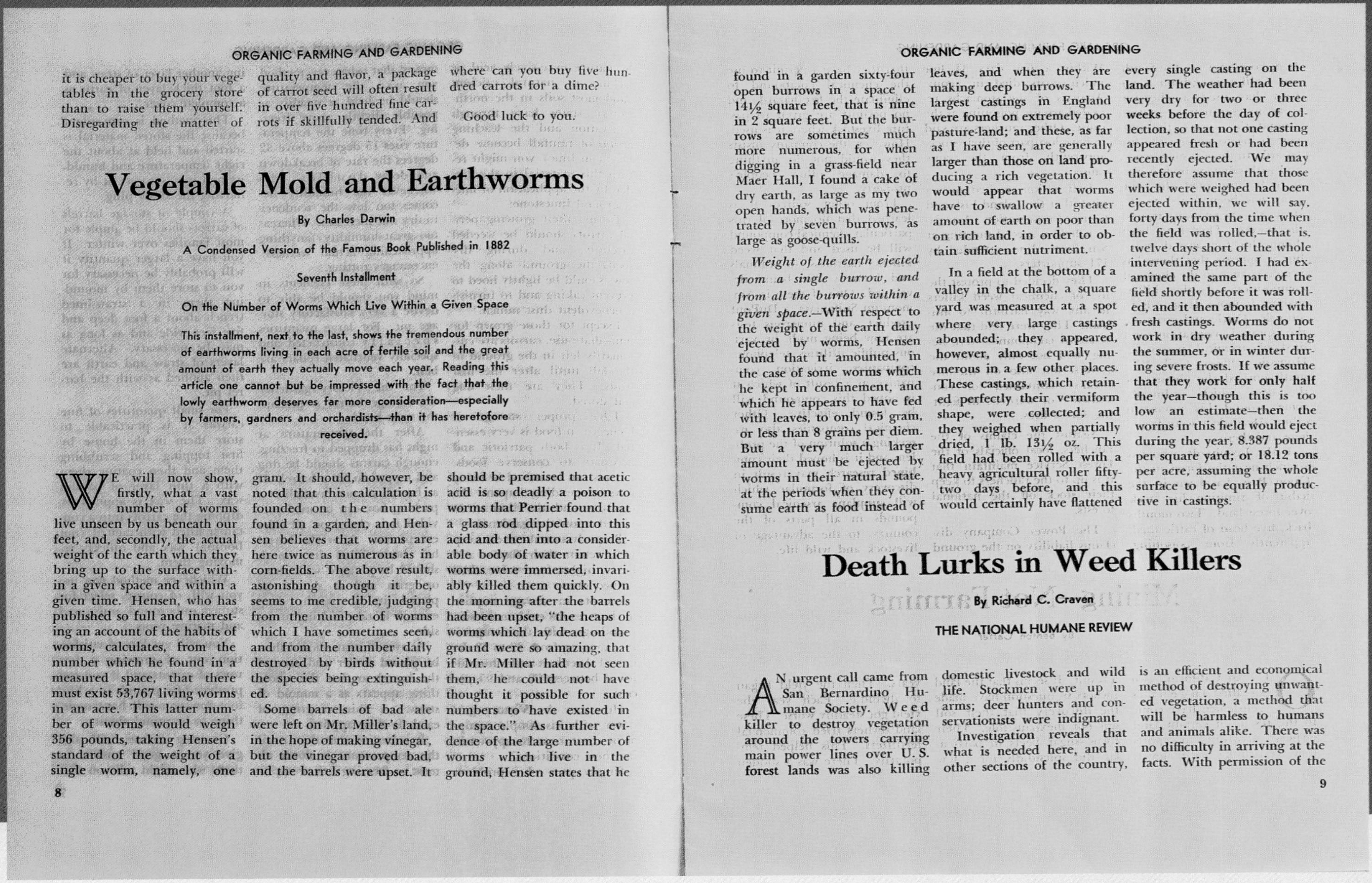

it is cheaper to buy your vegetables in the grocery store than to raise them yourself. Disregarding the matter of quality and flavor, a package of carrot seed will often result in over five hundred fine carrots if skillfully tended. And where can you buy five hundred carrots for a dime?

Good luck to you.

Vegetable Mold and Earthworms

By Charles Darwin

A Condensed Version of the Famous Book Published in 1882

Seventh Installment

On the Number of Worms Which Live Within a Given Space

This installment, next to the last, shows the tremendous number of earthworms living in each acre of fertile soil and the great amount of earth they actually move each year. Reading this article one cannot but be impressed with the fact that the lowly earthworm deserves far more consideration—especially by farmers, gardners and orchardists—than it has heretofore received.

WE will now show, firstly, what a vast number of worms live unseen by us beneath our feet, and, secondly, the actual weight of the earth which they bring up to the surface within a given space and within a given time. Hensen, who has published so full and interesting an account of the habits of worms, calculates, from the number which he found in a measured space, that there must exist 53,767 living worms in an acre. This latter number of worms would weigh 356 pounds, taking Hensen's standard of the weight of a single worm, namely, one gram. It should, however, be noted that this calculation is founded on the numbers found in a garden, and Hensen believes that worms are here twice as numerous as in corn-fields. The above result, astonishing though it be, seems to me credible, judging from the number of worms which I have sometimes seen, and from the number daily destroyed by birds without the species being extinguished.

Some barrels of bad ale were left on Mr. Miller's land, in the hope of making vinegar, but the vinegar proved bad, and the barrels were upset. It should be premised that acetic acid is so deadly a poison to worms that Perrier found that a glass rod dipped into this acid and then into a considerable body of water in which worms were immersed, invariably killed them quickly. On the morning after the barrels had been upset, "the heaps of worms which lay dead on the ground were so amazing, that if Mr. Miller had not seen them, he could not have thought it possible for such numbers to have existed in the space." As further evidence of the large number of worms which live in the ground, Hensen states that he found in a garden sixty-four open burrows in a space of 14½ square feet, that is nine in 2 square feet. But the burrows are sometimes much more numerous, for when digging in a grass-field near Maer Hall, I found a cake of dry earth, as large as my two open hands, which was penetrated by seven burrows, as large as goose-quills.

Weight of the earth ejected from a single burrow, and from all the burrows within a given space.—With respect to the weight of the earth daily ejected by worms, Hensen found that it amounted, in the case of some worms which he kept in confinement, and which he appears to have fed with leaves, to only 0.5 gram, or less than 8 grains per diem. But a very much larger amount must be ejected by worms in their natural state, at the periods when they consume earth as food instead of leaves, and when they are making deep burrows. The largest castings in England were found on extremely poor pasture-land; and these, as far as I have seen, are generally larger than those on land producing a rich vegetation. It would appear that worms have to swallow a greater amount of earth on poor than on rich land, in order to obtain sufficient nutriment.

In a field at the bottom of a valley in the chalk, a square yard was measured at a spot where very large castings abounded; they appeared, however, almost equally numerous in a few other places. These castings, which retained perfectly their vermiform shape, were collected; and they weighed when partially dried, 1 lb. 13½ oz. This field had been rolled with a heavy agricultural roller fifty-two days before, and this would certainly have flattened every single casting on the land. The weather had been very dry for two or three weeks before the day of collection, so that not one casting appeared fresh or had been recently ejected. We may therefore assume that those which were weighed had been ejected within, we will say, forty days from the time when the field was rolled,—that is, twelve days short of the whole intervening period. I had examined the same part of the field shortly before it was rolled, and it then abounded with fresh castings. Worms do not work in dry weather during the summer, or in winter during severe frosts. If we assume that they work for only half the year—though this is too low an estimate—then the worms in this field would eject during the year, 8.387 pounds per square yard; or 18.12 tons per acre, assuming the whole surface to be equally productive in castings.

Death Lurks in Weed Killers

By Richard C. Craven

THE NATIONAL HUMANE REVIEW

AN urgent call came from San Bernardino Humane Society. Weed killer to destroy vegetation around the towers carrying main power lines over U. S. forest lands was also killing domestic livestock and wild life. Stockmen were up in arms; deer hunters and conservationists were indignant.

Investigation reveals that what is needed here, and in other sections of the country, is an efficient and economical method of destroying unwanted vegetation, a method that will be harmless to humans and animals alike. There was no difficulty in arriving at the facts. With permission of the

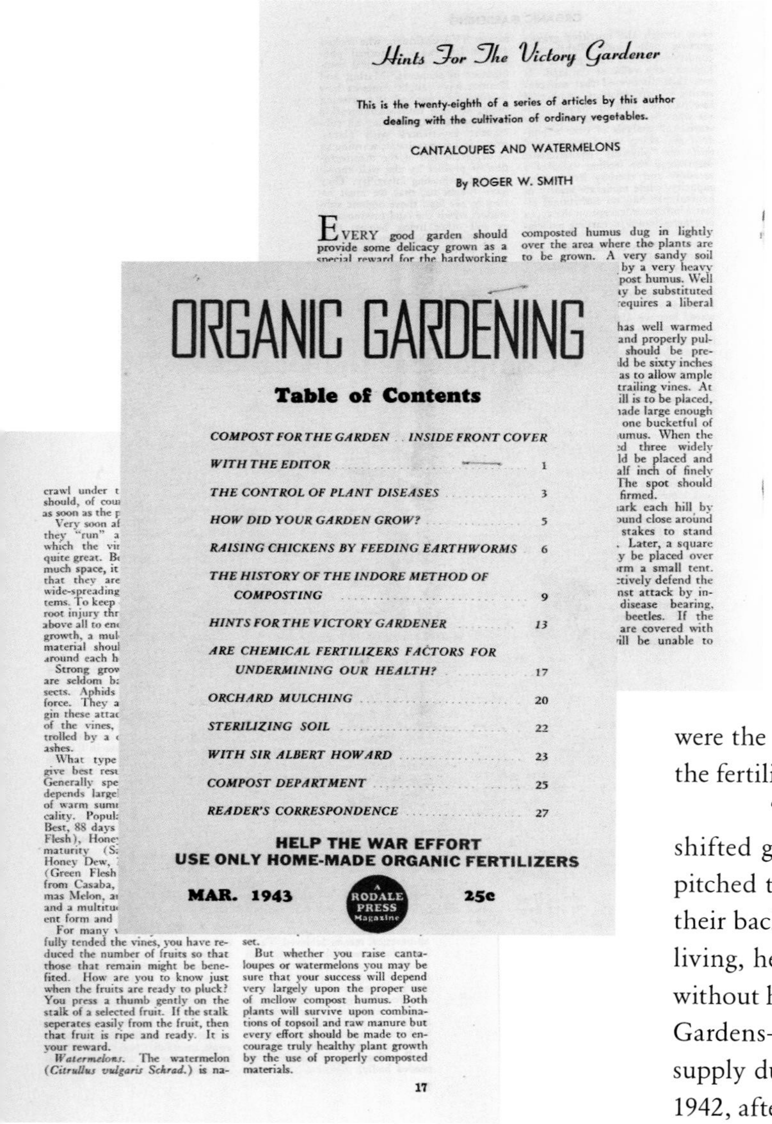

Hints For The Victory Gardener

This is the twenty-eighth of a series of articles by this author dealing with the cultivation of ordinary vegetables.

CANTALOUPES AND WATERMELONS

By ROGER W. SMITH

EVERY good garden should provide some delicacy grown as a special reward for the hardworking ... composted humus dug in lightly over the area where the plants are to be grown. A very sandy soil ...

ORGANIC GARDENING

Table of Contents

HELP THE WAR EFFORT
USE ONLY HOME-MADE ORGANIC FERTILIZERS

MAR. 1943 A RODALE PRESS Magazine **25c**

fully tended the vines, you have reduced the number of fruits so that those that remain might be benefited. How are you to know just when the fruits are ready to pluck? You press a thumb gently on the stalk of a selected fruit. If the stalk seperates easily from the fruit, then that fruit is ripe and ready. It is your reward.

Watermelons. The watermelon (*Citrullus vulgaris Schrad.*) is na- ... set.

But whether you raise cantaloupes or watermelons you may be sure that your success will depend very largely upon the proper use of mellow compost humus. Both plants will survive upon combinations of topsoil and raw manure but every effort should be made to encourage truly healthy plant growth by the use of properly composted materials.

17

Tapping into the patriotic drive to bolster the food supply during war, *Organic Gardening* offered practical advice for Victory Gardeners.

and will pay for eggs, meats, vegetables, etc., according to how they were produced. A substantial premium will be paid for high quality products such as those raised by organic methods."

That "fine day" would remain far off, and the initial response was less than overwhelming. J.I. printed about 14,000 copies of the first issue and sent them gratis to farmers in what he viewed as representative rural communities in an effort to win readers. "We received but 12 paid subscribers out of this first month's mailings," he wrote. From the beginning, J.I. realized that he was trying to reach two separate audiences with one magazine: professional large-scale farmers and amateur gardeners. Judging by the results of the first mass mailing, farmers weren't quite ready to adopt the organic method en masse. After all, the prevailing wisdom at the time held, since after World War I when synthetic chemicals were first used in pesticides, that chemical fertilizers and pesticides were the keys to increased yields, and hence profits. And powerful forces—from the government to the fertilizer companies—were encouraging more, rather than less, use of these products.

"Our prospects looked bleak. But I was not discouraged," J.I. recalled. Undaunted, he shifted gears. Instead of targeting farmers, he made smaller print runs, sent out circulars, and pitched the content more toward gardeners. Inducing people to experiment with a small plot in their backyard was probably an easier sell than urging farmers to change the way they made their living, he reasoned. Individuals could experiment with small compost piles just as J.I. had—and without having to make large investments of time or money. And with the proliferation of Victory Gardens—small plots in which civilians were encouraged to grow vegetables to guarantee a food supply during the war—the population of home gardeners was growing rapidly. So in December 1942, after just five issues, J.I. changed the name of the magazine to *Organic Gardening and Farming* (*OG&F*) and soon after that to *Organic Gardening* in January 1943.

The name may have changed, but Sir Albert Howard remained the magazine's guiding spirit. Virtually every issue featured an article by him, and a recurring feature allowed readers to ask

Howard specific questions. Throughout the war, J.I. and Howard, who never met, sustained a correspondence, and the Rodales occasionally mailed butter and other food to Howard and his wife.

Organic Gardening slowly built an audience. Readers included U.S. vice president Henry Wallace, who had founded the Hi-Bred Seed Company. "I shall look over the copies of your magazine with much interest because I have been busy trying to compost some vegetable material for my own gardening operation." And in 1943, when it was clear to him that the magazine had a future, J.I. decided to make the magazine the exclusive focus of his publishing efforts. In March 1943, the magazine formally took over the operations of the farm as an experimental farm. And that year, he sold *Fact Digest* and *Science and Discovery* to a company in New York, which melded them together into *Read* magazine. In 1943, J.I. reported a salary of $27,683 from Rodale Manufacturing and a loss of $2,291 on the farm.

Meanwhile, the Rodale family was adjusting to the different rhythm of life. When the Rodales moved to the farm, Ruth and Bob attended a one-room country school. The kids warmed their lunches over a potbellied stove and left school to harvest potatoes. Ultimately, Anna and J.I. decided they wanted to keep their children in the Allentown schools, so they purchased a house on South 17th Street in Allentown in the early 1940s. They lived in that house primarily during the school year and spent vacations and the summer at the farm. J.I. took to waking up at 4 in the morning so he could get more done around the house and the farm before going into the office.

The Rodale family in the early 1940s. *From left:* J.I., Nina, Robert, Anna, and Ruth.

1943
January 5: Death of George Washington Carver, pioneering African American scientist and inventor

There are 21 million Victory Gardens in the United States.

September 8: General Dwight D. Eisenhower publicly announces the surrender of Italy to the Allies.

The Little Prince, by Antoine de Saint-Exupéry, is published.

J. I. Rodale sells *Fact Digest* to concentrate on *Organic Gardening*.

Lady Eve Balfour publishes *The Living Soil*, making a case for an alternative, sustainable approach to agriculture.

The Rodale family in the late 1940s. *From left:* J.I., Nina, Bob, Ruth, and Anna

In *Organic Gardening* (*OG*), J.I. forged a style of journalism—a mix of personal essay and reporting—that was rarely practiced at the time. His activities—and those of his family—were fodder for the pages of the magazines. "We are practicing mulching in our vegetable garden," he wrote in May 1943. "Last summer we were fortunate to get a large quantity of hay cuttings from a nearby park system, tons and tons of it merely for the hauling. . . . We are raising apples not only for our own consumption but for that of a herd of steers which we are fattening." To the 14 steers and 100 chickens, "all fed with the products raised on our own farm," he planned to add sheep and pigs "so that we will be in a position to raise over 80 percent of the food we consume." In November 1943, he reported on the corn crop, which yielded almost as much from 9 acres as it had from 21 acres when farmed using fertilizer a few years before. The September 1944 issue featured photos of large sunflower plants on the farm. "The reason for these large plants is the organic treatment of the soil and also the spacing," he wrote.

Young Bob helped care for the livestock on the farm.

J.I. was frequently unabashed in revealing intimate details of his and his family's life, especially when he wrote about the effects of an organic lifestyle on health and hygiene—an early and recurring theme. "A few years ago I decided to try and do something about my tendency to catch cold very easily. After reading up on the subject, I eliminated all forms of grain from my diet," he wrote in October 1943. "After about three or four weeks my head became much clearer, and a mild catarrhal condition cleared up." And when the whole family went on the same diet, he reported, "it cleared up a stubborn case of constipation for Mrs. Rodale" and freed young Robert temporarily from the scourge of poison ivy.

At root, all of J.I.'s ventures were family businesses—as much as the grocery store on Norfolk Street in New York had been. "Bob was a growing boy, and he went around hauling rocks for the rock garden," Anna wrote. "The others helped in the garden, and we all helped with weeding." Robert was also developing as a young sportsman. An Angler's Record Book dated 1945 documents fishing outings in the Little Lehigh River. Using a Ganger Special rod, an Indian small fly reel, and a range of bait, Bob, then 15, caught several trout in one outing. Bob got his first

1944
June 6: D-day invasion of Normandy.

November 7: Franklin D. Roosevelt wins reelection over Republican challenger Thomas E. Dewey to become the only U.S. president to be elected to a fourth term.

D-day Normandy invasion

Swedish author of children's books Astrid Lindgren publishes *Pippi Longstocking.*

Mayo Clinic physicians say cigarettes may harm wounded men by constricting blood vessels.

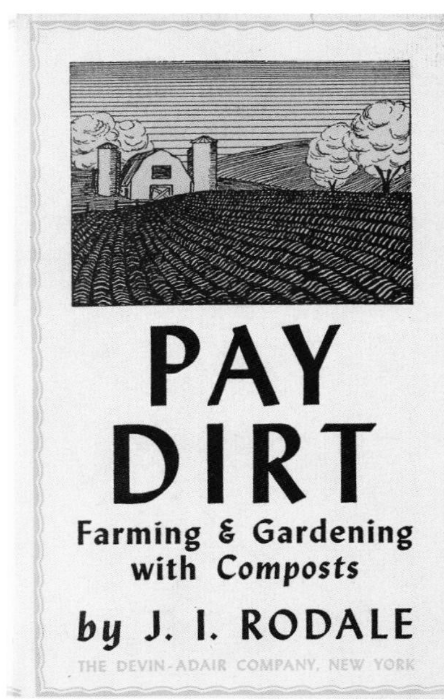

Pay Dirt (1945), the first book written by J.I. to be published by a commercial publisher, was a breakthrough success.

gun—a .22 rifle—shortly after the family moved to the farm. As a teenager, he occasionally shot pheasant with a 20-gauge single-barrel shotgun. He became interested in skeet shooting, and initially he practiced by shooting at birds out of a moving car. On one occasion, he shot a hole in the side door of J.I.'s Cadillac.

At Rodale Manufacturing, Joe and J.I. remained partners, taking virtually identical salaries. After J.I. and Anna moved to the farm, Joe, the onetime cavalry soldier, wanted to raise horses on the property. In 1944, Joe purchased an Arabian stallion and several purebred mares. He ultimately bought his own farm southwest of Allentown. There, he built a stone house and raised horses. By 1952, his stable grew to house more than 40.

During the war years, the Rodales faced a constant race to keep up with demand at Rodale Manufacturing and simultaneously to develop *OG*, the farm, and the book publishing operation. As the war came to an end in the spring of 1945, it would mark a moment of important transition. The peacetime economy would unleash consumer demand that would continue to drive Rodale Manufacturing's rapid growth, thus providing J.I. with more resources to develop his other ventures. The end of the war also brought an end to paper supply quotas, which meant that J.I. was free to invest in the expansion of *OG*—which claimed 30,000 subscribers—and that publishers had greater leeway to introduce new books to the reading public.

With the end of the war and the dawning of what promised to be a new era, J.I. felt it was a ripe moment for the organic movement. The publication of his book *Pay Dirt*, in August 1945, gave him reason for optimism. *Pay Dirt*, a summary and exposition of many of the arguments about soil and health that had been aired in the pages of *OG*, was not published by Rodale Press, but by Devin-Adair, a commercial New York publisher. For the first time, another company was investing in J.I.'s writings, and the book would be sold primarily through bookstores, not through mail order as many of his previous publications had.

To the readers of *OG, Pay Dirt* was a twice-told tale. But to new readers, the message was bracing and new. J.I. summarized Howard's findings, discussed good and bad farming practices, and

1945
May 8: Germany's unconditional surrender goes into effect.

August: Publication of J. I. Rodale's *Pay Dirt*.

August 6: The United States detonates an atomic bomb on Hiroshima, Japan.

Germany surrenders

November 1: John H. Johnson publishes the first issue of *Ebony* magazine.

The U.S. Census Bureau reports that nearly twice as many U.S. citizens died of cancer during 1942 to 1944 as were killed by enemy action in WWII.

Grand Rapids, Michigan, and Newburgh, New York, become the first cities to add fluoride to drinking water.

Meillands Nursery in France releases the 'Peace' rose. Single blooms are given to members of the United Nations.

November: Death of Bertha Cohen, J. I. Rodale's mother.

J. I. Rodale saw a direct connection between human health and environmental health. In 1945, he was one of the first critics to warn of the dangers posed to humans by the insecticide DDT.

Over the Fence by H. K. MEYER

DDT is on the market now. Paul F. Frese of the *Flower Grower* says that this material is death to the honeybees. While Elmer Carroll of *The Beekeeper's Magazine* wrote us recently that there is no concern, the well-known bee expert of the University of California, Dr. J. E. Eckert seems to be worried about the increased poison spraying. On August 25, the conservative *Wall Street Journal* published an item about the danger of DDT to beekeepers. "There is a vital need for state or federal regulation to control insecticide applications," Dr. J. E. Eckert, University of California apiologist, says. "Now any farmer in California except in one county, may release poisonous arsenate or cyanide sprays whenever and wherever he likes. Even if he dusts crops that bees don't visit (such as tomatoes) with power sprayers or by airplane, poison often spreads two miles away into adjoining fields or orchards where bees are working." Nearly 1,500 colonies of bees were killed and more injured in one California county last year by calcium arsenate spraying of tomatoes. The same poison two weeks ago *killed half of the University of California's highly-bred bees* when it drifted into dew (bees' drinking water) and into star thistle weeds alongside a tomato field.

Vegetable-rich Imperial County, at the bottom tip of California, controls insecticide applications rigidly for the sake of the expensive perishables it markets in the East.

—o—

Science News Letter, August 18, 1945, had an item as follows: "Eight or more sprayings of apple orchards are now required to accomplish the results of a single spraying forty years ago. The coddling moth of today is the descendant of the worms that proved best able to resist poisoning in the past." How well this scientific finding agrees with the practical observation and intuition of the plant breeder Allwood, from whom we quote in the article *Carnations and Organics!*

—o—

Both Mr. Faulkner and Mr. Pretzer replied to an item in this column and state that there is no doubt that earthworms dragged celery plants down into their burrows. "Ours is not a lone experience," writes Mr. Pretzer, "as our whole area could substantiate the fact by similar experience." The Cleveland region must offer very little organic feed to the earthworms who prefer half decayed matter to fresh plants. Or the area is otherwise so unique, since there can be *no doubt about Mr. Pretzer's statement*, that an earthworm species living on young plants could develop. This is unusual in the light

22

As farmers were reluctant to adopt the organic method, J.I. refocused the magazine on home gardeners.

J.I.'s notoriety attracted visitors to his farm, such as actress Gloria Swanson.

included testimonials from farmers and gardeners who had followed this advice and produced excellent results. He declared that "a revolution in farming and gardening is in progress all over the world" and concluded that a "new era of agricultural research is in the making."

Pay Dirt was a breakthrough for J.I. It was reviewed in dozens of newspapers and magazines. The *Omaha World-Herald* concluded that ". . . along with Louis Bromfield's *Pleasant Valley*, Mr. Rodale's *Pay Dirt* belongs on every farmer's living room worktable." Russell Lord, editor of *Land Magazine*, reviewed the book prominently in the Sunday *New York Times* book review section. "Much of the stuff he cites seems to me the outcome of a flaming will-to-believe, and a bit 'screwy'; but most of it makes sense, plainly." By December 1945, *Pay Dirt* was in its third American edition and about to be printed in England.

The commercial success of the book—it sold more than 50,000 copies—elevated J.I.'s status. "It more or less made me 'Mr. Organic,'" he wrote. "I was considered the leader of the movement. I was called on to speak all over the country, received important visitors at our farm, had lunch with notables at the Colony Club on Park Avenue, and once hobnobbed with Louis Bromfield at an affair at the swank River Club." The exuberance of the period was dampened in part by the death in November 1945 of J.I.'s mother, Bertha Cohen.

Increasingly, his writings took a more crusading, almost evangelical tone. In the December 1945 issue of *OG*, he proudly reported, "my seven-year-old daughter, Nina, was chosen by the school nurse as having the finest teeth in her class." J.I. postulated that "if all the statesmen of the world, if all government officials could eat food produced organically from a fertile soil rich in minerals, the possibility of future wars would be greatly diminished." Rather than promulgating a new method of gardening and farming, J.I. viewed his efforts as leading an "organic cause." He enlisted subscribers to sell subscriptions to their friends and neighbors and even developed a coat of arms—its quadrants featured a sunflower, worms, crossed pitchforks, and a shovel.

With the wartime restrictions on publishing lifted, J.I. also began to publish books again. In 1947, *The Word Finder* was introduced in a new edition as a single volume and was reviewed in

1946
January 10: First meeting of the United Nations.

February 14: ENIAC, the first general-purpose electronic computer, is unveiled at the University of Pennsylvania.

March 5: In a speech in Fulton, Missouri, Winston Churchill introduces the term "Iron Curtain."

Winston Churchill

Frank Capra's *It's a Wonderful Life*, starring Jimmy Stewart, premieres.

Penicillin is produced synthetically.

It's a Wonderful Life

***The Word Finder*, published in 1947, was a compilation of J.I.'s earlier word books.**

Publisher's Weekly and the *Saturday Review of Literature*. Bennett Cerf, the cofounder of Random House, was cited as calling it "the most useful" book to arrive on his desk. *The Word Finder* would sell 150,000 copies in its lifetime. In 1947, Rodale Press also introduced *The Glossaries for Anyone Who Writes*, which took the adjectives, adverbs, and verbs he had collected and aggregated them around different concepts and words in small pamphlets.

J.I. had begun collecting a set of richly illustrated limited edition books and liked them so much that he decided to publish a series of short story collections, the Story Classics line. The first, in 1948, was Thomas Hardy's *The History of the Hardcomes*, featuring full-color reproductions of oil paintings by local artist Walter Emerson Baum. Virtually all the Rodales—Anna, Ruth, Nina, and Bob—attended classes at the Baum Art School and were strong supporters of the school. Anna developed a passion for painting and fine arts and became president of the Allentown Art Museum auxiliary group. The series included works of Henry Wadsworth Longfellow, Chekhov, Voltaire, and Cervantes. Rodale engaged in a range of promotional efforts for the series. One circular, written in Old English type, noted that celebrities, such as "Irving Stone, Mrs. Darryl Zanuck, Louis Untermeyer, Ellery Queen, and many others in public or literary life," had subscribed. The Story Classics weren't profitable, but they helped J.I. make important connections. Once he realized it was cheaper to have the books printed in Great Britain, he established contact with London-based publishers William Green and John Frost.

Right after the war, Rodale Press was still run as a one- or two-person partnership out of a room in the southeast corner of Rodale Manufacturing's plant. But the years 1947 and 1948 were a remarkably productive period for J.I. as he focused on producing magazines and books related to organic farming and gardening and the collateral effects of these methods on human health.

The question of how eating organic foods could improve health had always been addressed in *OG*, but J.I. placed the topic at the center of his work in the late 1940s. In 1947, he began to construct a diet based on organic foods. He wrote to officials and professors at colleges in New Hampshire, Michigan, Wyoming, and Tennessee to inquire about local crops that were

1947
February 21: Edwin Land demonstrates the first "instant camera," the Polaroid Land Camera.

April 15: Jackie Robinson breaks baseball's color line.

Jackie Robinson

August 7: Thor Heyerdahl's balsa-wood raft, the Kon-Tiki, completes a 101-day, 4,300-mile journey across the Pacific Ocean.

October: J.I. introduces the Rodale Diet in *OG*.

October 20: Death of Sir Albert Howard.

November 2: Howard Hughes performs the maiden flight of the Spruce Goose, the largest fixed-wing aircraft ever built.

December 3: Tennessee Williams's play *A Streetcar Named Desire* opens on Broadway.

The Soil and Health Foundation is formed.

grown organically. "I was very happy to see that you found something similar to Penicillin in mushrooms," he wrote to a researcher in Australia, "because I am the originator of the Rodale Diet which represents foods that are usually grown without chemical fertilizers. Mushrooms are one of them."

In the October 1947 issue of *OG*, J.I. formally introduced his 60,000 subscribers to an eating plan that he dubbed the Rodale Diet. He viewed it as a temporary stopgap measure until the organic revolution took hold. Essentially, he listed foods and categories of foods that people wishing to maintain an entirely organic diet could safely eat: fish, kelp, mushrooms, coconut, watercress, pine nuts, lychee nuts, berries, palm cabbage, wild rice, and wild game such as deer. "This is an elementary statement of about one-half of the Rodale Diet," he wrote. "More material will be given next month."

Inspired by Sir Albert Howard, J.I. had taken a scientific approach to the organic method from the outset. While he was largely self-taught, he continually corresponded with and took cues from professionally trained biologists, chemists, and nutritionists. He knew the sensibility he advocated went against the prevailing grain, and he believed that the use of sound science, research, and investigation would legitimize the organic movement. He sought not so much to debunk the scientific establishment as to enlist it in his cause. To provide a spur to such efforts and to push the organic revolution into its next stage, J.I. decided to form a nonprofit foundation, the Soil and Health Foundation. As he noted in the May 1947 *OG*, "Competent chemists, biologists and other experts will be employed to place the theory of organic farming on a basis where all the claims made for it are proven scientifically."

His plans for the foundation were typically ambitious. "Let the Foundation go out to our American courts and ask for the application of eminent domain in the matter of the production of our food. Let the Foundation bring legal action against one of these large vegetable factories, and get an injunction issued against such evil practices. The Revolution has begun." So, in October 1947, the Soil and Health Foundation met formally at 46 South West Street in Allentown.

J.I. saw in the organic method the possibility of devising a system of producing and consuming food that could improve human health.

Endowed with a $1,000 donation from Rodale Manufacturing, its board elected J.I. as president, University of Vermont professor Dr. B. F. Lutman as vice president, Joe Rodale as treasurer, and William Eyster, the managing editor of *OG*, as secretary.

Rodale Manufacturing could afford to make such donations because it was prospering. In 1947, the company paid J.I. a salary of $32,400 and $37,772 in dividends. But Rodale Press was just as consistent a money loser. In 1947, it lost $120,337. The revenues from subscriptions and book sales ($212,270) and advertising ($38,755) were far outweighed by expenses, which included $116,000 in salaries and wages.

J.I. found proof for what he'd long assumed: Organic food can be the key to a long and healthy life.

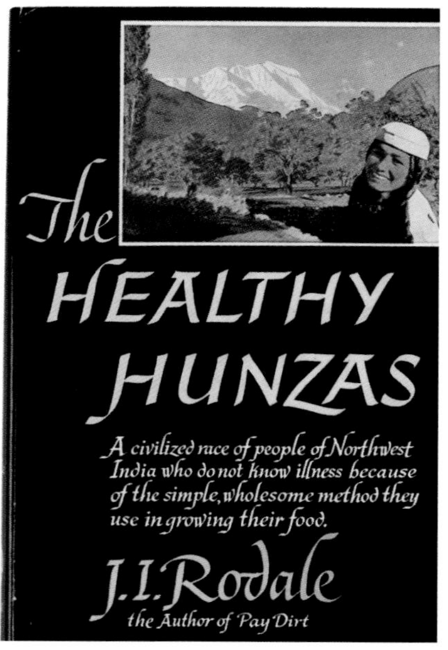

The enthusiasm of fall, however, was tempered by sadness. On October 20, Sir Albert Howard died at the age of 74. "It is one of the insolaceable regrets of my life that I never had the honor of meeting Sir Albert personally," J.I. wrote. "Yet I feel that our relations have been as close as if we had had weekly meetings in the intimate sessions of personal friends." And he described Howard in terms that others may well have used to describe J.I.: "He fought the chemical companies, the college professors, and all the vested interest that placed considerations of financial profit ahead of the welfare of man and that of the soil. Fearing no one, he gave others the courage to fight, himself setting the example and the pattern."

J.I. consciously tried to emulate Howard's sense of curiosity and open-mindedness. In 1948, he visited a farm in Alabama where the owner, who raised earthworms, argued that the castings of earthworms made an excellent component for compost. "Well, the force of his answer hit me like a ton of bricks," J.I. wrote. "I am sure that were Sir Albert alive today, he would strongly advocate such experimental work." J.I. resolved to send this new compost to be analyzed at the Soil and Health Foundation, which by the spring of 1948 had received more than 500 contributions from readers, farmers, and organic enthusiasts.

With the passing of Sir Albert Howard in 1947, one of the primary guiding spirits of *OG* had departed. But the next year saw the arrival of a young man who would prove enormously influential to the magazine and who would become a prominent leader of the organic movement.

1948
January 30: Winter Olympics open in St. Moritz, Switzerland.

April 7: The World Health Organization is established by the United Nations.

August 15: The first network nightly newscast, *CBS-TV News*, debuts with Douglas Edwards.

Adi Dassler renames his athletic footwear company Adidas and adds the trademark three stripes the following year.

Fairfield Osborn writes *Our Plundered Planet*.

J. I. Rodale publishes *The Healthy Hunzas*.

Rodale publishes the first of the Story Classics series, Thomas Hardy's *The History of the Hardcomes*.

While a teenage student at Lehigh University, Robert Rodale started working alongside his father.

In February 1948, 17-year-old Robert Rodale, who had decided to study journalism at nearby Lehigh University, was listed on the magazine's masthead as staff photographer. J.I.'s children had long been involved in the magazines. In the 1940s, J.I. would drive Robert and Ruth to towns in the area to hand out copies of *OG*. Ruth left Emmaus in 1946 to attend Wellesley College in Massachusetts and was studying botany.

Just as J.I. believed that diseases of plants and animals could be avoided by sound farming practices, he increasingly came to believe that human diseases could be prevented by sound eating practices. "There is a definite proven connection between the quality of our foods and our health," he told a group of organic gardeners in Michigan in 1948. But because society failed to recognize this truth, it misdirected massive resources. "Much money is being collected these days in every community in the country to be used in research to cure cancer, heart disease, poliomyelitis, and many other diseases. Fine. But practically all of this is going to the search for cure procedures. Probably nothing for prevention. But some of these diseases are increasing so fast that soon there may not be enough physicians to apply the cure, even if it is discovered."

The Soil and Health Foundation was intended to sponsor and back the sort of scientific inquiry into organic methods of farming and gardening that J.I. couldn't hope to do on his own. It was an effort to create a sort of counterestablishment, albeit with limited resources. "During the first several years of its existence, the Soil and Health Foundation was an almost total failure. J.I. could find very few universities and colleges to undertake organic experimentation," J. I. Rodale biographer Carlton Jackson wrote.

But it did report some results. "Preliminary results have been obtained in our studies of earthworms in relation to artificial chemical fertilizers," J.I. reported in August 1948. Nutrition studies of cancerous mice had been set up. "A chemist has now been added to our staff and we are now setting up and equipping a biochemical laboratory.... this laboratory will be set up in a temporary building in the hope that an experimental farm will soon become available where a permanent laboratory building and other necessary buildings can be erected."

The Story Classics came out three times a year and were marketed like a book club. Eventually, they were printed in Great Britain.

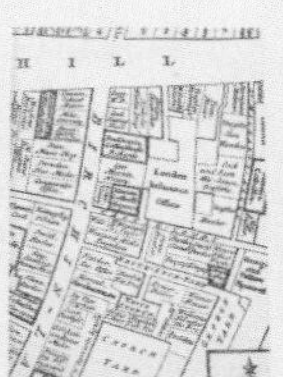

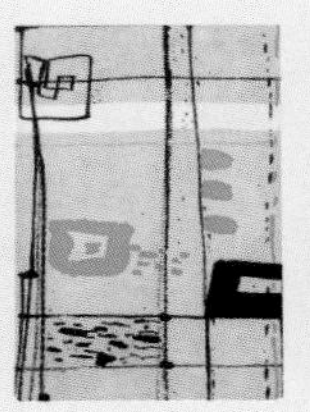

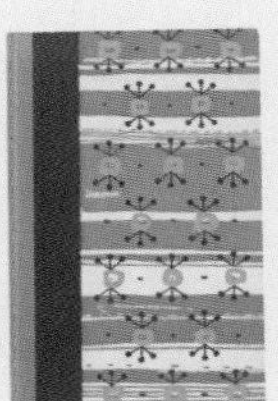

Friday, September 30, 1949 FALL

FALL BROWN & WHITE

Entered as second-class matter at the post office at Bethlehem, Pennsylvania, under the act of March 3, 1879.

Published by students of Lehigh University, Bethlehem, Pa. Office — Basement, Drown Hall Telephone 6-0331

Represented for National Advertising by NATIONAL ADVERTISING SERVICE, INC. College Publishers Rep. 420 Madison Ave., New York

Editor-in-chief .... Alan Yost
Managing Editor .... Les Whitten
Asst. Man. Editor .... Jack Carroll
Editorial Man. .... James Crawford
Assistant .... James Gill
News Man. .... J. Robert Cairns
Assistant .... Peter Lamana
Desk Editor .... Hugh Craig
Assistant .... Don Whitaker
Sports Editor .... El Cornog
Assistant .... Wm. Cornelius
Makeup Editor .... Harry Ramsey
Assistant .... Ira Handwerk
Photo Editor .... Jack Kelsey
Feature Editor .... Robert Rodale
Business Manager .... Wm. Clayton
Assistant .... Wm. Tracy
Financial Man. .... William Jones
Assistant .... Ken Hankinson
General Ads. .... Robert Bannister
National Ads. .... Bruce Hill
Local Ads. .... Michael Imbriani
Circulation .... Charles Segui
Assistant .... C. W. Ridinger
Faculty Advisers .... C. W. Wynn
J. B. McFadden

As a college student, Bob got journalism experience working at Lehigh University's *Brown & White.*

The Foundation published its first annual bulletin in October 1948. In 1949 the Foundation supported experiments on mice conducted by Dr. Ehrenfried Pfeiffer. The results, reported in Bulletin 2 of the Soil and Health Foundation in November 1949, found that mice that ate an organic diet fought less, were less irritable and nervous, and were less likely to die of stomach disorders than those that had eaten food raised with chemical fertilizers.

The connection between diet and health was vividly drawn in a book J.I. wrote and published in 1948, entitled *The Healthy Hunzas.* Written in what had become J.I.'s trademark style—a discursive mix of facts, trivia, and personal reflections—*The Healthy Hunzas* told the story of a tribe in northern India that practiced ancient and organic methods of farming and enjoyed what seemed to be remarkable health. In the same period, he also produced volumes on topics covered in the pages of *OG*, including *Stone Mulching in the Garden* and *Humus and the Farmer.*

As J.I. continued to investigate the connection between nutrition and health, he "began to study medical journals trying to find material in which doctors had studied the relations between the method of growing and food and its nutritional value." After reading a criticism of organic gardening that appeared in the *Journal of the American Medical Association*, "I began to browse in medical journals and was amazed to find how much valuable nutritional data of a preventive nature was hidden away there, mouldering, which the medical men were not disseminating to their patients." He resolved to start disseminating the information in *OG.* In the spring of 1949, he started using his Editor's Letter column to run a 13-month-long series on cancer.

As the magazine grew, and as J.I.'s interests changed, it became clear that *OG* was really three magazines in one. As it had always been, *OG* was a magazine about organic gardening. But with increasing numbers of farmers beginning to catch on to the organic message, it was also building a substantial base among professional farmers. Finally, given J.I.'s evolving and increasingly consuming interest in health, *OG* was emerging as a conduit for dispensing medical information. And while many of the magazine's 100,000 subscribers were interested in all three topics, J.I. sensed that it might be useful—and more profitable—to allow the magazine to focus on its core gardening audience and to create new vehicles to reach readers. So J. I. Rodale, with the assistance of son Robert, decided to spin off two new publications.

First, in the summer of 1949, Rodale Press introduced *The Organic Farmer.* As J.I. put it in his editor's letter, "One morning a few months ago in my mail there was such an earnest letter by a reader, asking that we start a special magazine devoted exclusively to the needs of the organic farmer, that we decided to do so." After the announcement, "subscriptions began to pour in, along with letters of elation and commendation. So much money has come in in advance subscriptions that it will furnish all the capital needed to start the new magazine."

The first issue of *The Organic Farmer* carried features on which organic products were easiest to sell by mail order, as well as goings-on at the Rodale Experimental Farm. One article in the September 1949 issue documented how workers there had managed "a perfect score" in raising chicks: "100 out of 100 chicks alive, healthy and growing after 12 weeks of age." In the same issue, Robert Rodale, who was listed as managing editor, wrote and took pictures for a photo essay about John Moyer, "an eastern Pennsylvania farmer who has combined elements of Edward Faulkner's 'no plow' theory with portions of the Organic Method to develop a method of farming that shows promise of making possible the production of large, naturally raised crops at little cost."

In the fall of 1949, Robert had started working at the magazines on a more informal basis. First he reviewed galley proofs of *The Organic Farmer,* and within a few months he was managing editor of the magazine. Robert learned a great deal simply by watching his father and absorbing. But he quickly developed his own opinions. In 1950, when J.I. wanted to reduce the size of *Organic Gardening,* "We had a big argument about it. In fact, I told J.I. I wasn't going to work at the Press anymore! For several days I thought about going off and doing something else, but I got over it."

The second spin-off came in the spring of 1950. Some readers expressed resistance to the appearance of so many health-related articles in a gardening magazine. But many others responded by asking pointed questions. And J.I. relished his role in dispensing advice and information to readers who had come to trust his judgment and knowledge. "I would not take Vitamin C unless a

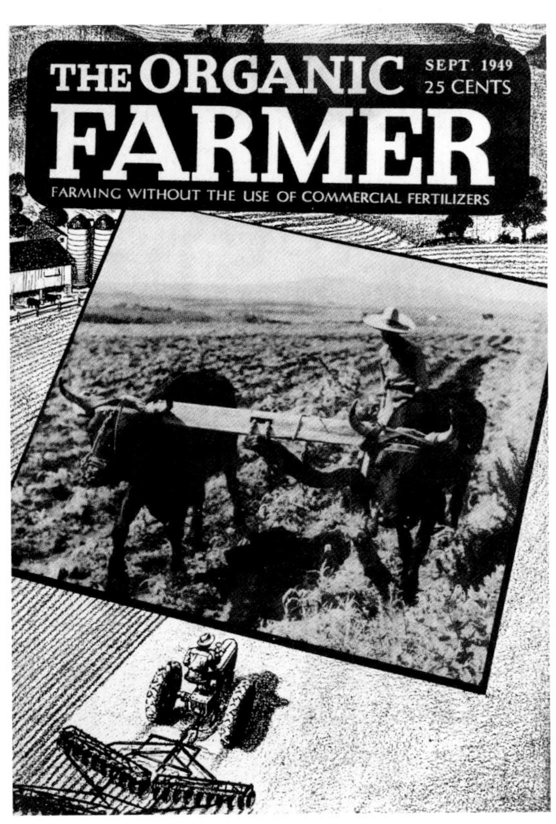

In the summer of 1949, Rodale introduced *The Organic Farmer.*

1949
February 27: Research presented at American Cancer Society and National Cancer Institute meetings links increased cigarette smoking to rise in lung cancer.

August 16: U.S. Public Health Service reports Americans' average life span is 66.8 years, up from the prewar average of 65.

August 29: Soviet Union tests its first atomic bomb.

October 1: Birth of the People's Republic of China.

Nineteen Eighty-Four, by George Orwell, is published.

***OG* starts a 13-part series on cancer.**

Rodale introduces *The Organic Farmer* magazine.

Robert Rodale begins working with J.I. at the magazines.

physician feels that it is needed because you can get so much Vitamin C out of fruit that there would be a danger of oversupplying yourself with Vitamin C if you took it with fruit as well as in Vitamin form," he advised one Mrs. O. Salle in March 6, 1950. In the same letter, he informed her that she would no longer have to write letters to receive such useful information. "We are starting a magazine to be called *Prevention* that will deal with the conservation of human health and in which we will go more into health problems."

The first issue of *Prevention* focused exclusively on polio.

Initially, Robert opposed the creation of a new magazine, since he thought they were courting sufficient controversy by taking on the agricultural establishment. Meanwhile, they were still losing money from the Press's publishing efforts. In 1950, Rodale Press had revenues of $473,467 and expenses of $556,000. But J.I. was less fearful of controversy or of losses. With the arrival of Robert, he felt comfortable devoting less time to *OG* and *OF*. And, as he had done with everything from writing to gardening, he set out to create a system that would allow those with the interest and attention to improve the way they approached a core function of life. "We're going to have the Prevention System," he said. "I'm going to keep tight control, and our articles will be backed up in the literature." To forestall criticism from the medical establishment—expected to be far more vitriolic than criticism from the agricultural industry—J.I. decided to rely largely on research findings published in medical journals.

After nearly 20 years of publishing books and magazines, J.I. had great faith in his ability to launch new ventures on a large scale. J. I. Rodale, the self-described revolutionary, was an internationally recognized authority and advocate on issues relating to agriculture and health. In 1949 two men from El Salvador came to visit Emmaus, "full of enthusiasm about a compost factory they were considering building there." In 1950, he testified before the House Select Committee to Investigate the Use of Chemicals in Foods and Cosmetics, chaired by Congressman James J. Delaney. The hearings led to an amendment to the Food and Drug Act that prohibited cancer-causing additives to the food supply. And J.I. traveled frequently to give unpaid speeches. In 1950 alone he was

J.I. and Robert Rodale formed an editorial and business partnership that would last for two decades.

invited to speak at a U.S. Department of Agriculture conference in College Park, Maryland; the Chicago Horticultural Society; the Lower Perkiomen Rotary Club; the Mennonite Soil & Health Association; the State Chiropractic Society of New Jersey; and the Tri-State Society of Physical Medicine in Cincinnati.

In the spring of 1950, Rodale Press began running advertisements in *Organic Gardening* that solicited subscriptions to *Prevention*, which J.I. dubbed "a medical journal for the people." The response was overwhelming. By the time the first issue appeared in June 1950, it had already attracted 50,000 subscribers. *Prevention*–"a magazine devoted to the conservation of health"–was different from other Rodale magazines. Unlike *OG* and *OF*, it didn't feature graphics, drawings, or photographs. With its plain brown cover, straightforward design, and advertisements confined to the inside of the front and back covers, it had more of the appearance of a journal.

The entire first issue was devoted to polio. A long article by Rodale Press staff member Edward J. Fluck profiled the work of Ralph R. Scobey, M.D., who investigated whether poisons in mussels produce polio. Another article discussed the findings of Dr. Benjamin Sandler, who had developed a preventive diet for polio. J.I. penned an article that addressed the question of whether the disease was caused by inoculation for other conditions. After reviewing the medical literature, he concluded, "I will stay neutral on the general subject of inoculations until I can secure more data, but surely where there is a question of polio, it would be the better part of wisdom not to inoculate in dangerous periods unless it is a matter of life and death."

The launch of *Prevention* put the cap on a decade of growth and evolution for J. I. Rodale, his family, and his company. In the 10 years from 1940 to 1950, by taking substantial risks–moving his family to a farm, launching a new magazine in the face of a war, and publishing his own books–J. I. Rodale had gained recognition, experience, and legitimacy. Firmly ensconced on the farm, and with a second generation of Rodales beginning to work in the family publishing business, J.I. had turned the ideas of Sir Albert Howard into reality. In the next decade, J.I. and Robert Rodale would transform Rodale's publishing operations into a solid, profitable business.

1950
February 9: In a speech, Wisconsin Senator Joseph McCarthy accuses the United States State Department of being filled with 205 Communists.

June: Debut of *Prevention*.

June 25: The Korean War starts.

October 2: The comic strip *Peanuts*, by Charles M. Schulz, debuts in seven newspapers.

Census shows U.S. population nears 150 million.

Conflict in Korea begins.

J. I. Rodale testifies before House Select Committee to Investigate the Use of Chemicals in Foods and Cosmetics.

Three generations of Rodales: Bob *(center)*, J.I. *(right)*, and David *(bottom left)*

CHAPTER 4

1951 TO 1961

An Avocation Evolves into a Business

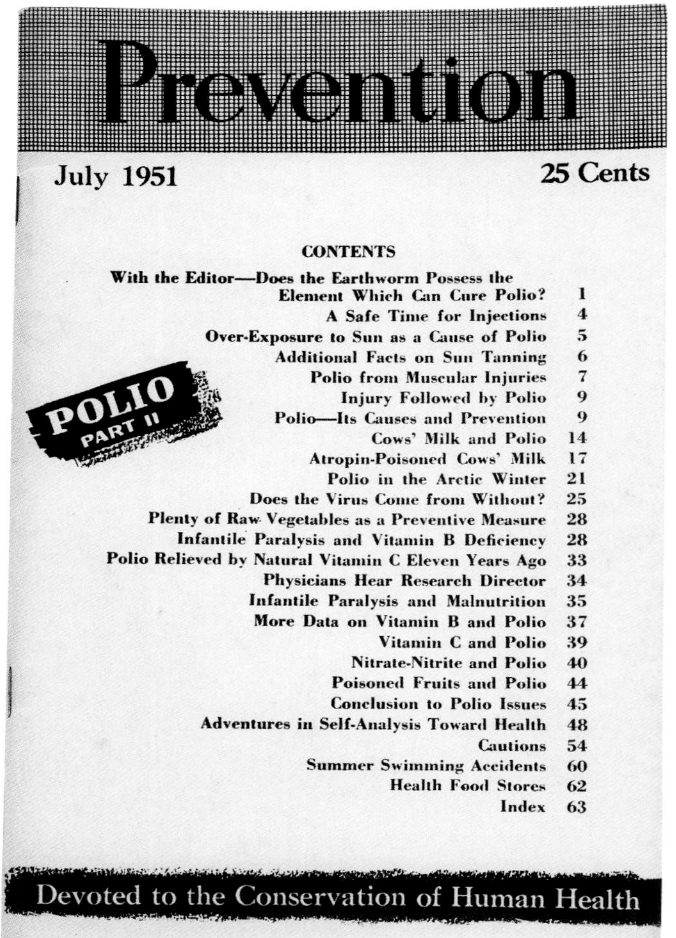

Prevention

July 1951 25 Cents

CONTENTS

With the Editor—Does the Earthworm Possess the Element Which Can Cure Polio? 1
A Safe Time for Injections 4
Over-Exposure to Sun as a Cause of Polio 5
Additional Facts on Sun Tanning 6
Polio from Muscular Injuries 7
Injury Followed by Polio 9
Polio—Its Causes and Prevention 9
Cows' Milk and Polio 14
Atropin-Poisoned Cows' Milk 17
Polio in the Arctic Winter 21
Does the Virus Come from Without? 25
Plenty of Raw Vegetables as a Preventive Measure 28
Infantile Paralysis and Vitamin B Deficiency 28
Polio Relieved by Natural Vitamin C Eleven Years Ago 33
Physicians Hear Research Director 34
Infantile Paralysis and Malnutrition 35
More Data on Vitamin B and Polio 37
Vitamin C and Polio 39
Nitrate-Nitrite and Polio 40
Poisoned Fruits and Polio 44
Conclusion to Polio Issues 45
Adventures in Self-Analysis Toward Health 48
Cautions 54
Summer Swimming Accidents 60
Health Food Stores 62
Index 63

POLIO PART II

Devoted to the Conservation of Human Health

Prevention magazine enjoyed a surge of success early in its history.

UNLIKE THE dozen-odd magazines J. I. Rodale had started in the previous years, *Prevention* found a large–and unexpected–audience of paying customers immediately. Some 50,000 readers responded to the 250,000 circulars with subscriptions. And since the first issue had been intended only as a test, J.I. had to rush to slap together a second issue. He reprinted an entire book Rodale Press had acquired, a translation of a memoir by Louis Cornaro, a Renaissance-era Italian who lived to nearly 100 and "who represents a wonderful example of what a diet containing a reduced amount of food can do to prolong a person's life." By the third issue, he was ready to resume slaughtering sacred cows with original articles. The lead editorial in the September 1950 issue took on baseball and hot dogs. "The frankfurter is one item of food that should be eliminated from the diet," assistant editor Edward J. Fluck wrote. Hot dogs contained sodium nitrates, which destroy hemoglobin, and the buns were made of white flour. For their part, carbonated drinks led to defective vision. The same issue contained a warning about antihistamines, citing an article in the *Journal of the American Medical Association.*

J.I.'s reliance on published scientific information was part of his strategy to position *Prevention* as, if not quite a scientific journal, then something quite close to it. "When we began publishing about a year and a half ago, we decided on a policy. We would quote only from conservative M.D. sources," he wrote in an exchange of letters with Dr. Austin Smith of the American Medical Association (AMA). "We would print no articles about chiropractic and osteopathy. We definitely would not print anything by Naturopaths."

At the same time, he affirmed the important role that nonscientists—readers and writers—played in advancing the cause of health. J.I. told his readers that they would be engaged in a cooperative experiment in finding better ways to live. "One year I might say, 'Eat this food,' and in another year I might counteract my own suggestion. It will be done in good faith and will be based on sound scientific research." The goal, as it always was for J.I., was to create a system, "a perfected molded plan" that would allow people to live until the age of 100. The *Prevention* ethos held that patients could heal themselves. As part of a recurring feature dubbed "Adventures in Self-Analysis toward Health," J.I. wrote in 1951, "For the last 10 years I have never permitted any new pain or other negative conditions that appeared, to stay with me too long. By concentrating on it and studying everything I did daily, I always found something new, which by its elimination always cleared up whatever it was."

At first, J.I. essentially worked alone on *Prevention.* But the staff grew quickly. In 1951, Ruth Adams, whom J.I. had met at a secondhand bookstore owned by his friend Helen Papashvily in Allentown, was hired as associate editor. Adams, a longtime *Organic Gardening* reader, thought J.I. a little eccentric. But once she met him and he assigned an article on constipation, "I realized then that there was nothing of the crazy faddist about him." Adams wrote many articles and

J. I. Rodale on one of his many trips to Europe

Bob and Ardie Rodale on their wedding day, June 23, 1951

earned a salary of $35 a week. "He came into my office loaded with clips from perhaps 20 journals or general news publications and just let me decide which was most important and which might wait for the next issue," she recalled.

Prevention, like all the ventures J.I. had started, was to be a family business. In the early 1950s, J.I. and Joe remained partners in both the manufacturing and publishing ventures. But a second generation was starting to arrive. Ruth Rodale, who graduated from Wellesley with a degree in botany in 1950, worked as an editor at *Organic Gardening* and frequently contributed articles to the magazine. In 1952, she was listed as managing editor. In her spare time she occasionally rode horses with her uncle Joe, who had built up the Rodale Stud Farm, several miles southwest of Allentown, to house more than 40 thoroughbreds.

Turning the publishing operations into a viable company would fall largely to J.I.'s son, Robert. Bob, who began working part-time at Rodale when he entered college at nearby Lehigh University in 1948, quickly shouldered an enormous amount of responsibility at the publishing operations, which by 1951 employed nearly 100 people. "I had the clear feeling, after I was there for six months, that I was a very necessary person." And his life was remarkably full. While living at home, he attended the university part-time, studying journalism. In December, he and Ardath Harter, a spirited Allentown native who was studying arts education at nearby Kutztown State Teachers College (later known as Kutztown University), began to date. Their families had known each other while they were growing up, and Ardath was friends with Bob's sister Ruth. In January 1951, they became engaged. And on June 23, the couple married at St. Michael's Lutheran Church in Allentown.

A division of labor quickly emerged between father and son—along with a difference in styles.

1951
Jack LaLanne's show premieres on television.

June 23: Bob Rodale and Ardath Harter are married.

July 5: Engineer William Shockley invents the junction transistor.

August: J.I. travels to Germany, his first European trip.

MSG is added to Gerber baby foods to make taste more appealing to mothers.

November 24: The Broadway play *Gigi* opens, starring little-known actress Audrey Hepburn playing the lead character.

J. D. Salinger's *The Catcher in the Rye* is published.

Rodale Press shows first operating profit.

J. D. Salinger

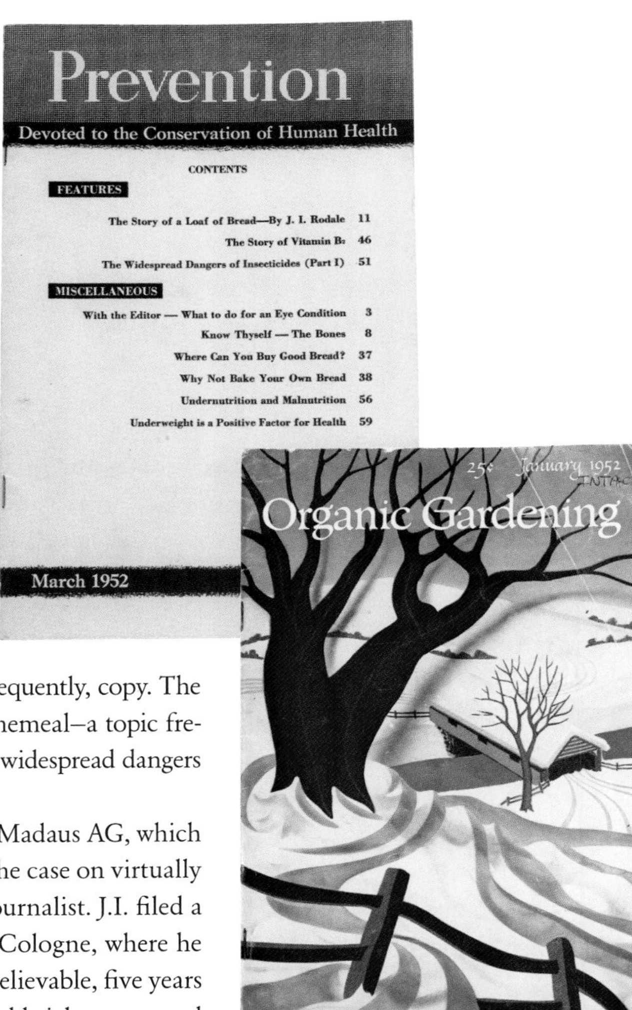

Early issues of ***Prevention*** **and** ***Organic Gardening*** **shared stories that J.I. thought important for both audiences.**

J.I. had studied business as a young student but spent much of his adult life writing. Bob studied journalism but would bring a new sense of business management to the publishing operations. "As soon as *Prevention* came along, he basically said to me, 'It's all yours now,'" Bob recalled J.I. saying. "You don't tell me how to run *Prevention*, and I won't interfere with how you run *Organic Gardening*." To run *Prevention*, J.I. set up an office on West Street in Allentown, across from his house. Although they were separate, the magazines shared management, ownership, and, frequently, copy. The January 1952 issue of *OG*, for example, featured a lead article on the virtues of bonemeal–a topic frequently covered in *Prevention*. And the March 1952 issue of *Prevention* warned of the widespread dangers of insecticides, specifically mentioning DDT–a topic frequently covered in *OG*.

In the summer of 1951, J.I. traveled to Germany to hold discussions with Madaus AG, which made pharmaceuticals from organic materials, about a joint venture. As would be the case on virtually all his travels to Europe and South America, he went as a businessman *and* as a journalist. J.I. filed a 12-part description in the Allentown *Morning Call* of his visits to Dusseldorf, to Cologne, where he visited a synagogue for Friday night services, and to a still-ravaged Berlin. "It is unbelievable, five years after the war, to see such unrepaired destruction! … Blocks and blocks of mangled brick, stone, and steel!" J.I.'s first visit to Europe opened a new world for him–he and Anna would return to Europe time and again in the coming decade. But the proposed venture collapsed before it got started, in part because J.I. rejected Madaus's suggestion that a doctor vet material for *Prevention*: "I would never agree to this and I insisted on always maintaining absolute independence in my magazine."

By 1951, *Organic Gardening* had 60,000 subscribers. *Prevention* was off to a promising start. Books such as *Pay Dirt* were still in print and selling. *The Word Finder* sold 25,000 copies in 1951 alone. That year, Rodale Press had net revenues of nearly $750,000, although advertising accounted for just $87,320 of the total. For the first time, it showed an operating profit of $42,578. Still, J.I. took no salary, subsisting on the salary and dividend from Rodale Manufacturing, which continued to thrive. In 1951 a third floor was added to the factory, bringing the total manufacturing space to 75,000 square feet.

Rodale Press was more than a hobby or a gentleman's publishing company. The livelihoods of scores of people depended on it. Hundreds of thousands of readers looked forward to receiving its products. The publications dealt with matters of life and death, human health, and big business. And yet there was a sense that the enterprise was also about connecting with people on an individual level. At the time, as Bob recalled, "the organic movement was very vital; it was small but full of enthusiasts who really understood what they were talking about and felt good about it but also felt that, you know, we're like a tiny little minority among this vast number of Philistines who don't understand." A woman in the summer of 1951 wrote to J.I. about her husband, a carpenter, who found working on his knees painful. "My suggestion is that your husband use a sponge rubber mat when he has to kneel at his work. My suggestion also is that he try to assume a different position, like squatting instead of kneeling." Violinist Yehudi Menuhin wrote to ask what kinds of bread were made without chemicals on the West Coast.

By intentionally tilting at the health and agricultural establishments, Rodale invited scrutiny. And J.I.'s tendency toward salesmanship and promotional exaggeration brought challenges. In 1951, the Federal Trade Commission objected to the way Rodale had advertised claims made in the October 1942 issue of *Organic Farming and Gardening,* which dealt with polio. Faced with the government's resources and, for the first time, the threat of serious legal repercussions, J.I. was in the mood to accommodate. "Evidently I can see that looseness developed in the wording of advertising matter in our organization, but I have recently issued instructions that no advertising copy can be used without my approval," he wrote to an FTC lawyer. Nonetheless, he signed an affidavit of discontinuance in May 1952, confirming that the ads in question were no longer in use and would not be used in the future. J.I. cited avoiding expense as the main reason for doing so.

In the fall of 1952, Anna and J.I. returned to Europe. While in Switzerland, they received the startling news that Joe Rodale had died of a heart attack, at the age of 56. Joe's untimely death set into motion a series of changes. J.I. lost not only the older brother he had looked up to for so many years, but also his partner of three decades. As J.I. pursued his range of ventures, Joe had

J. I. Rodale chronicled his travels to Germany and elsewhere in the pages of *Prevention*.

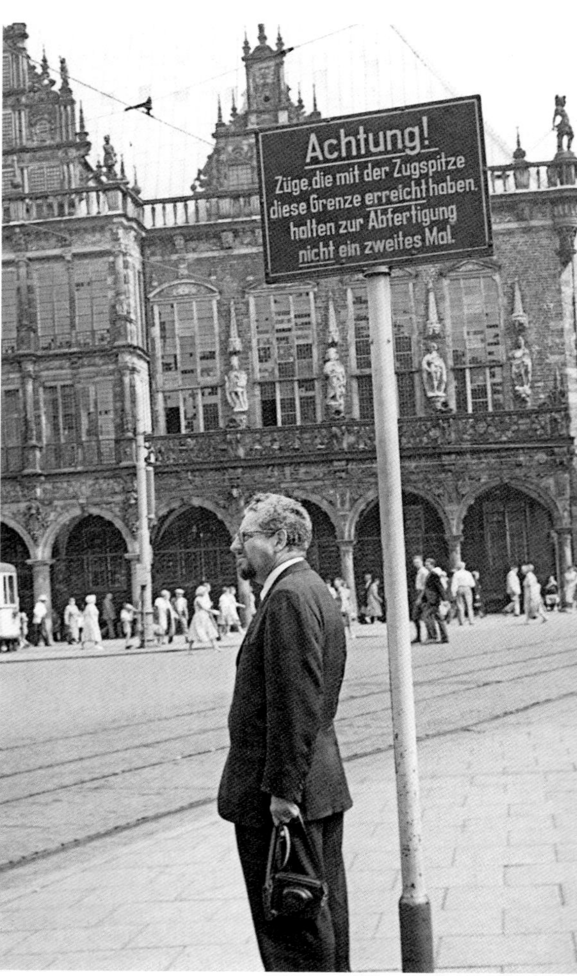

1952
Rachel Carson's *The Sea Around Us* becomes a bestseller.

Reader's Digest headline: "Organic Farming—Bunk!"

Kirsch Beverages introduces sugar-free NoCal soda.

June 15: The first American edition of *The Diary of a Young Girl*, by Anne Frank, is published.

September: Death of Joe Rodale.

November 1: The United States detonates the first hydrogen bomb near Bikini Atoll in the Pacific Ocean.

Anne Frank

November 3: Frozen bread is marketed.

November 4: Republican Dwight D. Eisenhower defeats Democrat Adlai Stevenson for president.

Bob and Ardie Rodale return from the hospital with their firstborn, Heather, in 1952.

focused intensely on building Rodale Manufacturing into a profitable, durable company—one whose profits enabled J.I. to build the publishing business. In 1952, the last year of Joe's life, Rodale Manufacturing had sales of $2.8 million and profits of $170,000. While Joe frequently chafed at the losses at the publishing company, he was a partner in everything J.I. did, from the magazines to the Soil and Health Foundation. At one point, Joe had given up his half interest in the publishing operations. As Bob recalled, "They had a fight over these illustrations, and to punish my father he gave him his half of the company."

Upon his return to Emmaus, J.I. assumed responsibility for Rodale Manufacturing. "Joe's death was a great blow to me, as we were always very close together," J.I. recalled. In typical fashion, he threw himself into the business, all while continuing to run *Prevention*. Editorially, both *Organic Gardening* and *Prevention* magazines were on solid ground. Financially, they were less so. Despite its 10-year history, *OG* was essentially still a niche magazine and one that failed to generate large sums of advertising. From the outset, *Prevention* was intended to be free of advertisements. The first issue contained a one-page ad for Nu-Age Products, a Pennsylvania company that made bonemeal—ground-up cattle bones that J.I. believed were an excellent nutritional supplement. J.I. reasoned that most readers would have no outlet from which to purchase bonemeal. When Nu-Age received orders of about $100,000 after the issue came out, it wanted to run advertisements in *Prevention*.

J.I. ultimately changed the policy. The fact was that a magazine like *Prevention* couldn't subsist on subscriptions alone. And since *Prevention*'s readers were hungry for ideas and products that could improve their lives, the magazine seemed a natural outlet for vitamin and food supplement companies. J.I. later rationalized the acceptance of advertisements humorously. "As it is, I'm not paying income tax because I'm losing money. It's not being a good citizen not to pay taxes. So, from now on, you'll see advertising in *Prevention* because I want to be a good American."

An early Rodale Press picnic
at Hunsicker's Grove, August 1951

Wide Bottom

Move over

Tete-a-tete

Pressman's Conference

Cooling off

Out

Rodale Press picnic - Hunsicker's Grove

Contentment

My! How refreshing

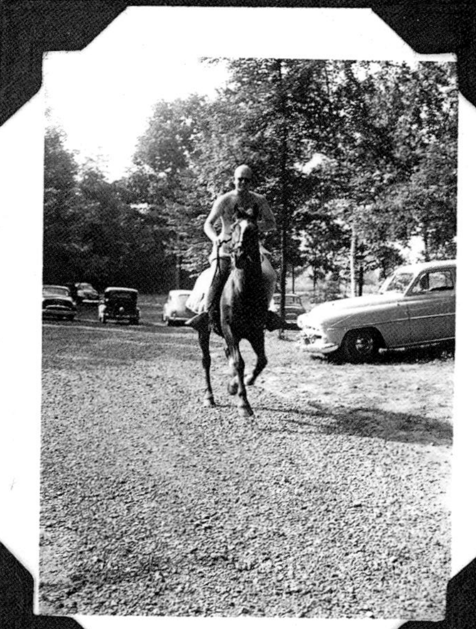

Hi-Ho Silver

"You don't say"

Watch the birdie

Nice Girls! nice suits!

Nice figures

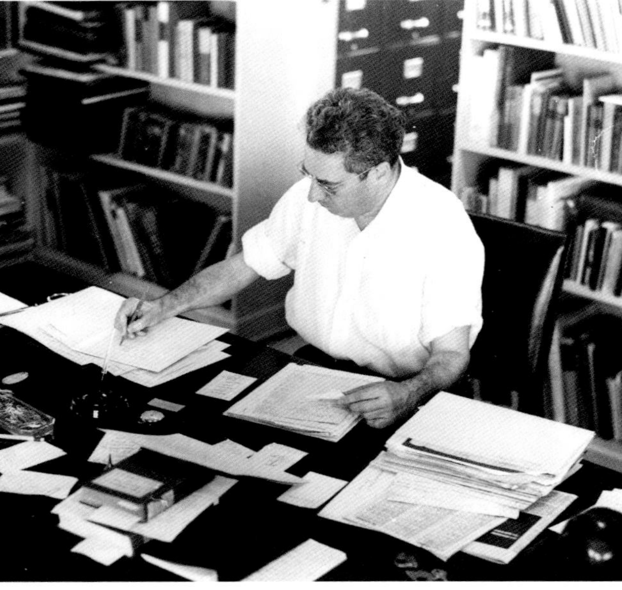

J.I. had an insatiable curiosity and capacity for work; he was often found in his library researching an idea or writing.

In 1952, John Larmer joined Rodale as advertising manager for the company's three magazines. Many of the early advertisements were for nutritional supplements. Others were for products such as Arrowhead whole wheat flour and blender manufacturer Whiz-Miz. Larmer pioneered the practice of having advertisers run multipage advertisements for mail-order products, so they could essentially run catalogs in *Prevention*.

In the spring of 1953, J.I. kept a meticulous journal that described his busy life in great detail. In the mornings, he would often go to the *Prevention* office in Allentown. Afternoons were frequently spent at the Rodale Manufacturing plant, dealing with issues such as "whether we should make small electric lightbulbs." In between, he worked on a system of learning foreign languages and kept abreast of developments on the farm. "Today for lunch we ate the first vegetables that were grown in our outside garden on the farm. They were parsley and asparagus," he reported on April 18. That evening, he met with architect Fred Genther to discuss an addition to the house on the farm.

Amid his responsibilities, J.I. found time to produce his own books as well. The mid-1950s was perhaps his most prolific period. J.I. was interested in his past. He wrote a memoir, never published, entitled *The Promised Land*. And on his frequent trips to New York, he would go to the Lower East Side. He reported in July 1953 in his journal, "I make my usual pilgrimage around the corner on Broome Street to the yard where as a boy I went to Red Donkey's." But he was also looking forward. In 1954 he published *This Pace Is Not Killing Us*, which examined the rise in the rate of death from heart disease. While many people argued that the quickened pace of life in the emerging jet age was responsible for many health woes, he reached the opposite conclusion. The use of escalators instead of stairs, riding in cars instead of walking, and the decline in manual labor meant that people were growing more sedentary, he concluded. J.I., of course, was living refutation of that maxim. He didn't do much manual labor, but he was extraordinarily active. In 1954 alone, he published several others books, including *How to Eat for a Healthy Heart* and *The Nutritional Way to Stop Smoking*—both of which were serialized in some form in the Rodale magazines.

1953
February 28: James D. Watson and Francis Crick announce that they have determined the chemical structure of DNA.

March 5: Soviet leader Joseph Stalin dies.

March 26: Jonas Salk announces the polio vaccine.

Jonas Salk

May 29: Sir Edmund Hillary and Tenzing Norgay ascend to the summit of Mount Everest.

Kellogg's introduces Sugar Smacks, a breakfast cereal that is 56 percent sugar.

Responding to evidence on links between cancer and smoking, cigarette makers add "safer" filter-tipped cigarettes.

Edmund Hillary and Tenzing Norgay

J. I. and Anna spent time in Palm Beach, Florida, in the '50s—a respite from cold Pennsylvania winters.

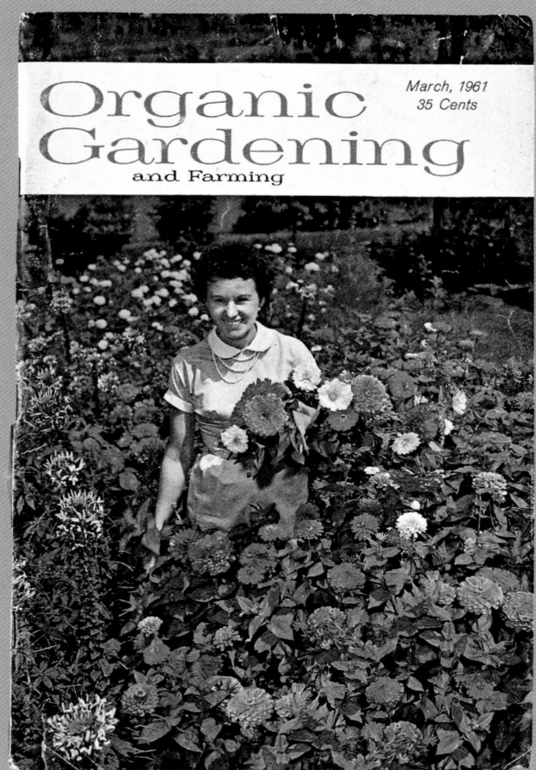

Through the years, members of the Rodale family made cameo appearances on the cover of *Organic Gardening* magazine. *This page, starting far left:* Ardie, Heidi, and David. *Opposite page:* Heather, Maria and Anthony, and Anthony (with carrot)

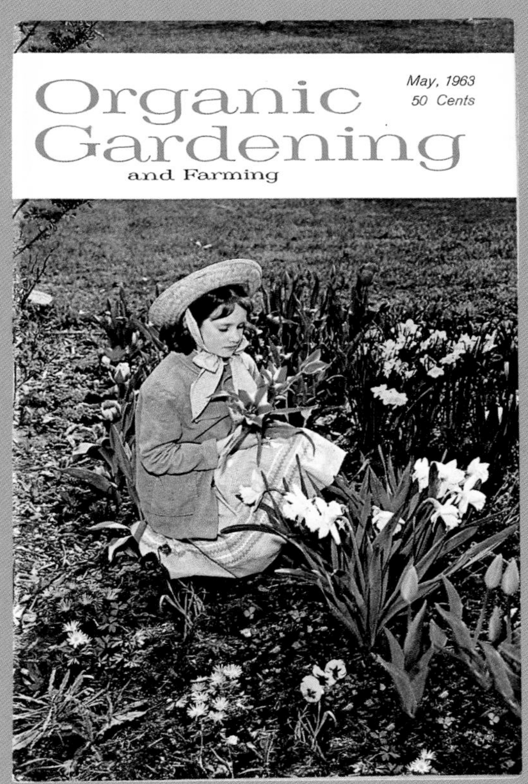
Organic
Gardening
and Farming
May, 1963
50 Cents

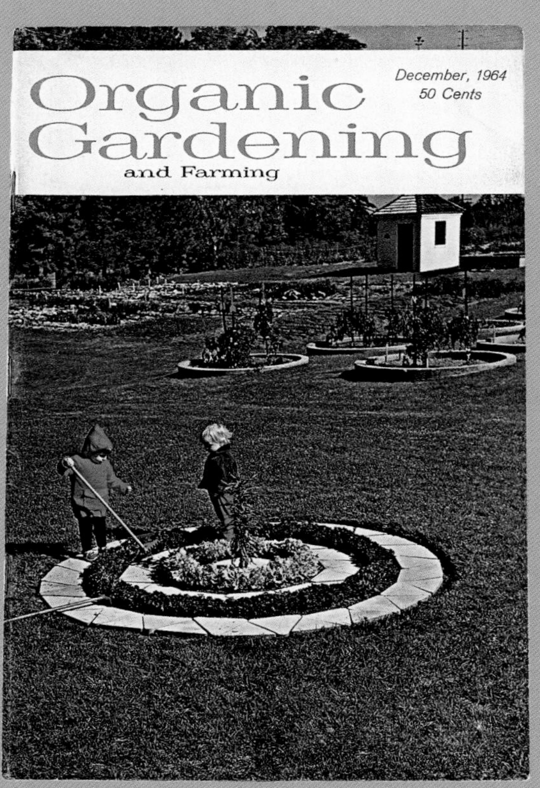
Organic
Gardening
and Farming
December, 1964
50 Cents

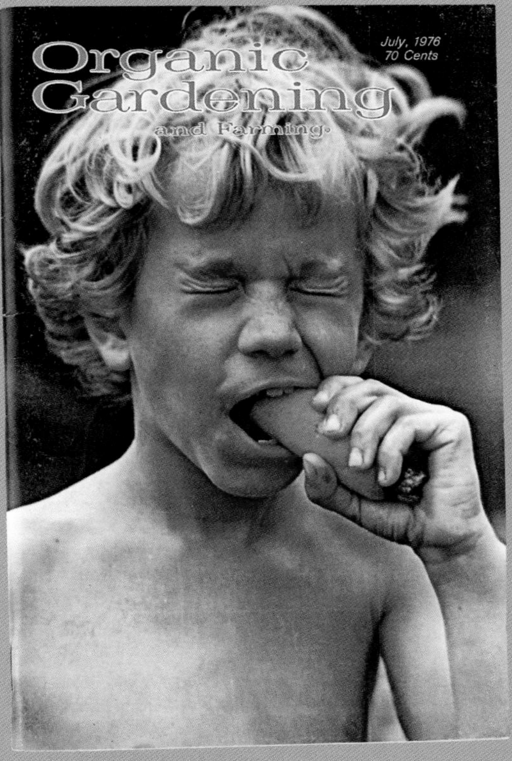
Organic
Gardening
and Farming
July, 1976
70 Cents

Constantly seeking systems that would improve health, J. I. Rodale published a guide to healthy eating in 1954, in which he charted the fat content of common foods.

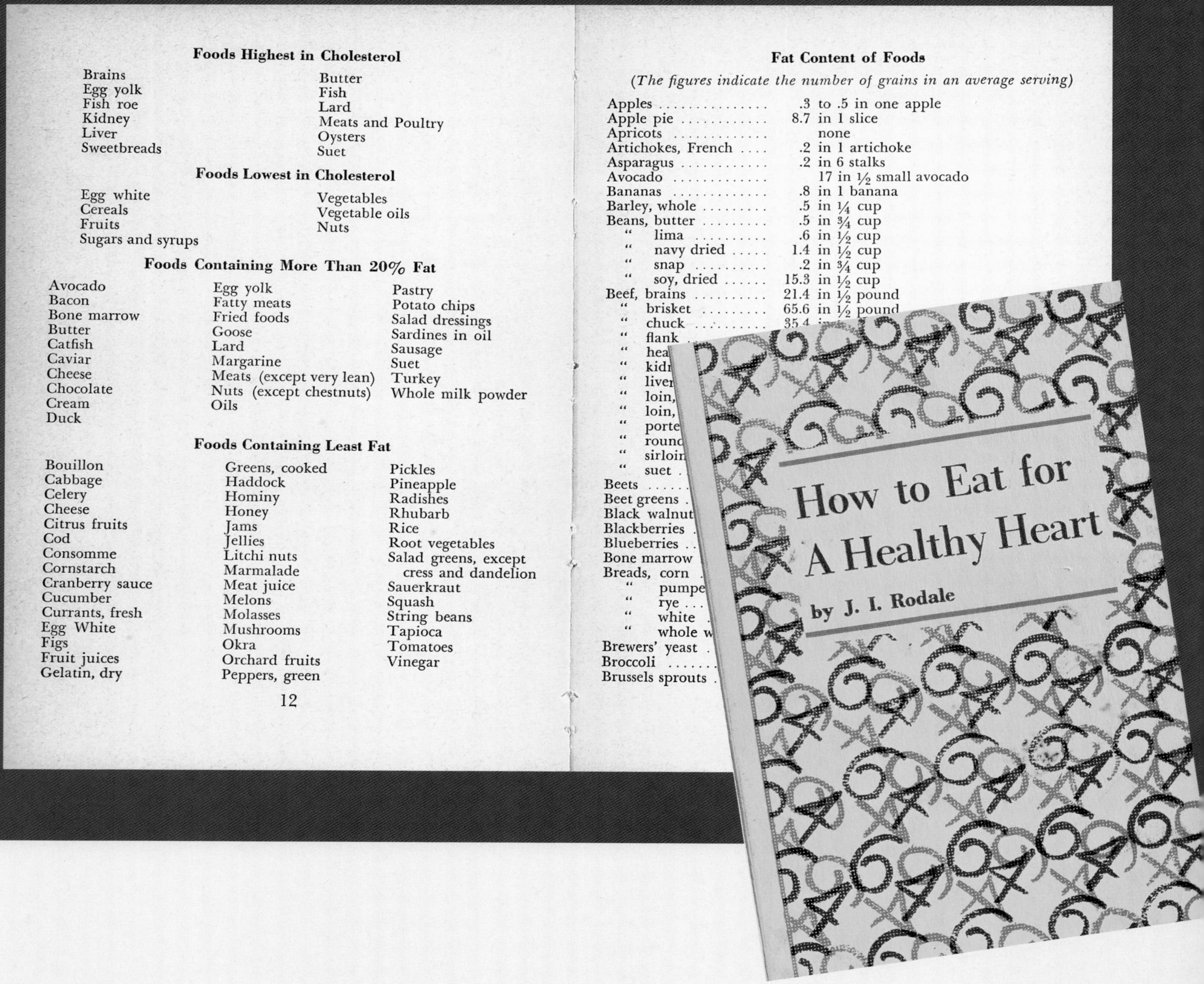

Foods Highest in Cholesterol

Brains
Egg yolk
Fish roe
Kidney
Liver
Sweetbreads
Butter
Fish
Lard
Meats and Poultry
Oysters
Suet

Foods Lowest in Cholesterol

Egg white
Cereals
Fruits
Sugars and syrups
Vegetables
Vegetable oils
Nuts

Foods Containing More Than 20% Fat

Avocado
Bacon
Bone marrow
Butter
Catfish
Caviar
Cheese
Chocolate
Cream
Duck
Egg yolk
Fatty meats
Fried foods
Goose
Lard
Margarine
Meats (except very lean)
Nuts (except chestnuts)
Oils
Pastry
Potato chips
Salad dressings
Sardines in oil
Sausage
Suet
Turkey
Whole milk powder

Foods Containing Least Fat

Bouillon
Cabbage
Celery
Cheese
Citrus fruits
Cod
Consomme
Cornstarch
Cranberry sauce
Cucumber
Currants, fresh
Egg White
Figs
Fruit juices
Gelatin, dry
Greens, cooked
Haddock
Hominy
Honey
Jams
Jellies
Litchi nuts
Marmalade
Meat juice
Melons
Molasses
Mushrooms
Okra
Orchard fruits
Peppers, green
Pickles
Pineapple
Radishes
Rhubarb
Rice
Root vegetables
Salad greens, except cress and dandelion
Sauerkraut
Squash
String beans
Tapioca
Tomatoes
Vinegar

12

Fat Content of Foods

(The figures indicate the number of grains in an average serving)

Apples	.3 to .5	in one apple
Apple pie	8.7	in 1 slice
Apricots		none
Artichokes, French	.2	in 1 artichoke
Asparagus	.2	in 6 stalks
Avocado		17 in ½ small avocado
Bananas	.8	in 1 banana
Barley, whole	.5	in ¼ cup
Beans, butter	.5	in ¾ cup
" lima	.6	in ½ cup
" navy dried	1.4	in ½ cup
" snap	.2	in ¾ cup
" soy, dried	15.3	in ½ cup
Beef, brains	21.4	in ½ pound
" brisket	65.6	in ½ pound
" chuck	35.4	
" flank		
" hea		
" kidn		
" liver		
" loin,		
" loin,		
" porte		
" round		
" sirloin		
" suet		
Beets		
Beet greens		
Black walnut		
Blackberries		
Blueberries		
Bone marrow		
Breads, corn		
" pumpe		
" rye		
" white		
" whole w		
Brewers' yeast		
Broccoli		
Brussels sprouts		

How to Eat for A Healthy Heart

by J. I. Rodale

Every month, ***Organic Gardening and Farming*** **showed readers how to put organic methods to use in their backyards.**

There were signs that after nearly two decades, J. I. Rodale was taking steps to run the press more like a business. The company formally incorporated in 1954. And the losses were no longer quite as tolerable. In January 1954, in an effort to stem the tide of red ink, *Organic Farmer* was merged back into *Organic Gardening* and the publication was renamed *Organic Gardening and Farming.* But efforts were also made systematically to increase revenues, and books would lead the way. *Health Finder,* a compendium of the wisdom amassed in *Prevention,* was published in December 1954 with a first printing of 10,000. It proved remarkably popular. A second printing of 10,000 came in March 1955, with a third printing of 15,000 in August 1955.

In 1954, John Larmer left to form his own agency, and Marshall Ackerman took over responsibility for selling advertising. Working with Jerry Goldstein, the circulation manager, Ackerman and the Rodales embarked upon new efforts to boost circulation and advertising—a mutually reinforcing process that would increase revenues. One tack was to publish premium booklets—32-page collections of articles on a single subject from the magazines. The first was *Make Compost in 14 Days.*

As was his wont, J.I. pursued multiple new lines of business at once—some of which had nothing to do with *Prevention.* In 1954 he became interested in developing a system for learning several languages at once. He planned to publish books that would have the same page in English, French, Spanish, and German, and he arranged to have them printed in Holland. In 1955 he started a company in England, taking an office at 123 Bond Street in Mayfair, in London. "Our British project is in its third month and we already have four staff members," he reported proudly in *Prevention.* It was viewed as a foothold to sell Story Classics and other Rodale

The Kemp shredder produces a very suitably fine consistency of ground material, is fed easily and safely.

Feeding the Keston shredder, which comes equipped with an electric motor, costs least of machines tested.

bors that composting did not have to drag on over two seasons. First, we began putting through the machine several bushels of iris that a friend had contributed. They were mashed up admirably, but the stringy stalks could stall the engine if they were fed too fast. We found that feeding a corn cob with each large handful of iris cleared the machine nicely.

The cobs themselves were shredded all right, but they made a lot of noise inside the machine. That started us feeding some hay with the cobs, in order to cushion them. Finally we ran through the hay and manure. Both were shredded into quite small particles.

2

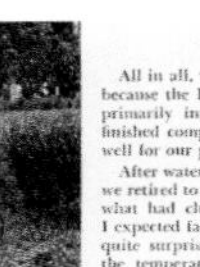
All in all, we were quite impressed, because the Kemp (and the W-W) is primarily intended as a grinder of finished compost and soil. It worked well for our purpose, however.

After watering our compost mound, we retired to the bathroom to soak off what had clung to our own bodies. I expected fast developments, but was quite surprised next morning to see the temperature up to 130 degrees. Even more interesting was the color, which had changed from a light yellow to a light brown overnight.

By afternoon, the temperature was up to 140. I was using my wife's meat thermometer, and the red line was up to "beef rare." So you can see that the compost was really cooking. Monday evening I turned it for the first time, noting that the color was even darker and the heat greater. A ring of white, air-loving fungus had begun to grow around the edges of the heap. According to scientists, the area around the edges of a compost heap breaks down first, because of the action of these fungi. The strongest decay-causing organisms need plenty of air. That is why the heap should be turned often.

The following Saturday—one week after the heap was made—it was turned for the second time. The ring mold was very noticeable. From a distance of a few feet, the heap looked finished already. But close up you could see that it needed some time to simmer down.

Ten days after the heap was made it was inspected by Phillip Wells, well known compost authority. He was surprised to hear that it was just recently made, for by that time it was quite dark brown in color and soft to the touch. Together, we transferred the heap to a Keston-Lehigh compost bin, in order to get some photos of the bin in use.

Three days later—two weeks after it was made—I judged the heap finished and ready for use. It had not stopped

Small heap of completed speed-compost, finished in the remarkably short time of 14 days. For gardeners, the advantages of this up-to-date method are many. It's a richer compost because it is exposed to climate changes a far shorter period. And, of course, you can make what you need as it is required, save space, time and fertilizer value.

On the afternoon of the day following establishment of this heap, the temperature had risen to 140 degrees Fahrenheit, a quick climb which aided the rapid breakdown of the raw materials. Shredding of all material with new garden-size equipment before it is added to the heap proved the key to fast composting.

1954
May 6: Roger Bannister runs the first 4-minute mile.

May 7: The Battle of Dien Bien Phu in Vietnam ends in a French defeat.

May 17: U.S. Supreme Court hands down its decision in *Brown v. Board of Education of Topeka, Kansas.*

Roger Bannister

First Burger King restaurant opens in Miami.

Ernest Hemingway wins the Nobel Prize in Literature.

August 16: *Sports Illustrated* debuts.

J. I. Rodale publishes *How to Eat for a Healthy Heart.*

December: *Health Finder* is published.

Marshall Ackerman joins Rodale.

Rodale Press incorporates.

To create an international presence for his growing company, J.I. opened a small office in London.

books. But it went slowly at first. "We sent a check of $14,000 to our little English project," he wrote in his journal on April 29, 1955. "I will admit that we have been sending them rather large amounts of money, all out of proportion to the sale of books up to this point, but I feel that it will pay out in the end." Within 16 months, J. I. Rodale & Co., Ltd., of England would launch a British version of *Prevention* and begin selling vitamins in England, Germany, Australia, South Africa, and elsewhere.

Bob and J.I. had very different styles—as executives and as writers. "He was more of a personal storyteller, and I was more of a journalist," Bob recalled. Where J.I. was intellectually frenetic, Bob's mind was more focused. He enjoyed fly-fishing. In April 15, 1955, Bob dutifully noted in an angler's diary that he and Jerry Olds, the managing editor of *Organic Gardening and Farming,* caught two brook trout on the Little Lehigh, below the Salisbury church. J.I. frequently found that the most intriguing subject to write about was himself—he had seemingly endless capacity to reminisce and to discuss his own health. In a column in January 1954, J.I. wrote of how he tackled heart problems in 1952 by removing desiccated liver, an iron-rich nutritional supplement made from cow's liver, from his regimen. He also described pulse studies in which he would eat certain foods and then check his heart rate. J.I. found that coffee did not make his pulse rise, contrary to the conventional wisdom. "It is another example of typical misinformation which is so generally prevalent in connection with so many ideas that the public subscribes to."

J.I. relished telling audiences that the things they had accepted for years were simply wrong. In 1955 he published the book *Poison in Your Pots and Pans*—a brief diatribe against using aluminum, tin, and copper for cooking food. He continually hammered on the virtues of bonemeal and railed against the growing use of fluoride in water supplies. In July 1955 the entire issue of *Prevention* was devoted to milk.

ANGLING RECORD

Accompanied By JERRY OLDS — Date APRIL 15 1955

Name of Water Fished LITTLE LEHIGH — Locality BELOW SALISBURY CHURCH

Condition of Water RUNNING STILL SALT FRESH CLEAR MUDDY WARM COLD TIDE — Weather CLEAR

Tackle Used SPINNING ROD AND REEL — Line LIGHT MONOFILAMENT

Rod — Reel AIREX

Hooks and Bait Used #8 SNELLED HOOK, WORM FOR BAIT

Boat Used — How Propelled —

FISH CAUGHT

Species	No.	Length	Girth	Wgt.	Kind of Bait	Stomach Contents	Time Taken
BROOK TROUT	1	12½"	–	–	WORM	3" MINNOW IN MOUTH	6 A.M.
BROOK TROUT	1	11"	–	–	WORM	–	6:45 A.M.

Remarks: JERRY CAUGHT THREE SMALLER FISH. THIS WAS HIS FIRST OPENING DAY. CATCH SEEMED NORMAL FOR OPENING DAY. FISHED ONLY UNTIL 7 A.M.

An outdoorsman and sportsman from a young age, 25-year-old Robert Rodale kept careful records of his fishing outings.

J. I. Rodale relished going after sacred cows. This *Prevention* issue explored the potential damage caused by milk.

July, 1955

Prevention

devoted to the conservation of human health

Is Milk Related to the Incidence of Cancer?

The following is reprinted from *Degeneration and Regeneration* by Melvin E. Page, D.D.S. published by the Biochemical Research Foundation, 2810 First Street North, St. Petersburg, Florida. Dr. Page discusses in this book the relation of good diet to the health of the glands and hence of the individual. He does not recommend milk as food for adult human beings.

ANOTHER factor which I believe has been almost totally overlooked is the rôle that milk plays in cancer cases. To say anything against milk as a food partakes of the nature of heresy. It is accepted by practically everyone including our best nutritionists as our most excellent food. Perhaps it is the universal acceptance which protects it from inquiry and investigation.

Just what is milk? It is that fluid, usually from a cow, used by the cow for the purpose of feeding her calf up till a certain age when she weans it. Man uses it as a drink for himself and his family for all of his life.

As far as I know, he and a certain species of ant are the only ones who use an animal secretion after the age of weaning.

Now there must be some good reason why nature weans children at six or eight months of age, for nature goes to great pains to see that this is done. The infant begins to eat food other than his mother's milk after a few months and then at

July, 1955 75

"I say to you who are really health-conscious, who want to live to 100 and over without the usual signs of crippling senility—don't drink milk, which means also don't eat butter or cheese or any other dairy product." J.I. reported that he had been off the stuff for more than five years, "and as yet there have been no signs of any deficiencies or repercussions of any kind."

Bob was more methodical, more circumspect, less declarative, and less polemical. He approached the crucial topics of human health and the health of the soil as an advocate of the organic cause, but also as an observer. While J.I. devised systems, Bob frequently described the small steps necessary to put them into practice. Where J.I. put himself and his opinions front and center, Bob wrote himself out of the picture—even when he was in it. In the December 1955 *OG&F* issue, Bob wrote an article entitled "The Editors Build a Greenhouse," which featured several staffers—including Bob—in a photo essay. But it didn't list their names.

And yet in many ways, father and son found their skills were complementary. On Fridays, Bob, Ardie, and their children—Heather, born in 1952, and Heidi, born in 1954—would come over for dinner. As Ardie put it, "The harmony between Bob and J.I. was real, if not always as serene as it seemed. His father's tendency to act on a whim kept Bob off-balance." Bob was more risk-averse, perhaps because he saw Rodale Press from the beginning as a business, as a way to make a living and support a family. J.I. had always been able to rely on the steady profits generated by Rodale Manufacturing.

One of the fundamental challenges father and son confronted in the mid-1950s was a realization that they could no longer rely upon Rodale Manufacturing's profits to fund the publishing operations. Upon Joe Rodale's death, his wife, Esther, inherited Joe's 50 percent share in Rodale Manufacturing. The brothers had an arrangement whereby the surviving brother would buy out the other's widow. J.I. did not have anywhere near the

1955
July 17: Disneyland opens in Anaheim, California.

August 28: Emmett Till is murdered in Money, Mississippi.

Fall: *The Village Voice* is founded.

Emmett Till

J. I. Rodale publishes *Poison in Your Pots and Pans*.

J. I. Rodale & Co., Ltd., is established in London.

First McDonald's opens in Des Plaines, Illinois.

amount necessary to do so, as the company that had started 30 years before was now valued at $1.65 million. As a result, he crafted a plan to have Rodale Manufacturing borrow $500,000 so it could ultimately pay Esther $650,000 in cash and give her a $175,000, four-year note. That meant there would be far less cash left over to pay dividends and salaries to J.I. and hence to subsidize the publishing operations. The magazines and books had to be made to pay their own way—and fast.

J.I. reluctantly made the decision to sell off the printing presses.

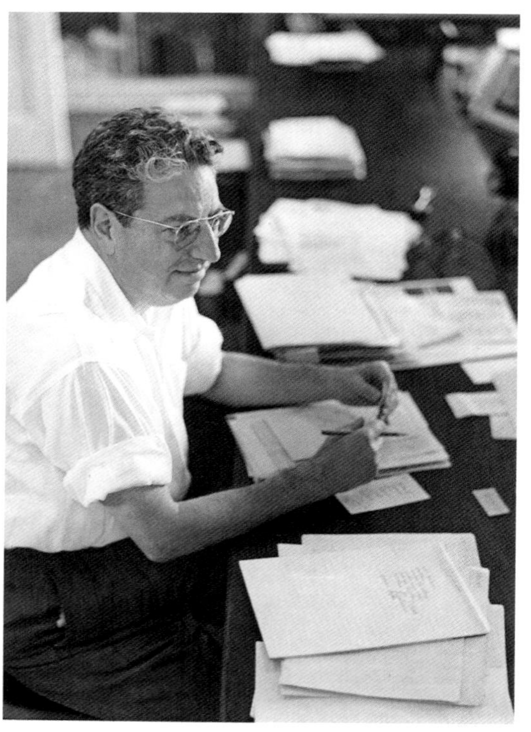

While attempting to come up with a means of meeting his commitment, J.I. took stock of his resources and his disparate businesses. After more than 20 years in publishing, it seemed as if he were doing so for the first time. Rodale Press didn't have many hard assets to sell—except the printing press. Virtually all large magazine companies had captive printing plants. But Rodale wasn't large, and Bob realized that having in-house printing capacity wasn't necessary for the publishing company, much as J.I. loved the smell of ink. It accounted for 25 of the company's 90 employees, and there were significant periods of downtime between publication runs. Meanwhile, the company wanted to expand by building a new headquarters on several acres it owned at the corner of Minor Street and Kline's Lane in Emmaus.

So on the morning of March 14, 1956, Rodale auctioned off its printing plant: nine printing presses, two Linotype machines, two folding machines, and two guillotine cutters. First to go was the paper drill—for $125. "So I thought, 'Oh, this is a good sign,'" Bob recalled. J.I. later wrote that the sale of the printing equipment brought $93,000.

Next to go was the Story Classics line of books, which had long been unprofitable. In the summer of 1956, the Jewish Book Guild agreed to buy the American inventory of Story Classics for $25,000, and the British line for $36,000. "It removes, in one fell swoop, a phase of our business that has been a serious drain on it for many years," J.I. wrote. More important, it provided a source of cash to "finance the largest edition we have ever printed at one time of any book, namely 35,000 copies of *Health Finder.*"

Bob typically saw the glass as half empty. The sale of the presses, he thought, was enough to keep the publishing operation going for another several months. But J.I., just as typically, saw the

1956
February 22: Elvis Presley's "Heartbreak Hotel" becomes a hit.

March: Rodale auctions off its printing plant.

Elvis Presley

March 15: *My Fair Lady* opens on Broadway.

October 8: New York Yankees pitcher Don Larsen pitches the first perfect game in World Series history.

November 25: American Cancer Society announces that cigarette smoking and lung cancer are clearly related. Sierra Club and other environmental groups block construction of the Echo Park Dam in Dinosaur National Monument on the Utah-Colorado border.

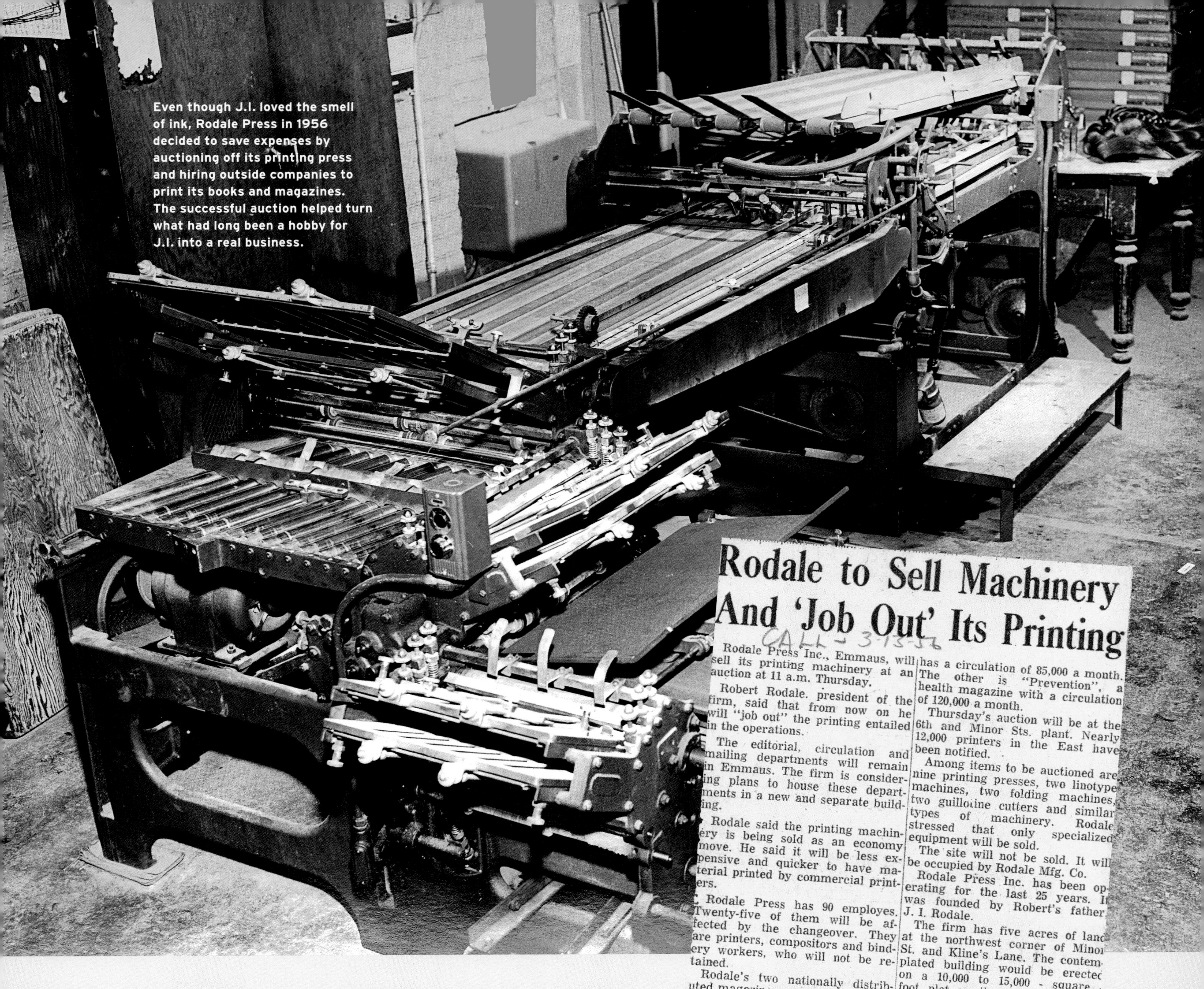

Even though J.I. loved the smell of ink, Rodale Press in 1956 decided to save expenses by auctioning off its printing press and hiring outside companies to print its books and magazines. The successful auction helped turn what had long been a hobby for J.I. into a real business.

Rodale to Sell Machinery And 'Job Out' Its Printing

Rodale Press Inc., Emmaus, will sell its printing machinery at an auction at 11 a.m. Thursday.

Robert Rodale. president of the firm, said that from now on he will "job out" the printing entailed in the operations.

The editorial, circulation and mailing departments will remain in Emmaus. The firm is considering plans to house these departments in a new and separate building.

Rodale said the printing machinery is being sold as an economy move. He said it will be less expensive and quicker to have material printed by commercial printers.

Rodale Press has 90 employes. Twenty-five of them will be affected by the changeover. They are printers, compositors and bindery workers, who will not be retained.

Rodale's two nationally distributed magazines are printed in Harrisburg and will continue to be printed there. One is "Organic Gardening and Farming", which has a circulation of 85,000 a month. The other is "Prevention", a health magazine with a circulation of 120,000 a month.

Thursday's auction will be at the 6th and Minor Sts. plant. Nearly 12,000 printers in the East have been notified.

Among items to be auctioned are nine printing presses, two linotype machines, two folding machines, two guillotine cutters and similar types of machinery. Rodale stressed that only specialized equipment will be sold.

The site will not be sold. It will be occupied by Rodale Mfg. Co.

Rodale Press Inc. has been operating for the last 25 years. It was founded by Robert's father, J. I. Rodale.

The firm has five acres of land at the northwest corner of Minor St. and Kline's Lane. The contemplated building would be erected on a 10,000 to 15,000 - square - foot plot on the tract. The president said preilminary plans call for a one-story building to measure 100 by 150 feet. The lot is now vacant.

Early Rodale Press staff. *Standing:* Maurice Franz, Bob Rodale, Al Moyer, Al Barrett, Jerry Goldstein, Jim Hare. *Seated:* Karl Manahan, Marvin Tannenberg, Marshall Ackerman, Lee Goldman

glass as two-thirds full. "The publishing company must be looked at in a new light," he wrote in a report intended to be read by bankers. "The days when it suffered consistent yearly losses are gone." *OG&F* and *Prevention* had paid circulations of 90,000 and 135,000, respectively. For the first eight months of 1956, advertising revenues had risen for both magazines, from $157,000 to $245,000. And J.I. was planning a 25 percent rate increase for the October 1956 issue. The magazines were finally beginning to sustain themselves. "I have sunk my life's earnings, almost every penny of it—a real fortune—into this business. It is now going to begin to pay off. For more than two years now, I haven't put a cent into the business." For its part, Rodale Books was already profitable, according to a report compiled by James Hare, who had joined Rodale from the Book-of-the-Month Club. Sales, which came in at $177,000 in the fiscal year ending September 30, 1955, rose sharply to $328,000 in the first three-quarters of fiscal 1956. "I expect total sales for the current fiscal year to be between $450,000 and $500,000," Hare wrote.

Selling the equipment meant Rodale had to find a new printer for the 6- by 9-inch magazines. Rodale had previously bought rolls of higher-quality paper that had been rejected by the *Saturday Evening Post.* Now it contemplated going down several grades. But it quickly struck a deal with Telegraph Press, which had made 6- by 6-inch telephone books for AT&T that were being discontinued. "We have found a very large printer in Philadelphia who is doing our printing at amazingly low prices and printing the jobs faster than we used to do it ourselves."

Reducing overhead and cutting printing costs were only part of the battle. The company faced higher costs in the form of rising third-class postage rates. So Bob next implemented the counterintuitive idea of raising prices. "We were charging three dollars a year for the magazines. So I said, 'We're going to have to charge four dollars.'" They found that the magazines were plainly delivering

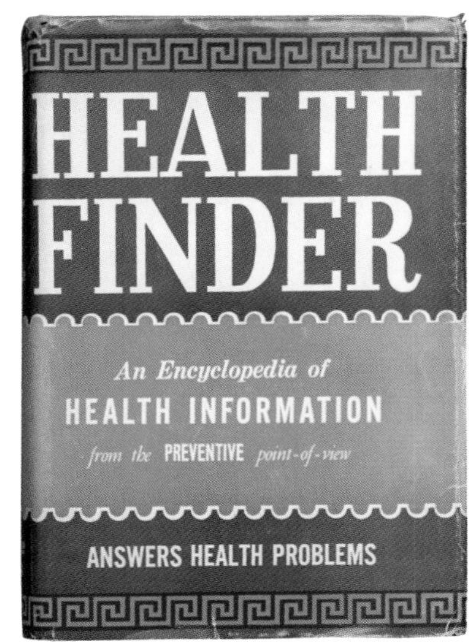

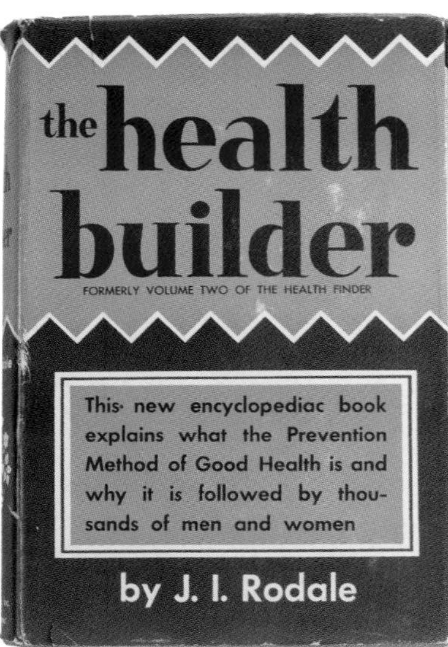

Rodale's books in the mid-1950s focused almost exclusively on empowering readers to take responsibility for their own health.

a value, for the renewal rates rose with the subscription rates. Bob recalled this episode as a turning point. "Soon after that, the strings with the manufacturing company were cut completely—and we didn't go under." By September 1957, magazines were driving the editorial train. With revenues of $1.09 million, the magazines eked out a gross profit of $40,991. The book division essentially broke even on book sales of $543,000, of which more than half—$279,000—came from *Health Finder.*

The growth of the magazines—and the desire and need to sell more advertisements—created both opportunities and tensions. Marshall Ackerman led efforts to get larger, established companies to sign on and frequently went to great lengths to sell ads. Once he chartered a plane to fly to the headquarters of farm machinery manufacturer W. W. Grinder in Topeka, Kansas. W. W. Grinder signed on. But other companies resisted placing ads in *OG&F* and *Prevention.* The magazines were sufficiently small and off the beaten path that they couldn't attract blue-chip advertisers like Ford and General Electric. And large advertising agencies, which worked on commission, didn't have much incentive to place ads in Rodale publications—in which advertising space was cheaper than it was in mass circulation magazines.

The penchant of contributors to criticize large commercial interests also inhibited advertising sales. In the late 1950s, Ruth Adams wrote a withering critique of Tang, the orange-flavored drink mix recently introduced by General Foods. "The best thing you can say about this product is that if you drink it with enough water, it won't kill you. The same can be said for carbolic acid." When Ackerman went to see General Foods' advertising agency—Young & Rubicam—to see if it would place ads in Rodale magazines for Postum, a coffee substitute, the advertising agents complained about the Tang article and asked *Prevention* to stop running such articles. The answer was a firm no.

Nonetheless, as the years went by and *Prevention*'s circulation increased, it became more difficult for advertisers to ignore. The same couldn't be said for *OG&F,* which was a continuing drag on resources. In the late 1950s, "J.I. came in one day and said, 'Enough of this organic gardening stuff,'" Bob recalled. As a publisher, J.I. had always been willing to discontinue magazines and lines of books if they weren't working. But Bob, who had spent virtually his entire young career at

1957
January 4: After 69 years, the last issue of *Collier's* magazine is published.

September 4: Ford introduces the Edsel.

September 25: Nine black students enter Central High School in Little Rock, Arkansas, protected by U.S. troops.

October 4: Launch of *Sputnik I*, the first artificial satellite to orbit the earth.

Rodale publishes *The Health Builder.*

Sputnik I

Rodale Press's new main building brought employees and operations together under one roof—for the time being.

OG&F, was adamant that it continue. He and Jerry Goldstein created a new direct-mail pitch—Country Homesteading—that received a highly favorable response.

In 1958, Bob wrote in a report that Rodale Press's sales were running at a rate of about $2 million annually, nearly twice the pace of 1956. After nearly 25 years, J.I.'s publishing operations were a viable concern. The magazines had large subscriber and advertising bases. New books based on material from the magazines were continually rolled out, including *The Health Builder* in 1957 and the *Encyclopedia of Organic Gardening* in 1958. "In recent months we have been able to pay our bills promptly and have accumulated some cash in the bank," Robert stated proudly in a report in the summer of 1958. Thinking of the long term, he resolved to build a cash balance of $100,000. "Once we establish a reserve, we can expand operations [or] invest in stocks." He also decided to use some of the excess cash to increase publicity and boost circulation of the two main magazines, "even if it means losing a little money on some mailings."

Rodale was taking on the accoutrements of an established company. In 1959, Bob introduced a plan under which "each employee is given a stake in the welfare of Rodale Press and Rodale Books." With $260,000 in the bank, the company created profit-sharing and pension plans. In the first nine months of 1959, *Prevention* alone had a profit of $353,000. That year, J.I. received a salary of $12,620 from Rodale Press and $15,000 from Rodale Books. Rodale still lacked a home, however. Its operations had been housed in offices in Allentown and in Rodale Manufacturing. On October 21, 1959, Rodale opened its 125,000-square-foot Organic Park, inviting the public in for a three-hour open house. Designed by Fred Genther, it contained 20,000 square feet of open space for the company's 100 employees, as well as vacant land that could be used for demonstrations. Thomas W. Sears, a prominent landscape architect, was hired to design an external environment in keeping with the company's ethos.

But while the profits were gratifying, there was still a pervasive sense that the effort was about something larger than dollars and cents. By the late 1950s, with nearly 20 years of *OG&F* and 10 years of *Prevention,* with the encyclopedias and reference books, Rodale had gone a long

1958
July 29: Congress formally creates the National Aeronautics and Space Administration (NASA).

Shoe company J. W. Foster & Co. becomes Reebok.

August 18: Vladimir Nabokov's controversial novel *Lolita* is published in the United states.

Amendment to Food, Drug, and Cosmetic Act bans cancer-causing artificial substances from food.

People reading *Lolita*

April, 1957
35 Cents
ORGANIC
Gardening and Farming
SPECIAL ISSUE
THE GOOD LIFE ON 1 ACRE homestead
Including a plan for the ideal organic

The
HEALTH SEEKER
by
J. I. RODALE
and Staff

Bright colors vividly brought the promise of good health and organic gardening to life.

Encyclopedia of
ORGANIC
Gardening
By J. I. Rodale and Staff

Rodale publishes *Encyclopedia of Organic Gardening*.

J. I. Rodale publishes *Skits and Conversations toward Better Health*.

J. I. Rodale's play *The Girl and the Teenager* is produced in summer stock in Allentown.

way toward developing the systems about which J.I. had long dreamed. "*Prevention* magazine is not a magazine in the ordinary sense of the word. Rather, it is a system, and to get the best results with it, it is best to follow it as a complete system," J.I. wrote in the April 1959 issue of *Prevention*.

The next paragraphs in the article distilled the wisdom on better living that J.I. had amassed in the previous 20 years:

- Avoid chemically fertilized and sprayed foods. "We are in favor of a low-carbohydrate, high-protein diet, including meat, fish, and eggs."
- Avoid bread, excess salt, and processed and canned foods, since they contain chemicals. "We are not vegetarians, for our research indicates that a high-protein diet is the best diet."
- Avoid milk (adults) and eat lots of nuts, fruits, and vegetables.
- Shun aluminum cooking utensils, plastic utensils, and tap water. "Never fry your food. Rather broil or bake."
- Eat sunflower seeds, avoid caffeine, and exercise.
- Test pulses, avoid toothpastes, and never wear rimless eyeglasses.

Bob took over enough of the responsibilites of running the company that J.I. could pursue other interests.

"This looks like a lot of things to do and to remember, but all can be worked out on a gradual basis," J.I. wrote. "You can study the reasons for each item by looking it up in the *Health Finder* (Rodale Books, Inc., $5.95)." Here was J.I. in a nutshell–systematic, reusing information, and plugging other Rodale products all the while.

In the late 1950s, as J.I. approached the age of 60, his interests began to shift away from the manufacturing and publishing businesses and toward leisure and less overtly commercial activities. In the winter of 1958 to 1959, he and Anna rented a house in Palm Beach, Florida, "so that I would be able to do my walking every day." He enjoyed traveling and went on frequent trips to Europe and Central America, always with Anna. On one trip in 1958, the actress Jayne Mansfield was next to them on the plane. "She knows about *Prevention* magazine and is a regular taker of bonemeal,"

1959
January 3: Alaska is admitted to the United States as the 49th state.

March 9: Barbie doll debuts.

July 24: Vice President Richard Nixon and Soviet premier Nikita Khrushchev engage in informal kitchen debate at the opening of the American National Exhibition in Moscow.

Richard Nixon and Nikita Khrushchev

Parathion, used as a chemical weapon during World War II, is sprayed aerially on farms throughout the South and Midwest and destroys far more than insects.

J. I. and Anna Rodale enjoyed a prosperous semiretirement in the late 1950s, traveling frequently and spending time with their growing family.

he proudly reported. "I gave her some sunflower seeds." He organized tours to Europe in the summer of 1958 and formed the J. I. Rodale Tour Office. With more professionals added to the staff at the magazines—assistant editor Charles Gerras and editorial adviser W. J. McCormick, M.D., at *Prevention*—and with Bob at the helm of the business, J.I. was liberated to pursue new interests. "He felt he could trust me, and when I got involved, he could relax, and then he could go out and do his own thing," Bob recalled.

In the latter half of the 1950s, the tone—if not the content—of J.I.'s writing began to shift. Rooted squarely in fact for nearly three decades, J.I. began increasingly to dabble in fiction. In February 1957, *Prevention* published "The Man with the Unopened Umbrella," a futuristic short story. Set in 2007, it described Illinois as a place where medicine was socialized, where the use of aluminum utensils in cooking was banned, and where doctors sought out preventive health measures. It was a Brave New World according to *Prevention*. In 1958 J.I. published a book, *Skits and Conversations toward Better Health*, that featured whimsical conversations between a reporter and a chicken farmer who was raising his birds through unnatural methods; and a fable, entitled "The Honest Counterfeiters," that compared synthetic foods and vitamins to currencies debased by alchemists. J.I. saw fiction as a new way of getting ideas across to people who might not subscribe to a Rodale publication.

The dustcover of the book featured a picture of J.I. and Anna that reflected J.I.'s expansive sense of self and stature. He described himself as "businessman, traveler, patron of the arts, originator of the *Prevention* method of good health and the Word-at-a-Time language system, compiler of the standard reference work *The Word Finder*." But it noted that "Mr. Rodale looks forward to a new career as a playwright." Indeed, while he

October: Rodale Press "Organic Park" office building opens.

October 21: The Solomon R. Guggenheim Museum, designed by Frank Lloyd Wright, opens in New York City.

Guggenheim Museum

November: Cranberries from Washington and Oregon are ordered off the market due to contamination by the chemical weed killer aminotriazole.

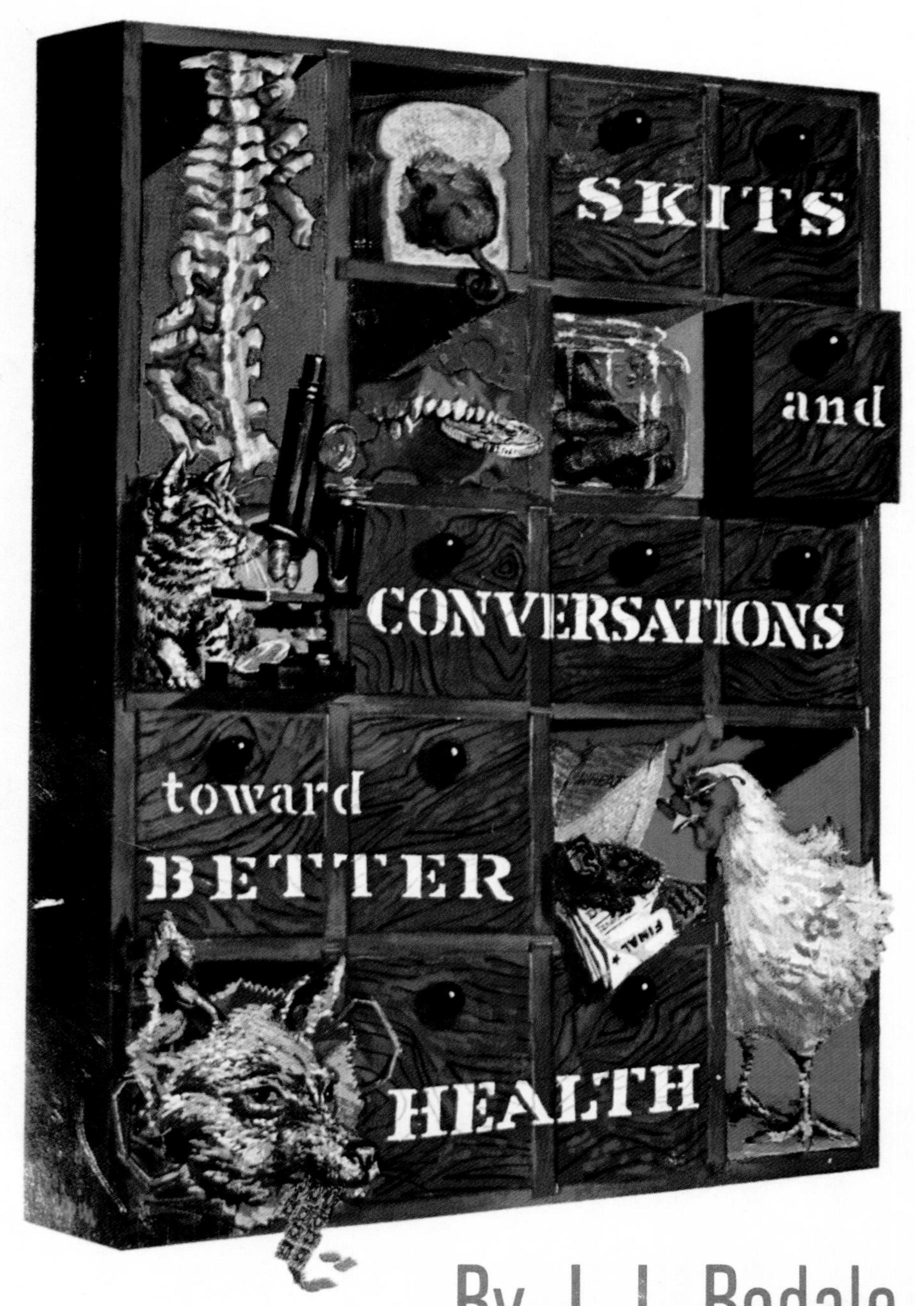

J. I. Rodale had spent virtually his entire career trafficking in fact. But in the late 1950s, he shifted gears. *Skits and Conversations toward Better Health* (1958) was his first real work of fiction.

would be involved in the magazines and remain their guiding spirit for the next decade and a half, much of J.I.'s creative efforts would henceforth be geared toward the stage.

In the October 1958 issue of *OG&F,* an advertisement appeared for a "serious comedy on health" to be presented by a Bethlehem theater group. Written by J.I. and entitled *Doctor and the Tramp,* it dealt with a "young man who owns a skyscraper in New York City and also [has] a very painful case of prostate" who is "cured through nutrition when he befriends a tramp-like, but wonderful, doctor." In December 1958, J.I. reported that his play *The Girl and the Teenager* played for a week at summer stock theater in Allentown. The plot: A social worker helps juvenile delinquents transform their lives through diet.

J.I. constantly revised his plays and pushed for them to be produced on larger stages. *The Girl and the Teenager,* later renamed *The Goose,* was ultimately staged at the off-Broadway Sullivan Street Playhouse in New York in March 1960. J.I.'s early plays—willfully quirky, didactic, containing a mix of humor and a serious message, and relatively short on plot—typically didn't find much critical success. The *New Yorker* reviewer wrote, "In this world there are a few things indeed that oblige me to speak of perfection. To any list of such things we may now add J. I. Rodale's *The Goose*.... It's perfectly awful. It is supremely inept. It is magnificently foolish. It's sublimely, heroically, breathtakingly dreadful. It inspires sacred terror. It is beyond criticism." After the play closed, J.I. bought a large advertisement in the *New York Times* defending the play against its critics. He told a *Times* reporter that the play received such bad reviews in part because *Prevention* "is telling the truth, is a menace to certain powerful and industrial interests."

In May 1960, J.I. was still actively in control of his health. He toted up his daily intake—9 tablets of bonemeal a day, 15 tablets of desiccated liver, 15 tablets of rose hips, and others. "In all, my wife and I take 93 tablets a day and are very happy and hearty because of our intake." In June 1960, the 10th anniversary of *Prevention* featured an oil painting of J.I. on the cover. Circulation had grown to 260,000. "We have become the second largest health magazine in the world," he wrote. "We have been jabbing at the vested interests. Without fear we have questioned the moves of the

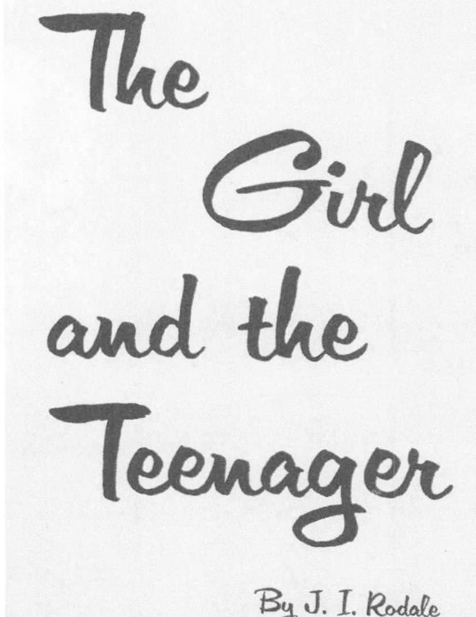

J.I.'s first play was performed in Allentown in 1958.

1960
March: J.I.'s play *The Goose* is staged in New York City.

Rodale starts *Compost Science: The Journal of Waste Recycling.*

May 1: Soviet missile shoots down the U.S. U2 spy plane piloted by Francis Gary Powers.

May 9: The Food and Drug Administration approves the sale of the birth control pill.

November 8: Democrat John F. Kennedy defeats Richard M. Nixon to become the youngest man elected president.

Alfred Hitchcock's *Psycho* premieres.

Nixon-Kennedy debates

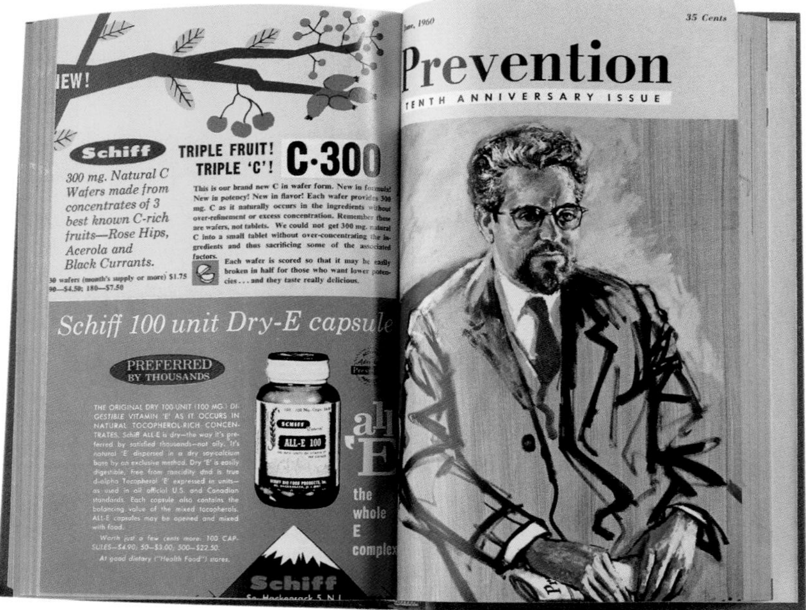

The tenth anniversary issue of *Prevention* featured an oil painting of J.I. on its cover.

large food producers who place profits and dividends above the physical well-being of their customers." He predicted that "the next 10 years will undoubtedly show far more regulation over food chemicalization than at anytime in the past."

Indeed, there were signs that J.I.'s ideas were gaining traction. In the late 1950s, public awareness of the problem of chemicals in foods was growing. In 1958 an amendment to the Federal Food, Drug, and Cosmetic Act banned from food any artificial substance that could be shown to cause cancer in lab animals. And in November 1959, Secretary of Health, Education, and Welfare Arthur Flemming announced that cranberry sauces were contaminated because farmers had sprayed the bogs with aminotriazole, which was found to cause cancer in laboratory rats. The announcement ruined countless Thanksgiving dinners nationwide.

And at a time when communities across the country were deciding to put fluoride in their municipal water supplies, J.I. led campaigns locally and nationally against the practice. *Prevention* carried a recurrent feature entitled "On the Fluoridation Front," offering encouragement and ammunition for readers who opposed local fluoridation efforts. In 1961 he published a local paper, *The Anti-Fluoridationist*, modeled on the *Federalist Papers*. Approaching an age at which many of his contemporaries were retiring, J.I. was still a self-proclaimed revolutionary.

Sensing a shift in the market, Rodale started a new publication, *Compost Science: The Journal of Waste Recycling,* in the spring of 1960. Whereas virtually all the company's prior publications had been geared toward consumers, this was intended for a professional audience. It was marketed to large companies and to city governments that had to deal with large amounts of waste. The first issue included an article on how the sewage treatment department in Schenectady, New York, had sold its sludge.

But for J.I., the stage would be the most important new medium through which to spread

1961
January 25: President Kennedy holds the first live presidential news conference.

February 11: Trial of Nazi Final Solution architect Adolf Eichmann begins in Jerusalem.

March 1: John F. Kennedy establishes the Peace Corps.

March: J. I. Rodale announces plans to buy the Royal Playhouse in New York City and renames it the Rodale Theater.

April 12: Soviet cosmonaut Yuri Gagarin is the first human in space.

April 17: Cuban exiles start failed invasion at Bay of Pigs.

Joseph Heller's *Catch-22* is published.

Cosmonaut Yuri Gagarin

In 1960, J.I.'s play *The Goose* was staged at the Sullivan Street Playhouse in New York City.

his message. In 1961, J.I., who saw an estimated 100 plays annually, bought a substantial interest in *Backstage* and started writing a weekly column called "In the Theatre with J. I. Rodale." And in March 1961 he announced plans to buy the Royal Playhouse at 62 East Fourth Street and turn it into the Rodale Theater. "Unless plans change, the first play will be *The Streets of Confusion*. The main theme is how certain people with less-than-average intelligence, through their social dexterity, monopolize positions in high places. The secondary theme is that people are eating infertile eggs laid by hens without benefit of roosters, which medical evidence reveals are of inferior nutritional qualities. Those who have read the script of this play claim it is the best thing I have done thus far."

J.I. relished his role as editor, propagandist for the organic cause, scourge of corporations, and advocate for the public health. And while many of his arguments were still controversial, many of his ideas had been in large measure ratified in the marketplace of public opinion. Far from retiring, J.I. maintained a hectic pace. And he was finally getting recognition—in his mind, likely well deserved—for the crucial role he had played. In August 1961 the Annual Convention of the National Health Federation gave J.I. its humanitarian award.

Over the previous decade, J.I.'s avocation—the publication of magazines and books devoted to helping people improve their lives—had evolved into a viable, profitable business. With Bob Rodale at its helm, Rodale Press, which was in 1951 an unincorporated entity that borrowed space in an electronics manufacturing plant, had transformed into an independent corporation with its own headquarters, a healthy balance sheet, and hard assets. Having established legitimacy among the constituencies that mattered most—its readers and advertisers—Rodale's future seemed bright. In the next decade, the larger culture would continue to move in Rodale's direction and to embrace the concepts Rodale had been advocating for decades. This shift would provide tremendous opportunities for growth. But the 1960s, a decade filled with so much promise, would also bring the greatest challenge and threat to the company's existence.

When this photo of J. I. Rodale, walking in a field on the Rodale farm, appeared on the cover of the *New York Times Magazine* in June 1971, the organic movement had achieved a certain critical mass.

CHAPTER 5

1962 TO 1971

The Message Resonates in a Changing Culture

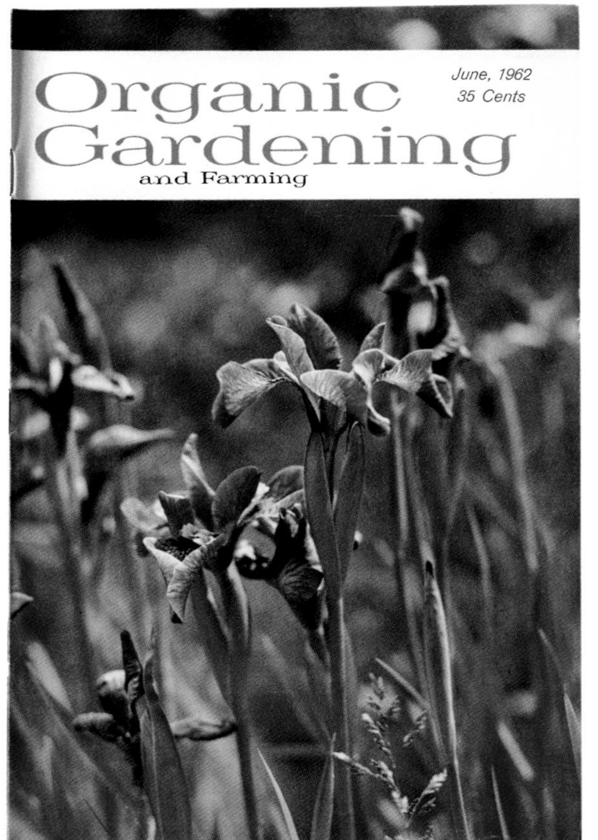

The year 1962 marked two decades of growth for *Organic Gardening and Farming* magazine.

IN THE EARLY 1960S, the publishing company that J. I. Rodale had founded and that his son, Robert, had helped build seemed finally to be on sound footing. With its own building, relatively solid finances, and professional full-time management, the company seemed poised for growth. "Today we are securing advertising from certain large companies that wouldn't look at us even as recently as five years ago," J.I. wrote in the 20th anniversary issue of *Organic Gardening and Farming (OG&F)* in June 1962. "When several million gardeners are practicing the organic method, their weight is felt." Even as J.I. began to devote more time to what would become his third or fourth career—playwriting—he continued to maintain an active role in the company's magazines, to publish nonfiction books with Rodale at the rate of nearly one

Rachel Carson's book *Silent Spring* echoed themes familiar to Rodale readers.

per year, and to speak publicly. In the 1960s, the themes he had been sounding for decades about health, the benefits of an organic lifestyle, and the dangers posed to humans, animals, and the environment by chemicals began to resonate in the larger culture. As the turbulent decade unfolded, the civil-rights movement, the antiwar movement, the women's movement, and the beginnings of the consumer and environmental movements would change the face of American politics and culture. The rise of these last two, in particular, would provide new audiences for Rodale publications and allow the company to report sustained and impressive profits for the first time.

The 1962 publication and instant success of *Silent Spring,* by Rachel Carson, a biologist with a gift for prose, proved a harbinger. *Silent Spring* was a lucid, scientifically literate lament about the ravages of chemicals on the land, water, and air as well as on animals. Serialized in the *New Yorker* in June 1962, it remained on the *New York Times* bestseller list for 31 weeks. From its language about the necessity to view soil as a living organism to its call for greater government action to prevent further damage, *Silent Spring* echoed themes familiar to readers of *OG&F* and *Prevention.* By the end of 1962, more than 40 bills had been introduced in state legislatures to regulate pesticides. Bob Rodale praised "Rachel Carson's Masterpiece" in *OG&F* in September 1962. J.I.'s book *Our Poisoned Earth and Sky,* published in 1964, would cover much of the same ground.

For decades, J.I. had been publicly calling for the government—particularly the U.S. Department of Agriculture—to change its policies regarding nutrition and health. On occasion he had been called to testify before Congress on issues such as chemicals in food. But in the early and mid-1960s, with the advent of new programs like Medicare and Medicaid and a growing sense of the need for greater consumer protection, Rodale Press began covering breaking news in Washington more comprehensively. In December 1962, *Prevention* started a new department, Your Government and Your Health. And in 1963 the company launched a weekly newsletter, *Health Bulletin,* in collaboration with Washington-based journalist Wade Jones. Its format—four to six pages of simple typed copy, no advertising, and no graphics—relied entirely on circulation. "We lost money on it, but circulation went up to 80,000 copies," Bob recalled.

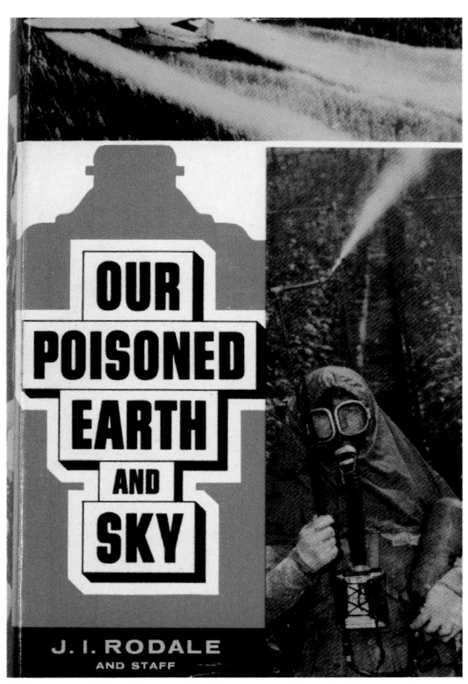

Rodale's alarms about the effects of pollutants and chemicals on the environment began to resonate in the broader culture.

1962
February 20: John Glenn becomes the first American to orbit the earth in *Friendship 7.*

June 15: Students for a Democratic Society (SDS) issues the Port Huron Statement.

June: Rachel Carson's *Silent Spring* is serialized in the *New Yorker.*

John Glenn

June: Twentieth anniversary issue of *OG&F.*

August 5: Marilyn Monroe found dead in Los Angeles.

October 1: James Meredith becomes the first African American student to register at the University of Mississippi.

October: Bob Rodale competes in world skeet-shooting championships in Cairo.

November: Cuban Missile Crisis ends.

health BULLETIN

Weekly Coverage of Health News

Editors WADE JONES ROBERT RODALE

Publisher J.I. RODALE

March 16, 1963 Vol. 1, No. 1

AMA DROPS TOBACCO STUDY

Claiming that it "has had difficulty finding appropriate scientists and physicians to serve on a special committee to carry out the work," the American Medical Association has decided to discontinue its investigation of the effect of tobacco on various diseases.

The announcement, made on March 12, caused tobacco stocks on the N.Y. Exchange to spurt upward.

NEW FLU VIRUS DISCOVERED

A potent new strain of the Asian flu virus, against which vaccines are largely ineffective, was mainly responsible for the seriousness of this winter's flu epidemic across the nation, the Associated Press reported Wednesday.

THOUGHTS OF CRANBERRIES HAUNT POTATO GROWERS

North Carolina farm authorities have cancelled permission for the use of the insecticide Aldrin on white potatoes in an effort to head off another cranberry-type crisis.

Here's the story: Aldrin is a chlorinated hydrocarbon insecticide (like DDT) that has been in use for 10 years. It is effective against potato pests, such as wireworms and white grubs. Because of Aldrin's toxic effect on the human nervous system, the FDA permits only a very small residue on potatoes -- one tenth of a part per million.

Until recently, no available testing equipment could make an accurate analysis of Aldrin in such a low quantity. When new, more sensitive equipment came into use last fall, it was found that some lots of white potatoes grown in the Pacific states had as high as .17 ppm of Aldrin and FDA made several seizures.

Now Eastern states are using the new test equipment, and they don't like what it is revealing. "The information which has come to us is alarming," North Carolina Assistant Commissioner of Agriculture John L. Reitzel said last week. "The samples now being run show one out of ten to be contaminated with Aldrin." Most of the insecticide is concentrated in the skin of the potatoes, but some has penetrated to the inside.

Chemical dealers in North Carolina have been told to instruct farmers not to use Aldrin on potatoes. Other Eastern states are likely to take similar action. Frank McFarland, director of FDA's pesticide branch, told Health Bulletin that the rest is up to the farmers. "If a grower follows label instructions," said McFarland, "he'll avoid violative residues." The cranberry crisis of 1961 was caused when FDA seized several lots of berries contaminated with weed killer residues.

The U.S. Department of Agriculture reports that Shell Oil Co., manu-

Rodale launched the weekly *Health Bulletin* in 1963.

Health Bulletin read something like a modern Web log, providing constant updates on areas of interest to readers, documenting advances and setbacks in the progress of legislation affecting health, and disseminating news of contaminated products. The first issue, on sale March 16, 1963, contained items about the American Medical Association's decision to stop an investigation of the effect of tobacco on various diseases, North Carolina's cancellation of permission for the use of the insecticide aldrin on white potatoes, and an antifluoridation vote in Seattle.

Even though the momentum for the organic cause was building, J.I. still saw himself as a member of an embattled minority–and one who continually sought vindication. On December 6, 1963, he spoke at the Tulsa Town Hall, "the first I had ever made for an honorarium." He spoke about bonemeal and vitamin C and noted that his arguments were still controversial. "Those who criticize should remember that the steps in the development of any theory are ridicule, discussion, and adoption. We are still in the ridicule stage."

For Rodale Press, however, ridicule was not nearly as dangerous as an outright assault from the government. And assault is precisely what J.I.–and, increasingly, Robert–had to contend with for much of the 1960s. A natural salesman, J.I. had long made exuberant, florid claims for his companies' products, whether they were Rodale Manufacturing's door buzzers or the Story Classics. (Consider this from a piece of sales literature for Story Classics: "You will be struck by the sheer beauty of the volume that has been designed for pure reading pleasure.") But claims that dealt with health were more likely to attract scrutiny. In 1952, J.I. had quickly settled charges by the Federal Trade Commission (FTC) that claims about polio he made in advertising *Organic Farming and Gardening* were misleading.

A decade later, government lawyers were again paging through Rodale's magazines. In April 1961, the FTC sent a letter to Rodale asking for a copy of each publication. When agents visited the company in October 1962, they said they were responding to complaints made about *Health Finder,* a popular reference book first published in 1954 that was compiled from material in *Prevention* and two

1963

February 1: *New York Review of Books* founded.

March 16: *Health Bulletin* debuts.

March 21: Alcatraz federal penitentiary closes.

August 28: Martin Luther King Jr. delivers "I have a dream" speech on the steps of the Lincoln Memorial.

Martin Luther King Jr.

November 22: President John F. Kennedy is assassinated.

Jean Nidetch incorporates Weight Watchers.

December 6: J.I. delivers first paid speech in Tulsa.

Kennedy assassination reports

other books. It wasn't clear precisely who had made the complaint. But Rodale had plenty of enemies. In January 1963, Dr. Robert Shank, chairman of the American Medical Association council on foods and nutrition, would mention J.I.'s *Complete Book of Food and Nutrition* before a U.S. Senate Special Committee on Aging discusing quackery. According to J.I., his long-running opposition to an Allentown-area water fluoridation movement had also induced Stephen Barrett, a local fluoridation advocate, to complain to the FTC about *Prevention*'s acceptance of advertisements for bonemeal. Meanwhile, the FDA in 1962 initiated a broad effort to regulate the growing health food business.

For one or all of these reasons, the FTC came to focus on Rodale's publications. It quickly emerged that the agency was concerned with the claims the company made in marketing its books, particularly *Health Finder.* Bob Rodale was somewhat mystified because sales of *Health Finder* had fallen dramatically from 53,480 in 1956 to 586 in 1963. In April 1963, when Rodale ran the last ad for the book, only 240 copies remained.

Nonetheless, in February 1964, the FTC demanded that Rodale sign an agreement that it would no longer make certain claims about the content of *Health Finder,* especially about its potential to help readers prevent or remedy particular diseases. Even though *Health Finder* no longer contributed significantly to the company's revenues and the main advertising brochure in question had been essentially discontinued in 1960, J.I. thought that accepting limits on what they could say about the content of the books would be both damaging and unconstitutional. The books themselves and the advertisements for them were protected by the First Amendment. Because it sold its books almost entirely through mail order, the company relied on attention-grabbing circulars and advertisements that ran in its magazines. What's more, the company's entire business was predicated on the notion that people could improve their lives and health through taking proactive measures. "It would literally put us out of business," Bob said.

Even as he spent much of his time working on plays, J. I. Rodale continued to write books on health.

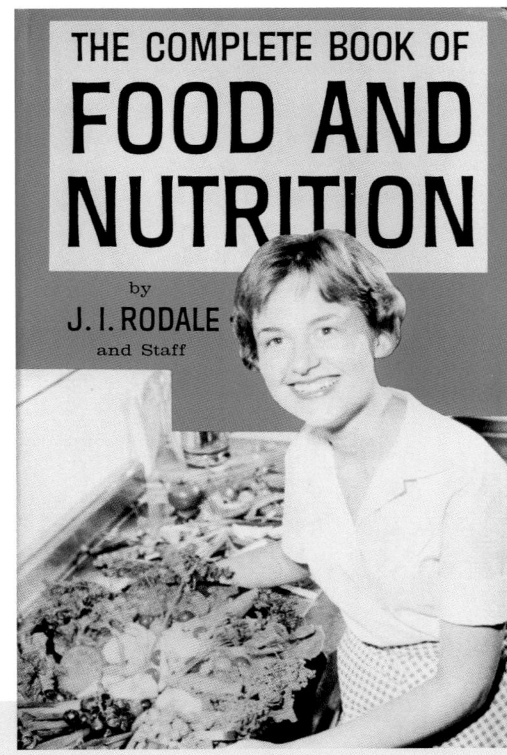

Always full of ideas, J.I. made small metal litter cans for downtown Emmaus and named the company after his mentor, Sir Albert Howard.

The FTC softened its position, saying it would apply the restrictions only to the marketing of Rodale's books, not to the magazines. Rodale's lawyer, Morton Simon, found this more reasonable and said that the company might view the action as a spur to installing new practices to ensure accuracy in all its publications. "You've got to move toward getting everything cleared, and making claims that can be backed up," he said. Bob was inclined to make a deal. But J.I. was emphatic. "We're not giving in to the government," he told Bob. "We're going to fight, and you're going to do it."

On April 3, 1964, the FTC issued a formal complaint. It argued that an ad for *Health Finder* that intimated that the book's contents could "add years to your life" was misleading and deceptive. What's more, the FTC charged that the book didn't contain the answer to all health problems, as it allegedly promised. The agency also charged that ads for the books *How to Eat for a Healthy Heart* and *This Pace Is Not Killing Us* falsely said that they contained information that would benefit in the prevention, treatment, or cure of heart disease.

Once again, the small company in Emmaus, which by geography, temperament, and editorial stance had defined itself in opposition to the publishing establishment, was tangling with the biggest establishment of them all—the federal government. But this time it wasn't without resources. Simon recommended the company seek out Thurman Arnold, a prominent Washington lawyer. A former assistant attorney general in the Roosevelt administration, Yale law professor, and appellate judge, Arnold had founded the influential Washington law firm Arnold, Fortas & Porter. Arnold was enthusiastic about taking the case, which had significant First Amendment implications. He was confident of victory but noted, "It's going to cost you a lot of money." Stewart Land, Arnold's assistant, was less sanguine. "We're going to buy you like five years of time, but be ready at the end of five years. You may lose, and you may be out of business."

Bob shouldered most of the burden. J.I. was enormously busy: writing plays, writing about his life and interests, dividing his time between Emmaus and an apartment in New York, traveling to Europe with Anna, and starting new ventures. In the 1960s, Rodale built a small business making

1964

January 11: Surgeon General Luther Terry reports that smoking may be hazardous to health.

January 13: "I Want to Hold Your Hand," the Beatles' first North American hit, is released in the United States.

April 3: Federal Trade Commission files complaint against Rodale.

July 3: President Lyndon B. Johnson signs the Civil Rights Act of 1964 into law.

August: *Quinto Lingo* debuts.

The Wilderness Act establishes the National Wilderness Preservation System to designate sections of forests as protected wilderness areas.

J. I. Rodale had a long-standing interest in the systematic study of languages. *Quinto Lingo*, a magazine he started in 1964, printed the same content in five different languages.

AFFE ALS BAUERNGEHILFE IST STEUERABZUGSFÄHIG

Melbourne, Australien.—Das Bundessteueramt bewilligte dem Schafzüchter Lindsay Schmidt einen Steuerabzug für seinen Affen, Johnnie, den er als rechtsmässigen Landarbeiter beschäftigt.

Dem drei Fuss und 6 Zoll grossen Rhesusaffen wurde das Traktorfahren beigebracht.

"Johnnie ist ein vorsichtiger Fahrer", sagte Herr Schmidt. "Er würde niemals auf den Anlasserknopf drükken, wenn die Kupplung geschaltet ist. Er versichert sich zuerst, dass die Kupplung neutral ist, drückt auf den Anlasser und springt dann wie ein Blitz auf den Fahrersitz und ergreift das Lenkrad."

Johnnie beaufsichtigt auch die Schafherde, berichtet Schmidt. Er wurde angelernt, die Tore zu öffnen und zu schliessen, und sammelt die verstreuten Schafe.

Der Affen isst gewöhnlich mit den anderen Farmarbeitern sein belegtes Mittagsbrot, Obst und trinkt Sodawasser.

RIDUZIONE DELLE TASSE PER LA SCIMMIA BRACCIANTE DI FATTORIA

Melbourne, Australia.—

I Funzionari delle Tasse Federali hanno garantito una riduzione al proprietario di fattoria ovina Lindsay Schmidt per la sua scimmia, Johnnie, autorizzando a considerarla un legittimo lavoratore della fattoria.

La scimmia, alta tre piedi e 6 pollici era stata addibita a dirigere un trattore.

"Johnnie è un guidatore prudente" disse il Signor Schmidt. "Egli non premerà mai il bottone dell'avviamento mentre il trattore è ingranato. Egli si assicura che il motore sia in folle, preme l'avviamento ed allora scatta al posto di guida come una saetta ed impugna il volante.

A Johnnie è anche affidato l'incarico di raccogliere le pecore, riferì Schmidt. Egli è stato istruito ad aprire e chiudere i cancelli ed a riunire quelle smarrite.

La scimmia mangia abitualmente la sua colazione di panini imbottiti, frutta e gasosa con gli altri braccianti della fattoria.—

SIMIO LABRIEGO ES DEDUCIBLE DE IMPUESTOS

Melbourne, Australia — Funcionarios fiscales federales han permitido una deducción al criador de ovejas Lindsay Schmidt por su mono, que aquél alega es un empleado legítimo de la hacienda.

El mono rhesus, de 3 pies 6 pulgadas de altura, ha sido enseñado a manejar un tractor.

"Johnnie es un conductor cuidadoso," dijo Mr. Schmidt. "Jamás aprieta el botón de arranque si el tractor está en velocidad. El se asegura de que la caja de velocidades está en neutro, aprieta el arranque y entonces se tira como un rayo al asiento del conductor y coge el volante."

A Johnnie también se le confían las obligaciones de pastor de ovejas, comunicó Schmidt. Se le ha enseñado a abrir y cerrar puertas y a juntar ovejas extraviadas.

Por lo general el mono come su almuerzo de sánwiches, fruta y alguna bebida gaseosa con los otros labriegos.

KRIEG GEGEN DIE ALBATROSSE

In den letzten zwei Wochen wurden von der U.S. Navy über 20.000 Albatrosse auf Midway im Pazifik vernichtet, ein Krieg der die Radarflugzeuge und deren Besatzungen schützen soll. Im Laufe der letzten Jahre sind viele Flugzeuge in Zusammenstoss mit den Albatrossen geraten.

Die Navy versuchte, die Vögel durch Abfeuern von Flackerlichtern, Mörserhülsen und Bazookas zu verscheuchen, mit Hilfe von Lautsprechern und sogar mit Mörserkrähen, aber die Albatros näherten sich nur, um die Ereignisse zu beobachten, als wäre es eine Unterhaltung,' die zu ihrem Vergnügen veranstaltet wurde.

Die übriggebliebene Zahl der Albatrosse auf diesen Inseln beträgt ungefähr 150.000 und eine weitere Verminderung wird nicht nötig sein. Diese Vögel haben eine Flügelspanne von sieben Fuss.

LA GUERRA CONTRO L'ALBATRO

Nelle ultime 2 settimane, circa 20.000 albatri sono stati distrutti sull'isola Midway nel Pacifico dalla marina statunitense in una guerra per proteggere gli aerei da radar ed i loro equipaggi. Negli ultimi anni molti aerei hanno urtato contro gli albatri.

La marina ha cercato di spaventare gli uccelli lanciando razzi da segnalamento, proiettili da mortaio e bazooka, usando altoparlanti ed anche spaventapasseri, ma gli albatri si fermarono solo per guardare le attività, come se fosse uno spettacolo allestito per loro divertimento.

La rimanente popolazione d'albatri su queste isole ammonta a circa 150.000 ed ulteriore riduzione non sarà necessaria. Questi uccelli hanno un'apertura alare di sette piedi.

GUERRA A LOS ALBATROSES

Durante las últimas dos semanas alrededor de 20.000 albatroses han sido destruidos en Midway, en el Pacífico, por la Armada de Guerra de los Estados Unidos, en una guerra para proteger a los aviones de radar y sus tripulaciones. En años recientes muchos aviones han sufrido choques con los albatroses.

La armada ha tratado de espantar a los pájaros tirando luces de señales, cartuchos de morteros y bazookas, con el uso de altoparlantes y hasta con espantajos, pero los albatroses únicamente se detenían al pasar para contemplar las actividades como si fuesen diversiones proporcionadas para su deleite.

La población de albatroses que quedan en estas islas asciende a alrededor de 150.000 y no será necesario disminuirla más. Las alas extendidas de estos pájaros alcanzan siete pies.

ÂOUT • AUGUST • AGOSTO • AGOSTO • AUGUST

Quinto Lingo

J. I. RODALE • EDITOR

Français
English
Español
Italiano
Deutsch

PUBLICATION MENSUELLE
ISSUED EACH MONTH
PUBLICADO MENSUALMENTE
PUBLICAZIONE MENSILE
ERSCHEID MONATLICH

50¢ PER COPY • ENGLAND 3/6

albatrosses have been ... Midway in the Pacific, by the U. S. Navy in a war to protect radar planes and their crews. In the past few years many planes have been in collisions with the albatrosses.

The navy has tried to scare away the birds by the firing of flares, mortar shells and bazookas, by the use of loud speakers and even scarecrows, but the albatrosses just stopped by to watch the activities as if it were entertainment provided for their enjoyment.

The remaining population of albatrosses on these islands amounts to about 150,000 and further reduction will not be necessary. These birds have a wingspan of seven feet.

... a tué à Midway, ... environ 20.000 albatros. Ces dernières années, beaucoup d'avions se sont heurtés contre ces albatros.

La Marine a essayé d'effaroucher les oiseaux en lançant des fusées éclairantes, des obus et des bombes, ainsi qu'en utilisant des haut-parleurs et même des épouvantails; mais les albatros, croyant à un spectacle organisé spécialement à leur intention, s'installèrent à regarder les activités.

La population restante d'albatros dans ces iles se chiffre par environ 150.000; aussi la reduction de celle-ci n'est plus nécessaire. Ces oiseaux ont une envergure de sept pieds.

... 19 creduloni ...

Italienische Fopperei

Ein unternehmender italienischer Gauner, der anscheinend die Höhe der menschlichen Intelligenz geringschätzte, schaltete ein Inserat in einer römischen Zeitung ein, in dem er eine Anzahl von Gramophonplatten mit den Geräuschen des Alten Roms, einschliesslich der Stimme Julius Cäsars, zum Verkaufe anbot. 29 leichtgläubige Personen antworteten.

November 3: President Johnson defeats Republican challenger Barry Goldwater in a landslide victory.

Phil Knight and his former track coach, Bill Bowerman, each invest $500 to launch Blue Ribbon Sports, the predecessor to Nike.

J. I. Rodale publishes *Our Poisoned Earth and Sky*.

Jean-Paul Sartre awarded Nobel Prize in Literature.

Jean-Paul Sartre

In 1965, as a "birthday gift," J.I. started working on a magazine about New York.

RODALEAN REACTIONS TO BROADWAY '64-'65

Nichols the directing, while at the same time adding a bit of humor here and there, it couldn't have been anything but funny.

I liked *Luv* for another reason. About 3 years ago I wrote and produced a play down at my theatre on 4th Street, called *The Man on the Bridge*. The setting is almost the same as that of *Luv*. But my play wasn't too bad. In the back of the stage is a parapet of a bridge . . . in *Luv* it is a railing. In *The Man on the Bridge*, there is a fellow who wants to jump off and various people who try to discourage him. In *Luv* it is much funnier. A man wants to jump off and another man comes to discourage him and gets so involved that eventually he wants to jump off himself. Both stories differ radically from each other . . . there is no common ground. There is a terrific amount of sex in *Luv*. But my play wasn't too bad. We had nice audiences, who laughed and applauded, and a man with a sinister looking face said that it should have been on Broadway.

FIDDLER ON THE ROOF

This could also be my number 1 choice, but since there is some nostalgia added, and a bit of stark drama, I must put it down as number 2, even though I think that Zero Mostel is the greatest . . . In later generations he will be considered one of the big greats of our time, and I'm glad I saw him in *On the Way to the Forum*, and *Rhinoceros*, – both classics! Don't miss seeing Zero or you'll feel as I do today in regard to Caruso. I was of age at the height of his fame, but never went to hear him.

Oh yes, I must tell you about how I met Zero in a Second Avenue restaurant, about 15 years ago. My wife and I and two of our children were sitting at the next table to him, his wife and one boy child, or maybe it was a girl child. The previous winter he had entertained at a Florida Hotel where we were vacationing. So I went over to tell him how much we had enjoyed him there. I think in part of his stand-up comic routine in Miami, he had given a hilarious imita-

(Cont. on page **43**)

31

metal litter cans in Emmaus. J.I. named the line Howard Metalcraft, after his mentor, Sir Albert Howard. He was also interested in working out systems to improve people's use of language. In August 1964 he launched a new 32-page magazine, *Quinto Lingo*. Much like *Fact Digest*, it was filled with short, informative articles—"sprightly news items, essays, health articles, short stories, and a page or two of jokes"—but in several languages at once: English, French, Spanish, German, and Italian. The content was largely free. The third issue contained one of J.I.'s *Prevention* articles. And the advertisements were mostly for other Rodale products—*The Word Finder*, a series of recordings J.I. published (*Harmony Sings*), and *Prevention*. One of the instructional items read: "Rachel Carson's book on poison sprays, *Silent Spring*, which is receiving such wide publicity, shows how Mr. Rodale's pioneer work *is finally bearing fruit*."

The back of *Quinto Lingo* featured a full-page ad for another new J.I. venture: *Rodale's New York*. J.I. noted in the summer of 1965 that on his birthday, "I began work on a new magazine.... In a way it was a birthday gift that I gave myself." While he was 67, "over the last few years, my mind seems to have become quite active," he noted. "Perhaps it is a mental vigor that comes from all the natural vitamins and minerals I have been taking." The new magazine would deal with city planning, water shortages, and juvenile delinquency and contain reminiscences and observations about the city of his birth. "For the past four years, I have maintained an apartment in New York, spending half my time there and half on our Pennsylvania farm, thus giving me an objective viewpoint." The first issue of *Rodale's New York* appeared in January–February 1966 and had seven articles by J.I., including "How to Survive in a Polluted City" and "1898: A Memory." The same year, J.I. also published his *Autobiography*—a short, anecdote-laden set of recollections.

J.I. continued to churn out plays and to produce them at his New York theater, renamed Theatre 62 in honor of his favorite school, P.S. 62 on Norfolk Street. In 1963, five of his plays were performed at the theater. And by the time the theater closed in 1965, 15 of J.I.'s plays had been staged there. These included *The Devil and the Nails,* which had Satan appearing on earth and speaking against smoking, and *The Hairy Falsetto,* a 1964 reimagining of the Little Red Riding Hood tale, in which the wolf is put on trial and Little Red Riding Hood is portrayed as a lawbreaker. The plays, like the magazines he launched in these years, *Quinto Lingo* and *Rodale's New York,* were not commercial successes—nor were they particularly intended to be. Frequently, admission to the plays was free, and J.I. would charter buses from Allentown to help fill the theater. Virtually all his plays were panned by New York critics, who looked down on his unrefined writing and efforts to inject morality tales about health into his dramas. In late 1961, the *New York Times* critic Howard Taubman called J.I.'s *Toinette,* a recasting of Molière's *Le Malade Imaginaire,* "witless, tasteless ... an alleged musical comedy," and wished for earplugs and glasses that would allow him "to ignore every offensive word, sound, and gesture on the stage." And the reviews never really improved.

J.I.'s obsession with his own health—and the poor health of his parents—had informed the tone and content of the company's successful magazines, *OG&F* and *Prevention.* J.I. was a man without many hobbies, aside from reading, writing, and starting new business ventures. But Bob, from his childhood on the farm, had a genuine interest in and affection for the outdoors. And in the 1960s, as he pursued sporting interests in his private life, he would weave them into Rodale's publications. In 1957 he began skeet shooting as a hobby, frequently going with his friend Ben Ruhe, the son of Allentown *Morning Call* editor Percy Ruhe, to shoot clay on Tuesday nights at the North End Gun Club in nearby Weisenberg Township. The sport requires a steady hand and an ability to focus and concentrate for prolonged periods of time. Bob excelled. After winning several tournaments,

Having long drawn on his own life experiences, J.I. finally published a formal brief autobiography in 1965.

J. I. Rodale relished his role as playwright and producer and began to spend more time in New York in the 1960s.

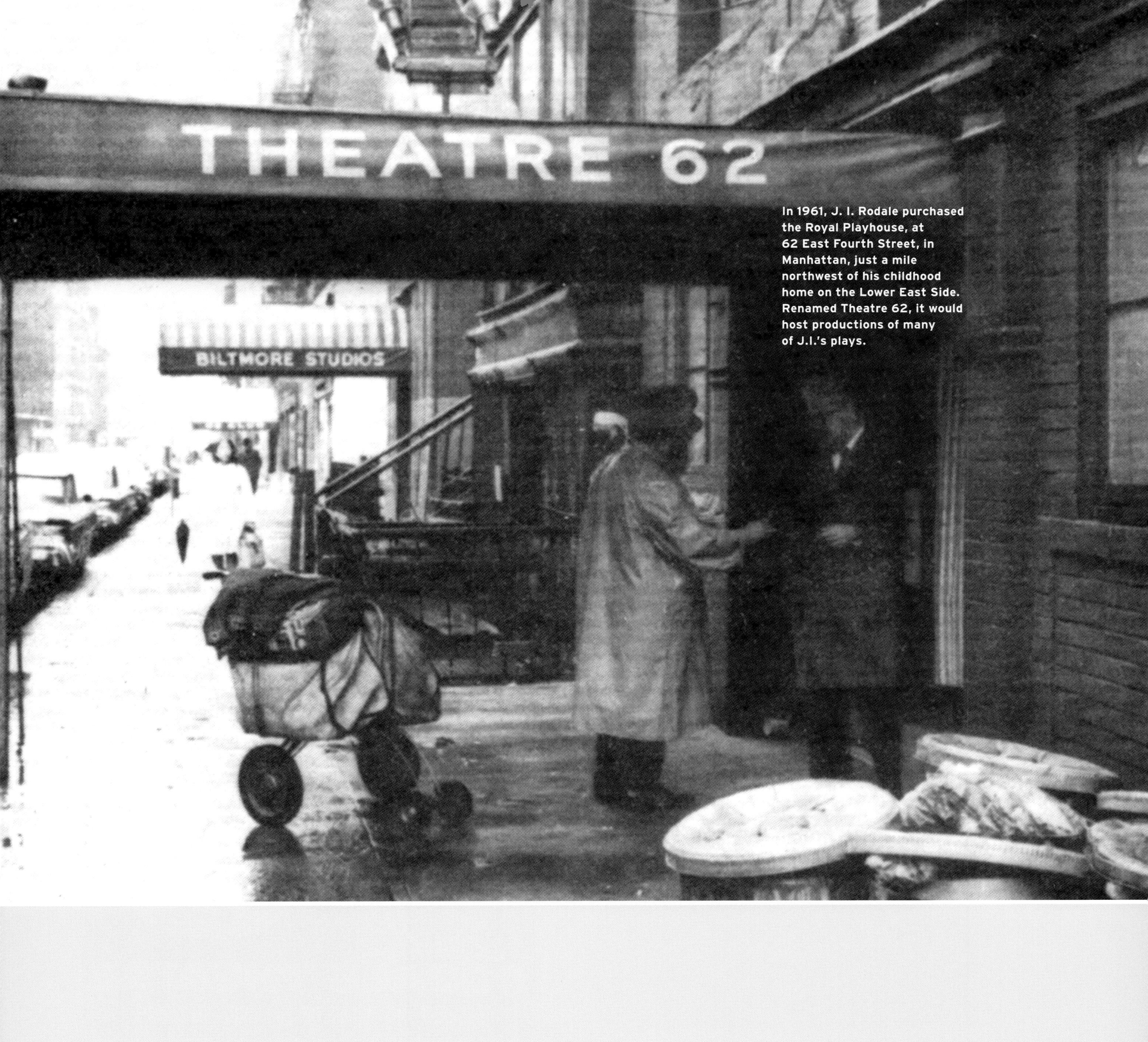

In 1961, J. I. Rodale purchased the Royal Playhouse, at 62 East Fourth Street, in Manhattan, just a mile northwest of his childhood home on the Lower East Side. Renamed Theatre 62, it would host productions of many of J.I.'s plays.

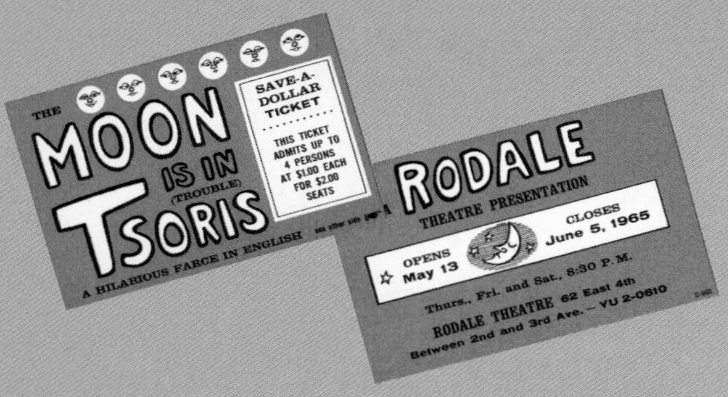

THE
MOON
IS IN
(TROUBLE)
TSORIS
A HILARIOUS FARCE IN ENGLISH
SAVE-A-DOLLAR TICKET
THIS TICKET ADMITS UP TO 4 PERSONS AT $1.00 EACH FOR $2.00 SEATS
A RODALE
THEATRE PRESENTATION
OPENS May 13
CLOSES June 5, 1965
Thurs., Fri. and Sat., 8:30 P.M.
RODALE THEATRE 62 East 4th
Between 2nd and 3rd Ave. — YU 2-0610

In the 1960s, much of J. I. Rodale's creative energy was spent writing and producing plays.

MAN ON THE BRIDGE
RODALE WEEK-END THEATRE
$2.50
A RODALE COMEDY

OP
FRI.–SAT. EV
62 EAST 4th –

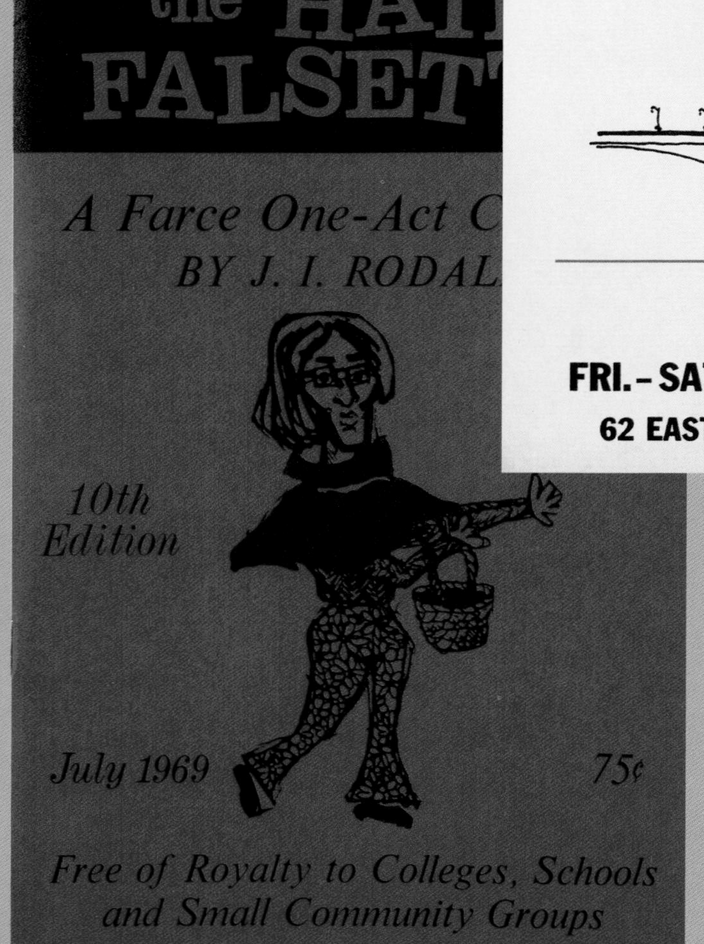

the HAI
FALSET
A Farce One-Act C
BY J. I. RODAL
10th Edition
July 1969
75¢
Free of Royalty to Colleges, Schools and Small Community Groups

DEVIL ON THE BRIDGE
A SPRIGHTLY, HILARIOUS MUSICAL COMEDY
NOW PLAYING
FRIDAY and SATURDAY
NIGHTS ONLY — 8:30 P.M.

$1.75

RODALE THEATRE
62 EAST 4th - WEST OF 2nd AVE. - YU 2-0610

Bob decided in the fall of 1962 "to try out for a place on the four-man skeet team which was to represent the United States at the 38th World Shooting Championships in Cairo, Egypt." Finishing second, he made the team.

On October 1, 1962, Bob left New York for two weeks in Cairo. The team won the team championship with a world record. In the team event, Bob shot 99 out of 100, and he placed seventh in the individual competition.

Much as J.I. did, Bob saw the world and events through an organic prism. Bob expressed dismay that he couldn't get close to the farms and gardens of Egypt, but he noted people roasting ears of sweet corn, clipping grass by hand, and irrigating crops from the Nile. And Bob believed that the Russians performed better than Americans in the individual meets in part because of their diet of unprocessed foods. "If the Russians ever start eating instant mashed potatoes and TV dinners, they will be a lot easier to beat in international sports events, and in other more serious events also," he wrote in *OG&F.*

In the fall of 1964, however, the FTC proceedings were foremost in Bob's mind. Formal hearings before FTC examiner John Lewis began in November 1964. From the beginning, Thurman Arnold tried to paint the government's efforts as censorship—the only other instance in which the government banned advertisements for books, he noted, was for obscenity. The government, for its part, argued that the ads made promises on which the content of the book didn't deliver. Each side called medical experts to comment on the nature of the claims made both in *Health Finder* and in the advertisements for it. A government witness, Modestino G. Criscitiello, professor of medicine at Georgetown University, noted that for patients with a congenital heart problem, the solution would be surgery—not any of the ideas contained in *Health Finder.* The most prominent pro-Rodale witness was Louis Lasagna, an associate professor of medicine and associate professor of pharmacology and experimental therapeutics at Johns Hopkins University, who had previously testified for the FTC. "As I read these books, it seems to me they contain reasonably accurate reports of a great deal of published literature," he said in his testimony on December 8, 1964.

Bob traveled the world to compete in international skeet-shooting competitions.

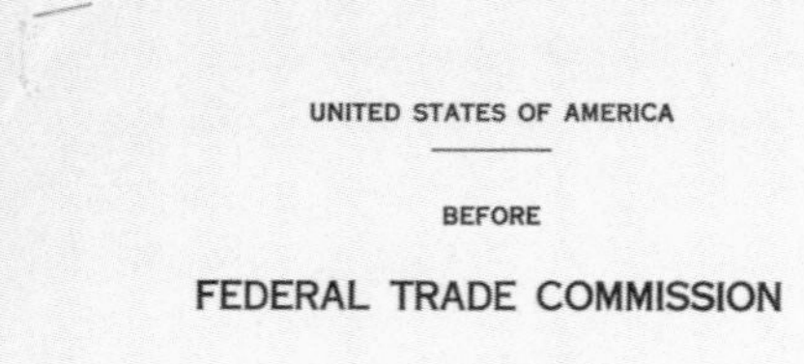

UNITED STATES OF AMERICA

BEFORE

FEDERAL TRADE COMMISSION

DOCKET NO. 8619

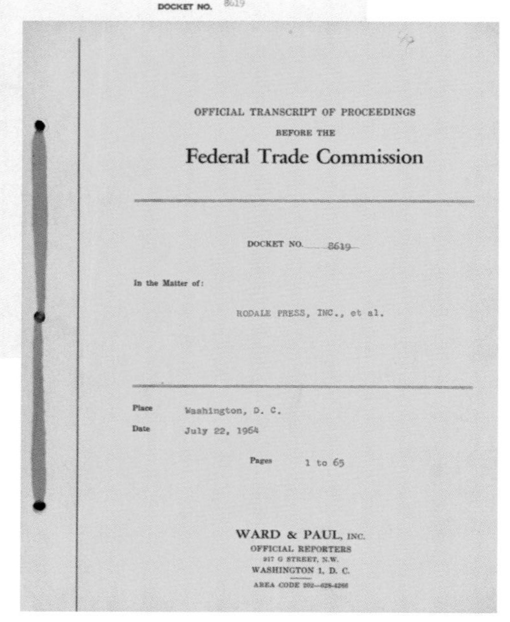

OFFICIAL TRANSCRIPT OF PROCEEDINGS
BEFORE THE
Federal Trade Commission

DOCKET NO. 8619

In the Matter of:

RODALE PRESS, INC., et al.

Place Washington, D. C.
Date July 22, 1964
Pages 1 to 65

WARD & PAUL, INC.
OFFICIAL REPORTERS
917 G STREET, N.W.
WASHINGTON 1, D. C.

For much of the 1960s, Rodale fought off the Federal Trade Commission's assault on its business.

"They make many admirable recommendations, focusing primarily on the suggestion of a generally nutritious diet and recommend to patients the avoidance of excessive reliance on drugs."

Bob was actively involved in preparing the case, writing memos and doing research on the government witnesses. He described the fight in the February 1965 *Prevention*. "They are not putting their hand on our shoulder and saying that we can't say certain things in our publications. All they are saying is that we can't advertise the ideas we are writing about.... Above all, the FTC emphasized, don't tell people that your writings will be of value in helping people to improve their health." Rodale was vigorously resisting the charges, defend to both its business and the principle of freedom of the press. "The cost of this legal battle will be enormous—possibly as much as $100,000. But freedom cannot be measured in dollars."

The FTC examiner's report, released on April 16, 1965, brought bad news for Rodale. Lewis found that "respondents have made statements and representations in the advertising for their publications that are false, misleading and deceptive in a number of material respects." He concluded that following the advice could lead to a delay in obtaining necessary medical treatment and may result in irreparable injury to health or even loss of life. The brochure used between 1956 and 1960 to advertise *Health Finder* was problematic, Lewis found, because it promised specific cures to specific ailments, such as the common cold, even though nothing in the book would stop people from getting the common cold. A week later, Lewis issued an order requiring Rodale to stop making such claims in ads for the three books named in the complaint or for any other similar books. They could advance "any theory they wish in their publication, no matter how ill-conceived and misguided. However, if they wish to advance the sale of their publication, as a commercial product, and to induce the public to purchase it, then they have no right to falsely advertise the therapeutic benefits which purchasers of their product will receive, merely because that product is a book."

The verdict brought Rodale much negative press. But others in the media recognized the nature of Rodale's continuing crusade. In the summer of 1965, the conservative columnist James Kilpatrick railed against the government's case and coined a phrase that would neatly define J.I.:

1965
February 21: Malcolm X is assassinated in New York City.

March 8: The first U.S. combat troops are sent to South Vietnam.

Malcolm X

Gold's Gym is founded in Venice Beach, California.

Medicaid is created.

April 16: FTC examiner releases report on Rodale case.

September 28: Oral arguments in FTC case begin.

Ralph Nader publishes *Unsafe at Any Speed.*

Three generations of Rodales. ***From left:*** **Heidi, David, Maria, Ardie, Bob, Heather, Anthony, and J.I.**

Thus far, 17 months of litigation "already have cost this small apostle of nonconformity some $50,000."

There was no question that Rodale would appeal. There was a great deal at stake here, far beyond advertising *Health Finder.* The company, or rather the companies–Rodale Press (the magazines), Rodale Books, and J. I. Rodale & Co., Ltd., which sold vitamins in England and Europe–were synergistic. Ads in the magazines helped sell Rodale books, many of which were in turn serialized in Rodale magazines. Magazines helped launch new books and other new magazines. Scrappy marketing gaining attention and advertisers in a frequently crowded field dominated by larger, more well-heeled competitors had been a hallmark of Rodale's style since J.I. first published *The Clown* in the 1930s. And by 1965 it was a substantial enterprise. Rodale Press Inc. had revenues of $3.7 million and $30,000 net profit. It reported $1.04 million in total current assets, including $262,000 in marketable securities and $190,000 in cash. Rodale Books produced sales of $633,000 in 1965 and an operating loss of $1,500 and was more of a vanity operation for J.I., who still owned the profitable Rodale Manufacturing Company. "He had a strong rule that every book that Rodale Press published had to have his name as the author on it . . . and every one had to have his picture in it," Bob recalled.

But for Bob, the books, the magazines, and the vitamins represented his future and that of his growing family, which now included five children: Heather, Heidi, David, Maria, and Anthony. The Rodale enterprise now involved multiple members of two generations of the family. Anna Rodale had been a participant in all of J.I.'s ventures, was a full partner in moving to the farm and

Ardie was an active participant in the Rodale business.

As a columnist for *Skeet Shooting,* Bob Rodale was able to combine two of his great passions—magazine writing and competitive skeet shooting.

OFFICIAL BULLETIN OF THE NATIONAL SKEET SHOOTING ASSOCIATION

Vol. 20 • No. 12 • Dec., 196

SKEET SHOOTING Review

—THE ROYAL PALMS OPEN—

SKEET GAB: Avoid 'Shotgun Deafness' By Plugging Your Ears

GAIN IN MEXICO CITY

February, 1967

$50,000 U.S. cy For The "FLYERS"

XII Championship Of Las Americas

From Feb. 18th To Feb. 25th 1967.

...... MAKE YOUR PLANS NOW!!

developing it, and received occasional credits as photo editor in the early magazines. But she had not been involved specifically in Rodale's businesses. Bob's wife, Ardath Rodale, assumed a different position, at a time when women generally were not involved in high-level decision making at corporations. As the company added new facilities and buildings in the 1960s, Bob would ask for advice on what color to paint the walls. But Ardie wanted to do more than give advice: "Not only am I going to decide the color, but you're going to sign this piece of paper saying that from here on out, I will decide all the colors," she said. As Rodale's physical plant grew, Ardie would be responsible for everything from working with architects to maintenance. "We knew about the company business," Ardie recalled. "We talked about it at home, at work; it was a total involvement."

Bob and J.I. not only served as editors and publishers of the main magazines but also continued to produce a large portion of the copy. But non-family members also held important positions. Longtime employees Jerry Goldstein and Marshall Ackerman both served as executive vice presidents. Goldstein was in charge of editorial for *OG&F* and in charge of circulation, while Ackerman was the chief ad salesman. Bob Teufel, who had joined Rodale Press in 1961 as a circulation assistant, was by 1965 promoted to run the fulfillment, purchasing, and production departments. Most of the company employees worked in areas such as circulation and marketing. The magazines were run by small editorial staffs—*Prevention* had just four full-time employees until 1965.

For the Rodales, and for the company's employees, there was a great deal at stake in the FTC case. Oral argument before the full FTC started on September 28, 1965. Each side was granted 45 minutes, and the American Civil Liberties Union (ACLU), which had joined as a friend of the court on Rodale's behalf, was given 10 minutes. Essentially, the lawyers recapitulated the arguments made in the initial hearings, with the Rodale defense team relying heavily on First Amendment grounds. Thurman Arnold charged that the government "criticized excerpts from the book as if it was a textbook designed for medical students." Arnold also pointed out that the examiner had no way of knowing that there wasn't a way of preventing the common

A world-class skeet shooter, Bob Rodale frequently represented the United States in international competitions.

With starry eyes and a nose for profit, J. I. Rodale writes plays, sells electrical supplies and designs gadgets, but his passion is the art of growing food.

Apostle of the compost heap

By ELEANOR PERÉNYI

Photographs by Hans Namuth

An article in the *Saturday Evening Post* in 1966 drew attention to J.I.'s many ventures.

cold, just because the witness said so. Indeed, the U.S. Department of Health published material on precisely that topic! Besides, he argued, the books contained opinions, which the FTC had no authority to regulate. Arguing for the ACLU, William Warfield Ross posed a simpler question: "Can the commission proscribe the advertising of a book of opinions which is nothing more or less than a truthful reflection of the content of the book, of the author?"

Amid the tension of the hearings, Bob found time to pursue skeet shooting. A regular on the U.S. national team, he became a columnist in *Skeet Shooting Review*. In the fall of 1965 he traveled to San Antonio, Texas, to try out for one of four spots on the national team. Tied for sixth place after two days, Bob returned to the hotel to relax one day and was dismayed to smell the insecticide chlordane. Figuring he would perform better if he were to sleep in a cleaner environment, Bob moved to another hotel. The next day he shot 99 out of 100 and qualified for fourth place, becoming the only civilian member of the team. In November, in Chile, Bob shot two perfect rounds, which enabled the team to win a shoot-off for the team championship; he placed tenth in the individual competition. Afterward, he traveled to Peru–to Machu Picchu and Cuzco. As J.I. had always done, Bob shared his experiences with readers, mixing observations about agriculture with his comments on tourist sites.

Although its business practices were under assault from the government, Rodale in the 1960s saw that the issues it championed were growing in popularity. For example, the magazines were a vocal voice against the widely used insecticide DDT, which was ultimately banned in the United States in 1972. Still, there was a sense that the Rodales' crusades to reform agriculture and revolutionize health care weren't particularly realistic. The *Saturday Evening Post* in 1966 dubbed J.I. "the Don Quixote of the compost heap, tilting his lance against the dangers and curses of the technological world." But as the decade wore on, and as critical masses of subscribers, consumers, and citizens came to embrace J.I.'s ideas, the crusades seemed less and less quixotic. The power of

1966
January–February: *Rodale's New York* debuts.

April 21: An artificial heart is installed in the chest of Marcel DeRudder by Dr. Michael DeBakey in a Houston hospital.

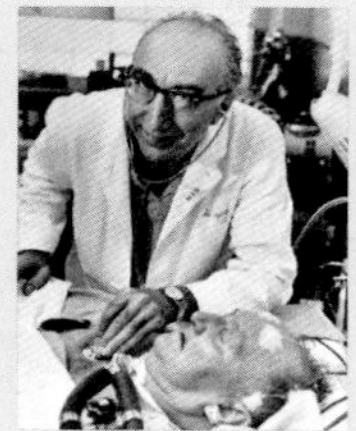

Dr. Michael DeBakey

May 25: St. Louis' Gateway Arch is dedicated as part of the Jefferson National Expansion Memorial.

July 4: President Lyndon B. Johnson signs the Freedom of Information Act into law.

U.S. Congress introduces first bills recommending use of electric vehicles as a means of reducing air pollution.

Gateway Arch

August 15: *New York Herald Tribune* stops publication.

September 16: Metropolitan Opera house opens in New York City.

J. I. Rodale publishes *Rodale's System for Mental Power and Natural Health.*

what was emerging as an organic lobby was first seen in 1966. In June 1966, Dr. James Goddard, the new head of the FDA, was poised to issue new regulations on the sale of dietary supplements and minerals. One would have limited the potency of vitamins that could be sold in stores, or through the mail, to the recommended daily allowances. "It became apparent to us that the vitamin food supplement industry was under attack," Bob recalled. Vitamin companies were among the Rodale magazines' leading advertisers and were the dominant advertisers in *Prevention.* More broadly, vitamins and supplements were a key component of Rodale's notions about improving health.

In the August 13, 1966, *Health Bulletin,* an editorial declared, "The battle on food supplement anti-vitamin labels is joined." Quentin Miller, an official at the National Health Foundation, had suggested that Rodale and others interested in vitamins try to influence Congress by encouraging citizens to write letters to their representatives. *Prevention, Health Bulletin,* and *OG&F* encouraged readers to do just that. In a *Prevention* article entitled "The Government Starts to Control Our Diet," Robert Rodale pointed readers to places where they could read the new regulations. "What is the way to stop them?" J.I. asked in *Prevention* in the fall of 1966. "Write a typewritten letter to your congressman, with a carbon copy to go to President Lyndon Johnson, telling what vitamins and food supplements have meant to you." Ultimately, more than 55,000 citizens wrote to complain. "The Vietnam War generated a lot of letters to Congress," Bob Rodale recalled. "But this issue generated the second largest amount of mail." In the end, Congress passed a bill unanimously that ordered the FDA not to regulate vitamin potency.

The episode represented a gratifying triumph over the government. But the jury was still out—literally—on Rodale's other long-running battle with a federal bureaucracy. The FTC's decision on Rodale's case finally came out on June 20, 1967. The majority opinion concluded that the advertisements were intended only to sell books, rejecting Rodale's argument that the advertising was just an extension of the book. At the same time, the full commission found the advertising for *Health Finder* to be not false, deceptive, and misleading but rather an *exaggeration* of what was in

The Government Starts To Control Our Diet

Robert Rodale

FDA Issues Supplement Restrictions

Robert Rodale

A DRASTIC REDUCTION in the sale of vitamin and mineral food supplements seems to be the object of just-released Food and Drug Administration regulations covering the sale of dietary foods. Although the new regulations also set food standards for many enriched foods and clarify confusion over low-calorie food items, most interest has been concentrated on the many changes required in the formulation and marketing of food supplements.

The FDA first issued its proposal for sweeping changes in dietary foods and supplements in 1962. There was vigorous opposition then from the industry and the public, and the proposal was withdrawn for further study. Four years later, FDA has now issued substantially the same proposals in the form of a final order. Legal opposition by the food and food supplement industries is almost certain to develop, especially to provisions limiting promotion claims and requiring a label on vitamins saying they aren't really needed. Although FDA Commissioner James L. Goddard has stated that he hopes there will be no need for public hearings on the regulations, lawyers who are expert in the nutrition field have predicted that hearings will be held and that it will be several years before the regulations are enforced. If valid objections are not filed within 30 days, and supporting evidence within another 30 days, the order will be enforced 180 days from June 20, the date of its publication.

Here are the main provisions of the food supplement regulations:

Label Disclaimer: All bottles of food supplements will have to carry the statement that "Vitamins and minerals are supplied in abundant amounts by the foods we eat," that dietary needs should be satisfied by foods, and that "there is no scientific basis" for routine use of dietary supplements.

Nutrient Limits: Formulators of vitamin and mineral supplements will be limited to the use of 17 nutrients. Multivitamin supplements will be required to contain 6 specific vitamins, with 5 others optional. There will be 2 required minerals for supplement use, with 4 others available as optional ingredients. Potencies will be limited by FDA to specified minimum and maximum ranges.

Terminology: FDA wants to junk the words "minimum daily requirement," which it says leads people to believe that it is advantageous to take amounts of vitamins larger than the recommended minimum. It plans to substitute the phrase "recommended dietary allowance."

Expiration Date: All bottles of vitamins will have to be marked with the date which the manufacturer feels states the maximum time the product will retain its rated potency.

Identification of Ingredients: Vitamins and minerals can be made from synthetic or natural substances, says FDA, but manufacturers will have to name the ingredients used.

Other provisions of the new dietary food regulations will have far-ranging effects on foods used for special diet purposes – a rapidly-growing segment of the food market. Vitamin and mineral fortification standards have been set for alimentary pastes (such as Chinese noodles), milk products, fruit juices and juice drinks, infant fruit products, breakfast cereals, salt and infant formulas. Disclosure of ingredients will be required on labels of infant and hypoallergenic foods – a measure strongly advocated by some allergists. Foods advertised as low in calories will have to be at least 50% lower in calories than standard foods.

AUGUST, 1966

35

Bob Rodale and Rodale Press led a successful grassroots campaign to stop the government from regulating vitamin potency.

the book. "In sharp contrast to the flamboyant claims in respondents' advertising of the therapeutic benefits which readers will gain from reading the book and pamphlets, the publications themselves make no such claims." The 4-to-1 opinion, written by Mary Gardiner Jones, ordered Rodale to cease and desist from advertising, directly or by implication, that readers of *Health Finder* and its subsequent editions could add years to their lives and save on medical and dental bills. It also enjoined ads for *How to Eat for a Healthy Heart* and *This Pace Is Not Killing Us* from promising to deliver therapeutic benefits.

At J.I.'s urging, Rodale started *Theatre Crafts* magazine in 1967.

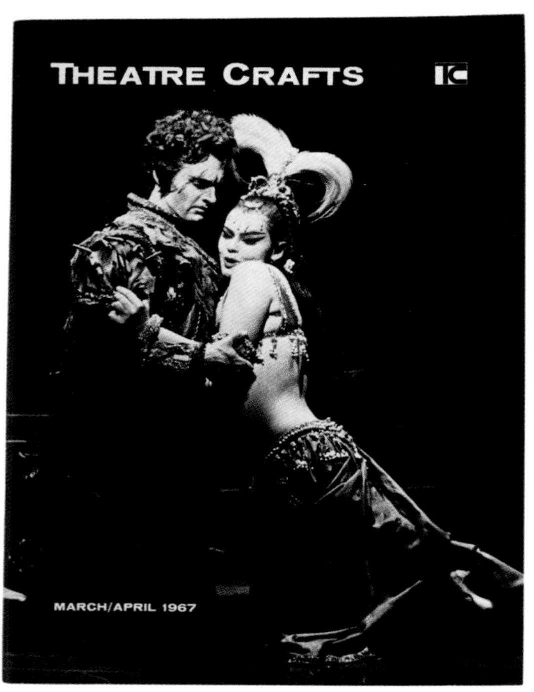

It was a mixed decision, and again the company's future hung in the balance. On November 22, 1967, Rodale filed a petition to have the U.S. Court of Appeals in Washington, D.C., hear the case. Thurman Arnold argued that the ruling violated the First Amendment and that the FTC had overstepped its bounds and jurisdiction by changing course midstream. Arguments were held before the U.S. Court of Appeals in February 1968.

Even as it was dealing with potentially ruinous legal problems, Rodale continued to press ahead. Since the launch of *Prevention* in 1950, Rodale Press had not successfully rolled out a new, large-scale magazine. But in the late 1960s, emboldened by the growth and profits in both *Prevention* and *OG&F*, Bob and J.I. began to invest in new publications. In 1967, J.I. had the opportunity to purchase the magazine *Theatre Arts*. J.I. knew it wouldn't make a good prospect because the magazine was pitched primarily to actors, who tended not to have much disposable income. Still, he saw that drama was a growing industry, with the growth of off-Broadway and regional and nonprofit theater companies. So in 1967, Rodale hired Guy Cimbalo, who had a theater-production and editing background, to start *Theatre Crafts*, a sort of trade publication for directors, costume and set designers, and theater administrators.

Later that year, Rodale unveiled a second new magazine—one that explicitly

1967
June 5: Start of the Six-Day War in the Middle East.

June 20: FTC hands down decision in Rodale case.

October 2: Thurgood Marshall becomes the first black member of the U.S. Supreme Court.

Thurgood Marshall

November 7: President Lyndon B. Johnson signs the Public Broadcasting Act of 1967, establishing the Corporation for Public Broadcasting.

November: *Fitness for Living* debuts.

Rolling Stone magazine is founded.

Rodale launches *Theatre Crafts*.

bore Bob's stamp. *Fitness for Living*, perhaps the first broad-based fitness magazine published in the United States, debuted in November 1967, with Bob as publisher, John Haberern as editor, and Glenn Johns, a high school English teacher whom Rodale had hired to work on a book about bugs in 1967, as managing editor. The cover featured five Allentown YMCA members of the 100-mile Run Club in an early morning workout. At the outset, Bob Rodale defined the ethos of the magazine. Along with nutrition and preventive medicine, personal fitness was yet another area in which individuals could exert control and improve their lives. "In past times, only the fittest survived," he wrote. "Today, only those who are fit will be able to sense the true pleasure of living." J.I. had endeavored to lay out systems whereby people could improve the way they farmed and managed their health. *Fitness for Living* offered readers a system to improve their quality of life. As in previous magazines, the Rodales figured prominently. One of the first issues featured a photo of J.I., striding forward—in an unlikely exercise outfit of black pants, white shirt, and black shoes—and extolling the benefits of his daily one-hour walk.

While Bob had started slowly to develop a personal style of journalism in *OG&F* and other venues, he had not yet become comfortable writing in the first person as frequently as J.I. did, or using his own life—and the lives of family members—as material for articles. But in the late 1960s, and with *Fitness for Living* as a vehicle, Bob began to do so more regularly. In 1968 he wrote a great deal about his experience in the Olympics in Mexico City. Bob chronicled his experiences qualifying for the games—he was the number-one shooter; altitude training in Santa Fe, New Mexico; sharing the charter plane to Mexico with rowers, fencers, boxers, and the women's track team; and living in the Olympic Village. "For the past several weeks

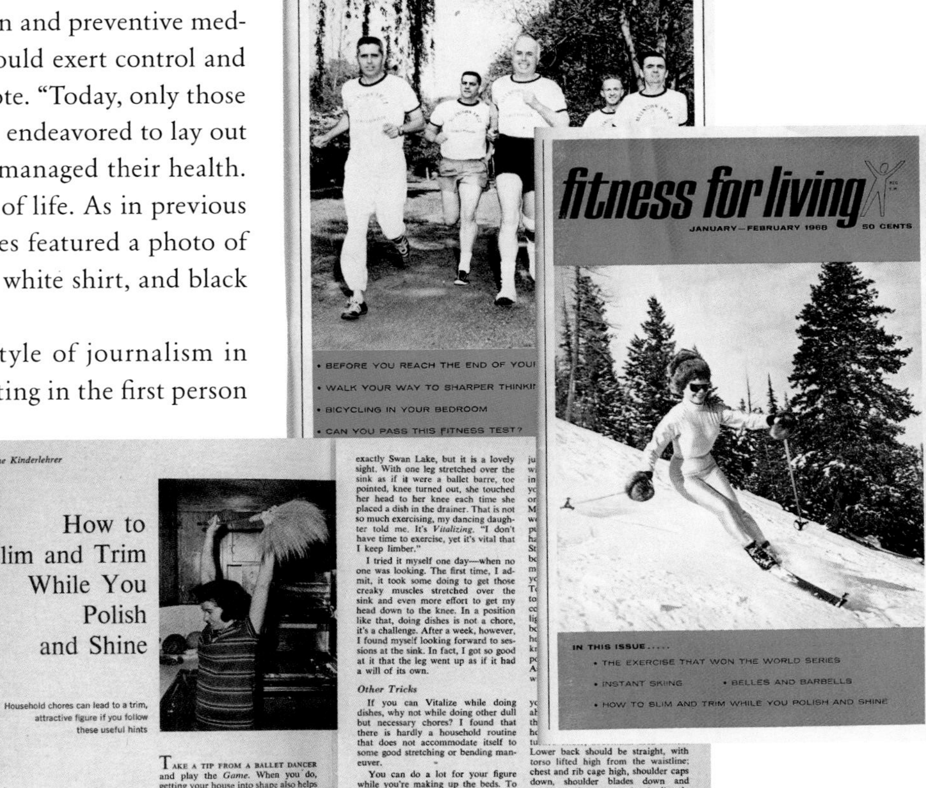
fitness for living
NOVEMBER—DECEMBER 1967 REG T.M.

• BEFORE YOU REACH THE END OF YOU
• WALK YOUR WAY TO SHARPER THINKI
• BICYCLING IN YOUR BEDROOM
• CAN YOU PASS THIS FITNESS TEST?

fitness for living
JANUARY—FEBRUARY 1968 50 CENTS

IN THIS ISSUE.....
• THE EXERCISE THAT WON THE WORLD SERIES
• INSTANT SKIING • BELLES AND BARBELLS
• HOW TO SLIM AND TRIM WHILE YOU POLISH AND SHINE

Jane Kinderlehrer

How to Slim and Trim While You Polish and Shine

Household chores can lead to a trim, attractive figure if you follow these useful hints

TAKE A TIP FROM A BALLET DANCER and play the *Game*. When you do, getting your house into shape also helps *you* get into shape. Even though you can't squeeze a daily exercise session in between the diapers, dishes, doorbells and dusting, you're still going to get the movements into your day that contribute tone to your muscles, get rid of unwanted flab, and keep your waistline slim as a school girl's.

The Game is not football, tennis or golf. It's *Association*. You associate each chore with a specific routine. After a week of warming up to those routines, you will find yourself doing them automatically as soon as you tackle the chore. Besides being a built-in personal fitness scheme, the Game takes the bore out of the chore.

The idea hit me when I watched a ballet dancer doing dishes. It's not exactly Swan Lake, but it is a lovely sight. With one leg stretched over the sink as if it were a ballet barre, toe pointed, knee turned out, she touched her head to her knee each time she placed a dish in the drainer. That is not so much exercising, my dancing daughter told me. It's *Vitalizing*. "I don't have time to exercise, yet it's vital that I keep limber."

I tried it myself one day—when no one was looking. The first time, I admit, it took some doing to get those creaky muscles stretched over the sink and even more effort to get my head down to the knee. In a position like that, doing dishes is not a chore, it's a challenge. After a week, however, I found myself looking forward to sessions at the sink. In fact, I got so good at it that the leg went up as if it had a will of its own.

Other Tricks

If you can Vitalize while doing dishes, why not while doing other dull but necessary chores? I found that there is hardly a household routine that does not accommodate itself to some good stretching or bending maneuver.

You can do a lot for your figure while you're making up the beds. To reach the far side of the bed, keep your feet on the floor and stretch your upper torso. People with any hint of back pain should be cautious here. In this way you lift your rib cage and promote the separation between your rib cage and hipbone. Work for a separation that is as wide as the span of your hand and your waistline will whittle away. If you must walk around the bed to complete the job, walk on your tiptoes, stretching your finger tips up, reaching for the ceiling. Next time around the bed, walk on your heels and feel the stretch in your hamstrings and calf muscles. You'll feel a nice tingle and stretch the first time you do that.

When you scurry down the hall to get the broom or floor mop, don't

Lower back should be straight, with torso lifted high from the waistline; chest and rib cage high, shoulder caps down, shoulder blades down and together. Keep your head directly over the top of the spine, neck long and chin slightly in. After you've got yourself into correct alignment once or twice, it will come naturally and you will walk with a new grace. Now, keeping yourself in correct alignment, use the mop or broom for the purpose it was originally intended.

After you have finished one room, push the mop into the next room walking like a drum major, lifting your knees smartly to your chest. That is a great movement when done to music. Put on a Herb Alpert record and your knees will come up higher with less effort. You'll soon feel a nice tingle, like champagne bubbles in your arteries.

42 Fitness for Living

January/February, 1968 43

Bob Rodale expanded the organic message to include a broader view of health that encompassed physical fitness, exercise, and sports. In 1967, he started *Fitness for Living*, the first magazine devoted to the notion that improving personal fitness could enhance the quality of life.

Abiquiu, N.M.
3/4/67

Dear Mr. Rodale:

I have taken Organic Gardening for years but
I am sorry to have to say to you that you will
find my garden a rather sorry affair —
It should be a lovely garden but it isn't.
I just don't have time for it and the men who work
for me have other ideas —
Come by and see my failures

Sincerely

Georgia O'Keeffe

My village is 50 miles north west of Santa Fe.
— the road — 84 is marked.

J. I. Rodale enjoyed the fame he earned, and he corresponded frequently with prominent people the world over who shared his interest in organic gardening and health. The painter Georgia O'Keeffe, shown here with J.I., was a longtime *Organic Gardening* subscriber.

J.I. visits Georgia O'Keeffe's garden in New Mexico.

CERTIFICATE OF AWARD
PRESENTED BY THE ORGANIZING COMMITTEE OF THE
V PAN-AMERICAN GAMES
JULY 22 TO AUGUST 7, 1967 • WINNIPEG, MANITOBA, CANADA
FIRST PLACE
TO
ROBERT RODALE
IN
SHOOTING, SKEET, TEAM

The 1968 U.S. Olympic skeet shooting team, Bob Rodale on far right. Bob was proud to represent the United States at the 1968 Summer Olympics in Mexico City, finishing 19th in the individual competition.

I have had the wonderful experience of living in a town of health, inhabited by the most perfect physical specimens of humanity," he wrote in *Prevention*. "Ten thousand people lived in that town, and almost every one of them was the kind of ideal person we could gladly use as a model for our efforts to gain positive health and fitness. Just the simple act of walking down the street was a thrill."

1 PAYS / COUNTRY / PAIS: ESTADOS UNIDOS DE AMERICA
2 NOM ET PRENOMS / NAME / NOMBRE COMPLETO: RODALE, ROBERT
3 NATIONALITE / NATIONALITY / NACIONALIDAD: U.S.A.
4 QUALITE / STATUS / CATEGORIA: SHOOTING - SKEET
5 PASSEPORT Nº / PASSPORT Nº / PASAPORTE Nº
6 DATE DE NAISSANCE / DATE OF BIRTH / FECHA DE NACIMIENTO: 27 MARCH 1930
7 LIEU DE NAISSANCE / PLACE OF BIRTH / LUGAR DE NACIMIENTO: NEW YORK, NEW YORK
ESTADOS UNIDOS DE AMERICA
COMITE ORGANIZADOR DE LOS JUEGOS DE LA XIX OLIMPIADA
PRESIDENTE — SECRETARIO GENERAL

The 1968 Summer Olympics, which actually took place in fall, were a tumultuous two weeks, marred by riots in Mexico City. They were best remembered for American long-jumper Bob Beamon shattering the world record and for sprinters Tommie Smith and John Carlos giving a black-power salute on the medal stand. The results for the skeet shooters were disappointing; Bob finished 19th in the individual competition. But perhaps the most important result for Rodale during the games came in a Washington courtroom. On October 18, 1968, while Bob was in Mexico, the Federal Appeals Court ruled on Rodale's appeal. It essentially ignored the First Amendment arguments and noted that the FTC had changed theories in the middle of the case. It concluded that Rodale should be given an opportunity to present an argument against the new theory of violation. So it vacated the commission's order and remanded the case to the FTC for further hearings and arguments. The FTC chose not to pursue the matter further, and Rodale had quietly prevailed. "Well, we won," Robert told J.I. "How do you feel now?" J.I., ever distrustful of credentialed professionals, responded: "I still think I should have defended myself. It would have been cheaper, for we wouldn't have had to pay all those lawyers and doctors."

Representing his country in the 1968 Olympics was a defining moment in Bob's sporting career.

It was satisfying for Rodale to find vindication in the courts. But it was even more satisfying to find it in the marketplace. And in the late 1960s, with the litigation behind it, Rodale began to ride a wave of growing public interest and enthusiasm in the organic cause. The ideas, products, and theories Rodale had been promulgating for decades suddenly seemed

1968
January 30: The Tet Offensive begins when Viet Cong forces launch a series of surprise attacks in South Vietnam.

April 4: Martin Luther King Jr. is assassinated by James Earl Ray in Memphis, Tennessee.

Tet Offensive

April 11: Premiere of the musical *Hair* on Broadway.

Food and Drug Administration bans cyclamates (a sugar substitute), which cause cancer in lab animals.

October: Bob Rodale competes in the Mexico City Olympics.

Cast of *Hair*

October 18: Federal Appeals Court rules in Rodale's favor in the appeal of the FTC decision.

November 5: Republican challenger Richard M. Nixon defeats Vice President Hubert Humphrey.

New York magazine is founded.

Whole Earth Catalog is published by Stewart Brand and others.

From one of 60,000 productive fruit trees at their northern California orchard, Ruth Waltenspiel and daughter Pam pick heavy clustered pears, plus apricots and peaches.

The Sharp Rise in Organic Food Demand

California growers reflect the upbeat in interest—and why the West is wild about organic foods!

M. C. GOLDMAN

THERE'S A CHANGE going on.

Direct contact with people in the organic food business—both large and small—is one key way we've been taking the pulse of public interest. On a state-long field trip in California, for example, I visited with over a score of growers, distributors and others wrapped up in organic foods. Teamed with all the additional signs, the facts and comments from these businessmen reflect a phenomenal upbeat—a real turn to the "age of organics."

Take the folks at Rancher Waltenspiel's orchards, for instance. Located at Healdsburg, about two hours' drive north of San Francisco in the refreshing environs of Sonoma County, the orchards consist of some 600 acres, with an average of 100 hardy-looking trees per acre. Ten years ago, after a

Young workers ready apricots and peaches—two of Rancher Waltenspiel's big crops—for drying, then packaging for shops.

try at "straight" farming, Ron and Ruth Waltenspiel decided to package their own and other naturally-grown California fruits.
with unsul
that doesn
cers"), and
come the c
of organic
shipped ov
last year's fi
ily from that
Besides tl
orchards grc
and IMPERIA
BOSC pears,
THOMPSON aı
addition, ther
climate fruits
Covalda Dat
firm in the so
To ready apr

showed me the huge "tunnel" equipment with an automatic thermostat, where the fruit is dried at 105 degrees for 24 hours. The apricot harvest runs nine weeks each summer, about three weeks at each of three farm locations. A refrigerated room as big as a jet hanger keeps the unsulfured ripe fruit at 34 to 36 degrees. (Bees won't touch them if sulfur is added, I was told, but would eat all but the skins of unsulfured apricots. Guess they know what's best!)

Of 175 on the Rancher Waltenspiel payroll, 150 are young workers needed mainly for harvesting, sorting, grading and packaging. Fruit not up to eating-quality standards is sold for animal feed. Apricot pits, another waste by-product, are also sold at 5¢ a pound to a manufacturer who grinds them up for use as an abrasive to clean jets, in preference to soap-powders which leave a residue.

In the orchards, Waltenspiel tests by leaf analysis for tree-feeding, then applies dolomitic lime, composted grape pomace from nearby wineries, and a mulch of crushed, dry grape stems ("almost like a nylon net"), which holds the soil, keeps it from washing in heavy spring rains. Potash rock, some dried kelp and an occasional layer of chicken

At the time of the first Earth Day on April 22, 1970, Rodale Press's two primary magazines were thriving.

April, 1970
60 Cents

Organic Gardening
and Farming ®

Citrus-rancher Phyllis Pavone adjusts sprinkler in her 500-tree orchard at Escondido, Calif., where natural soil-improvement and pest controls have overcome deficiencies, bugs and spring frosts, to produce top harvests.

that it has been produced naturally, allowed to ripen fully on the trees before harvesting, dried and then preserved with pure honey instead of the usual commercial methods—all of which contributes to its superior flavor.

The Lady Is a Citrus-Rancher

Phyllis Pavone has to rate as the prettiest citrus-rancher imaginable. Not only does Mrs. Pavone's 5-acre grove near Escondido produce some of the best-tasting oranges, tangelos

Each year's harvest of large, juicy oranges has increased, says the attractive "businessman," who attributes her Pavone Ranch success to organic orcharding—plus a sharp rise in the public's demand for better foods.

and tangerines in the West, it's proving by successful example to chemical growers in the area that organic methods work.

And it *is* enthusiastic, determined work that's created business success for the attractive rancher. Planted 6 years ago, her well-spaced grove includes 500 orange trees, divided be-

tween VALENCIAS an
gerines and tangelo
with three post hol
down around each
deep root-feeding
ground phosphate a
Last spring, when ar
sent the mercury dow
(20 at the grove), Pl
rigation system on a
few smudge pots to
trees and crop. "Better
have more viscosity,"
"They resist freezing
ter than chemical-fed c

No Bugs — or Jackr

Insect trouble—or r
of it—is another way
methods have prove
Mrs. Pavone says the
at all by now, and that
she introduces into the
good job on aphids an
"Each year my trees
more resistant," she poi
dog keeps bark-nibblin
and other neighborhood
of the groves, which a
weeded, she added. "No
control on this ranch." St
falfa go on as a mulch—
save water, which is expe
section—and the rotary-
tings stay in the wide ais
the trees as an additional s
The Pavone Ranch ora
brush cleaning after harve
lis, now working with
she's "converted," sorts al
allows none to be packed
breaks. So far, she ships
her crop to two markets,
for Life shop in Burbank
berg's in West Los Angeles,
order deliveries to pleased
all over the country. The "la
ist," whose fresh-squeezed
orange juice went down swe
hot July afternoon, also gro
apricots, pecans, cherries, gr
mulberries—and hopes to
her fruit-marketing productio

decades solved the magnesium problem by mixing powdered dolomitic limestone in their feeds, and also that rock powder had been used widely as a fertilizer. J.I. saw that dolomite was an ideal magnesium source for people, and is completely responsible for its current popularity. Now, anyone who knows about dolomite can be sure of getting adequate magnesium in his diet.

A Prophet

thought of by more than a handful of city planners. During the middle 1940's he and I were walking through an old section of Allentown and J.I. said to me, "The government ought to buy up these houses, tear them down, and make a park." I thought to myself, boy, that is blue sky stuff, but today Allentown is working on its second round of urban renewal. (The first project still looks in places like a blitzed section of Rotterdam after World War II, but that is beside the point.) You might also be interested to know that J. I. Rodale is the proprietor of the Howard Metalcraft Division, a small but mighty manufacturer of premium quality litter baskets for municipal use. If there are attractive green baskets mounted on the parking meters or light poles in your city, chances are they are J. I. Rodale's brain child.

Returning to the history of PREVENTION, many of the tenets of the PREVENTION System didn't seem like prophecies when J. I. Rodale first stated them, but that is what they have turned out to be. His indictments of food additives, pesticides and synthetic chemicals of all kinds were hard for some people to accept years ago, but they are now being echoed almost every day by experts of the highest academic repute. Here is an interesting story. One day about 15 years ago my father was either driving or walking along a country road and saw a few dead geese in a gutter partly filled with soapy wash water. "Those synthetic detergents are no good," he thought, and proceeded to write an article condemning them at a time when no one else even suspected that they were harmful. Some people scoffed when the article appeared, but no one is laughing today.

I well remember the furor that was caused by J.I.'s statements

PREVENTION

Prevention®

THE MAGAZINE FOR BETTER HEALTH

June 1970 • 60 Cents

J. I. RODALE, Editor

20th Anniversary Issue

As a young and successful businessman, J. I. Rodale harbored a dream of pioneering in health.

Prevention is One Man–J.I. Rodale

Robert Rodale

PREVENTION was first published in 1950, and was a success from the start. A letter announcing the birth of the new magazine went out to all the subscribers of *Organic Gardening and Farming*, which was then the flagship publication of Rodale Press, Inc. As a result of that solicitation, 50,000 people subscribed and the course of PREVENTION has been a continual upward march ever since. Today, over 700,000 people subscribe to PREVENTION, and many more feel the impact of the natural health

JUNE, 1970

151

roundabout fashion is the confession that when J.I. came home to dinner one evening and said he was going to publish a health magazine, I told him I thought it was a bad idea.

A Different Health Magazine

Being propelled by all those previous years of dedication and preparation, he didn't for a moment let my feebly stated objection sway him. And in my own defense, allow me to say that my negative feeling persisted only until the first issue appeared, and I could see that this was, in fact, a different and better kind of health magazine. If I had listened more closely when J.I. first explained his concept of a health magazine, no doubt I would have been a fan from before the start.

"No health magazine published today is any good," he told me. "On the one hand you have the popular magazines put out by doctors, which are full of articles telling how good it is to let doctors operate on you. And on the other hand you have magazines not associated with doctors which range all over the map, covering all sorts of strange and sometimes useless ideas. They have no self-discipline, no organized approach to health. I don't think they even understand what health is, sometimes."

My father told me that his mag-

Editor Rodale in a portrait made on the fifth anniversary of PREVENTION.

146 PREVENTION

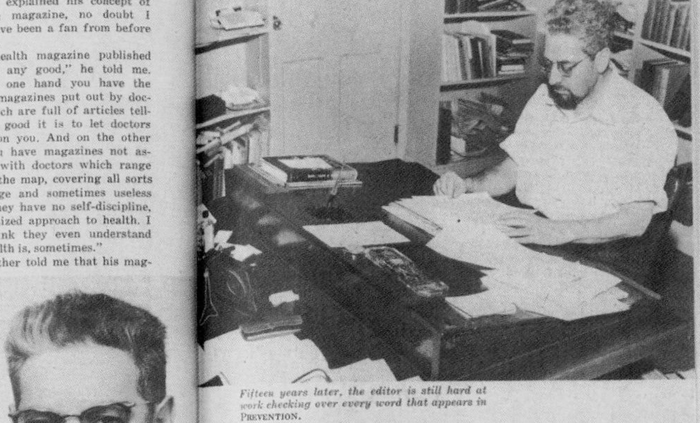

Fifteen years later, the editor is still hard at work checking over every word that appears in PREVENTION.

azine was going to be different. PREVENTION, he said, would extend the sound organic concept into the much broader field of organic living. "All our articles will be based on facts," he said. "And heaven knows, there are tons of facts important to health which are buried in the medical literature, not even being used by doctors, let alone by the public." He knew the scope of the medical literature, because for decades he had been reading it, seeking ideas and articles for his more general and scientific magazines.

"Most important, we are going to be very careful about the advertisements in PREVENTION," he told me. "Other health magazines are open to ads for all kinds of products and services, and many of them don't create health." The far-out things advertised in other health magazines had a very strong impact on his thinking, because he felt sure that such uncontrolled commercialism was holding back the growth of the natural health movement. His first issues of PREVENTION had no display advertising at all, only classified ads for organically grown food. Only after he saw that use of the PREVENTION system by readers required use of certain natural foods supplements that were not then available in stores did he open the pages of the magazine to advertisements for natural products. At no time did he

JUNE, 1970 147

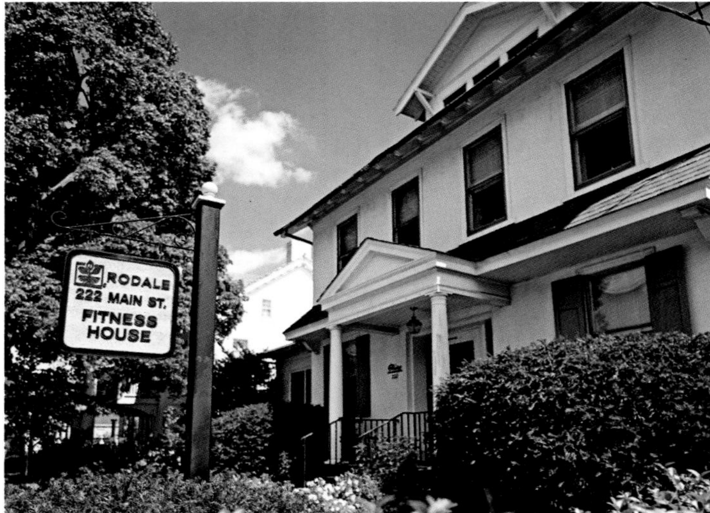

Fitness House became the site of the first Rodale dining room where lunch was served on a first-come basis for $1.25.

J. I. continued his prolific book publishing in the 1960s.

to burst into the mainstream. Consequently, in the late 1960s, readers and, almost as important, advertisers began flocking to *Prevention* and *Organic Gardening and Farming*.

In placid Emmaus, Rodale was somewhat removed from turbulent college campuses and urban areas roiled by the unrest of the late 1960s. And for all their unconventionalities, the Rodales—both J.I. and Bob—were essentially bourgeoisie. J.I. said he liked Governor Ronald Reagan of California but was shocked that "Reagan was addicted to such an unhealthy food item as jelly beans." On a trip to San Francisco, he and Anna made a detour to Sacramento and tried to go into Reagan's office to determine if it was true. J.I. also disapproved of drug use. Nor was Bob fully in sync with the prevailing ethos of the late 1960s. "Basically, the youngsters of the new left are rebelling against the affluent society," Bob wrote in a September 1969 *OG&F* article about people going back to the land. "Hippie farm life is better than burning the flag or locking up the dean."

But the organic business and movement were growing up rapidly around Rodale. In 1967, the Environmental Defense Fund was formed, and it spearheaded the move against chemical pesticides. By October 1968, *OG&F* had 400,000 readers. In 1968, the magazines reported revenues of $5.49 million and net income of $56,000. Books continued to grow, but not much more beyond J.I.'s impressive ability to pump them out: *Rodale's System for Mental Power and Natural Health* (1966); *Smoke and Die, Quit and Live* and *Walk, Do Not Run, to the Doctor* (1967); *Natural Health, Sugar and the Criminal Mind* (1968). The company was expanding. In 1968, it bought property at 151 East Minor Street in Emmaus, and in 1969 it added on to the main building at 33 East Minor Street. The following year, it bought 222 Main Street in Emmaus, later dubbed Fitness House.

Not all the new initiatives succeeded. *Fitness for Living* failed to find a large audience and ultimately folded. But the company noticed that executives had responded well to the magazine. So in 1970, Rodale started the biweekly *Executive Fitness* newsletter—four pages of brief items, in the model of *Health Bulletin*. Meanwhile, *Health Bulletin* continued enthusiastically to chart the growth of the organic movement. In June 1970 it noted that more than 700 major organic food outlets were in operation in the United States.

1969
January 10: Last issue of the *Saturday Evening Post* is published.

June 27: The Stonewall Riots in New York City mark the start of the modern gay rights movement in the United States.

July 20: Neil Armstrong and Buzz Aldrin take first steps on the moon.

August 15: Woodstock music festival starts.

November 10: *Sesame Street* premieres.

Neil Armstrong

In May 1970, just weeks after the first Earth Day on April 22, 1970, Rodale convened the first Organic Food Symposium in Allentown. Some 175 people attended, including organic growers and owners of organic food chains. A special report in *OG&F* documented the growth of the organic food scene. Meanwhile, Rodale's flagship magazines were growing thick with advertisements. The 20th anniversary issue of *Prevention,* June 1970, with a drawing of J.I. on the cover, was 240 pages thick.

For J.I., these years were particularly sweet. He and Anna continued their travels—they went to Russia in 1970—and they enjoyed spending time at their apartment in New York and at the farm, which had grown to include a tennis court and swimming pool, and seeing their children and grandchildren. Anna Rodale had become an accomplished painter, and J.I. continued to write plays. In the late 1960s he also established an arts award through Brandeis University, in Waltham, Massachusetts. Perhaps most significant, J.I. was finally gaining widespread recognition and acclamation for his life's work. In May 1970, a testimonial 72nd birthday dinner was held for him at the George Washington Motor Inn in Allentown. Friends, colleagues, and six original *Prevention* subscribers gathered to hear performers read excerpts from his plays. "It is odd how history sometimes turns nuts into prophets," Roderick Cameron, executive director of the Environmental Defense Fund, wrote in a letter read at the dinner. "If we survive our present insanity, it will in part be due to the organic agricultural science J. I. Rodale has been so influential in developing."

Rodale had long since gained critical mass as a business. Now Rodale—and J.I. in particular—was gaining critical mass as a cultural phenomenon. A slew of newspaper and magazine articles about J.I. and his company in the fall of 1970 and the spring of 1971 pushed him further into the public's consciousness. *Life* magazine featured the organic

In 1970 and 1971, the organic movement drew attention from the mainstream media.

Eleven tons of coho salmon are seized in Wisconsin and Minnesota due to excessive DDT contamination.

Oil-soaked Cuyahoga River near Cleveland catches fire and becomes a symbol of outrage by many Americans troubled by the growing number of environmental problems in the country.

The Los Angeles Board of Education, along with the county's medical association, warns children not to "run, skip, or jump inside or outside" on smog alert days.

Mo Siegel and Wyck Hay, founders of Celestial Seasonings, produce their first batch of teas in Colorado.

For J. I. and Anna Rodale, the late 1960s were sweet, satisfying years. With the company thriving, they had the time and resources to travel and to pursue their interests—writing plays, attending the theater, and painting. As the culture increasingly came to accept the Rodale worldview, they could reflect on their accomplishments.

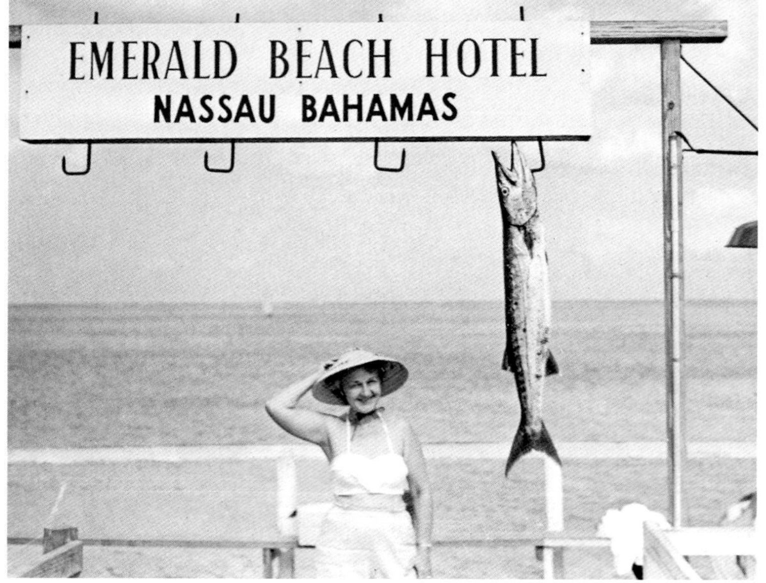

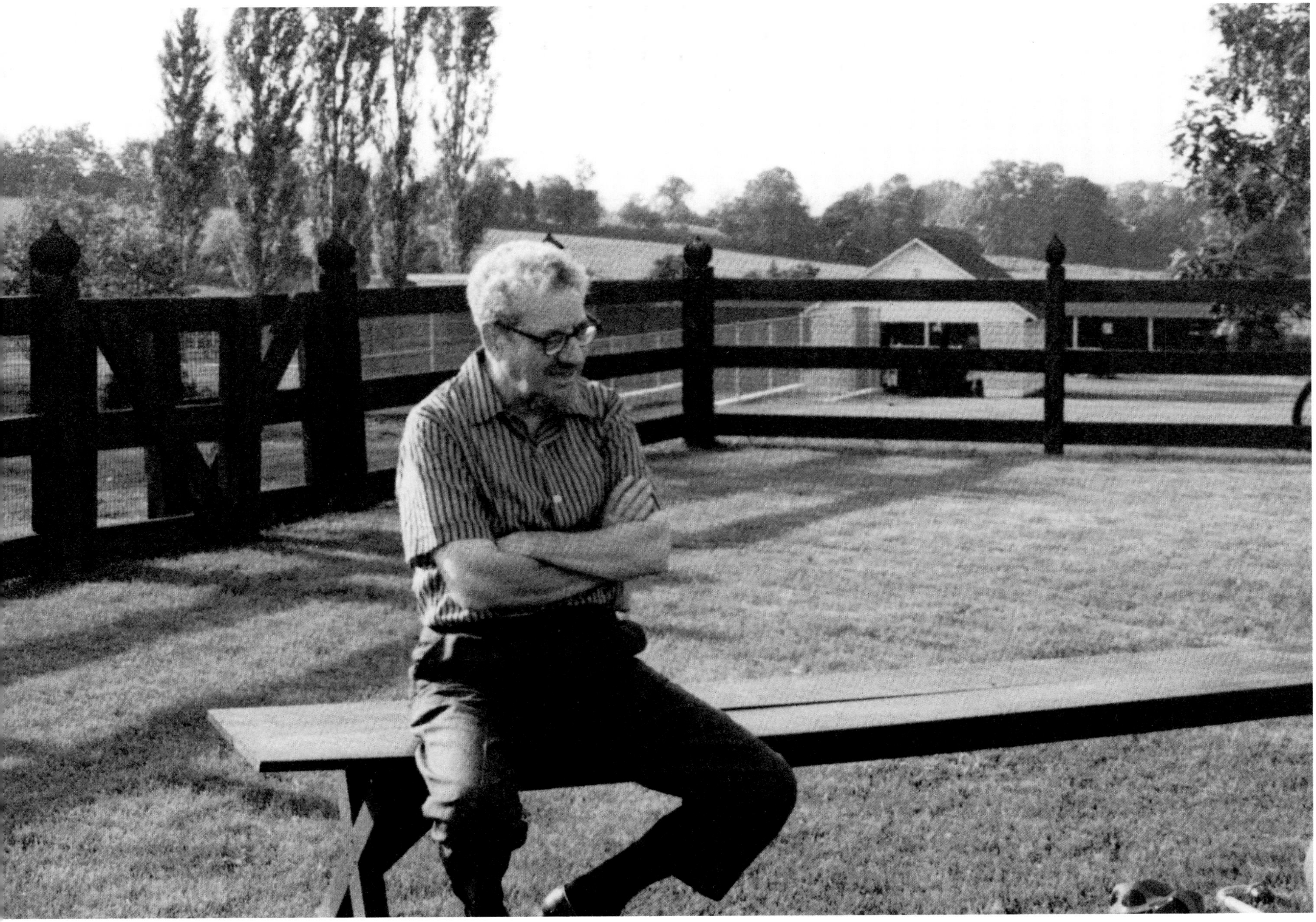

An Organic Gardening®/Ballantine Book
Original $1.25
22102
The Basic Book of Organic Gardening
Edited by Robert Rodale

Interest in organic food production accelerated during this time; *The Basic Book of Organic Gardening*'s first printing sold out in two weeks.

movement on its December 11, 1970, cover. The article estimated that there were about 5,000 organic farmers and included photos of the Rodale farm. The *National Observer* noted in May 1971 that "the real spurt in organic-food sales has come less from food cultists than from ecology-minded housewives. They fear that herbicides, pesticides, fungicides, and chemical fertilizers may really be bad for their families' health, and they view their higher food bills as a way of lessening the poisonous chemicals in the environment." By the spring of 1971, *OG&F*'s circulation had shot up to 720,000 from about 400,000 in three years. *Prevention* had risen from 520,000 to 920,000 in the same period. The first printing of 100,000 copies of *The Basic Book of Organic Gardening*, edited by Bob and published by Ballantine, was sold out within two weeks.

"I have worked for 30 years trying to encourage [organic growing's] acceptance by the authorities, but in a short year or two the youth of our nation have taken hold of it, and it is now seeping into unbelievable places," J.I. wrote in the March 1971 issue of *OG&F*. "It is glorious to behold! God bless our youth!" An organic world was emerging, and Emmaus was at the center of it. *The Christian Science Monitor* in April 1971 noted that "growing numbers of commune hippies as well as Agnew-prone retirement villagers are making this little Pennsylvania town something of a mecca." *Barron's* in May 1971 reported that the health food industry was growing at a 30 percent annual rate "and is the nation's new 'glamour' business."

By far the most important article on the Rodales in the spring of 1971 was one that appeared as the cover story of the *New York Times Magazine* on Sunday, June 6. The cover showed J.I. in a suit and tie walking through a field on the farm. Writer Wade Greene identified J.I. as the "foremost prophet" of the organic movement and noted that J.I. and Robert disseminated "a brand of secular fundamentalism through two immensely prosperous monthly magazines." The company had come through the storm of litigation and had matured.

1970

April 1: President Richard Nixon signs the Public Health Cigarette Smoking Act, which bans cigarette television advertisements.

April 10: Paul McCartney announces that the Beatles have disbanded.

April 22: Twenty million Americans take part in the first Earth Day celebration.

Leaders of several prominent environmental groups join together to form the League of Conservation Voters.

May: Rodale holds Organic Food Symposium.

June: Twentieth anniversary issue of *Prevention* is published.

The Nixon administration establishes the Environmental Protection Agency.

First Lucille Roberts Health Club opens in New York City.

The Clean Air Act regulates emissions of 189 specific pollutants.

September 13: First running of the New York City Marathon.

October 28: U.S. Food and Drug Administration orders makers of baby food to label the nutritional value of their products.

December 11: *Life* magazine features a story on J. I. Rodale.

But the Rodales still saw themselves as members of an embattled minority. "We are afraid of becoming legitimate," Bob said. "We have a lot of freedom now.... So I'm comfortable being in a small minority and I don't know how to operate if we're in a majority." Despite all the attention and growth, J.I. never lost the sense that he was an occasionally oppressed outsider, struggling to be heard. "I'm a Jew from the ghetto," he said in a May 1971 interview.

After the *Times* article ran, *The Dick Cavett Show* called and asked J.I. to appear. So on Monday, June 7, J.I. traveled to New York. That day, producers for *The Johnny Carson Show*—then produced in New York—asked if he would appear on *that* show on Thursday. After spending the day at the family's apartment on 58th Street, J.I. walked down to the ABC Studios on 42nd Street. Anna remained at the apartment during the taping. In the Green Room he made notes on the yellow slips he always carried with him. Cavett introduced J.I., who came on stage as the band played "Doing What Comes Naturally." They began to banter—about Sir Albert Howard, carrots, and organic farming. "When do we start with the jokes?" J.I. asked. After a commercial break, Cavett asked J.I. about his age. "I'll be 73 in August," he said, to applause. "I am so healthy that I expect to live to 101. I have no aches or pains. I'm full of energy." He and Cavett shared some raw asparagus.

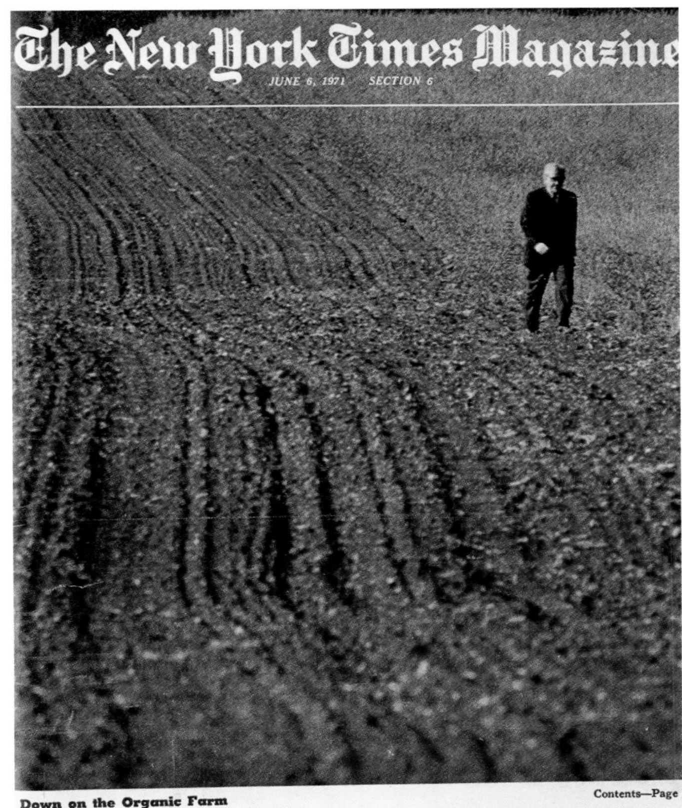

The New York Times Magazine
JUNE 6, 1971 SECTION 6
Down on the Organic Farm
Contents—Page

At 72, J.I. had become the "foremost prophet" of the organic movement.

After another break, a new guest, the journalist Pete Hamill, was brought on. Suddenly, J.I. had a heart attack. Hamill heard J.I. make what he described as "a low, soft whooping sound" and saw J.I.'s head slump on his chest—as if he had fallen asleep. Two physicians in the audience, Eric White and Richard Kaslow, took his pulse and found none—

1971
February 8: The NASDAQ stock market index debuts.

March 10: Twenty-sixth Amendment to the U.S. Constitution lowers voting age to 18.

May 3: First broadcast of *All Things Considered* on National Public Radio.

June 6: J. I. Rodale is featured on the cover of *New York Times Magazine* as "Guru of the Organic Food Cult."

June 7: J. I. Rodale dies after suffering a heart attack.

June 13: *The New York Times* begins to publish the Pentagon Papers.

August: Rodale publishes *The Ruth Stout No-Work Garden Book.*

October 1: Walt Disney World opens.

November 15: Intel releases world's first microprocessor.

December 23: President Nixon signs into law the National Cancer Act, which appropriates $1.5 billion to combat the nation's second leading cause of death.

Ruth Stout

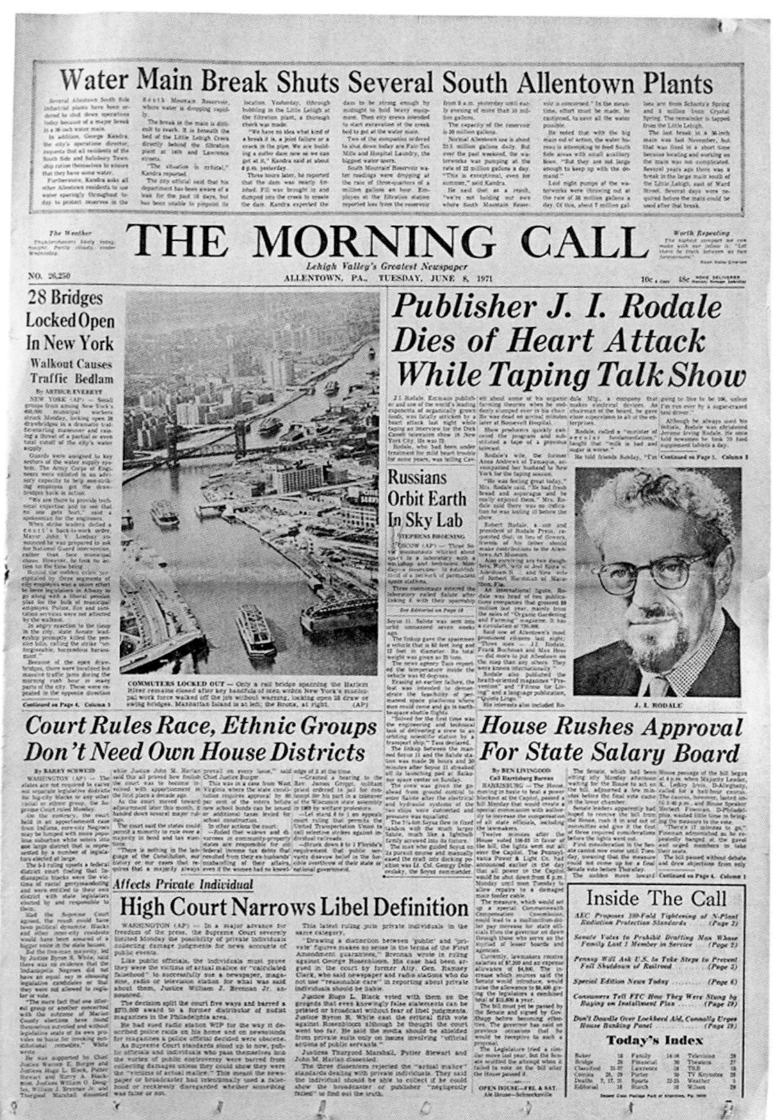

Water Main Break Shuts Several South Allentown Plants

THE MORNING CALL

Lehigh Valley's Greatest Newspaper

NO. 26,250 ALLENTOWN, PA., TUESDAY, JUNE 8, 1971

28 Bridges Locked Open In New York

Walkout Causes Traffic Bedlam

Publisher J. I. Rodale Dies of Heart Attack While Taping Talk Show

Russians Orbit Earth In Sky Lab

COMMUTERS LOCKED OUT

J. I. RODALE

Court Rules Race, Ethnic Groups Don't Need Own House Districts

House Rushes Approval For State Salary Board

Affects Private Individual

High Court Narrows Libel Definition

Inside The Call

Today's Index

The local newspaper in Allentown breaks the news of J. I. Rodale's sudden death.

J.I. had suffered cardiac arrest. Doctors and firemen who came from across the street tried to revive him, and an ambulance rushed him to nearby Roosevelt Hospital, located just a few blocks from DeWitt Clinton High School, where Jerome Irving Cohen took his first tentative steps outside the Lower East Side ghetto. There, doctors again labored to revive him. But after 15 minutes, at about 7:35 p.m., J.I. was pronounced dead. The producers of the Cavett show called Rodale's office in Emmaus, and word began to spread. In Emmaus, the Rodale family was preparing for Heidi's high school graduation, when the phone rang. It was a newspaper reporter, calling with the news of J.I.'s death. At first, Bob thought it was a joke. He and Ardie sent their children to the graduation and rushed to New York to be with Anna.

In accordance with the Jewish tradition–which J.I. had found so burdensome as a child but with which he had reached a grudging accommodation later in life–J.I. was buried quickly. The rites were set for 10:00 a.m. on Thursday, June 10, at Temple Keneseth Israel in Allentown, with a viewing the night of the 9th at the J. S. Burkholder Funeral Home in Allentown. Rabbi Steven Shafer gave the main eulogy. "There was a sense of humanity which inspires us, a kind of excitement which life generated in him," Shafer said. "He was generous, he was concerned, he knew how to create. He had a sense of drama and timing, and he had that humor." J. I. Rodale was buried in Northwood Cemetery in Emmaus.

J.I. outlived his brothers and many of his family members. His 72 remarkably full years far exceeded the typical life expectancy of someone born in 1898. But for J. I. Rodale, who had been so determined to live to see the 21st century, and who once said he had enough projects to keep him going for 200 years, it wasn't nearly long enough.

The remarkable father-son partnership between J.I. and Bob allowed the company to thrive under a second generation of family management.

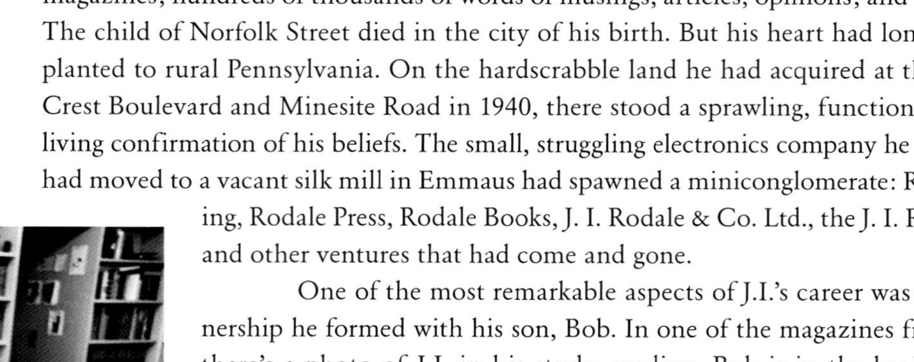

As Bob and Ardie Rodale raised their five children (including Anthony, in this picture), it was clear that building the organic movement would be a multi-generational commitment.

J. I. Rodale left behind a huge legacy: dozens of plays and books; thousands of issues of magazines; hundreds of thousands of words of musings, articles, opinions; and millions of readers. The child of Norfolk Street died in the city of his birth. But his heart had long since been transplanted to rural Pennsylvania. On the hardscrabble land he had acquired at the corner of Cedar Crest Boulevard and Minesite Road in 1940, there stood a sprawling, functioning organic farm—a living confirmation of his beliefs. The small, struggling electronics company he and Joseph Rodale had moved to a vacant silk mill in Emmaus had spawned a miniconglomerate: Rodale Manufacturing, Rodale Press, Rodale Books, J. I. Rodale & Co. Ltd., the J. I. Rodale Tour Office, and other ventures that had come and gone.

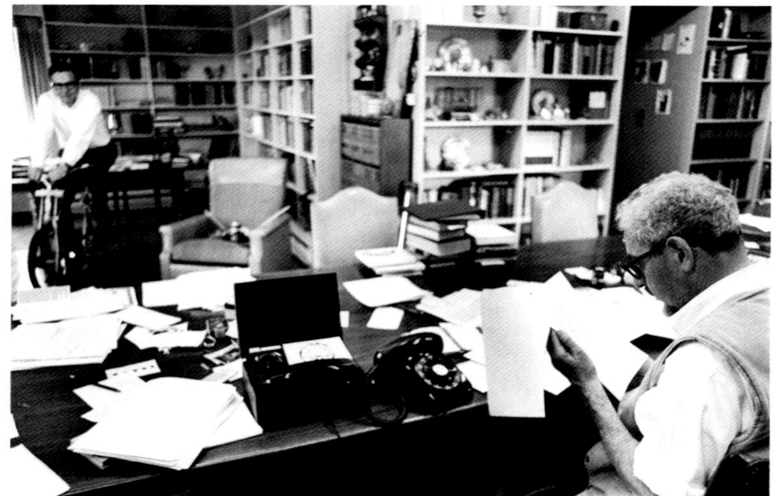

For nearly 20 years, J.I. and Bob collaborated in good cheer.

One of the most remarkable aspects of J.I.'s career was the enduring partnership he formed with his son, Bob. In one of the magazines from the late 1960s, there's a photo of J.I. in his study, reading. Bob is in the background riding an exercise bike. It's a testimony not just to their interests but to the way they worked together—with J.I. in the foreground and Bob in the background. J.I. and Bob had different styles—of writing, and of working. And there must have been times when Bob found it difficult working with J.I., who had a riot of interests and a constant desire to pursue projects that were of dubious commercial value. But the relationship nonetheless seemed remarkably free of friction.

More than a single magazine, or book, or relationship, J.I.'s legacy is remarkably broad. He left his relatives and readers with a self-made ethos and worldview that would continue to inspire future generations. J.I.'s life, and his life's work, embodied a series of attitudes and convictions: the importance of family, the need to speak truth to power, the ability of individuals to improve their own lives, and, perhaps above all, the capacity of an indefatigable mind and spirit to overcome obstacles. The day before he died, J.I. told his son: "Stick to a thing for a long time and you'll make it work."

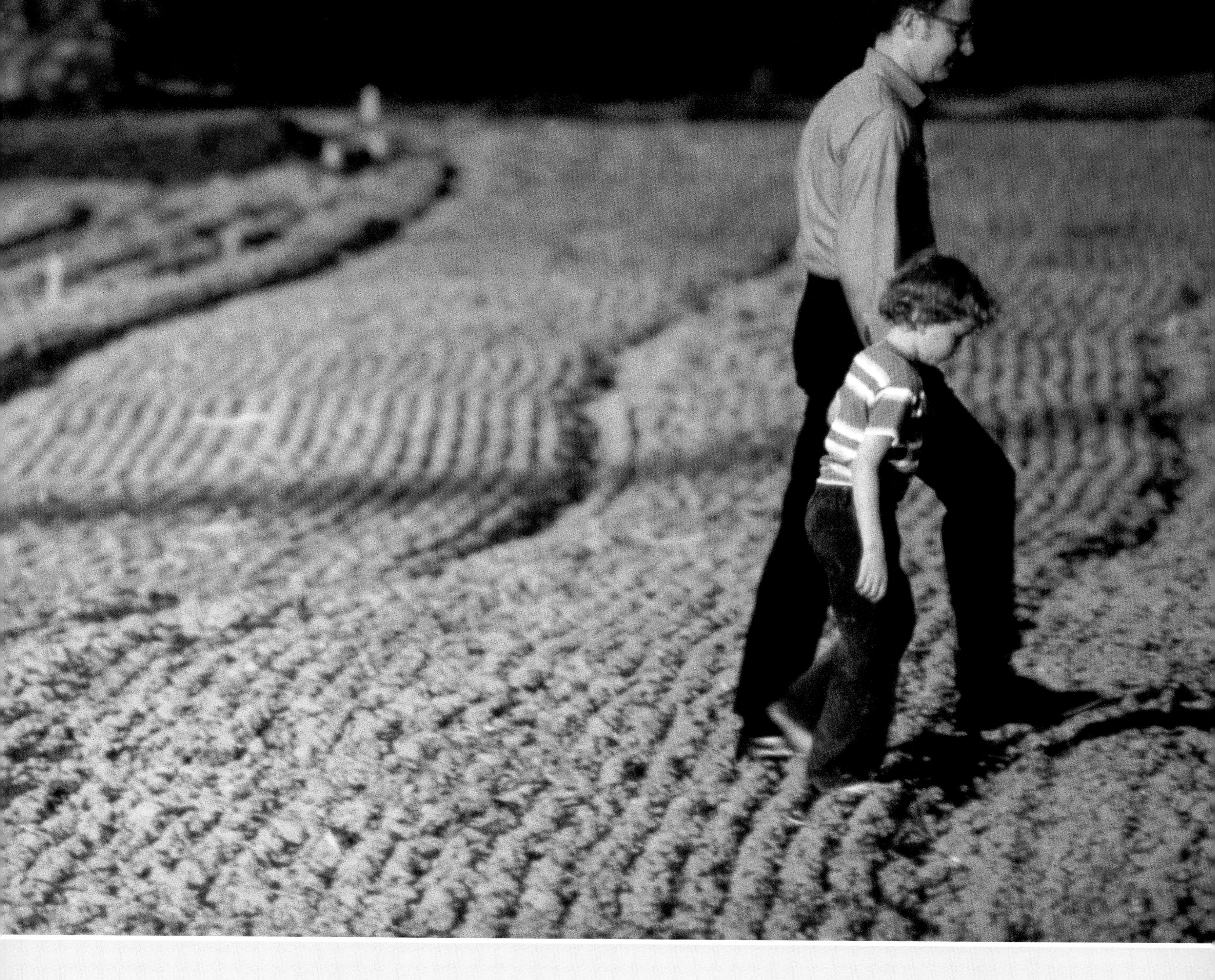

business, but as a means of communicating with people all over the world. He was thrilled to exchange ideas with readers—anonymous and well-known.

den 31.Oktober 1938

Herrn J.I.Rodale,President
Rodale Press
Emmaus,Pa.

Sehr geehrter Herr:-

Ich erlaube Ihnen gerne von meinem Brief an Upton Sinclair für den von Ihnen genannten Zweck Gebrauch zu machen.

Mit ausgezeichneter Hochachtung

A. Einstein.

EDDIE ALBERT

719 Amalfi Drive
Pacific Palisades, C

February 19, 1957

Mr. J. I. Rodale, Editor
The Organic Farmer
6th and Minor Streets
Emmaus, Penna.

Dear Mr. Rodale:

I am very much interested in organic farming and have read and enjoyed your writings on the subject. At present I am indulging a wish of long standing in that I am setting aside a small plot at my home for this purpose.

I would like very much to exchange information with someone in this area whose interest is the same. I wonder if you could help me get in touch with somebody ou here -- in the Santa Monica area of Los Angeles -- with whom I might discuss this fascinating subject.

Thank you for the pleasure and information you have provided.

Sincerely,

Eddie Al

Eddie Albert

Le Régina. Cimiez.
NICE. A.M.

Le 10 Avril 1952.

Monsieur David M. GLIXON.
Story Classics.
Sixth and Minor streets
EMMAUS.

Monsieur,

J'ai bien reçu vos deux lettres mais je n'ai toujours pas reçu vos quelques livres déjà édités que vous m'annonciez si je comprends bien pour que je puisse me rendre compte de vos réalisations.

Dès que je les aurai vus je vous donnerai ma réponse définitive quant à ma participation à vos éditions.

Je vous prie d'agréer, Monsieur , mes salutations distinguées.

HENRI MATISSE.

H Matisse

July 2, 1952

Mr. Yehudi Menuhin
P.O. Box 32
Alma, California

Dear Mr. Menuhin:

Mr. Rodale has left on an extended trip to Europe. I cannot at the moment find the clipping which you sent from the San Francisco Chronicle, but I am certain he has filed it carefully away and is extremely grateful for it, because he gets so much help from the clippings that interested people send in from all over the world.

I would like very much to be able to advise you on what brands of bread you can obtain, without chemicals, on the west coast. But we got ourselves into considerable difficulty with our readers recently when we recommended a brand of bread sold here in the east which appeared at the time to be just the finest bread imaginable. These bakers began to use a chemical preservative, to keep their bread from molding during the summer months. We have had several thousand letters from readers asking why we didn't check more carefully before recommending the bread.

Actually the only safe thing to do is to study the wrapper on each loaf of bread carefully and, when you find one that appears to be free of chemicals, write to the baker telling him what you want in a loaf of bread and asking whether his bread comes up to your standard. Usually bakers are honest about telling you the ingredients they use and many of them will tell you very proudly if they do use chemicals. It's a long, hard road -- this road to good eating -- but we are convinced it's worth it in the end.

Sincerely yours,

Ruth Adams, Asst. Editor
Prevention

RA/mk

For the third generation of Rodales, and for Rodale Press, the 1970s would represent a coming-of-age period.

CHAPTER 6

1972 TO 1980

Coming of Age

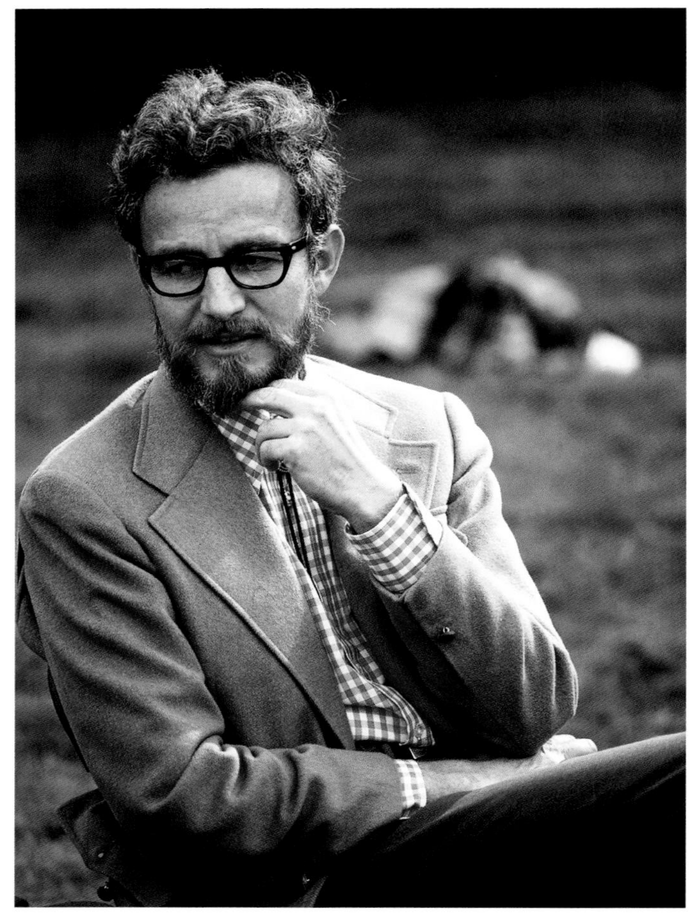

Robert Rodale in 1972

J. I. RODALE DIED in the summer of 1971, just as the organic movement he had brought to America was gaining momentum. For Rodale Press, the death of its guiding spirit proved to be a turning point. Bob Rodale, a self-confident and experienced magazine editor and executive, had been running the company for more than a decade. He was surrounded by a core of executives with long tenures. And having come through the attacks and challenges of the 1960s, Rodale Press was on solid financial footing. Over the next decade, Bob would put his own stamp on Rodale in a period of rapid growth, creating new institutions in and around Emmaus and pursuing new ventures influenced by his personal interests and vision.

In his 40s, J.I. had been a playwright with the day job of a manufacturing executive. Bob, a journalist by training and vocation, had the mind of an engineer and philosopher. Bob was interested in building systems to make the company run better, and in developing products—beyond magazines and books—that could allow people to assume greater control over their lives and health.

The former Olympic athlete found ingenious new ways to integrate fitness, the outdoors, and athletics into the organic lifestyle. One of Bob's most significant business innovations was using the strengths of markets and consumer behavior—and not simply argument, evidence, and opinion—to win more converts to the organic cause.

In the 1970s, history—rather than sheer nostalgia—would inform Bob Rodale's strategy to build and expand the company in his father's image. "Here at Rodale Press, we keep an eye on the past but we apply those observations to the present; even the future," as he once put it.

Rodale Press in the early 1970s was dominated by magazines, and by one magazine in particular: *Prevention*. In the fiscal year that ended July 1972, *Prevention* brought in about half the company's total revenues. *OG&F* was about half the size of *Prevention*. Immediately after J.I.'s death, Bob set out to alter the company's business. He shuttered or sold the unprofitable magazines that J.I. had founded and run, like *Quinto Lingo* and *Theatre Crafts*. Intent on expanding the audience for the core publications, Rodale hired Fawcett Publications to test the potential of selling *Prevention* and *OG&F* on newsstands and in supermarkets. And in August 1971, Bob hired Burton Fox, who had made a film about J.I. for a Philadelphia television station, to run the newly created Rodale Press Film Division. In the fall of 1971 Fox and his colleagues traveled around the United States to make a film entitled *Looking for Organic America*.

Bob soon found out that he needed to answer to a new boss—his mother.

Bob didn't operate with complete independence, since J.I. had left effective control of the company to Anna. "Suddenly I had a new boss," he recalled. And it was only after J.I.'s death that Bob realized what an important influence his mother had been on the company. "It turned out that J.I. would come up with ideas and talk about them, and on the fourth day, she'd say, 'Enough talk already—get out there and do it,'" said Bob.

1972
February 21: President Nixon starts visit to China.

March: Rodale purchases the 306-acre Siegfried Family Farm in Maxatawny, Pennsylvania.

June 4: J. I. Rodale's grave is unveiled at Northwood Cemetery in Emmaus.

Nixon meets Mao Tse-tung

June 14: The Environmental Protection Agency, following the lead of several individual states, bans the use of DDT.

June 17: Five White House operatives are arrested for breaking into the offices of the Democratic National Committee.

September 5 and 6: Eleven Israeli athletes are taken hostage and killed by terrorists at the Berlin Olympics.

As teenagers, members of the third generation of Rodales began to work at the company, interning at magazines and serving as tour guides at the organic farm.

J.I. and Anna's marriage was in many ways utterly conventional for their generation–she was primarily responsible for managing the household and the children's upbringing, and he was primarily responsible for making a living. But in the Rodale household, the boundaries between work and home, between business and family were blurry. For years, the Rodale home was the base for J.I.'s publishing activities; for decades, J.I. and Anna had lived on and built the farm that played such an important role in the genesis of *OG&F*. And Anna accompanied J.I. on virtually all his travels.

Grief-stricken at her husband's death, Anna nevertheless vigorously embraced an independent life. She would start a host of new ventures aimed at ensuring and expanding J.I.'s legacy. In 1972, she formed Annar Productions, a theatrical company that would stage shows in the Allentown area. She traveled extensively, embarking upon a six-week tour of South America, Africa, and Europe in 1972 to continue spreading the organic gospel. A year after J.I.'s death, she supervised production of a special issue of the company newsletter, *What's Going on Here?* "No longer the cracked pot. We proved a cracked pot can hold brown rice," she wrote–and oversaw the unveiling of J.I.'s grave on June 4. The large marble slab in the Northwood Cemetery, a few blocks away from the company's headquarters, read: "He urged man to live in harmony with the world." And, to the occasional annoyance of Bob, Anna routinely inquired about the company's operations and weighed in on goings-on at Rodale.

As the company grew, so did Ardie Rodale's role as the executive in charge of facilities management and design.

Bob and Ardie Rodale replicated J.I. and Anna's partnership. In the 1960s, Ardie's role as the executive in charge of the company's interiors and the management of its working spaces had been institutionalized. And as the company vastly expanded its physical plant in the 1970s, so too did her role grow. What's more, Bob and Ardie's five children, who had appeared in Bob's

1972
October 25: Belgian cyclist Eddy Merckx sets a new world hour record in Mexico City.

The Godfather premieres.

Fall: Rodale publishes Bob Rodale's Sane Living in a Mad World.

Eddy Merckx

Landmark U. S. Surgeon General report warns that nonsmokers exposed to cigarette smoke may suffer health hazards.

Congress enacts the Clean Water Act, intended to regulate the release of pollutants into waterways, storm sewers, and reservoirs and to restore waters that are already polluted.

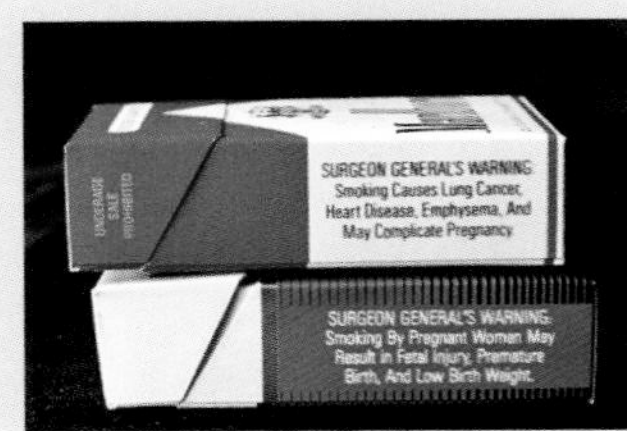

Smoking warning

WHAT'S GOING ON HERE?

1 December 1970

THE DRINKING PROBLEM

Remember last month when we said we were going to stop buying the plastic cups because they were a pollution problem? Remember how awful you felt?

Well, buck up. Thanks to a suggestion box item from Jim Stitt, we will buy paper cups for the coffee instead of plastic ones. We still hope you'll buy a real cup instead of using throwaways, but you won't have to.

THE TV STARS

On 8 November, the Roger Mudd Sunday night news program had a five-minute feature on the spread of interest in organic foods around the country. It included a few words from Bob Rodale and a shot of Mary Gulla and her machine.

The film was made back on 16 September, and we couldn't be sure just when the program would be on. So Mary faithfully watched every week at 6 p.m. The news wasn't even on for several weeks, because of football games. Finally, the big day arrived. Mary hurried home, turned on the television set, and dozed off. She woke up right after her picture had been on the screen. Goodnight Chet. Goodnight Roger. Goodnight Mary.

If you missed the show, you can't see it again, but if you want to hear it, ask Bob

ON THE THEATRICAL SCENE:

Audiences, especially in colleges, continue to gobble up plays by J. I. A little over a week ago, "Funeral Jazz" was presented at Cedar Crest. And a month before that, Lehigh University staged "The Hairy Falsetto."

On the 6th through the 8th of this month, Brandeis University will put on "The Hairy Falsetto" and "20 Years From Now." Then on the 11th through 13th, five or six of J. I.'s plays will be presented at the College Of Artesia, New Mexico.

Altogether, more than 20 requests for permission to produce J. I.'s works came in during November alone.

AND THIS REMINDER

Anna Rodale says don't forget "A Man For All Seasons" at Cedar Crest. We had a big block of tickets which were purchased for us by J. I., and there were a very few left at press time. Check with Judy New if you didn't get yours. Our tickets are for 8:15 p.m. on the 10th.

IS IT CHRISTMAS ALREADY?

If you haven't been here a full year, you don't know what a great spread of food is in store for you at the company Christmas party, the afternoon of the 24th. Serving will be buffet style out in the employee's lunchroom, and you can flop down to eat wherever you please.

Nancy Albright and her helpers are working ahead to prepare homemade cake and other goodies, which will make this even better than the feasts we've had in the past.

OY, VEY!

The Jan/Feb 1971 issue of Yiddish Lingo will be its last. Although both readers and critics were enthusiastic about the magazine, the economics of publishing such a specialized buch caused us to drop it. We felt the money could be better used to promote a public concern for environmental matters.

GARBAGE AS YOU LIKE IT

There's going to be a big waste conference in Denver, Colorado, 20 and 21 May 1971, sponsored jointly by Compost Science and the National Association for Composting and Waste Recycling. Maury Franz and Jerry Goldstein are members of the conference steering committee.

WHAT'S GOING ON HERE?

1 August 1971

VISITORS OF THE MONTH:

Sometimes you see people in Fitness House or in someone's office, and you wonder who they are. Well, no need to wonder about these two. The one on the right is familiar to many in the promotion department--he's Austin Ettinger, President of Jameson Advertising, Inc. His firm does all those great ads which we have in the New York Times and other prestigious papers. On the left is Hugh J. Kelly, Group Vice President of the Purchasing and Special Divisions areas for Howard Johnson's. Bob Rodale wrote a letter directly to Howard B. Johnson one day, asking about the possibility of Howard Johnson's using organically-raised foods in their giant chain. As a result, Mr. Kelly visited with us, and discussions are under way to explore the possibilities of Howard Johnson's getting more organic. You can read more of the story in a coming issue of Prevention--probably September. Meanwhile, we understand that Mr. Kelly and his wife really dug our Fitness House food.

COOL THOUGHT FOR A HOT AUGUST DAY:

Just remember back to the Christmas party. Fressing at the steam table, from left, are Barbara Dries, Linda Dunton, Peggy Dilliplaine and Mildred Flexer. ←

FINALLY, THE FTC SEES THINGS OUR WAY

Many of you remember the Rodale Books and Rodale Press case with the Federal Trade Commission, which dragged on in fits and starts from about 1960 to 1969. Summarizing and simplifying, the government was trying to censor ads for our books, claiming that we couldn't explain our editorial ideas in book advertising because those ideas were considered to be wrong by established medical authority, namely the A.M.A.

Well, the FTC finally lost, thanks to a ruling by the Washington Circuit Court of Appeals in our favor. Faced with that court decision, the FTC dismissed the case.

Now, we are pleased to note that the FTC, under a new chairmanship and revitalized concept of its mission, has gone further and disavowed its old activities as a censor of book advertising. The following release was published by the Commission on July 2. We note with pleasure that the new policy extends to all publishers the principles for which we argued in our case.

"The Federal Trade Commission today announced the following enforcement policy in regard to advertising which promotes the sale of books and other publications, and which involves issues arising under the First Amendment

What's Going on Here?, Rodale's corporate newsletter, built a sense of community among employees.

columns as sidekicks, companions, and occasionally as cover models for *OG&F*, began to join the family business. In the winter of 1972, *What's Going on Here?* noted that Heather Rodale would be working at the company over a Christmas break from Lehigh University, coordinating the work-study program of 19 Cedar Crest College students, and that Heidi Rodale would be working as a "moveable artist for various departments." The Rodale children also worked as tour guides at the organic farm.

What's Going on Here? which had started as a typed news bulletin for management written by Bob Compton, Bob's assistant at the time, was expanded into a full-fledged employee newsletter (*WGOH*) in 1971. And it marked one of the first attempts by Bob Rodale consciously to build a cohesive corporate culture at a company whose operations were increasingly spread throughout different locations. "Us old-timers can remember when you could walk from one end of the building to the other, glancing from side to side, and see all of our employees," Compton wrote in November 1971. "Now we've got branches in Fitness House, the Book House, the Studio in Allentown and the old Post Office Building in Emmaus." *WGOH* was filled with items on the annual clambake, vacation news of employees, anniversaries, personnel changes, and condolences.

"Rodale Press is building again!" *WGOH* noted in February 1972, trumpeting plans to add 25,000 square feet to the main building. The space, designed by architect Jim Harter, Ardie's brother, was expected to be completed in early 1973.

1973
January: Bob Rodale travels to China with a group of journalists.

January 22: U.S. Supreme Court issues ruling in *Roe v. Wade*.

Roe v. Wade resolved

May 14: *Skylab* space station is launched.

May: Rodale opens a new distribution center on South Fifth Street in Allentown.

One of Rodale Press's first annual reports

Annual Report 1973

the Rodale people

To cope with the growing volume of books, magazines, and mail it sent out, Rodale continually expanded its distribution capabilities. In the early 1970s, Rodale leased a building in Allentown that had housed the Skateland roller rink as a book distribution center. In September 1973, the company opened a new distribution center on South Fifth Street in Allentown.

In the fall of 1972, Bob released the company's first-ever annual report. "Why an annual report? For us it is a way of letting our employees and friends know in more detail the total operations of the company." The publication provided figures on advertising pages and circulation for the magazines (1.106 million for *Prevention*, up 25 percent; 750,000 for *OG&F*), the number of pieces of direct mail sent (more than 30 million), and other news on the changing business operations. Bob noted with satisfaction that "many of the large mass-marketed food and drug companies (like Quaker Oats, Ralston-Purina, Borden, Squibb, Parke-Davis, etc.) have recognized the rationale and the consumer demand for better quality food products and natural source supplements, and we anticipate a large new body of advertising prospects." Meanwhile, he conceded, *Fitness for Living* was struggling: "We have found a good deal of consumer resistance both in initial magazine subscription sales and in advertising space sales."

The Book Division remained something of a stepchild. Book sales in 1971 were only about 10 percent of overall sales, and the division operated out of Book House, a small stone house on Minor Street that Rodale had acquired a year before. Because J. I. Rodale had dominated the book division—he wrote most of the company's books, and all book marketing literature featured his photograph—Bob had generally treated books as J.I.'s exclusive province. "When he died,

September 11: Chile's democratically elected government is overthrown in a military coup.

October 6: Yom Kippur War begins as Egypt and Syria attack Israel, setting off oil crisis.

October 10: Vice President Spiro T. Agnew resigns.

Spiro T. Agnew

Rodale publishes *Stocking Up*, by Carol Hupping Stoner.

Rodale publishes *The Rodale Cookbook*, by Nancy Albright.

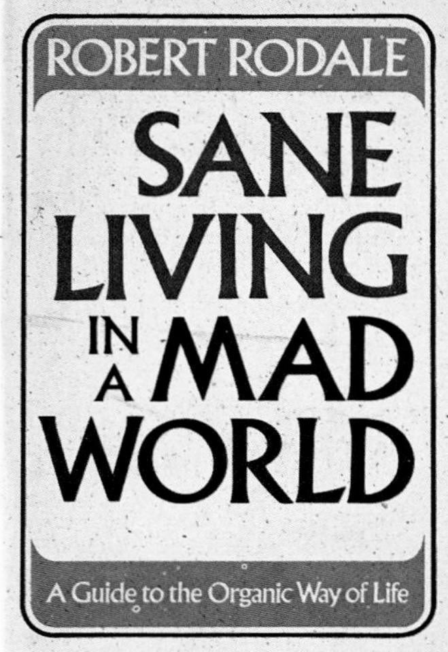

Bob Rodale began to invest his personal time and the company's resources in the company's book division.

I didn't really pay attention to the book division for three or four years because I figured I'm more of a magazine person." Run by veteran Jim Hare, Rodale Books focused on selling large books like the *Encyclopedia of Organic Gardening.* Operating on a cash-only basis, the book division eschewed bookstores and wholesalers and instead marketed books almost entirely through the direct-mail lists the magazines generated.

But over the course of the 1970s, books would assume greater importance as a business in its own right. In the early 1970s, Rodale essentially started a second book division, which was run out of Rodale Press by Jerry Goldstein. Goldstein had joined the company in the 1950s and was working on the business side of *OG&F.* By the late 1960s, he was in charge of editorial for *OG&F* as well as its circulation. The unit commissioned original books and repackaged material from magazines into smaller books that were marketed to members of the rapidly growing *Prevention* and *OG&F* book clubs, which each had more than 40,000 members in 1972. In 1971 and 1972, the *OG&F* book club included titles such as *Confessions of a Sneaky Organic Cook*, in which *Prevention* editor Jane Kinderlehrer described how she surreptitiously used nutritious ingredients when cooking for her family. In the fall of 1972, Rodale released the first book written by Bob. *Sane Living in a Mad World: A Guide to the Organic Way of Life* was a collection of his articles and columns from *Prevention* and *OG&F.*

Bob Rodale also moved to invest some of Rodale's profits to expand the company's capabilities in agriculture. "I'm planning to buy a bigger farm—the old one is too small and too close to the city—and we'll get people with important credentials to work with us and demonstrate what we already know," he told John Haberern in 1971. In March 1972, Rodale purchased the 306-acre Siegfried Family Farm in Maxatawny, about 11 miles west of Emmaus, and called it the New Farm. Over the next few years, the property would be transformed into an organic showcase, with the addition of vegetable gardens, livestock, poultry, and community gardens. The farm, later renamed the Rodale Research Center and then the Rodale Institute, and headed by John Haberern, would become an important component of the company's larger efforts to establish the scientific credibil-

1974
February 4: Patricia Hearst is kidnapped by the Symbionese Liberation Army.

February 27: *People* magazine is published for the first time.

July: Rodale donates 5 acres in Lower Macungie Township to be used as an outdoor recreation center.

Patty Hearst as SLA member

August 8: President Richard Nixon announces his resignation.

Stephen King's *Carrie* is published.

Mark Bricklin is named editor of *Prevention.*

Rodale Press donation establishes J. I. Rodale Scholarship fund at Lehigh University.

Nixon resigns

The New Farm, purchased in 1972, was developed as a showplace for organic farming methods and research. It became a living embodiment of the Rodale philosophy.

ity of organic gardening and agriculture. It would be a place where visiting officials, scientists, and readers could see tangible results of the work featured in Rodale's publications.

Bob had a distinctive, inclusive management style. He wrote a large number of typed memos and routinely sent articles to colleagues to read. "As I mentioned to you," he wrote to a group of executives in October 1972, "I'm convinced the energy crisis is going to develop in future years and will present unavoidable challenges to industry and individuals." His concern proved prophetic. Even before the Arab oil embargo of late 1973, which caused the price of oil to skyrocket, Rodale was emphasizing the need to use energy more wisely. Typically, Bob believed that organic methods could help solve the looming crisis. "As the price of fuel goes up, more people are going to turn to gardening and small-scale farming as ways to produce needed food energy," Bob wrote in his February 1973 *OG&F* column. "We must do more walking, especially around cities and towns, and less riding in automobiles." For Rodale, the energy crises that roiled the country and sandbagged economic growth were something of a boon. Bob wrote in Rodale's 1974 annual report that the core magazines were unaffected by the economic slowdown in part because "our primary subjects–gardening and health–become more important in hard times." Over the course of the decade, the effort to profit and grow while helping to mitigate the ill effects of the nation's overreliance on fossil fuels would assume growing prominence at Rodale.

John Jeavon's bestseller *How to Grow More Vegetables (Than You Ever Thought Possible on Less Land Than You Can Imagine)* shows people how to transform postage-stamp backyards into productive kitchen gardens.

Rodale publishes *The Best Health Ideas I Know*, by Bob Rodale

Bill Mollison and colleague David Holmgren develop the principles of permaculture, a self-sustaining agricultural system based on a philosophy of working with nature rather than against it.

Rodale Research Center begins a study of amaranth, an ancient grain grown by the Aztecs. News of its nutritional value spreads around the world.

October: Whole Food Company (WFC) opens its doors in New Orleans.

Bob Rodale joined a group of journalists on a trip to China in 1973.

Much as he differed in style and temperament from his father, Bob continued to edit the magazines in his mold. In January 1973, Bob traveled to China with a group of journalists. As J.I. did, he used his experience as fodder for articles. He had a photo taken with a journalist from the Hsinhua News Agency in Beijing who had a copy of *The Word Finder* in his office. In *Prevention*, Bob recounted how when he got a cold, a Dr. Sheng prescribed certain medicines, herbs, and acupuncture.

More so than J.I. did, however, Bob thought strategically about how the company would have to change if it wished to match its recent impressive growth. "I think we will always be a publishing company basically, but we have to realize also that people are getting more information from films and TV, and also radio, so we should have some capability there," he wrote to Anna in March 1973. The company also needed to boost its human infrastructure. "We are successfully making the transition from a small company where most executives share several responsibilities to a more professionally run company with experienced and trained specialists in key functions," he wrote in the 1974 annual report. Given its size and scope, Rodale was one of the largest employers in Emmaus–Rodale needed to take issues of recruitment and training more seriously. As Bob would later say, one had to "institutionalize a family business, or professionalize it." In December 1973, the company started a program under which new employees would meet top executives, including Bob Rodale, receive an introduction to the publishing industry, and tour the company's operations. And Bob began writing a help-wanted column in *WGOH*. "Because of our size, I'm not familiar with every job opportunity that exists here and don't know all the people who are anxious to grow into new positions."

These efforts came at a time of change in the generally stable management team. In 1974, Harold Taub, executive editor of *Prevention* for 12 years, left and was replaced by Mark Bricklin. Bricklin, who had started freelancing humorous material for the magazine in the early 1970s, was promoted from associate editor to head the company's flagship magazine. And when Jim Hare retired in 1975, the book division he ran was folded into Rodale Press's books unit.

Bob Rodale regularly ate lunch at Fitness House and made a point to sit with all levels of employees.

Bob was involved in many aspects of the company, here discussing advertising in *Prevention* with *(from left)* Cerf Berkley, Mark Bricklin, Marshall Ackerman, and Mark Schwartz.

The Trexlertown velodrome, shown here in later years, became a training ground for Olympic hopefuls.

Bob takes an inaugural ride.

In the wake of the oil crisis of 1973 and 1974, the United States—a nation defined for so long by abundance—began to think seriously for the first time about the need for conservation, for efficiency, and for self-sufficiency in the production of food and energy. This changing mindset played directly into Rodale's strengths. Bob Rodale latched onto one phenomenon in particular—the bicycle—as both a symbolic and a practical solution. Since watching bike racing at the 1968 Olympics, Bob had become interested in bicycling as a recreational sport. After returning from Mexico City, he wanted to build a velodrome—the banked venue for cycling races, of which there were very few in the United States—near Emmaus. In 1969 and 1970, he sounded out architects about the possible cost. And in August 1974, the company announced it was going to move ahead with the project, which was expected to cost between $50,000 and $90,000. The velodrome would be built on part of a 22-acre parcel that he and Ardie had committed to donate to the Trexlertown Park Association.

At the same time that he made large new investments—such as in the farm or velodrome—Bob proved willing to cut his losses. In the summer of 1973, Rodale shut down the money-losing film business. And in 1974, Bob reluctantly closed one of his longtime pet projects, *Fitness for Living.* As he noted, it "never really clicked in terms of contributing to the profit picture at Rodale."

Bicycling had an appeal that went far beyond competition and recreation. For Bob Rodale, the bicycle was something like the perfect machine. Energy-efficient, environmentally friendly, and healthy, the bicycle offered people the ability to take greater control of their own lives. And increasingly, he used the company's resources to promote both traditional and new uses for the bicycle. In the 1975 annual report, which featured a picture of Bob on a bike at the nearly completed velodrome, Bob discussed the company's newly formed Research and Development unit. John Haberern was asked to develop and lead this division. Rodale had decided to hire professionals with expertise—and credentials—in areas such as nutrition, engineering, and food technology to conduct research and to develop ideas and products that Rodale could package as individual articles, as entire magazines or newsletters, and as products to be marketed and sold. One of the first products the R&D unit began to develop was "the energy bicycle, a concept conceived by Bob

1975
January: The Altair 8800 microcomputer is introduced.

March 3: Bob Rodale presents the deed to a 172-year-old house on South Keystone Avenue—the second-oldest house in Emmaus—to Mayor Pierce Randall.

Bill Gates and Paul Allen found Microsoft.

Bill Gates and Paul Allen

April 30: Communist forces take Saigon, and South Vietnam surrenders.

June 20: *Jaws* premieres.

July 5: Arthur Ashe becomes the first African American man to win the Wimbledon singles title.

Arthur Ashe

After becoming fascinated with bicycle racing at the 1968 Olympics, Bob Rodale resolved to build a velodrome near Emmaus. The facility opened on land donated by Bob and Ardie Rodale in 1974.

October 11: *Saturday Night Live* is broadcast for the first time.

October 12: The Velodrome opens in Trexlertown.

Rodale forms Research and Development division.

Saturday Night Live cast

Anthony and Susan Harnett purchase the first Bread & Circus store in Brookline, Massachusetts. The store sells natural foods and wooden toys, hence the unusual name.

Kent and Diane Whealy found the Seed Savers Exchange—a network of backyard farmers with a passion for saving and sharing heirloom fruit and vegetable varieties.

Rodale Resources explored projects designed for energy conservation and self-sufficiency—fishponds, pedal power for household tasks, a food dehydrator, a solar greenhouse, among others.

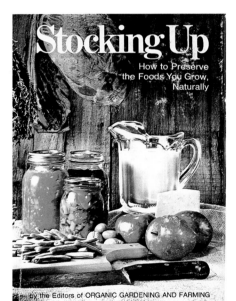

Rodale Press responded to the 1973–74 energy crisis by developing books that enabled readers to become more energy-efficient and self-sufficient.

Rodale." The idea was to harness energy created through riding a stationary bike to grind grain, chop food, churn butter, or generate electricity.

The new focus on self-sufficiency quickly manifested itself in different ways throughout the company. *OG&F* had designated 1975 as the Year of Personal and Food Security on the Land. At the Rodale Research Center, work continued on a fishpond and a windmill. "We are working for energy conservation, and possibly for eventual self-sufficiency," Bob wrote in the 1974 annual report. Books focused on the same theme. In 1975, among the nine books with sales of more than 100,000 copies were titles like *Stocking Up* and *Producing Your Own Power.* The following year, *Low-Cost, Energy-Efficient Shelter*, with a 130,000-copy first printing, was the book division's greatest success.

The ability to take a single idea, or a set of ideas, and roll them out into multiple media and sales channels simultaneously became a core component of Rodale's strategy in the mid-1970s. In November 1976, James "Chuck" McCullagh, a British-born graduate of Lehigh, was named editor of a series of books that would describe R&D projects. Bob suggested in 1976 that the company develop books on water purification and on pedal power. And a memo about the "Home Production Development Policy" in early 1976 demonstrated the new ambition to create synergies. The company could promote home production by making it a theme of *OG&F*, the topic of books, the subject of experiments at the farm, or part of the R&D unit—or a Rodale Home Production Catalog, "a business selling tangible products that will enable people to produce more goods and services in the home." In 1977, the division was renamed Rodale Resources, Inc. With John Haberern as president, it occupied a 39,000-square-foot building that had formerly been a silk mill in Emmaus. There, engineers and workers aimed to develop the energy-generating bicycle—known as the Energy Cycle—and pond aerators that would help fish grow.

The use of company resources to back experiments in everything from food to fitness helped produce ideas for the magazines and the book unit. In 1976, the company noted, R&D efforts generated produce dozens of articles. *OG&F* began to include a Fitness House Idea of the Month, for example. A regular feature in *Prevention*, entitled "Table Talk," noted that "all recipes

1976
April 1: Apple Computer Company is formed by Steve Jobs and Steve Wozniak.

June 1: Rodale holds groundbreaking ceremonies for library addition to headquarters.

Apple Computer

July 29: First attack by serial killer Son of Sam.

October 24: Bill Rodgers wins the New York City Marathon with a course record 2:10:10.

November 2: Georgia Governor Jimmy Carter defeats President Gerald Ford.

Bill Rodgers

November 21: Sylvester Stallone's *Rocky* premieres.

Saul Bellow wins Nobel Prize in Literature and Pulitzer Prize for Fiction.

Saul Bellow

Rodale publishes Low-Cost, Energy-Efficient Shelter for the Owner and Builder.

Perrier water is introduced into the U.S. market.

At its farm and in its publications, Rodale championed the benefits of amaranth, a protein-rich grain.

are tested under the direction of Anita Hirsch, home economist in our Research and Development Department."

The company aimed not simply to develop new recipes, but to find new sources of food. Bob had set as a goal the development and popularization of new foods that "can add to the spectrum of food experiences in the U.S." One of those was amaranth, a grain that was popular in Mexico. After learning that amaranth contained more protein than wheat or corn, the company sent an ethnobotanist to Mexico to retrieve seed. Throughout 1976 and 1977, Rodale featured amaranth in *OG&F*, planted 2.5 acres of test crops at the farm, conducted cooking tests at Fitness House Kitchen, and created the Amaranth Information Bureau. *OG&F* enlisted organic gardeners to grow the grain around the country and to keep records of their results—more than 3,000 subscribers responded and offered to participate.

Amaranth was a good example of Rodale thinking globally and acting locally. In the 1950s and 1960s, J.I. had led national antifluoridation efforts in *Prevention* while leading a lengthy antifluoridation effort in Allentown. In the 1970s, as magazines like *OG&F* cited the need for land preservation, Bob became involved in several local efforts. He joined and supported local organizations that fought efforts to tear down a historic bridge and to develop parkland. And he was a force in the creation of the Wildlands Conservancy, which in 1976 began acquiring property. In 1978, Bob would donate 92 acres of land in the South Mountain area near Emmaus for preservation.

Rodale Press also continued to expand in and around Emmaus. In April 1975, Rodale opened a new distribution facility in town, a 37,600-square-foot building at 400 South 10th Street, set on a 30-acre parcel the company owned. In 1976, the company made plans to add on to the main headquarters again. This time, it would add a new library wing complete with six large

1977
January: Mrs. Gooch's Natural Foods Market opens in West Los Angeles.

July 13: Blackout occurs in New York City.

August 3: Tandy introduces the TRS-80 home computer.

TRS-80

August 4: President Carter signs legislation creating the United States Department of Energy.

Summer: J. I. Rodale Theater, located in a former church in Allentown, opens.

Cars line up for gas ration

Rodale's main building gained a new library addition in 1977.

solar windows. Groundbreaking ceremonies were held on June 1, 1976, with Rosemary Bortz of *Prevention* Readers' Service wielding the honorary golden spade. Rodale had always had an intense interest in proceedings in Washington. And in 1977, it opened an office on P Street, several blocks from the White House, and stationed a reporter there to handle research requests, cover congressional hearings, and write for the magazines.

That summer, the J. I. Rodale Theater, located in a former church on Linden Street between Eighth and Ninth Streets in Allentown, opened with a production of Jean Anouilh's *Ring Around the Moon*. Backed by Rodale Press funds, Anna had spent three years converting the building into a 271-seat theater. David Rodale, Bob and Ardie's son, worked on the project with his grandmother and ultimately became general manager and artistic director.

As it grew in size—and in profitability and ambition—Rodale became a more paternalistic company. In the winter of 1977, Bob Rodale surprised the firm's 500 employees by giving each a bonus in the form of a $100 bill to help cushion the impact of higher heating costs. Rodale served low-cost meals at Fitness House and developed fitness and recreation activities for employees. The company also focused resources on bolstering the professional quality of its journalism. A research editor was appointed in 1974, tasked with fact-checking the material in the magazines. The new library subscribed to some 900 publications. And a staffer began to edit the Sieve, an in-house publication of abstracts from other scientific journals.

Even though *Fitness for Living* had failed as a business, Bob still believed fitness was a potential growth area for the company. *Prevention* had begun to focus more on fitness. In 1977, the magazine sponsored its first annual marathon, which began at the velodrome. And that year, Rodale considered a more significant investment in fitness: the purchase of the magazine *Bicycling!* While at the velodrome in early 1977, Bob Rodale had jokingly suggested to Barbara George, the owner of *Velo News*, that Rodale should buy her magazine. George responded by suggesting that he look into *Bicycling!* which was for sale. Founded three years earlier, *Bicycling!* which had a circulation of about 85,000, was owned by an investor who was not committed to publishing.

TUESDAY, APRIL 30, 1974 — THE SIEVE

A. DOCTOR HOUSE CALLS. A University of Connecticut Health Center due to open shortly will feature house calls by doctors as well as other family group practice services. The Health Center is part of the teaching program in family medicine offered by the University. (UNIVERSITY OF CONNECTICUT NEWS RELEASE, 4-18-74; pp. 2)

B. YEAST AND OIL. Large scale food production tests conducted by Standard Oil are scheduled to begin this year to determine whether yeast for human consumption can be grown on ethanol derived from oil. (CHEMICAL AND ENGINEERING NEWS, vol. 52 #16, 4-22-74; p. 29)

C. PESTICIDE PROBLEMS. At the 167th American Chemical Society meeting, scientists discussed the environmental problems pesticides cause, such as the ease with which pesticides travel in the air, soil, water and living organisms and the influence of pesticides on photochemical reactions, microbiological attack, and chemical decomposition. Pesticide misuse in El Salvador is also discussed in terms of pesticide poisoning of humans, pesticide residue in food, and increasing mosquito resistance to pesticides resulting in an upsurge of malaria. (CHEMICAL AND ENGINEERING NEWS, vol. 52 # 16, 4-22-74; pp. 32-33).

D. MARIHUANA AND MALE INFERTILITY. Studies conducted on 20 young men who used marihuana at least 4 days a week for at least six months revealed a significantly lower plasma testosterone level on this group as compared to the controls. Six of the marihuana users displayed oligospermia and 2 men were impotent. Chronic marihuana use may alter male reproductive physiology through hypothalmaic or pituitary action. (NEW ENGLAND JOURNAL OF MEDICINE, vol 290 #16, 4-18-74; pp. 872-874).

E. CRIB DEATHS. Medical research into the causes of crib deaths has been ignored up to now. However, Congress has passed a bill to set up regional diagnostic centers and the National Institutes of Health's National Institute of Child Health and Human Development has put more than half a million dollars into crib death research. The article also discusses some of the current theories on crib deaths. (SCIENCE, vol. 184 #4135, 4-26-74; pp. 447-449).

F. SMOG. Dr. Julian Heicklen has developed a process in which the chemical compound DEHA (diethylhydroxylamine) can inhibit smog formation. Dr. Heicklen discusses how this chemical would act in the atmosphere, not in the tailpipes of cars, how it will pose no hazards to living things when added to the atmosphere, and how much this new procedure would cost. (PENNSYLVANIA STATE UNIVERSITY NEWS RELEASE, 4-24-74; pp. 4)

G. ANOREXIA NERVOUSA. According to UCLA researchers, an abnormality in fat (lipid) metabolism may be involved in anorexia nervousa, a disorder in which young women starve themselves into emaciation. (UCLA NEWS RELEASE, 4-18-74; p. 2)

H. POTASSIUM, ARTHRITIS AND HEART ATTACKS. The author of the article discusses how rheumatoid arthritis and heart attacks can be classified as degenerative diseases resulting from loss of strength and breakdown of tissues derived from the amoeboid cells of the middle layer of the embryo. This tissue breakdown is closely related to a potassium deficiency. A complete bibliography is not included, but can be purchased from the International College of Applied Nutrition. (THE JOURNAL OF APPLIED NUTRITION, vol. 26 # 1 and 2, Spring, 1974; pp. 41-67).

In the 1970s, Rodale Press started the Sieve, seeking to institutionalize knowledge sharing in the company.

August 16: Elvis Presley dies in Tennessee.

November 22: Concorde supersonic jet service starts between London and New York City.

Rodale's in-house research publication, the Sieve, is formally started.

Elvis Presley

The baby-food industry agrees to remove extra salt and sugar from its products.

While serving a life sentence on an island near Cape Town, South Africa, Nelson Mandela cultivates a stony strip of soil in the prison courtyard and begins growing vegetables.

Baby food

Approximately 87.5 million U.S. adults over the age of 18 participate in athletic activities; 8 million of those are joggers.

Rodale executives in the late 1970s

But Rodale had avoided acquiring magazines for temperamental and philosophical reasons. "We had looked at other acquisitions in the past, but the magazines were usually heavily supported by cigarette and liquor advertising," Bob said.

Still, Rodale was interested. And since this would be the company's first major corporate acquisition, it proceeded carefully. Studies and memos were drafted on *Bicycling!*'s strengths and weaknesses, the demographics of its readership, its roster of advertisers, and possible editorial changes. In early December 1977, a team was sent to California to meet with the owner and iron out a deal.

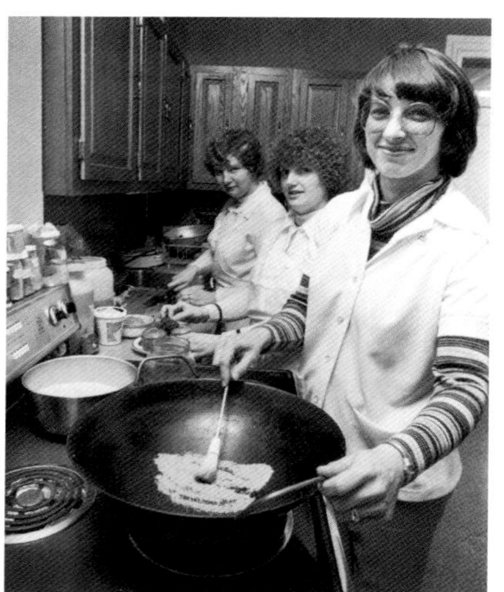

Anita Hirsch and staff at the Rodale Test Kitchen

Bob proclaimed *Bicycling!* a perfect fit. "Our company philosophy meshes perfectly with the interests of bicyclers," he wrote in the magazine's February 1978 issue. "We believe that most people have vast untapped potential to do more for themselves–both in creating enjoyment and in producing useful things–and we recognize the bicycle as the most efficient machine for such self-fulfillment." Immediately, Rodale installed a new team. Chuck McCullagh was named editor. Bob became the publisher and a columnist and announced plans to boost circulation to 250,000 in "about two years." Slowly, Rodale features were introduced. By June 1978, a food column, "Food for the Road," by Anita Hirsch of the Rodale Test Kitchen, had become a mainstay.

Another important transition came in 1978. With an expanding portfolio of businesses under the corporate umbrella and a desire to be less immersed in the details of the magazines, Bob Rodale assumed the new role of chief executive officer and promoted several executives to positions of higher responsibility. In November 1977, Marshall Ackerman took over Bob's post as publisher of *Prevention*. In July 1978, Bob Teufel was named president of Rodale Press, with responsibility for the company's day-to-day operations. At *OG&F*, Lee Goldman was named executive editor, and advertising executive Sandy Beldon became publisher.

By 1978, Rodale Press faced some difficult choices. The company had prospered and grown rapidly in a period in which many businesses had suffered and struggled. To a degree, however, the growth simply reinforced the need for diversification. *Prevention* remained a juggernaut.

1978
January 11: Health, Education and Welfare Secretary Joseph Califano calls cigarette smoking "slow-motion suicide."

February: *Bicycling!* debuts as a Rodale publication.

April 18: U.S. Senate votes to return the Panama Canal to Panamanian control by 1999.

June 19: *Garfield* comic strip debuts.

August: Residents of Love Canal in upstate New York are forced to abandon their homes after it's discovered that they are living on top of a chemical waste dump.

Love Canal

August 23: Rodale breaks ground for the new fulfillment center on South 10th Street in Emmaus.

Summer: Rodale introduces *The New Farm* magazine.

By purchasing *Bicycling!* magazine in 1977, Rodale Press diversified its magazine business to include a publication that focused on fitness as an overall component of health and well-being. It represented a first step in a sustained effort to build an important line of business: active sports.

The Well-Dressed Cyclist: A Complete Guide to Bicycle Clothing

by Rhonda Gainer

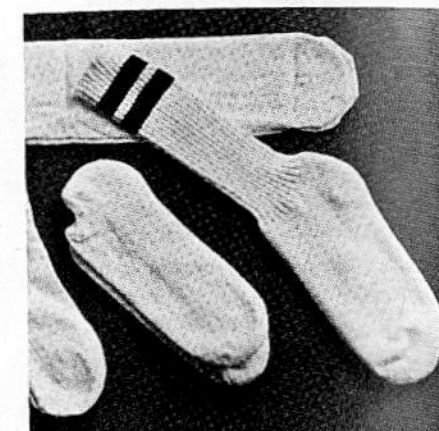

Newcomers to the sport of bicycling often look aghast at the outlandish outfits of converted bikies. Don't you remember the days when you thought to yourself, "Why would anyone want to look like that?" But as with most things, there's a reason for the design of bicycle clothing. Your comfort while riding is directly related to the shape, weight, permeability and absorption qualities of your clothes.

There are a number of characteristics one would desire bicycle clothing to have: light weight, streamlined profile, absorbency, breathability, ventilation, durability, easy care, safety, softness, ease in folding, ease in removing, extra length and pockets, and be economical. Let's look at how each of these affect you, the rider.

Light weight is important, for you don't want to carry around any more weight than you have to. Clothing should be streamlined so that it doesn't flap around in the wind and get in your way or slow you down. Bicycle riders get warm and sweat. If the clothing fabric breathes, then the hot air and moisture next to the body can escape. The cool air from outside can move in toward your body and evaporate the sweat. Thus your body is cooled.

Specialized clothing for bicyclists abounds. Shown here are shoe covers (these imported by Neel and Katz) for extra warmth on winter rides; gloves (those pictured are distributed by Bulk Bike) to protect palms from road shock and, in case of a fall, abrasions; and socks in an assortment of fabrics and styles.

One of the most interesting new developments is sew-it-yourself kits for jerseys, shorts and other garments. This one is a Patty Kit.

It is interesting to see how this actually occurs. Transmission of air and water vapor (perspiration) can occur because fabrics are permeable. That is, they allow the passage of air, water vapor and liquid water. However, permeability rates may vary from one fabric to the next. They are not all able to equally cope with wind, rain and perspiration. For example, if a fabric has a fairly high permeability, perspiration vapor can escape through it. But if it is not highly permeable, then the vapor condenses to liquid sweat and accumulates between the skin and the clothing and results in an uncomfortable feeling.

Permeability and absorption rates depend on fabric construction and the

nature of the fiber
a fabric is woven
stitches per inch,
is. With fibers,
or nonabsorbent,
more they hate
ble they are.

With rainwea
lem. Here you
let the rain lea
but you also w
perspiration
functions call
fabrics.

Another i
teristic is ve
lowed to circ
and the ski
body cool.
durable, w
made of fa
and pill-re
mation of
face of a
repeated

For co
be easy
and dryi
touring
thing th
wash it
it's dr
mornin

Safe
You n
cally safe
bility to motorists. Bright colors and/or reflective fabric are good safety features.

Soft and snug clothing aids comfort. Extra length also helps. If the sleeves and the back waist areas have added length, they won't pull up when you're riding the drops.

It's important to have clothing that is easy to fold and pack; in other words, that are compressible and compact. While riding you may want to strip or add layers of clothing, depending on weather conditions or how strenuously you are riding. Therefore, having easily removable clothing articles is important.

Many different lines of bicycle clothing in varying qualities and prices are available in the marketplace. Shop around and you can make sure you get the best product for the price you're willing to spend. The accompanying charts will give you a good idea of just what is available today.

Fiber properties and construction of the fabric determines the suitability of a fabric for bicycle clothing. Each has its own advantages and disadvantages and

There are different ty
percent virgin wool, good quality; Mexican wool, lower quality; superwash wool, good quality and treated to be machine washable and dryable without shrinkage.

Natural Fibers, Cotton

Advantages of Cotton

1) Comfortable;
2) high absorbency and wickability (ability to transmit perspiration moisture away from body);
3) free from static electricity;
4) durable—no pilling or seam slippage, strong;
5) easily dyed;
6) responds favorably to bleaches;
7) resistant to alkalies;
8) can be mechanically and chemically stabilized;
9) easy cleaning care—machine washable.

Disadvantages of Cotton

1) Lacks reiliency and elasticity—wrinkles;
2) degraded by microorganisms (such as mildew and rot), sunlight and

Disadvantages

1) Low moisture absorption;
2) retains body oils and perspiration;
3) accumulates static electricity;
4) damaged by sunlight;
5) affected by strong acid substances;
6) may pill.

Helenca nylon is a nylon commonly used in bicycle clothing, and its construction gives it added benefits. It is a stretch nylon with two-way stretch for body movement.

Synthetic Fibers, Polyester

Advantages of Polyester

1) Strong;
2) good dimensional stability;
3) resilient and wrinkle-resistant;
4) high abrasion resistance;
5) blends well with other fibers to increase wrinkle resistance;
6) easy cleaning care—machine wash and dry;
7) resistant to moths and mildew.

Disadvantages of Polyester

1) Low moisture absorption;

September 17: Israel and Egypt reach the Camp David peace accords.

October 16: Karol Wojtyla becomes Pope John Paul II.

Camp David peace accords

October: Rodale holds festival to commemorate J. I. Rodale's 80th birthday.

USDA issues regulations for reducing use of nitrates in bacon, after sodium nitrate is found to produce lymphatic cancer in laboratory rats.

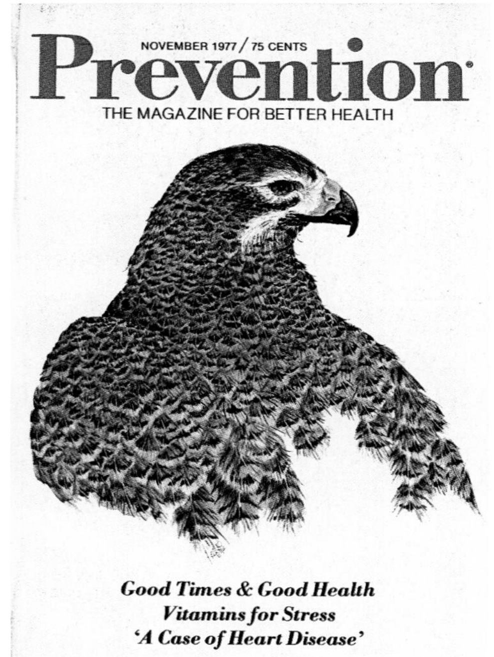
NOVEMBER 1977 / 75 CENTS
Prevention
THE MAGAZINE FOR BETTER HEALTH
Good Times & Good Health
Vitamins for Stress
'A Case of Heart Disease'

Prevention, which depended largely on mail-order advertising, sought to appeal to mainstream consumer advertisers.

In 1978, circulation topped 2 million, total revenues amounted to $22.89 million, and a single page of black-and-white advertising sold for $12,355. As it had for much of the past decade, the magazine alone provided about half of the company's revenues, as well as a disproportionate share of the overall profits.

For any company to rely so much on a single asset carries risks. And the risks seemed pronounced in Rodale's case because *Prevention* depended in large measure on direct-mail vitamin supplement advertisements. "We were both concerned and uneasy about the tendency of the company to rely on *Prevention* mail-order advertising and the gyrating base of *Organic Gardening and Farming* subscriptions," said Teufel. In 1979, Marshall Ackerman noted, food supplement direct-response advertising constituted 80 percent of the total. That was dangerous, especially given that vitamin and food supplements were increasingly sold in supermarkets, drugstores, and, increasingly, stand-alone vitamin stores. "The thing that changed the tide was when a vitamin store opened in Grand Central Station in New York City," said Mark Bricklin.

The magazine had evolved under Bricklin's leadership, adding more coverage of fitness and lifestyle, hiring new correspondents, and undergoing a redesign. But there was a sense that if *Prevention* were to build on this impressive base, to seek out new readers and advertisers, it would need to change. "*Prevention* hopes to become more than a 'vitamin magazine,'" Bob noted in the 1977 annual report. "We are developing research and selling techniques to interest the *mass market advertisers* of products that do not conflict with our philosophy."

The growing consumer interest in organic goods had helped create national brands that did advertise in *Prevention*, such as Hain vegetable soup mixes and Celestial Seasonings herb teas. But Rodale faced obstacles in reaching larger advertisers. Chief among them was inertia. As Ackerman noted, "Many of the most desirable positions have been committed for more than 20 years and would be difficult to change." What's more, convincing Fortune 500 companies to advertise was a labor-intensive process, and one made more difficult by Rodale's history of antagonizing the

1979
February 11: Ayatollah Khomeini seizes power in Iran.

March 28: Three Mile Island, Pennsylvania, nuclear power plant releases radiation.

Three Mile Island

June 18: President Carter and Soviet Premier Leonid Brezhnev sign the SALT II nuclear arms agreement in Vienna.

September 7: ESPN starts broadcasting.

September 12: Judith Krantz receives book advance worth more than $3 million for *Princess Daisy.*

establishment. Readers might also have been expected to react negatively to the sudden appearance of more corporate ads. Finally, *Prevention* maintained standards that were in some ways self-defeating. Some consumer products were welcome, while others weren't. *Prevention* would accept ads for Clairol shampoo, but not for Bayer aspirin, for example.

There were twin impulses behind such moves. On the one hand, Rodale, which had for so long defined itself in opposition to the establishment, wanted to be accepted by the business establishment. On the other hand, Rodale's corporate thinking had evolved to the point where it was no longer excessively dogmatic when it came to health issues. J. I. Rodale had fiercely opposed the use of aspirin. "But I had grown to the point when I could see people using these things in the overall context of taking responsibility for their own health," Bob recalled.

Marshall Ackerman drafted a plan called Target Marketing for targeting insurance, financial services, and health and beauty product companies, such as Beatrice Foods, Campbell Soup Company, and General Mills. But it was clear that Rodale would first have to educate the public and the business community about *Prevention*. "Before we crack this market, we will probably have to make an investment in an advertising space campaign, certainly in the trade press if not the *New York Times*," Ackerman wrote. And so in the late 1970s and early 1980s, Rodale made efforts to define and boost its corporate profile.

Rodale also sought to lessen its reliance on *Prevention* by further developing the magazine business. Rodale invested in *Bicycling!* by purchasing a smaller magazine, *Bike World*, which had a monthly circulation of about 30,000, and merging it into *Bicycling!* in early 1980. Meanwhile, Bob was enthused about many of the projects that centered on the larger experimental farm. At the same time, he had grown concerned that *OG&F* "had become too big to comfortably handle farming topics." So in the summer of 1978, Rodale rolled out *The New Farm*, a new magazine that (much as *The Organic Farmer* had attempted to do in the 1950s) sought to cover farm topics in great detail. Features centered on equipment, natural pest-control measures, and the experience of organic farmers. Steve Smyser, a former associate editor of *OG&F*, was executive editor.

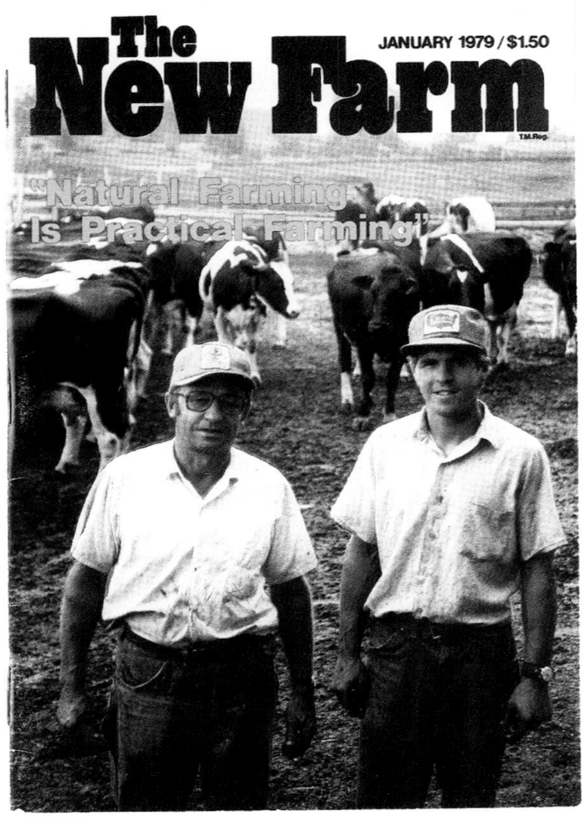

Rodale introduced *The New Farm* in the summer of 1978.

November 4: Iranian radicals seize the U. S. Embassy in Tehran.

December 24: Soviet Union invades Afghanistan.

Rodale publishes *Passive Solar Energy Book*.

U.S. Embassy in Iran

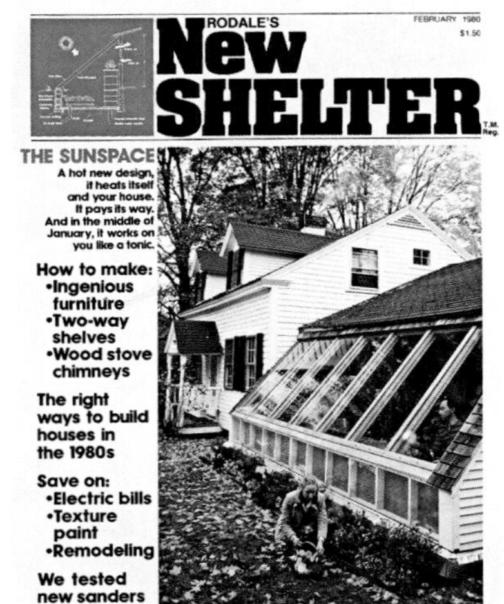

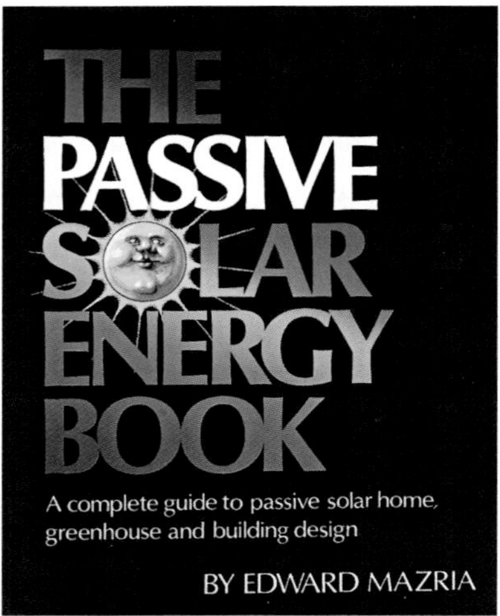

Interest in alternative energy brought about a new magazine—*New Shelter*—and related books, including *The Passive Solar Energy Book*.

With the introduction of *The New Farm*, *OG&F* changed its name to *Organic Gardening*. And in the January 1979 issue, at a time when the term *malaise* was being used to describe the nation's mood and economy, Bob Rodale painted a more optimistic picture. In his *OG* column, he wondered why there was such a sense of pessimism abroad in the country. Some of it could be blamed on technology and the rapid pace of change. But Bob looked ahead. "We could be entering a new age of renewable energy use that will allow many people to be more self-sufficient," he wrote. In the past 10 years, "people have learned some basic lessons about how to create happiness for themselves." This included the current interest in jogging and other exercises and the salutary benefits of gardening. "We need to think more actively about the role of gardening as a much needed booster of national morale," he wrote.

Rather than mope about the situation, Rodale declared it would do something about it. Bob Rodale was very interested in alternative energy projects. Rodale Resources had successfully built a solar greenhouse on the experimental farm, and the company had incorporated solar windows in the latest addition to the headquarters building. In February 1980, Rodale launched *New Shelter*, a glossy magazine that offered advice on how people could manage their homes in a more efficient manner. "We've just gone through a decade in which the cost of buying and operating a home shot up nearly 150 percent," Bob wrote in an introductory column. "Our mission is to put more of your home in your own hands." With energy shocks, there was a realization that "the systems that provided the energy to power our homes weren't as economical and reliable as we were taught to assume."

Solar power was a topic Rodale took seriously. The following year *The Passive Solar Energy Book* sold 250,000 copies. And in 1981, Rodale Press branched out for the first time into home building. It announced it would sponsor the first solar development in the Lehigh Valley, financing the design and construction of four solar houses in a development northwest of Allentown. "If we don't build solar homes there, someone else will come along and build ordinary homes," said Bob.

1980
February: Rodale launches *New Shelter*.

March 21: President Carter announces the United States will boycott the 1980 Summer Olympics in Moscow.

May 18: Mount St. Helens erupts in Washington, killing 57 people.

Mount St. Helens

June 1: CNN is launched.

August 14: Lech Walesa leads the first of many strikes at the Gdańsk shipyard.

October 14: Dr. Paul Berg receives the Nobel Prize in Chemistry for his work in recombinant DNA—a technique used to splice a gene of one organism into the DNA of another. The biotechnology industry is born.

Strikes in Poland

Rodale bought and restored unused buildings in Emmaus for use as company facilities: an old elementary school was recycled as the food center *(top)*, the old Emmaus post office as the photo lab *(middle)*, and an old silk mill as a facility for Rodale Resources *(bottom)*.

Indeed, while the economy was in the grips of stagflation, Rodale was in an expansive mode. It continued to add to its holdings in and around Emmaus. In 1980, it allocated space at the North Street building for what became known as the Energy Center, which would feature fitness and wellness classes for employees. The same year, it purchased the Thaddeus Stevens School in Emmaus and turned it into the new Rodale Food Center, with three separate kitchens. In January 1981, it started a new video division, Rodale Press Electronic Publishing, which produced documentaries on solar heating.

The developments were significant not just for their size, but for the way in which they were done. The buildings incorporated what Ardie Rodale had dubbed "holistic office planning." Rather than tear down buildings, Rodale chose to restore or renovate existing buildings where possible. The old post office had been turned into the Photo Laboratory; R&D worked out of an old silk mill on North Street; the company's new operations center was built on the site of the Emmaus borough dump. Wherever possible, the buildings utilized energy-saving design.

Rodale also self-consciously tried to project a new image to the world beyond the Lehigh Valley. With the assistance of Austen Ettinger, of Jameson Advertising, it began running a series of ads—so-called advertorials—on the op-ed page of the *New York Times* in 1980. The ads reflected Bob's view on the need for efficient housing, the future of bicycling, and America's state of health—a serialization of Rodale's philosophy. At the same time, the company consolidated its publicity and public relations efforts into a new corporate communications department and began more aggressively to seek outside press. During the first half of 1980, *WGOH* reported, "Rodale Press magazines, books, and research facilities were mentioned in over 300 separate stories." In May 1981, Rodale developed a new logo. And in June 1981, Bob appeared with the actress Brooke Shields, making a donation to the American Lung Association as part of an antismoking campaign.

Ten years after J. I. Rodale's death, the company he had founded in a corner of Rodale Manufacturing's plant had come a long way. No longer a niche business, Rodale Press was a large company, with revenues of nearly $100 million. The numbers were indeed impressive: *Prevention* alone had $31 million in revenues, and the company sold nearly $30 million in books.

November 4: Former California Governor Ronald Reagan defeats Jimmy Carter for president.

Rodale allocates space at the North Street building for an Energy Center.

Ronald Reagan

FDA advises pregnant women to stop or reduce consumption of coffee, tea, cola drinks, and other caffeine-containing products, which may cause birth defects.

Whole Foods Market opens in Austin, Texas, with a staff of 19 people.

Whole Foods Market

In the late 1970s, *Prevention* underwent a redesign that resulted in greater focus on fitness and lifestyle.

Tired of the Same Old Coffee Grind? Try Herb Tea!

Our erstwhile coffee hound catches scent of lemongrass, star anise and jasmine—and sets merrily off on the track of more healthful refreshment.

EMRIKA PADUS

Never mind the headaches and jitters. Don't mention the 10 or 12 trips to the john. And forget about the heart palpitations, high blood pressure and ulcers. Coffee cravers continue to chug their beloved brew at any cost—even at $4 and $5 a pound!

What drives them? Some say taste. But catch them gulping down a mug while gabbing on the phone or gallivanting around town on a Saturday morning. You can bet their taste buds barely register a hint of coffee flavor.

They might as well be drinking the overheated dregs of Chock Full o' Nuts as a delicately dripped brew of Jamaican Blue Mountain coffee for the amount of true taste pleasure they're getting out of their cup.

I know. I was once hooked on caffeine—unconsciously consuming some eight to 10 cups of coffee a day, and enjoying maybe one measly cup.

Now, I've cut down my habit to two cups and reduced my caffeine intake at least three-quarters—by discovering the exciting world of herb tea.

Herb teas are different. Differ-

apartm

The soft c about nigh wat dri po m

I took m —sitting erect and s neck over the steaming pot like puppy sniffing a stranger's hand. I surprised myself by not jerking my head back whiplash fashion. Instead, I let my nose drop a little closer to the vapors while my mind drifted to a summer day's stroll through a flower-filled, fra-

ca space with th taining as many as 20 gredients. A tea for every taste and any occasion.

I found what I was looking for and then decided to try out an-

In 1981, Bob Rodale appeared with actress Brooke Shields at an antismoking press conference.

The Encyclopedia of Natural Healing had become the company's first million-copy seller. In addition, new publications like *Bicycling!* and *New Shelter* had evolved into significant contributors. In 1981, *Organic Gardening* and *Prevention* had circulations of 1.3 million and 2.5 million, respectively, while *New Shelter* reported audited circulation of nearly half a million. The company had expanded its infrastructure to house and feed its 710 employees. Rodale now encompassed a vast new farm, the test kitchen, a larger headquarters, the North Street facility and a new operations center. Meanwhile, the company had made forays—some of them successful, some of them unsuccessful—into video, manufacturing, even home building. With new magazines covering different aspects of the human experience, Rodale was reaching a broader and expanding audience. The company was extending the concept of organic living beyond gardening, farming, and preventive health care into the realms of personal fitness and home design. And this notion that Rodale could create books, magazines, and products that would allow its customers to lead lives that were more full, and more whole, would help drive the company's growth.

At the beginning of the 1980s, and with the core of a third generation beginning to arrive, Rodale Press occupied a much larger footprint in both Emmaus and the larger culture. In the next decade, it would continue to expand. Like the tree in its logo, Rodale Press had grown into a company with deep roots, a strong trunk, and an expanding network of branches.

While supporting the company's expansion in the 1980s, Robert Rodale turned his thoughts to global issues.

CHAPTER 7

1981 TO 1990

Regenerating the Core Business

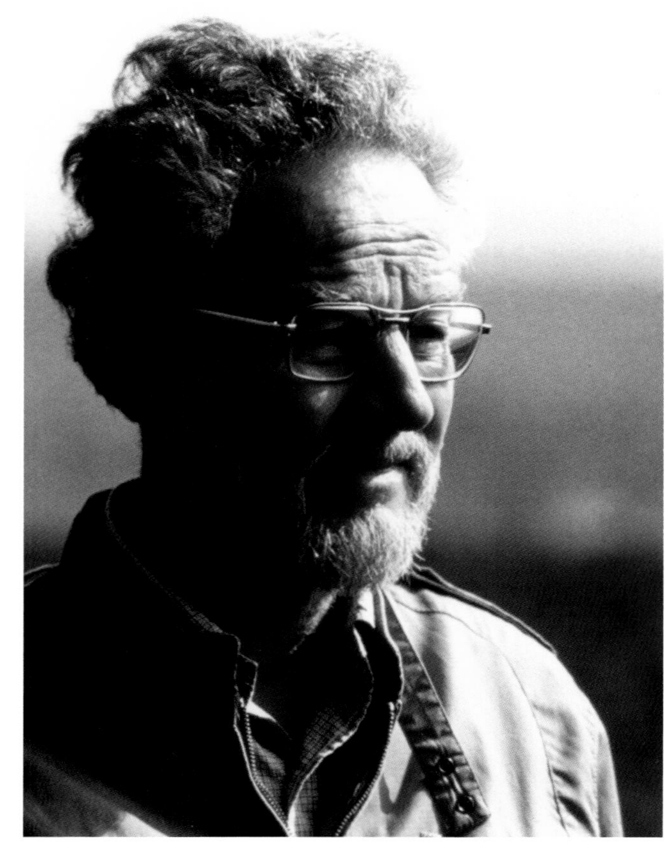

Moving into his 50s, Bob Rodale became a visionary.

IN THE 1970S, Bob Rodale had pushed the business in several new directions–manufacturing energy-saving devices, building a large new experimental farm–as the magazine and book business he had inherited enjoyed spectacular growth. In the 1980s, starting from a much larger base, Rodale would seek growth by returning to its core: publishing magazines and books, growing them organically and through acquisition. Rather than branch off into entirely new fields, Rodale Press innovated largely by leveraging the resources it possessed–a strong brand, editorial capabilities, and a large and expanding customer base. With the book division becoming a reliable source of profits, Rodale placed greater emphasis on sports-related magazines and on finding new channels through which to broadcast its message on health and wellness.

In the 1980s, the publishing company, which had its origins in manufacturing, effectively created a series of editorial assembly lines—books and newsletters, one-shot publications and magazines—through which it could test, develop, and bring to market new products. As the decade wore on, and as a third generation of Rodales began to find their places in the company, Bob Rodale maintained an intense interest in the company's progress and management. But he also began to think systematically about important global issues. He ultimately developed a management philosophy—regeneration—that had applications to agriculture at home and abroad, to the company that bore his name, and to society at large.

To a degree, Rodale in 1981 faced the same dilemma it had faced in 1971—an overreliance on *Prevention*. In 1981, the magazine alone provided 35 percent of revenues and more than half of operating profits. But the average age of *Prevention* readers, who were mostly women, was in the early 50s—and rising. Eager to deliver the health message to younger women—a group of readers many advertisers wanted to reach—a confident Rodale decide to create a new glossy magazine, *Spring*, aimed at women between the ages of 20 and 40. "*OG* and *Prevention* were doing extraordinarily well; *New Shelter* had launched and made money in its first year," said John Griffin, head of the magazine division. A pilot issue of *Spring* was produced in the spring of 1981, and plans were hatched quickly to launch it on a large scale.

While philosophically similar to *Prevention*, *Spring* represented a point of departure for Rodale. It more closely resembled a traditional women's magazine than *Prevention did*: full-size, lots of color, modern graphics. *WGOH* called it "our first attempt at a 'slick' magazine." And it was largely oriented toward New York. The art department set up its office on Spring Street, in Soho, so it could tap into New York–based illustrators and photographers. The advertising office in midtown Manhattan shared space with *Prevention*. Edited by former *Prevention* staffer Emrika Padus, *Spring* was officially launched in March 1982 with a party at Manhattan's Four Seasons restaurant and a circulation of about 680,000. The debut issue, subtitled "High Energy Living," featured articles on nutrition, smart small cars, and vitamin B_6. "You won't find much of the usual froth in

To expand its customer base, Rodale launched a new magazine, *Spring*, aimed at a younger readership than the successful *Prevention.*

1981
January: Rodale starts a new video division, Rodale Press Electronic Publishing.

March 6: Walter Cronkite ends 19-year run as anchorman of *CBS Evening News.*

March 29: First London Marathon is run.

Walter Cronkite

March 30: President Ronald Reagan is shot in the chest outside a Washington, D.C., hotel by John Hinckley Jr.

April 12: Space shuttle *Columbia* is launched.

August: IBM releases its personal computer.

September 25: Sandra Day O'Connor is sworn in as the first woman on the U.S. Supreme Court.

October 6: Egyptian president Anwar Sadat is assassinated.

Pac-Man video game is introduced in the United States.

Downtown Emmaus in the 1980s

Spring," Bob Teufel wrote in a letter to readers. "No high fashion, no miracle diets. No hot trends that turn out to be lukewarm fads."

Rodale simultaneously sought to reach new mass audiences by increasing single-copy sales of *Prevention*. *Prevention* had a massive circulation (2.55 million) in 1982. As a rule, Rodale's publications had always derived more revenues from circulation than from advertising. But virtually all circulation revenues came from subscriptions, sold at a substantial discount to the cover price; in 1981, *Prevention* ranked 2,000th among U.S. magazines in single-copy sales. Boosting such sales could help increase profits while attracting new readers and prospective subscribers. Led by executive Rich Alleger, the company in the early 1980s initiated a years-long effort to sell more single copies at retail outlets. The first success came in 1982, when Rodale convinced Florida's Publix grocery store chain to start selling *Prevention* at the checkout counter.

Launching *Spring* and pushing *Prevention* into new sales channels required significant investments. Rodale, which had revenues of about $96 million in 1982, was equipped to make them. From a corner of the old Rodale Manufacturing plant and J. I. Rodale's dining room table, Rodale had grown to occupy 250,000 square feet in 12 locations in and around Emmaus. With 800 employees—more than half of whom lived within a 4-mile radius of Emmaus—the company was a huge force in the local economy. In 1981, its payroll injected $11.3 million into the Lehigh Valley's economy, and the company bought $27.88 million in goods and services locally.

Given its size, however, Rodale was large enough to be affected by broad economic cycles. Some of the economic dislocations of the 1970s had played into the company's hands, as energy conservation and gardening became more appealing in times of economic stress. But when a deep national recession hit in 1981 and 1982, subscription renewals and advertising sales fell across the board. As a result, in the summer of 1982, Rodale enacted an austerity program, cutting jobs, freezing wages, and shutting down *Spring*'s New York editorial office. "Would we have started *Spring* had we known the economic recession would be so severe?" Bob Teufel wrote in the fall of 1982. "Of course not." And by the spring of 1983, after having racked up millions of dollars in losses, Rodale

1982
March: Rodale launches *Spring*.

May 2: The Weather Channel goes on the air.

June 11: *E.T.: the Extra-Terrestrial* premieres.

June 12: In New York City's Central Park, 750,000 people rally against nuclear weapons.

July 26: *Newsweek*'s cover story on gardening features Lee Goldman, of *Organic Gardening* magazine.

September: One hundred thirty-five people gather at Cedar Crest College in Allentown for Cornucopia Project meeting over Labor Day weekend.

October: *Prevention* Health Report, 2-minute news spots on health, fitness, and nutrition, debuts on more than 200 TV stations.

November 13: The Vietnam Veterans Memorial is dedicated in Washington, D.C.

Vietnam Veterans Memorial

Research trials at the Rodale Research Center in Maxatawny drew attention from research scientists in the government and around the world.

December 26: The computer is *Time* magazine's Man of the Year.

Alice Walker publishes *The Color Purple.*

Rodale buys *American Cyclist*.

Soil and Health Foundation is renamed the Regenerative Agriculture Association.

Alice Walker

Rodale leases the Keystone Building in Emmaus.

New England Journal of Medicine study suggests that the typical U.S. diet—high in meat and low in fiber—may increase the risk of breast cancer in women.

Bicycling magazine led the way in the growth of fitness as a Rodale business.

decided to shutter *Spring.* The poor economy was only one of the reasons for its relatively quick demise. The magazine faced stiff competition from *Shape* and *Self,* which debuted at roughly the same time and were backed by companies with deeper pockets. And Rodale still had difficulty penetrating large consumer advertisers. The November/December 1983 issue was the magazine's last.

Bicycling was one of Rodale's bright spots in the early 1980s. Since the 1977 acquisition, *Bicycling*'s circulation rose steadily to more than 200,000, and the magazine was consistently profitable. In 1982, Rodale bought *American Cyclist,* a regional publication, and folded it into *Bicycling. Bicycling* also started a new technical newsletter, *Bike Tech,* and began sponsoring races with 7-Eleven. The fact that *Bicycling* could thrive under difficult economic conditions highlighted the underlying growth in the businesses surrounding fitness. Running, biking, and weight lifting, which had caught on in the 1970s, continued to grow, even as new trends like aerobics gained strength. Rodale would capitalize on and help lead this growth by integrating fitness and recreation more tightly into its overall vision of health and wellness.

A new and larger Energy Center opened in 1985.

The company also integrated fitness into the lives of its employees. In 1983, Rodale approved plans to construct a 10,000-square-foot exercise facility in Emmaus. The new Energy Center opened in 1985. Budd Coates, a marathon runner who had joined the company in 1980 as fitness director, set up programs for employees to exercise at work. And Rodale began to field strong running teams in competitions such as the Manufacturers Hanover Corporate Challenge.

Much as J.I. had devoted himself to writing plays while remaining an important influence at Rodale in the 1960s, Bob Rodale in the 1980s began to develop his own theories about agriculture—ones that would be applied to other areas of the economy and society, and ultimately to the company he had built. But as he did, he remained a hard-nosed businessman. He didn't hesitate, for example, to shut down *Spring.* "Bob was very keen that the core businesses had to throw off enough profit for him to do the new things that he wanted to do," said Pat Corpora, who joined Rodale in 1980 as a project accountant.

1983
January: Rodale implements a smoking ban.

February: The People's Medical Society is formed in Emmaus, based in Health House and led by Charles Inlander.

February 7: Iran invades Iraq.

February 28: The final episode of *M*A*S*H* is watched by more than 125 million Americans.

Partial cast of *M*A*S*H*

Ninth in a series.

Beyond the bottom line.

It's that time of year again.

The voice of the Annual Report is heard in the land.

Scrupulously shepherded by accountants and lawyers, America's business executives in the coming weeks will

But what is likely to happen in future years, as the next generation of oil executives strives to maintain the same high levels of financial health?

The typical annual report isn't much concerned with looking that far

Sixth in a series.

The losing of America.

The United States will lose 26 square miles of its land today.

It will lose another 26 square miles tomorrow, and every day this year.

But not to a foreign power.

We are giving up our land to the ravenous demands of an unrealistic food system. And, before you turn the page, telling youself that land loss is someone else's problem — too remote, too big for you — *it isn't.*

You *can* help to face this dilemma. And help yourself, too.

If you know these facts:

Each time an Iowa farmer grows one pound of corn for you and us, he uses up five to six pounds of topsoil. And in the wheatlands, for each pound harvested, up to 20 pounds of soil disappear — never again to be available for growing food.

In 1980 — and again in 1981 — three million acres of farmlands will be lost to erosion. Five billion tons of topsoil are displaced annually — enough to cover all five boroughs of New York City with a 13½-foot-deep layer of soil.

And while this is going on, each year, another three million acres of agricultural land are lost to development: new homes, factories, and other structures.

Let's concede those three million acres to the requirements of "progress."

But why is it that, in the areas still being farmed, we're eating up more land than food?

Because today's food producers are "burning up" the soil with chemicals in order to maintain high yields. Because, when they over-use chemicals, the soil becomes more vulnerable to wind and water erosion. Because the ways of commerce are now overruling the wisdom of crop rotation. And because modern tractors don't permit the strip cropping and contour plowing that are most effective for preventing erosion.

Man-made blights, these. Symptoms of a food system that is dangerously out of touch with our new world of limited resources. A food system that is headed for disaster, unless we do something about it.

That's not easy to believe. Not with our bumper harvests almost every year, and our grain-clogged warehouses.

But the danger signals are inescapable: We have already lost half of our land. Each day, the U.S. population increases by 5,000 people while the farmlands shrink. And prices soar, because the food system needs more and more expensive energy to operate.

Is there still time? We believe there is.

America *can* produce food at less cost to the consumer, and to the environment. The nation's citizens *don't* have to pay for food today with fertile soil they'll need tomorrow.

That's why we launched *The Cornucopia Project* — a concentrated effort to collect information about the ways the U.S. food system must be restructured to prevent a food crisis.

The information we've already assembled could be of great importance to you, personally, and we'd be pleased to share it. No cost or obligation, of course. Just write: Robert Rodale, Rodale Press, 33 E. Minor St., Emmaus, PA 18049.

RODALE PRESS, INC.
Emmaus, PA 18049

Rodale publishes: *Prevention, Rodale's New Shelter, Organic Gardening, Bicycling, Executive Fitness Newsletter, New Farm,* and *Theatre Crafts,* as well as hardcover and paperback books under the Rodale Books imprint.

Rodale drew attention to the inefficiencies of the U.S. food production system in these *New York Times* op-ed pages.

In the early 1980s, Bob spearheaded the Cornucopia Project, an effort to systematically study the U.S. food production system and provide consumers with information on the true costs of food. Rodale ran its findings in a series of advertisements on the *New York Times* op-ed page, which were part educational effort and part brand-building exercise. One ad noted that transporting 24,000 tons of broccoli from the West Coast to New York consumed $6 million and 950,000 gallons of fossil fuel. In 1981, Rodale called a summit on the Cornucopia Project and began publishing a newsletter on its efforts.

Along with an interest in health and organic agriculture, Bob had inherited J.I.'s interest in searching for systems that could improve life. In the 1970s and 1980s, many activists and experts began to speak of sustainable agriculture. But Bob felt the word *sustainable* was too neutral, almost stagnant. "I felt that there was a larger concept waiting to be discovered that would take sustainable one step further–to encompass that missing sense of growth and improvement," he said. His understanding of farms and the human body–gleaned from decades working on *OG* and *Prevention*–taught him that organisms and other types of living systems could be strengthened and revitalized based on their own internal resources.

These insights became the basis for a theory of management Bob called regeneration, defined broadly as "a method of producing ideas and products that systematically makes more efficient use of all available inputs and resources and that continually improves both the resource base and the people involved in that process." Regeneration was first applied to agriculture at the farm research center. In 1982, *The New Farm* magazine, which had lost money for four straight years, was removed from under the aegis of Rodale Press and began to be published by the Soil and Health Foundation, which was renamed the Regenerative Agriculture Association. Starting with the November/December 1982 issue, the magazine was subtitled "The Magazine of Regenerative Agriculture." But in the 1980s, regeneration would be fleshed out in many areas at Rodale, influencing the way employees were trained, the content of the magazines, and the way people spoke.

THE CORNUCOPIA PROJECT
Working toward a safer, more secure and affordable food system in America

June 18: Sally Ride becomes first American woman in space on the space shuttle *Challenger.*

Bob Rodale leads delegation to Tanzania.

Sally Ride

Rodale launches *Prevention* Total Health System continuity series.

***Spring* is discontinued.**

Rodale Press clambakes provided fun, creative outlets for employees in the 1980s.

ARDIE-GRAS

MARSHALL ACKERMAN

ORB

Bob always made time to talk with visiting scientists and international dignitaries at the Rodale Research Center.

In a neat illustration of the circularity of great ideas, organic farming—which had come to Emmaus from the Third World, via Sir Albert Howard's description of his work in India—began to find a new audience in the developing world. David Miller, the newly appointed U.S. ambassador to Tanzania, took *The Complete Book of Composting,* and the volume found its way to the assistant to Tanzanian president Julius K. Nyerere. Intrigued, Nyerere invited a delegation from Rodale to visit. So in the spring of 1983, Bob led a group of five experts to conduct a workshop on "Resource-Efficient Farming Methods for Tanzania." For Bob, it was both recognition of the universal applicability of the organic message and a validation of ideas he and his father had been promoting for 40 years. "I get chance to make a brief speech," he wrote in a terse description of the trip. "Choke up slightly when talking about historical significance of a whole country being on the verge of endorsing organic methods—think of J.I.'s struggles against ridicule and statements about how many people would starve if the world 'went organic.' Now we see that the poorest countries have to go organic to be able to eat."

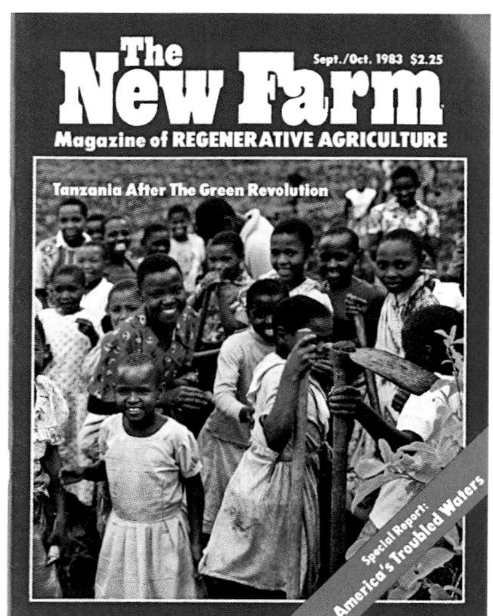

Bob and colleagues were invited to present a workshop on sustainable agriculture in Tanzania.

Twelve years after J.I.'s death, Bob still had a very strong sense of carrying on his father's work. In 1984, he wrote a column in *OG* entitled "What Would J. I. Rodale Say?" Bob took an inventory of the impressive array of activities at the Rodale Research Center—as the farm was now known—the test plots, amaranth collection, solar greenhouse, labs, and fishponds, and the presence of a soil scientist sent by the U.S. Department of Agriculture. "I think I can indeed hear what J. I. Rodale would say," Bob mused. "'I told you all this was going to happen.' Then his voice in my head trails off. I can't hear the words, but I get the message. And the message is, get back to work. There's plenty more to do."

As Bob Rodale saw it, Rodale didn't exist simply to make money by publishing books and magazines. Rather, its purpose was to sustain a long-term commitment to large ideas. "A family is more than just a chain of genes that goes from one generation to the next; it's also a heritage of ideas," he said. "You inherit ideas from your ancestors and add something to those ideas as you preserve their essence, interpreting them for your generation." For the five Rodale children of the third generation, these ideas and the company were part of their upbringing. From a young age,

Bob, with soil scientist William Liebhardt, PhD, who accompanied Bob and others to Tanzania in 1983.

In spite of being immersed in his work, Bob enjoyed spending time with his grandchildren.

all five of Bob and Ardie's children worked on the farm and at the company, and they witnessed first-hand the passion that the organic cause instilled. "Visitors would come in and say, 'This was my pilgrimage. I traveled across the country or from another part of the world to come and visit this farm,'" said Anthony Rodale.

Bob Rodale gave lots of thought to management and a great deal of thought to his family. But he didn't think systematically about managing a multigenerational family business. "Dad was very inspiring, but not very communicative about directing us," said Maria Rodale. "We had to kind of learn by watching." Bob had become an indispensable partner to his father at the age of 19. But with a cadre of executives, hundreds of employees, and a corporate structure with clear lines of authority and division of labor, Bob didn't need his children to work in the publishing operations the way J.I. had needed him. "He liked having his own space and things that we weren't involved in," said Heidi Rodale. And for the Rodale children of the third generation, particularly the younger ones, growing up as members of the family of the largest employer in a small town brought certain pressures. "Every one of us in the family has said at one time or another, 'I've got to get out of this place, I don't want anything to do with this!'" said Anthony. Both Maria and Anthony left to attend high school at Lawrence Academy in Massachusetts. But they also were aware that Rodale offered them opportunities. Maria returned to the Emmaus area after high school. In 1981, she gave birth to a daughter, Maya, and, while raising her as a single mother, enrolled at Muhlenberg College in Allentown.

To further complicate matters, although Ardie had carved out a prominent role for herself as director of facilities, Rodale in the 1980s remained largely a male-dominated company. In the 1970s and 1980s, there simply wasn't the expectation that Bob and Ardie's first two children, daughters Heather and Heidi, would pursue full-time careers at the company. Heather, the eldest, worked as a teacher after graduating from Lehigh, married Tom Stoneback in 1975, and was raising their four children while Tom rose through the Rodale ranks. Heidi, who had attended Carnegie-Mellon University and studied art, married Charlie Norelli, a doctor who had also grown up in Emmaus. She worked full-time in the book division and edited newsletters.

1984
January 1: Telephone monopoly AT&T is broken up into 22 independent units.

January 22: The Apple Macintosh is introduced.

Early Apple computer

February 8: 1984 Winter Olympics opens in Sarajevo.

Summer: The pilot issue of *Men's Health* newsletter is published.

Kraft buys Celestial Seasonings.

November 6: Ronald Reagan defeats Walter Mondale in U.S. presidential election.

The first *Prevention* Index appears.

Initially, Bob had assumed that David, his third child and eldest son, would naturally want to go into the family business and ultimately succeed him—just as he had done. But David had different interests. He studied music, art, and drama at Ithaca College, in London, and at Lehigh before moving to New York. In the late 1970s, he returned to Emmaus and worked as artistic director at the J. I. Rodale Theater. "Bob never, ever thought of doing anything but following in his father's footsteps," said Ardie. "Bob had a very, very hard time with David because he couldn't understand why David wouldn't follow in his footsteps."

Rodale's magazines had taken a hit from the recession and the failure of *Spring*. But the company began to regenerate itself by making more out of a long-overlooked resource: the book division. From the outset, book publishing at Rodale had always been smaller than and subordinate to magazines. In the 1950s and 1960s, aside from successes like *Health Finder*, the book business was generally a vanity business for J. I. Rodale. In the 1970s, the main focus had been to produce books for the *Organic Gardening* and *Prevention* book clubs. "When I arrived, the book division was at the end of a long hall at Rodale Press," said Rich Huttner, who joined the company as publisher of the book division in 1981. "It was considered an addendum to the Press." And while books were a significant business—about $29 million in sales in 1982—they didn't provide steady profits. Production was divided largely between health books and gardening and craft publications, the latter of which were photo-intensive and hence more expensive than all-text books.

The Prevention Total Health System launched in the fall of 1983.

A consultant brought in in the early 1980s suggested that Rodale not invest further in the book division because it had exhausted its subject matter. Fortunately, Rodale ignored the advice. Rather than seek out single ideas generated by the research division or the magazines, it decided to build a series of books around *Prevention*'s collected wisdom on interrelated topics such as exercise, diet, disease prevention, and natural foods. Under the guidance of executive editor Bill Gottlieb, Rodale in late 1982 conceived and tested the *Prevention* Total Health

BODY BULLETIN™

Bringing you the latest "feel better" news

April 1981

The New and Smarter Way To Exercise: The Easier the Better!

Set out to do *any* job as fast as you can and chances are you'll make a mess of it. We all know that but somehow forget it when we decide to become fit. And what we make a mess of is our bodies. A week after starting, we ache all over. Worse, we make a mess of all our good intentions when we call it quits.

Many of us have had that experience, but maybe it isn't our fault. We remember our high-school gym teacher, talking about "no pain, no gain" and yelling at us if we cheated a little bit doing calisthenics. Or maybe we've been overwhelmed by all this talk about "aerobics," and feel that the only way to travel the road to fitness is at a gallop.

Today, happily, there is a much better and more effective way to become fit. The easy way.

Take jogging, for instance. The average jogger feels that if you don't run at least five miles a day, and always strive to increase that distance, you'll miss the health magic jogging is supposed to deliver.

Truth is, new scientific research reveals, you can do just as muc
good for your heart and circulatio
by walking at a good clip as y
can by jogging. How *much* wa
ing? No more than about an h
or so a day, maybe half in the mo
ing, half in the evening. Eve
brisk 45-minute walk at luncht
will give you those same he
goodies joggers are huffing
puffing after. What walking
give you is shin splints, knee
and all the other problems so
joggers seem to develop.

Here's another example—s
The strict way most of u
taught to do them is jus
crazy. Today, fitness coac
vise doing sit-ups with you
fully bent. And one coach w
who specializes in training
people, not fitness nuts.
encourages his stude
"Use your elbows,
hands, to help do thos
advises. If your fitne
calls for any deep
cheat by holding on
of chairbacks for add
And be sure to quit be
any real pain. Pain

Diet Pills: What's the Truth?

Open most any women's magazine and you see the ads.

"The pill to end all diet pills!" they say. "Now you can eat more and weigh less! Shed 10, 20 or 50 pounds—the easy way!"

Sounds too good to be true, doesn't it?

That's ... it's mostly lies.

diet pills can make you seriously sick.

In a recent study done at the University of Melbourne, in Australia, it took only one pill to raise blood pressure to dangerously high levels in a third of the people tested, while others suffered from dizziness, headache, chest tightness ... nausea. And that was with a

May 1981
Volume 10, Number 2

The local supermarket can be a gold mine for natural food shoppers. Read on, as Executive Director Mark Schwartz tells you how to return from the supermarket with a plentiful supply of natural, wholesome foods.

page 3

Plant some lettuce seed and help improve the quality of food on tables across the country. The coated lettuce seed ...

A New Symbolism for Soil

Robert Rodale

Soil is basic. It is the skin of life stretching over almost all the land areas of the globe. In that thin layer are the minerals we need to live. Calcium, magnesium, zinc, chromium, strontium, copper and all the others are there. Plants slowly extract those minerals from the earth and present them to us graciously and healthfully in our food.

Unfortunately ...

20 years—topsoil that takes from 300 to 2,000 years to replace.

Each time an Iowa farmer grows one pound of corn, he uses up five to six pounds of topsoil. And in the wheatlands, for each pound of wheat harvested up to 20 pounds of soil disappear—never again to be availabl[e] for growing food ...

VOL. 1, NO. 1

THE RODALE REPORT

NOVE...

Good Ideas for Your Life and Business from Rodale Press

How to Run Two Miles in a Motel Room

by PORTER SHIMER
From *Fitness Through Pleasure*, Publication date: October, 1982

It's one of those trips you can't stand: too long to avoid the overnight stay, too short to bother booking truly "accommodating" accommodations. Needing to clear your head after a less than perfect flight, you ask the desk clerk about the exercise facilities.

"The what?"

You kick yourself for not packing your running shoes, and return to your room ... and to a TV that blinks.

Do not at this point head for the cocktail lounge. You can get a very good workout in a motel room.

Jumping jacks, sit-ups, push-ups, even chin-ups are possible (if the bar you hung your coat on is willing, and you don't mind bending your knees).

Start with jumping jacks. Five hundred may sound like a lot, but if you're in shape enough to be longing for a workout, you'll be through those 500 in about eight minutes, having burned about 100 calories (as many as you do jogging a mile) in the process. Because jumping jacks require you to spread your legs in a way that running does not, 500 of them could leave you a little sore. If you don't want to risk that, run in place for part of those eight minutes.

Next, some sit-ups. If you can manage to eke out 60 (at a rate of 20 per minute), chalk up 12 more calories.

Push-ups. A set of 30 (done in a minute) is worth seven calories.

Alternate these exercises, but keep moving. The idea is to keep your heart clicking along at about the same rate as you would jogging, cycling, swimming, walking, or whatever. (Side bends, toe touches, and/or some other light stretching can be a good way to catc[h] breath between exercise[s] push-ups or chin-ups tha[t] leave you puffing harder you're used to.)

If you can keep yourself ping along nonstop for abo[ut] minutes, you've gotten you a workout that's at least equivalent of a two-mile ru[n] and in the process you've go[t] to some muscle groups that j[og]ging doesn't.

Who knows—bounce arou[nd] enough and you might sha[ke] some sense into that TV.

Caloric Costs of Selected Calisthenics

	Rate of Exercise (completed sequences per minute)	Energy Cost (calories)
Push-ups	28	6.5
Sprinter's stretch	14	4.7
Sit-ups, hands behind head	20	4.0
Knee raises, supine position	14	3.3
Alternate leg raises, supine position	10	2.5
Alternate toe touch, sitting	14	1.4
Side bends	14	1.2

SOURCE: Adapted from *The Physical Fitness Encyclopedia*, by Charles T. Kuntzleman, Rodale Press.

Exercise: A Natural Tranquilizer

Last year, doctors wrote 50 million prescriptions for tranquilizers, those pills that turn your mind into a warm blanket. But while tranquilizers muffle anxiety (for a while, anyway), they can also put a damper on some things you'd rather keep alert, like your memory ... and your ability to react quickly. (A study shows that users of tranquilizers have more car accidents than nonusers.) To top it all off, even the mildest ones are addicting: You may actually have to go through a miserable withdrawal period if you take them regularly and want to stop. No, what we all need to cope with our anxieties—the worry, tension and frustration of modern living—is a *natural* tranquilizer, one that soothes without smothering.

A tranquilizer like exercise.

Did we say "exercise," the huff-and-puff action that seems anything but calm? True, you may not feel more relaxed *during* a jog or a swim. But researchers at the University of Florida found that only 10 percent of a group of people who exercised regularly (at least 15 minutes a day of brisk walking or jogging) had anxiety, compared to over 40 percent in a group of nonexercisers. What's more, the exercise group had 50 percent fewer medical problems. "Lack of exercise," the researchers say, "is associated with anxiety and numerous medical problems."

So the next time you feel upset, get set—and go exercise.

From *Body Bulletin*, October, 1982.

RODALE'S

health·bulletin®

August 7, 1971
Vol. 9 No. 16

Robert Rodale Publisher **Harald J. Taub** Editor **John Feltman** Managing Editor
Contributors: Joan Jennings, Jane Kinderlehrer, Rich Meislin, Ray Wolf

VITAMIN C STUDY BACKS UP PAULING

Medical literature is full of reports that vitamin C helps protect against infection. But how? A research team from Bowman Gray School of Medicine in Winston-Salem, N.C., has proposed that the process by which specialized blood cells called leukocytes engulf and kill invading bacteria may be stimulated by the vitamin. If their theory proves to be correct, it will, in their opinion, "do much to vindicate the name of Linus Pauling (Nobel Laureate author of the best-selling *Vitamin C and the Common Cold*) in medical circles."

Drs. Lawrence DeChatelet, Charles McCall and M. Robert Cooper, in a paper recently presented to the American Society of Biological Chemists in San Francisco, reported that while the process by which foreign microorganisms are destroyed by the body's natural defenses is known to involve increased oxygen consumption, a rise in hydrogen peroxide production and increased hexose monophosphate shunt activity (a complicated chemical cycle), nobody has yet been able to explain *why* the reactions occur.

The trio believes that vitamin C is the answer. Studies still in progress reveal that the addition of ascorbic acid (vitamin C) to leukocytes taken from victims of granulomatous disease—a rare ailment in which leukocytes fail to repel infection—resulted in a "dramatic" increase in shunt activity, which must take place if any bacteria are to be killed. Apparently the vitamin is somehow involved in the actual killing of invading microorganisms, Dr. DeChatelet told *Health Bulletin*. The observation that ascorbic acid can spark shunt activity, he noted, "suggests a therapeutic potential for this vitamin."

NO PORK IN "PORK AND BEANS"?

Housewives who have opened a can of pork and beans only to be perplexed by not finding any meat now have a reasonable explanation: There is very little, or none at all.

A study announced July 21 by the New York City Department of Consumer Affairs has shown that the amount of pork in a pork and beans mixture ranges from a modest 7% down to nothing. "In the department's analysis," an agency statement said, "it was found that half of the cans of the 10 brands tested contained 1% or less of pork. One brand, 'Campbell's Home Style Pork and Beans,' contained no pork at all. None of the cans tested had more than 7% pork."

Bess Myerson, the city's Commissioner of Consumer Affairs, said the results were sent to the U.S. Department of Agriculture, but "a spokesman replied with a lot of double talk about why no action could be taken." She added, "Not one of the reasons cited was valid."

"Therefore," said Miss Myerson, "we are now asking the FDA to help us put an end to this fraudulent practice. If the USDA will not regulate the content of so-called 'pork and beans,' the FDA should require the product to be relabeled so that consumers will be able to tell exactly what is inside the can."

Naturally, the Campbell Soup Company was upset by the claim there was no pork in their product, and issued a statement saying the products actually weigh in with "about 2% pork." There's just one catch: "The pork has been ground up and is not visible to the naked eye," a company spokesman said.

Perhaps in the future they could attach a magnifying glass to the side of their cans.

NOT ALL AMBULANCES SAVE LIVES

Thousands of Americans are losing their lives needlessly each year because there are too few ambulances, and those that are available are all too often poorly equipped and poorly staffed, according to Rep. Robert H. Mollohan (D-W. Va.). "Expert consultants returning from combat in South Vietnam have publicly asserted that, if seriously wounded, their chances for survival would be better in the zone of combat than on the average city street or highway here in this country," he told his colleagues on Capitol Hill July 19. Particularly in rural areas, the local ambulance in many cases is nothing more than a hearse operated by an undertaker.

"Of the 450,000 to 475,000 heart attack victims last year, 275,000 died en route to a hospital, but an estimated 35,000 of them could have been saved by prompt ambulance service with qualified personnel," he said. "Of the 55,000 traffic accident victims last year, 40,000 to 43,000 died en route to a hospital – and over half of them within the first critical hour after injury – but, with prompt and professional ambulance service, an estimated 12,000 could be saved."

To correct the situation, Mollohan introduced a bill to amend the Highway Safety Act of 1966. The legislation would require that every state upgrade its emergency services through the licensing of ambulances and personnel within one year of enactment. What does he think is needed? More ambulances, equipped with up-to-date life-support equipment, staffed by trained attendants, and hooked into central dispatching systems. As he put it, "We have all heard of traffic victims bleeding to death along our highways waiting for an ambulance that never comes, or comes too late; but what few realize is that it might be better if some so-called ambulances never come at all, for, in most states, a station wagon with an army cot in the back, driven by a garage mechanic, is called an ambulance."

MICROWAVE OVENS—SEALED LIKE A SIEVE

Many microwave ovens in home use are so poorly sealed against radiation leakage that they might as well be operated with open doors—the housewife is getting at least half as much dangerous radiation as she would with the door wide open! Such was the startling report of the U.S. Public Health Service released July 23.

After testing 5,000 household microwave ovens in 25

EXECUTIVE FITNESS

A RODALE PRESS PUBLICATION

What Light Weights Add To Your Fitness Routines

How to use extra pounds safely to improve your exercise results.

Weighted Walks and Runs

A RODALE PRESS PUBLICATION

WOMEN'S HEALTH

December 1983

Volume 1 Number 1

Part 1 of a Series

Taking Charge of Your Health

by Cathy Perlmutter

Volume 4, Number 1

January, 1988

Men's Health

A RODALE PRESS PUBLICATION

Fat Is Made, Not Born

9 Sex Secrets Women Wish We Knew

Newsletters—easy to start and stop—became the proving ground for new Rodale ideas.

System continuity series—a set of 15 books, each about 176 pages and in full color, that would mimic the highly successful Time-Life series.

The book division also took steps to modernize its business practices. Pat Corpora, who joined the book division in 1984, pushed for Rodale to abandon its long-held practice of working on a cash basis—people had to send in money and then they would receive the books—rather than sending books out first and then asking people to pay if they wanted to keep them. And he immediately increased the postage and handling charge, which had been flat for several years. By 1985, a turnaround was under way. The book division's revenues rose sharply from $35 million in 1984 to $47.7 million in 1985, turning a $1.5 million loss into a $13 million profit.

In early 1985, Chuck McCullagh, editor-in-chief of *New Shelter* and editor and publisher of *Bicycling*, spoke of a "new enthusiasm and realism" and a "kind of cautious aggressiveness" at Rodale. The failure of *Spring* had an impact not just on the company's magazine business but also on its attitude toward new ventures. But rather than simply rely on *Prevention* and *Bicycling*, Rodale began to roll out several new products on a smaller scale. The company had long had success publishing newsletters containing brief articles—frequently material recycled from or into the magazines—such as *Executive Fitness*. And so newsletters quickly emerged in the mid-1980s as a vehicle for testing expansion efforts. "Newsletters are easy to start, can be stopped without great expense, and are a good test for ideas," said Kim MacLeod, director of new ventures. *Spring* was essentially downsized into a newsletter, *Women's Health*. *Bicycling* introduced *Bicycling Touring* as a newsletter, and *Fitness Vacations*, an eight-page quarterly newsletter, grew out of a column in *Prevention*.

In late 1984, planning began for a newsletter aimed at what Rodale hoped would be a new audience for its health message: male baby boomers. Rodale knew from its experience publishing *Prevention* that most health publications were pitched toward women. But the company reasoned that young men, as they aged, would start to worry about their health. In the summer of 1984, a pilot issue of *Men's Health*, an eight-page newsletter that addresses "health challenges that are

Special publications were another way Rodale tested new ideas and concepts in the mid-1980s.

uniquely male," from male sexuality to stress disorders, brought a healthy response for 3,800 subscriptions. The first issue came out in January 1985. And by the summer of 1986, *Men's Health* had attracted 40,000 subscribers.

At about the same time, Rodale began to develop a second low-risk means of packaging information in magazine form. The specials department was formed, under publisher Mike Perlis, to produce "onetime, single-topic magazines" on topics in which Rodale had already amassed significant content or experience. It was held up as an example of Bob Rodale's new management theory. "The regenerative role of Specials is a good fit at Rodale Press," Bob Teufel said. "It enables us to focus on our editorial strengths and marshall existing staff resources." The first special, which appeared in October 1985, was *Women's Health: A Guide to Self-Care*, a 96-page semiannual publication.

One-shots, sold through retail channels, allowed Rodale to test the potential acceptance of magazine concepts at the newsstand without having to commit substantial resources up front. In 1986, after its success as a newsletter, *Men's Health* was tested as a glossy one-shot. The magazine, officially entitled *Prevention Magazine's Guide to Men's Health*, addressed its audience directly. "You've realized that taking care of the physical machine is not something only for wimps, women or doctors; it's for anybody who wants to live as fully as it's possible to live." Put together under the direction of Stefan Bechtel, a writer for *Prevention*, and longtime *Prevention* editor Mark Bricklin, it included articles about good fats, drug-free blood pressure control, friendship, and the Great Condom Test of 1986. The first issue was a huge success, selling over 40 percent of the copies at the newsstand.

A third unit—custom publishing—was formed to create low-risk print ventures. With its reputation for quality information about health and fitness and a vast reservoir of research, writing talent, and material, Rodale believed it could leverage its brand to create publications for companies and organizations. It produced a publication about AIDS for General Motors, a magazine sponsored by Reebok for high school coaches, and a magazine for the Boston Marathon.

The company also began, cautiously, to launch new magazines. *Superfit*, a magazine about high-performance athletics, debuted in the spring of 1985 as a quarterly, for example. *Superfit*

1985
March 4: U.S. Food and Drug Administration approves a blood test for AIDS.

March 11: Mikhail Gorbachev becomes leader of the Soviet Union.

Mikhail Gorbachev

May 8: Coca-Cola introduces the New Coke.

September 22: Farm Aid concert held in Champagne, Illinois, attracts 20 million viewers and raises approximately $10 million.

Rodale's new Energy Center opens.

Farm Aid concert

Superfit magazine was introduced as a quarterly publication in 1985.

signaled an intention to invest more resources in recreation and fitness. And with the success of the acquisition of *Bicycling*, Rodale began to look for other opportunities. One surfaced in 1985, when Rodale purchased *Runner's World* magazine and *Cross-Country Skier*. Both were seen as complementary to *Bicycling*. Together, the fitness-oriented magazines would become the platform for the Rodale Active Sports Group.

Long-standing titles were renovated or regenerated. With the energy conservation wave having crested, *New Shelter* shifted to focus on home improvement. In September 1986, with a circulation of about 700,000, it became *Practical Homeowner*. In August 1985, *Organic Gardening* changed its name to *Rodale's Organic Gardening*. Under the direction of editorial director Stevie Daniels, who had taken over when Lee Goldman suffered a stroke in January 1985, it underwent an internal redesign. As *OG* approached its 50th anniversary, Bob Rodale said, it "has begun the process of regeneration and will be ready to face the future with freshness and vitality."

Meanwhile, *Prevention* was extending its brand. In March of 1983, Bob had posed a question including "How are we, as a nation, doing in preventing disease and promoting health?" That set off an effort by *Prevention* to quantify the state of American health. Rodale formed the Prevention Research Center and commissioned Louis Harris and Associates to devise questions and conduct surveys on 21 factors: Were people taking steps to control stress and avoid home accidents, wearing seat belts, trying to restrict fat intake, and installing smoke detectors? The first *Prevention* Index appeared in July 1984, giving Americans a score of 61.5 on a 0-to-100 scale. "We're not getting a passing grade in creation of health," Bob wrote. "But we can improve." The Index became an annual feature and another means of projecting the *Prevention* name further into public consciousness.

As the company recovered, the third generation of Rodales began to find their way into positions. In 1985, Heidi Rodale became an editor at *Prevention*. Maria, a student at Muhlenberg College, worked at various positions in the company. In the mid-1980s, David Rodale worked in a series of jobs at *New Shelter* and helped to create the *Regeneration* newsletter. As one of the founding members of the International Electronic Networking Association, David was involved in early

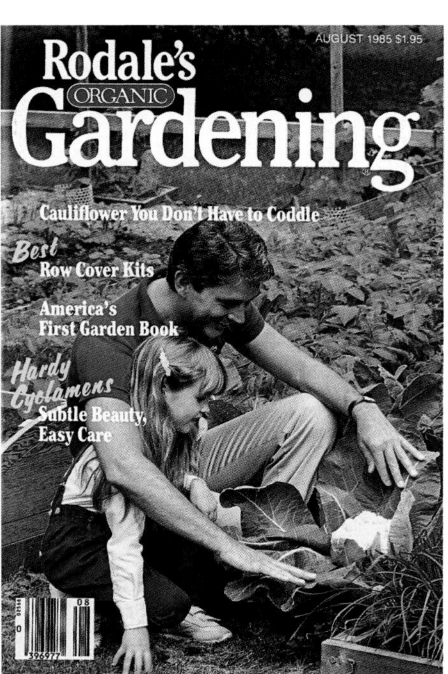

In the spirit of regeneration, *Organic Gardening* was redesigned and got a new name.

Rodale purchases *Runner's World*.

***Prevention* launches in Australia.**

October: Rodale Research Center hosts government representatives from Mali, Senegal, Togo, and Niger.

Rodale's library staff produces the *Vitamin A+ Sieve* newsletter.

THE VITAMIN A+ SIEVE

***New Shelter* is named one of the 10 hottest magazines of 1985 by *AdWeek*.**

November 14: The Center for Science in the Public Interest indicts fast food chains for deep-frying in beef fat rather than oils lower in saturated fats.

December 23: David Rodale dies.

Organic Foods Production Association of North America is formed.

U.S. life expectancy raises to 78.2 for women and 70.9 for men.

Along with *Bicycling*, *Runner's World* and *Cross-Country Skier* would form the Rodale Active Sports Group.

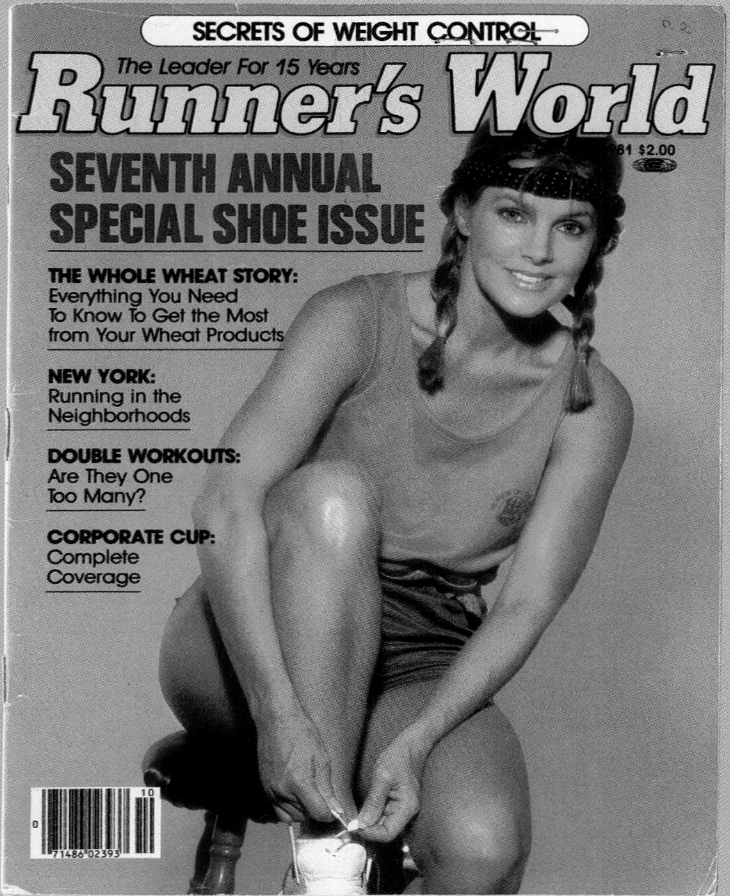

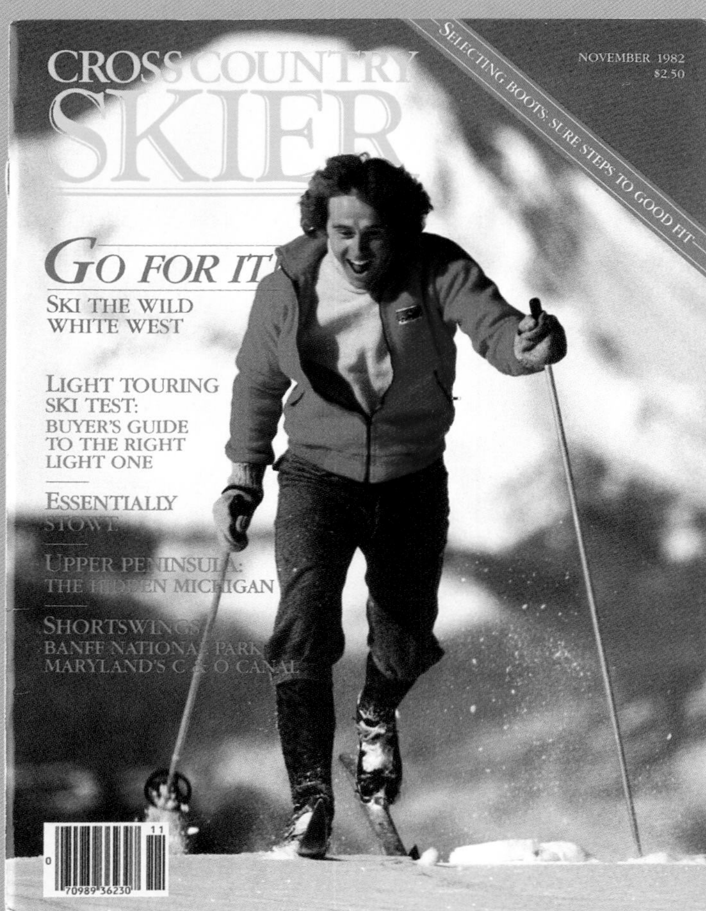

1986
January 20: First federal Martin Luther King Jr. holiday

Rodale launches *Children, for Today's Parent*.

March 20: *New England Journal of Medicine* study finds replacing dietary saturated fats with olive oil improves health.

July 5: The Statue of Liberty is reopened to the public after renovation.

Statue of Liberty

David Rodale

efforts to turn computers into communication tools. Several years before the advent of the networked office, David was working on creating a networking system for Rodale. But as David was settling in, tragedy struck. On December 16, 1985, just a few days after his 30th birthday, David was diagnosed with bronchitis. A few days later, when his condition hadn't improved, a specialist diagnosed pneumonia in both lungs. David was admitted to the hospital, and his condition began to deteriorate rapidly. On the 21st, David was officially diagnosed with AIDS. He died soon after, on December 23, 1985. For the extended Rodale family, it was a horrific and difficult experience. David's family had known for several years that he was gay. But in the early years of the AIDS epidemic, testing was not yet common and drugs that could forestall the illness had yet to be developed. As a result, many AIDS sufferers weren't diagnosed until their immune systems had already been fatally compromised.

David's premature and sudden death affected the lives of his family members in different ways. In the months after, Ardie found her voice as a writer. She wrote a heartfelt and moving memoir, *Climbing Toward the Light*, which was published in 1987, and became active in the fields of AIDS education and awareness. At a time when few women spoke publicly about the ravages of AIDS, Ardie traveled the country to deliver a poignant message of urgency and uplift. "Basically, what I did was tell a mom's story to help people understand and to help them take care themselves," she said. It also had the effect of pulling the family closer together in many ways. Bob Rodale rarely wrote or spoke about how his son's death affected him, but it clearly did. "It wasn't until after my brother died that we really were brought into the business more," said Heidi Rodale. "He kind of realized there was some benefit to teaching us." Family members began to take courses at a family business program at the Wharton School at the University of Pennsylvania, and the third generation began to commit more time to the company. With her children in school, Heather came to work on human resources issues. "I realized that what I liked to do could fit in at the Press," she said. After graduating from Muhlenberg in 1985, Maria worked at a public relations firm in Washington. But when her daughter was about to start kindergarten in 1986, Maria returned to Emmaus. She worked on the *Regeneration*

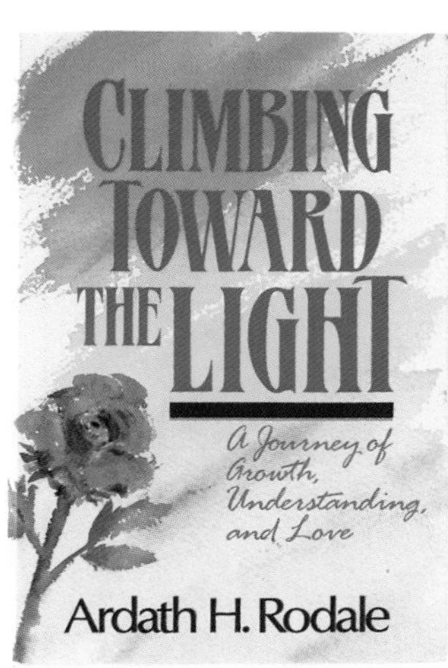

Ardie channeled her grief into writing her first book, a memoir, *Climbing Toward the Light*.

July: Greg Lemond becomes the first American to win the Tour de France.

September: *New Shelter* becomes *Practical Homeowner*.

October 11: Presidents Reagan and Gorbachev hold nuclear summit in Reykjavik, Iceland.

Greg Lemond

November 4: National Academy of Sciences calls secondhand smoke a real health risk for children and adults.

November 28: *Journal of the American Medical Association* study finds four out of five that middle-aged American males have unhealthy levels of cholesterol, which increases the risk of death from heart disease.

Rodale publishes Dave Barry's *Claw Your Way to the Top*.

Scientists discover a hole in the ozone layer over the Antarctic.

The Organic Foods Productions Association publishes a set of voluntary guidelines for the organic food industry.

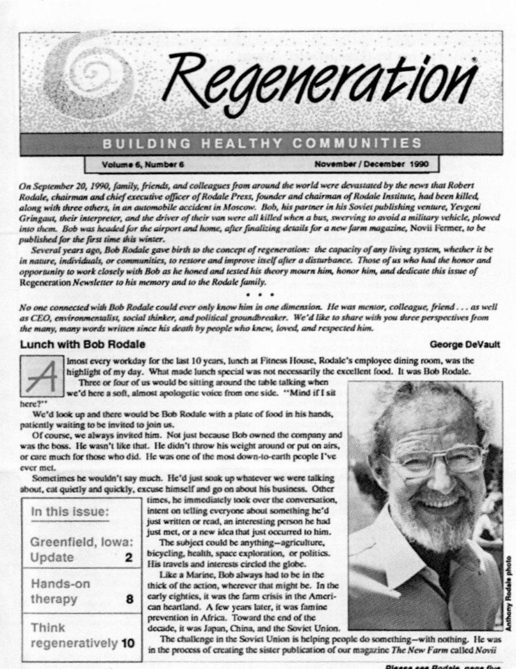

Regeneration

BUILDING HEALTHY COMMUNITIES

Volume 6, Number 6 November / December 1990

On September 20, 1990, family, friends, and colleagues from around the world were devastated by the news that Robert Rodale, chairman and chief executive officer of Rodale Press, founder and chairman of Rodale Institute, had been killed, along with three others, in an automobile accident in Moscow. Bob, his partner in his Soviet publishing venture, Yevgeni Gringaut, their interpreter, and the driver of their van were all killed when a bus, swerving to avoid a military vehicle, plowed into them. Bob was headed for the airport and home, after finalizing details for a new farm magazine, Novii Fermer, *to be published for the first time this winter.*

Several years ago, Bob Rodale gave birth to the concept of regeneration: the capacity of any living system, whether it be in nature, individuals, or communities, to restore and improve itself after a disturbance. Those of us who had the honor and opportunity to work closely with Bob as he honed and tested his theory mourn him, honor him, and dedicate this issue of Regeneration *Newsletter to his memory and to the Rodale family.*

• • •

No one connected with Bob Rodale could ever only know him in one dimension. He was mentor, colleague, friend . . . as well as CEO, environmentalist, social thinker, and political groundbreaker. We'd like to share with you three perspectives from the many, many words written since his death by people who knew, loved, and respected him.

Lunch with Bob Rodale — George DeVault

Almost every workday for the last 10 years, lunch at Fitness House, Rodale's employee dining room, was the highlight of my day. What made lunch special was not necessarily the excellent food. It was Bob Rodale.

Three or four of us would be sitting around the table talking when we'd here a soft, almost apologetic voice from one side. "Mind if I sit here?"

We'd look up and there would be Bob Rodale with a plate of food in his hands, patiently waiting to be invited to join us.

Of course, we always invited him. Not just because Bob owned the company and was the boss. He wasn't like that. He didn't throw his weight around or put on airs, or care much for those who did. He was one of the most down-to-earth people I've ever met.

Sometimes he wouldn't say much. He'd just soak up whatever we were talking about, eat quietly and quickly, excuse himself and go on about his business. Other times, he immediately took over the conversation, intent on telling everyone about something he'd just written or read, an interesting person he had just met, or a new idea that just occurred to him.

The subject could be anything—agriculture, bicycling, health, space exploration, or politics. His travels and interests circled the globe.

Like a Marine, Bob always had to be in the thick of the action, wherever that might be. In the early eighties, it was the farm crisis in the American heartland. A few years later, it was famine prevention in Africa. Toward the end of the decade, it was Japan, China, and the Soviet Union.

The challenge in the Soviet Union is helping people do something—with nothing. He was in the process of creating the sister publication of our magazine *The New Farm* called *Novii*

Anthony Rodale photo

Please see Rodale, page five

The *Regeneration* newsletter became the mouthpiece of the Regeneration Project.

newsletter and soon after began to work in circulation on Rodale magazines. Anthony was studying photography at the Brooks Institute of Photography in California.

Bob also seemed to respond by redoubling his efforts on regeneration—as a more spiritual, comprehensive philosophy that extended far beyond agriculture. Now in his 50s, the more practical adjunct to J.I. was becoming more visionary. "My belief that we can find new islands of peace and renewal within our minds comes from my conviction that regeneration is the most powerful force of our earth itself," he wrote in *Prevention* in April 1986, just months after David's death. "There is something about this planet that makes it keep getting better and better."

Rodale had always sought to break down the walls that separate publishers from readers. And regeneration offered yet another way to do that. The Cornucopia Project was transformed into the Regeneration Project, looking beyond food to energy production, housing, and health care. "The purpose is to help communities and regions become more self-reliant, to regenerate them and their economies." This posture was a combination of the longtime ethos of *Prevention* and the more proactive ethos Bob had developed as an athlete and through his involvement with magazines like *Bicycling* and *Runner's World*. Health was about not getting sick, about being well. But fitness was really about the human capacity to live life to its fullest potential and to excel. "So I was starting to think, if a person is fit, can a city be fit, too?" Bob wrote in the *Regeneration* newsletter.

Greenfield, Iowa—an appropriately named town—presented an opportunity to put the regeneration philosophy writ large into practice. The county seat of Adair County had never recovered from the 1980s farm crisis and was losing both its population and its hope. In the fall of 1986, Bob Rodale spoke to a large gathering of residents at a community meeting and challenged the town to use its own resources to recover. In early February 1987, Rodale staffer Jeff Burcovitz encouraged residents to post a list of 110 good things about Greenfield and to list communal priorities. In short order, a People's Pages was compiled, a vacant gas station became a mini-park hosting ice cream socials, and plans were made to create a museum and other economic development projects.

The connection between information, proactive action, and self-empowerment was emerg-

1987
March 20: The FDA approves AZT as an anti-AIDS drug.

June 19: *Journal of the American Medical Association* article states that a cut in dietary cholesterol can benefit those with symptoms of coronary artery disease.

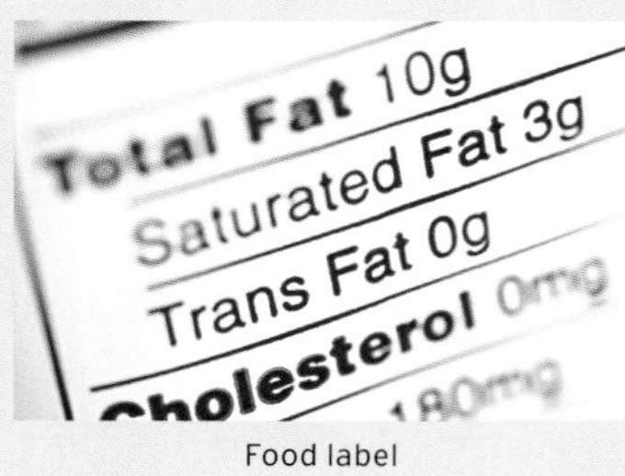

Food label

September 16: The United States joins other nations meeting in Montreal to agree on measures to protect the environment, including banning chlorofluorocarbons, which deplete the earth's ozone layer.

Wild Oats grocery chain is founded with the purchase of Crystal Market, the only vegetarian natural foods store in Boulder, Colorado.

NASA scientists warn that rising levels of carbon dioxide created by the burning of petroleum are causing a potentially catastrophic global warming. The phenomenon is dubbed the "greenhouse effect."

October 19: Stock market crashes.

ing as the basis of regeneration and as the reformulated mission of Rodale. "People plus information equals individual power," Bob liked to say. The magazines and books would allow readers not simply to avoid disease and grow food chemical free, but to "run faster, to bike longer, to lose weight, to beat depression," he wrote. "We give people more control over their lives; help them to depend less on outside inputs and more on themselves."

Rodale executives at an offsite meeting in 1990: ***Back row:*** **Bob Rodale, John Haberern, Bob Teufel, Sandy Beldon, Tom Wolf, Bob Kazlik, Bill Gottlieb, Chuck McCullagh.** ***Front row:*** **Mark Bricklin, Tom Stoneback, John Griffin, Pat Corpora**

Increasingly in the late 1980s, Bob Rodale seemed eager to use his position, wealth, and moral authority to support causes near and far. In 1987, when Allentown was planning to sell some parkland for development, Bob created an organization, Friends of the Park, and launched commercials successfully opposing the development. He agreed to help lead a campaign for a local group that wanted to build an Olympic-size swimming pool near Cedar Crest College. He also helped rescue New York's St. Mark's Bookshop with a $250,000 loan.

And yet he remained an important influence at Rodale Press. In 1987, when Rodale bought *The Runner* from CBS and began to fold it into *Runner's World*, the staffs of the two magazines were bickering over how to integrate the two magazines. After a while, Bob intervened. "He began speaking in his typically slow, understated manner, like a farmer leaning over the fence to chat with his neighbor," *Runner's World* editor Amby Burfoot recalled. "A magazine, he told us, is basically a group of people with a shared interest." And he asked them to think about how they could serve this community. After the combined magazine was relaunched, its circulation grew to 445,000.

The acquisition of *The Runner* was part of the broader push into recreation and fitness. In 1988, Rodale acquired *Backpacker* from Diamandis Communications, along with *Adventure Travel* and *Ski X-C*. But just as he had viewed *Bicycling* as a means of spreading a larger vision of the importance and symbolism of the bicycle in the 1970s, Bob believed running could be about more than simply keeping fit. *Runner's World* publisher George Hirsch recalled meeting with Bob and Amby Burfoot the morning of the Boston Marathon in 1988. "We talked about how running could serve as a motivating force for those who needed to beat a drug or alcohol addiction, lose weight, [or]

December 15: Digging starts on the train tunnel under the British Channel.

Tom Wolfe publishes *The Bonfire of the Vanities*.

Rodale buys *The Runner* and merges it with *Runner's World*.

Rodale decides to accept beer and wine advertising in some magazines.

Rodale acquires *American Woodworker*.

What's Going On Here?, Rodale's internal monthly communications newsletter, chronicles the story of Rodale. Shown here are some examples of *WGOH* in the '80s.

all the news that fits

What's Going On Here?

DECEMBER 1980

Life fulfilled, through the eternal streams of consciousness, ever flowing in the greater worlds beyond.

"Making Clean Money"

"Can you make money without injury? Some people have, and have actually gotten rich at it. For example, we have the Rodale Press in Emmaus, PA"

– *Nicholas Von Hoffman, Syndicated Columnist*

"Hope for the World"

"Visitors leave Emmaus, PA. after a visit to Rodale Press with a feeling that there's hope for the world. One sees solid answers for reducing reliance on fossil fuel, on lowering cost of food...the firm, dedicated to ecology and environment is the ultimate in publishing experience."

– *FRIDAY REPORT (Newsletter)*

RODALE IN THE PRESS

J. I. Rodale's Son Leads Way in Energy C

Rodale advertising its old ways, and advertising for advertisers

Rodale reaches out for the mainstream

magazines

New Shelter builds on the nitty-gritty

The old

They're best as it starts a

During the first 6 months of 1980, Rodale Press magazines, books and research facilities were mentioned in over 300 separate stories in the nation's press. Total circulation of the newspapers and magazines which those stories appeared is approximately 100 million! Add to this, pick ups on radio programs and TV shows – which are more difficult to monitor than print media – and you will double the impressions made on the public.

Why does the media find us so interesting? Why are our editors and researchers invited to participate in radio and TV programs? Because there is a broadened national interest in health and survival and because of a long-overdue recognition that Rodale Press IS the leader in the drive to healthier, more self-reliant, environmentally-sane living!

But it hasn't happened without careful prodding from us.

For some time now, Rodale Press has conducted an educational campaign to acquaint media with Rodale concepts. On... been an in-house generated "Media Informati... to and trend material to the press based on m... books; material which the press uses regularly... listeners. This material is sent to newspapers,... shows, syndicated columnists and news servic... Recently we retained the services of one of t... lations firms, Carl Byoir, to help promote the...

During the past few months we launched a... to reach editors and writers with expertise an... media people who are both opinion makers a...

In coming issues of WGOH? we will keep y... in the media and clue you in on important ar... company and our publications.

OCTOBER 1984

RODALE PRESS

WHAT'S GOING ON HERE?

Sharon Burklund

Elizabeth Karsch, John Grosz and Joyce Carp

Susan Meskill Drumm and Anne Rothsc...

Greg Cross

NEW YORK NEW YORK

Bryce Lubbert

New York – nerve center of the advertising business where major decision-making is done. Headquarters for the general national advertiser.

So it's no wonder that ad sales reps for all four of our magazines have set up "shop" in the media center of the country.

Organization and keeping informed are two priorities ad sales reps abide by. There to help them do this is New York's support staff.

What started out for John Grosz to be a temporary position about a year ago, turned permanent when he found that being a receptionist freed him to pursue his interests. John is writing his first novel. He also studies and teaches metaphysics as well as does volunteer counseling for people stricken with Acquired Immune Defficiency Syndrome.

Elizabeth Karsch, secretary for *O.G.* sales reps left Zabar's, the gourmet food company, seven months ago to join Rodale Press. A resident of Brooklyn Heights, Elizabeth likes the exposure she's getting to the publishing business. She often sets up calls or goes along to assist Greg Cross and Deborah Gardiner with presentations.

Secretary to half of the *Prevention* staff, Mardi Herrick has been working for Rodale Press for three years. Helping with travel plans, reservations and answering inquiries, Mardi says she enjoys working for a company whose goals are in line with her beliefs. Serving the other half of the *Prevention* sales staff is administrative assistant, Martha Fletcher. Previously art director with Telephone Marketing Program, she refers to the Rodale office as "an oasis set apart from the impersonality of most New York city businesses."

Alison Fletcher turned down the offer three times before becoming secretary for *Prevention*. Now three years later she's office manager serving a staff of 15 people and their needs. She calls herself "resident mom." Actually she's a combination of office services/personnel and liaison between New York City and Emmaus.

Representing *Organic Gardening* in New York are Manager, NY Sales Office, Greg Cross and Ad Sales Rep, Deborah Gardiner, who also represents *New Shelter*.

In the ad sales business for 20 years, Greg joined Rodale Press after he disbanded his own ad sales firm. Charged with non-gardening accounts (automotive, food, kitchen appliances, etc.) Greg has to make them aware that *O.G.* readers are an excellent audience for their products.

"We've got to match the magazine to their needs. Everyone wants to know what's in it for them, so it's important to give a strong marketing background," said Greg. He views New York competition as an advantage. "Competition means there's a lot of action going on." And he means to be a part of that action.

Selling ad space for *Prevention* are Ad Sales Reps Susan Meskill Drumm, Larry Duke and Anne Gallagher. Currently on maternity leave is Eastern Ad Manager, Anne Rothschild.

Reared in the advertising industry, Susan Meskill Drumm regards ad sales as a service that's always a challenge and never boring. It's especially "interesting to look at a new product, how it sells and how it's marketed to a particular audience," she said. A long-time *Prevention* reader, this ad rep strongly believes in what Bob Rodale is trying to accomplish and her conviction carries into her work. Her major accounts are Nabisco, Chesebrough-Ponds and Lipton.

After work Susan volunteers 10 hours of her week to a hospice. She enjoys the volunteering because "it sets my mind to what's important."

Anne Gallagher originally joined Rodale Press to represent *Spring* magazine in May '83. Dealing with major accounts like AT&T, American Home Products, Colgate and Kal Kan, Anne enjoys the challen... dispelling preconceived notions people have about *Prevention*.

Originally from Illinois, Northeast advertis... manager for *Bicycling*, Sharon Burklund mov... hattan in 1971 with her husband Herbert and... Lisa.

In the publishing business for nine years, S... previously served as director of research for n... with Whitney Communication.

Sharon says visual presence is vital to sales... contact is fine but you like people to see you... face," she said. "It's the only way they reme... you. In New York you need to establish a co... presence, because you may be competing agai... dred other publishers." Presence yes - but on... there's something important to say, otherwis... note or a copy of the magazine provides the i... she's after.

Now two years with Rodale Press, manage... the New York sales office, Bryce Lubbart, alo... Deborah Gardiner, has the responsibility of b... into new advertising categories for *New Shelte...*

New categories might include any consume... product like American Express, Owens-Corni... motive or home computers. "Breaking into new categories is a slow process, because you're asking the account to look beyond the focus of the magazine to the readers interest or point of view," Bryce said. From the *New Shelter* standpoint, most consumer oriented products are hard to sell because there is no particular editorial advantage. So what Bryce has to do is educate the account about the readership.

Bryce enjoys giving presentations, formulating unique selling propositions. "I enjoy the public forum," Bryce admitted, "and the presentation is the most creative part of what we do."

Larry Duke | Martha Fletcher | Mardi Herrick | Alison Fletcher | Anne Gallagher | Deborah Gardiner

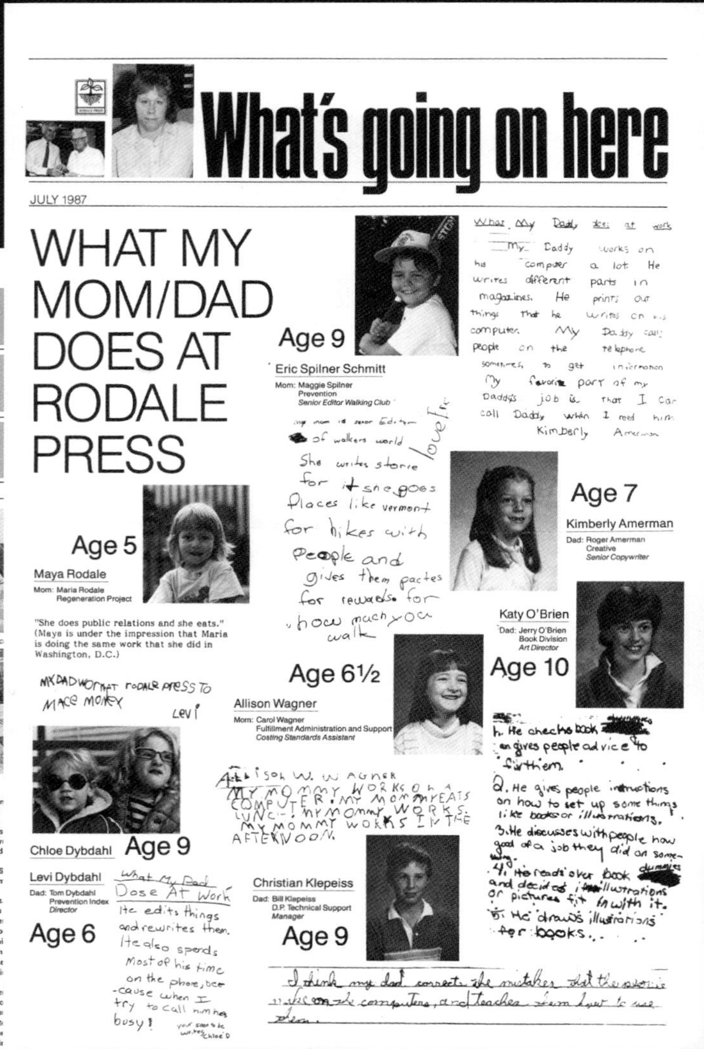

What's going on here

JULY 1987

WHAT MY MOM/DAD DOES AT RODALE PRESS

Age 9

Eric Spilner Schmitt

Mom: Maggie Spilner, Prevention, Senior Editor Walking Club

She writes stories for it she goes places like vermont for hikes with people and gives them pactes for rewords for how much you walk

Age 7

Kimberly Amerman

Dad: Roger Amerman, Creative, Senior Copywriter

What My Dad does at work

My Daddy works on the computer a lot. He writes different parts in magazines. He prints out things that he writes on his computer. My Daddy calls people on the telephone sometimes to get information. My favorite part of my Daddy's job is that I can call Daddy when I need him. Kimberly Amerman

Age 5

Maya Rodale

Mom: Maria Rodale, Regeneration Project

"She does public relations and she eats." (Maya is under the impression that Maria is doing the same work that she did in Washington, D.C.)

MY DAD WORKS AT RODALE PRESS TO MAKE MONEY

Levi

Age 10

Katy O'Brien

Dad: Jerry O'Brien, Book Division, Art Director

1. He checks book ... and gives people advice to fix them.
2. He gives people instructions on how to set up some things like books or illustrations.
3. He discusses with people how good of a job they did on something.
4. He reads over book ... and decides if illustrations or pictures fit in with it.
5. He draws illustrations for books.

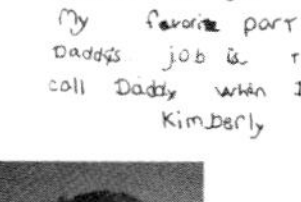

Age 6½

Allison Wagner

Mom: Carol Wagner, Fulfillment Administration and Support, Costing Standards Assistant

ALISON WAGNER
MY MOMMY WORKS ON A COMPUTER. MY MOMMY EATS LUNCH. MY MOMMY WORKS. MY MOMMY WORKS IN THE AFTERNOON.

Chloe Dybdahl

Age 9

Levi Dybdahl

Dad: Tom Dybdahl, Prevention Index, Director

Age 6

What My Dad Dose At Work

He edits things and rewrites them. He also spends most of his time on the phone, because when I try to call him he's busy!

Christian Klepeiss

Dad: Bill Klepeiss, D.P. Technical Support, Manager

Age 9

I think my dad corrects the mistakes that the people ... on the computers, and teaches them how to use them.

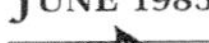

JUNE 1985

WHAT'S GOING ON HERE?

All Th

RODALE EXPA SPORTS MAGAZI

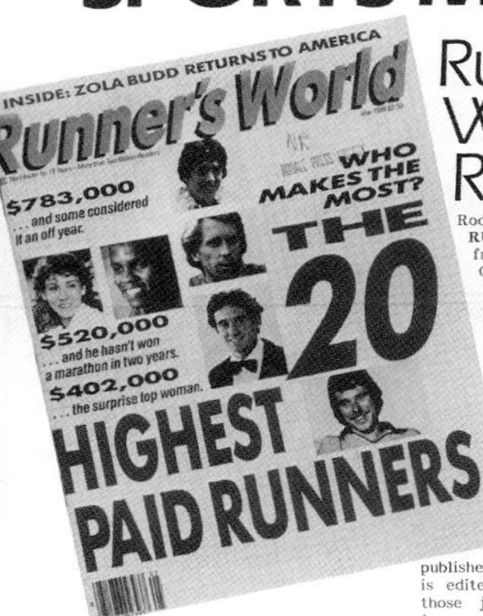

INSIDE: ZOLA BUDD RETURNS TO AMERICA
Runner's World
WHO MAKES THE MOST?
$783,000 ...and some considered it an off year.
THE 20
$520,000 ...and he hasn't won a marathon in two years.
$402,000 ...the surprise top woman.
HIGHEST PAID RUNNERS

Runner's World Races East

Rodale Press has purchased **RUNNER'S WORLD** magazine from the Runner's World Magazine Company in Mountain View, California. According to Bob Teufel, who made the announcement, "We bought **RUNNER'S WORLD** to round out our package of active sports magazines. It's a perfect complement to our **BICYCLING, CROSS COUNTRY SKIER,** and **SUPERFIT** magazines." Mike Perlis, currently publisher of magazine specials at Rodale, will be acting publisher of **RUNNER'S WORLD.** According to the publisher's profile, "**RUNNER'S WORLD** is edited for the mature runner, from those just beginning to discover the joys and benefits of running to veteran

Cross Country Skier Glides South

Rodale Press has acquired **CROSS COUNTRY SKIER** magazine from the Nordic Skico publishing company of Brattleboro, VT, announced President Bob Teufel.

CROSS COUNTRY SKIER is published five times a year, monthly from October through February. No change in frequency is planned at this time, Teufel said. It's current circulation is 35,000.

Rodale also bought the annual **NORDIC TRADE** from Nordic Skico. The advertising-supported trade publication is distributed free-of-charge at the national Ski Industries America Trade Show and regional trade shows each year.

CROSS COUNTRY SKIER is aimed toward the person who is or wants to become actively involved in the sport, explained Kim Mac Leod, director of Rodale's New Ventures Department. Cross-country skiing is compatible with Rodale's other sports-specialty magazine, **BICYCLING.** Many cyclists, in fact, cross-country ski during the winter months, Mac Leod said, as the two sports are both aerobic and use similar muscle groups. Cross-country skiing is popular among both young adults and families, she added.

Over a quarter of **CROSS COUNTRY SKIER**'s current circulation is in direct sales through sporting-goods stores. Rodale plans an even more aggressive drive in this area, Teufel said. Rodale will assume the subscription liabilities of Nordic Skico for **CROSS COUNTRY SKIER.**

The top positions will be filled on an interim basis by persons presently employed at Rodale. Chuck McCullagh, editor/publisher of **BICYCLING,** will be interim editor and publisher; Marcia Godelesky, advertising director of **BICYCLING,** will be ad director, and Peter Spiers, Project Analyst with New Ventures, will also serve as circulation manager for the magazine.

Several members of the present editorial staff will continue with the magazine. **CROSS COUNTRY SKIER** moved to Emmaus in early April.

What's going on here

OCTOBER 1985

ALL THE NEWS THAT FITS

A Diary of a Publisher in Africa

ADDIS

NAIROBI

ZIMBABWE

In late August, Bob Rodale traveled to Africa at the invitation of Ambassador David Miller of Zimbabwe to help develop new strategies for agricultural development in that country. While in Africa, Bob also joined the delegation of World Vision, a private aid organization, to study famine relief and development projects in East Africa. Here are some excerpts from his notes...

Creating a new source of food in Ethiopia as insurance against famine. Water from a nearby well—which did not go dry even during the drought—is being used to irrigate new gardens being set up in the Ansokia Valley.

Sunday, August 18

On arrival, I was met by Eric Witt, the U.S. A.I.D. Agriculture officer. We were traveling companions for 5 days and he helped me get a good general picture of the country in a short time.

Within 4 hours of my arrival, Eric and I were flying off in a twin-engine Beechcraft to Mutare in the east, within view of Mozambique. At the Mutare strip, we were met by Michael Leonard, director of AGRITEX in that region, and Tom Schaff Jr., horticulture specialist. AGRITEX stands for the Department of Agriculture Technical and Extension Services — and seems to operate much like our extension service.

Mike is very concerned about the apparently rapid degeneration of the soil in the communal areas, where most of the black population lives. These are somewhat like our Indian reservations, but more primitive. A true common area, with cattle (too many) grazing free. No fences. No electricity. People live in thatched huts and farm an acre or two of poor land by hand. Erosion is severe.

At the Solusi College airstrip are (left to right) Michael Leonard of Agritex in Mutare; Jim Rankin, head of the garden project at Solusi College; a reporter for the Solusi College news magazine; Joshua Mushari, assistant to Eric Witt in AID; and the assistant director of the garden project at Solusi.

Mike Leonard thinks it's too late to solve the problem. Too much good land has already washed away, and with much of the originally thin topsoil gone, the soil has little water-absorbing capacity.

Maybe he is right. Maybe time has run out for the communal lands of Zimbabwe. But I think they have not yet tried all the remedies that could help, and perhaps even restore the soil.

Took off again and flew about 15 minutes north to a short, rough dirt strip where our land rover was waiting. We drove on a graded dirt single lane road through the communal farming area. I saw erosion, mainly in stream beds but also some sheet erosion. However, the people all were in good health and vigorous. They were not underfed. Zimbabwe now has a surplus of maize, and it showed in the faces, bodies and spirits of the people in that communal area, at least.

Monday, August 19

Eric and I spent today with people of the Zimbabwe government's agriculture research and extension effort at Harare. In the morning, we were with Ron Fenner, a scientist who had visited our research center last year in search of information about amaranth.

Though friendly, he held fast to his background as a soil chemist. He praised the precision of his lab's soil analysis, yet his chief assistant told us that his research plots got the best yield when they used half the recommended amount of fertilizer. Ron shrugged that off as a problem of the dry weather, and not an indication of a problem with his analysis. A classic and perhaps typical confrontation between scientific "truth" and African reality.

In the afternoon, Eric and I returned to the government research center complex where we met in the main conference room with Peter Ivy, acting national director of AGRITEX, his colleague Peter Silk, Ron Fenner, and Mike Leonard.

After an hour of positive discussion about regenerative zones and economics,we began to talk about implementation of these concepts in Zimbabwe.

Peter Ivy then took the initiative to suggest next steps involving us beyond my visit. He spoke at some length about a Southern African Development Coordination Conference (SADCC) workshop. The AGRITEX people said a workshop on regenerative agriculture and regenerative zones "sounds interesting." They were surprisingly serious in their expressed interest in the zones -- which was encouraging. Also, they had been talking about this workshop before, apparently in reaction to our work in Tanzania.

Thursday, August 22

I then left Zimbabwe and flew to Nairobi, Kenya. The next day, I met with David Lumberg, the Agriculture officer for Kenya, at the U.S. A.I.D. office. Gave him my standard lecture on internal resources versus external inputs, and he reacted positively.

Friday, August 23

In the morning, I met the World Vision Group in a VIP transit lounge in the Nairobi airport--all friendly people. Only 6 of us are going to Ethiopia. We are a quiet, low-key group.

We are picked up at this Addis airport by World Vision staff people -- friendly, quiet, capable. They are making big sacrifices living for months or even years in a poor hotel, in a tough country, missing many American foods and other amenities, particularly newspapers.

What is Ethiopia like? First of all, it is green when we visit. Good rains have come, for the first time in several years. The drought is over, at least for the time being. The effects of the famine linger, though. Many people are weak and sick. Draft animals have been killed and many farm tools sold

(AFRICA continued on page 3)

What's Going On Here?

OCTOBER 1983

RGANIC GARDENING PICNIC/SEMINAR 200 GUESTS AT RESEARCH CENTER

ok Club members were selected for an all-expense paid weekend in the Lehigh e Press at the first Organic Gardening Picnic/Seminar.

Bob Rodale spoke to book club members about Tanzania at the close of the day's activities.

ntown may not
ray, but for Mrs.
kas, Mrs. Frances
lderaro of Pt. Reyes
Nally of Upper
of Wayne, New
field, Pennsylvania,
s. Martha Semon
has of Grayslake,
Brown of Springfield,
experience they'll

ning Book Club
esearch Center
attend the first
The event was
Marketing dept.
were extended to
f whom have been
have purchased
e 200 attendees
Rodale's guests

y of Rodale Press,

from their home towns to A.B.E. airport on Friday, September 9. They were escorted to the Allentown Hilton where they were invited to stay as guests of Rodale Press. Later our guests were joined by Bob and Ardie Rodale at the Cafe Carmel restaurant for dinner.

Registration for Saturday's festivities began at 9:00a.m. to coincide with an all-natural breakfast of orange juice and muffins prepared by our food services staff. The day featured seminars covering three topics. Suggestions for how to extend the gardening season was given by Jeff Ball, author of THE SELF SUFFICIENT SUBURBAN GARDEN. Gene Logsdon, author of WILDLIFE IN YOUR GARDEN spoke on what it means to be an organic gardener and Jack Ruttle, managing editor of *ORGANIC GARDENING* magazine discussed composting.

Also, included in the picnic/seminar were continuous guided tours of the Research Center and the showing of slide presentation "Meet Rodale Press." A luncheon, catered by Fran Wilson and food services staff was highlighted by Executive Editor, Lee Goldman, who spoke of the history of *ORGANIC GARDENING* magazine. An autographing session took place in the afternoon by Carol Stoner for STOCKING UP, Bob Rodale for OUR NEXT FRONTIER, Jeff Ball for THE SELF SUFFICIENT SUBURBAN GARDEN, Bill Hylton for BUILD IT BETTER YOURSELF and THE RODALE HERB BOOK and Anne Halpin for ENCYCLOPEDIA OF INDOOR GARDENING, Gene Logsdon for WILDLIFE IN YOUR GARDEN and Nancy Volk for HOME AQUACULTURE. Two hundred Rodale books were sold that day.

There was also a chance for everyone to mingle, exchange ideas and share gardening problems and answers. To close the festivities Bob Rodale spoke about Tanzania to what seemed to be more like a family than a gathering of strangers.

At dinner that evening, our 10 special guests were accompanied by various Book Division personnel and authors Jeff Ball and Gene Logsdon at the Good Spirit restaurant.

On Sunday they were treated to brunch at the Allentown Hilton and were presented certificates naming them honorary members of the book club's advisory board. Their testimonials and photos will be used in promotions and their opinions on book and marketing ideas will be considered.

The weekend was a special one, not only for the 10 folks who won a free weekend here, but also for the other 190 who found their way into the Lehigh Valley from all over the United States.

Special because these participants in the Organic Gardening Picnic/Seminar were invited by Rodale Press to spend the day with others who share their philosophy. And important for Book Division Marketing because it put the staff in touch with O.G. Book Club customers.

Book Club members line up for autographs from Jeff Ball, Carol Stoner, Bill Hylton and Gene Logsdon.

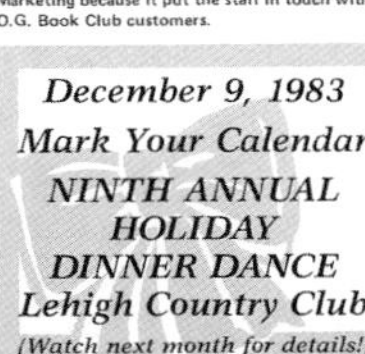

December 9, 1983
Mark Your Calendar
NINTH ANNUAL HOLIDAY DINNER DANCE
Lehigh Country Club
(Watch next month for details!)

Prevention magazine staff in the 1980s

quit smoking." In 1989 Bob wrote several "regenerative running columns" in the magazine. One highlighted Joan Benoit Samuelson's involvement with Drug Abuse Resistance Education in Maine. At about the same time, *Bicycling* started a Regeneration feature, urging readers to pursue the Path to the Golden Wheel–riding 10,000 miles and participating in a community cycling project.

Disruptions and the reactions they fomented were a fundamental component of the process of regeneration. Bob Rodale had believed that disruptions in the company's history–selling the printing presses in the 1950s, the battles with the FTC in the 1960s, the decline of *Prevention*'s direct-mail vitamin advertising in the 1970s and 1980s–had been crucial instigators of change. Another important disruption in the late 1980s helped revivify Rodale's two oldest magazines, *OG* and *Prevention*. In 1987, Telegraph Press, the longtime printer of the two magazines, went out of business. The switch in printers that operated different machines spurred a redesign of both publications. First, *OG* was redesigned and reformatted. Beginning in April 1988, it grew from its traditional digest size to a larger, 8- by 10-inch format, with full color and coated stock. With more and better-illustrated features, the redesigned *OG* became more appealing both to readers and to advertisers.

By contrast, *Prevention*, still Rodale's largest publication (1988 circulation was 2.975 million) and largest source of revenue, was made smaller. Its previous size had made it slightly too large for the standard *Reader's Digest* and *TV Guide* racks at checkout counters. Now, slimmed down and redesigned, *Prevention* became more accessible. And this proved a boon to the long-running effort to boost single-copy sales. *Prevention* in February 1987 sold 200,000 single copies. By June 1989, single-copy sales rose by 50 percent from the year before, and the number of national advertisements rose 18 percent. In May 1989, *Prevention* corralled its first back-page automotive ad. "This is a very regenerative time for *Prevention* magazine," Bob Rodale said. "It's the successful culmination of a transformation that we started planning eight or nine years ago."

1988
February 13: The 1988 Winter Olympics opens in Calgary.

1988 Winter Olympics

May 16: A report by Surgeon General C. Everett Koop says the addictive properties of nicotine are similar to those of heroin and cocaine.

August: *Prevention* appears in digest size.

C. Everett Koop

Clearly, Rodale's historic publications were reaching a remarkably broad audience. For much of the past two decades, the company's twin ambitions of cultivating and maintaining its antiestablishment identity on the one hand, while seeking to recruit large consumer advertisers on the other hand, had seemed to work at cross-purposes. But by the late 1980s, with Rodale's message having evolved and the culture having shifted, the two goals no longer seemed mutually exclusive. Beer and wine companies wanted to advertise in *Bicycling*, *Cross-Country Skier*, and *Runner's World*, and Rodale was prepared to accept them. But the biggest sign of the continued evolution was the rollout and market embrace of *Men's Health*.

After producing three specials—two of which were highly successful at the newsstand—Rodale decided in late 1987 to take *Men's Health* quarterly. Geared toward an audience of men, who were serious consumers, *Men's Health* could target a demographic similar to that of advertising powerhouses like *GQ* and *Esquire*. Having successfully worked with advertisers for footwear and exercise equipment in its athletic magazines, Rodale believed it could recruit many of them—who had little interest in advertising in *Prevention*—to support its new health magazine. Under the editorship of Mike LaFavore, the first quarterly issue of *Men's Health* appeared in the spring of 1988, with articles such as "Plastic Surgery: A Man's Guide" and "Why Women Cheat"; an excerpt from humorist Dave Barry's *Guide to Marriage and Sex;* and advertisements from, among others, Bufferin, Johnson & Johnson, and Casio. Plans were laid to turn *Men's Health* into a 300,000-circulation bimonthly by 1989 and into a 525,000-circulation monthly magazine by 1994. Some of the swagger surrounding the launch of *Spring* had returned.

Men's Health went from a newsletter in the early '80s, had success as a special publication, and transitioned to a quarterly magazine in 1988.

As the magazines broke new ground, Rodale's book business became more sophisticated. And under editorial director Bill Gottlieb, Rodale devised a system for creating books from idea to hardcover in two years, more like a factory than a traditional publisher. Three times a year, editors would send surveys with descriptions of 25 titles in health, gardening, and woodworking to Rodale readers. Based on their responses, the winners became the basis of the publishing program for the following year. Then the ideas were turned into proposals, reviewed by editorial and marketing

November 30: Kohlberg Kravis Roberts & Co. buys RJR Nabisco for $25 billion.

Rodale acquires _Backpacker_, _Adventure Travel_, and _Ski X-C_.

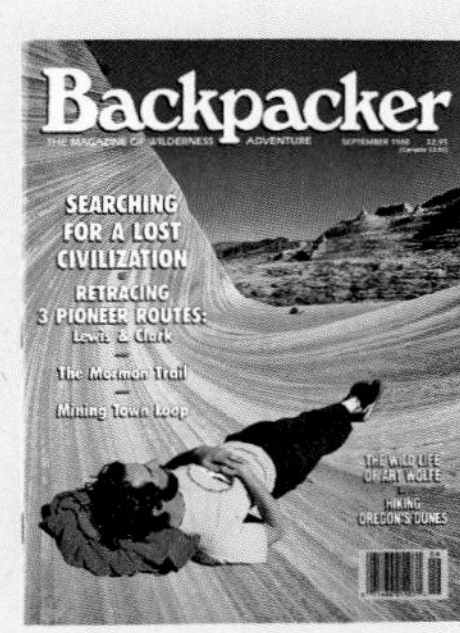

Rodale launches _Good Spirit_ magazine.

***Organic Gardening* staff in the 1980s**

Rodale's new Distribution Center, built in the late '80s, was twice as large as the previous facility. Using state-of-the-art scanning and sorting equipment, the DC ships books and magazine premiums around the world.

review committees, and written mostly by in-house writers. (But there was still room for some whimsy. Clause 8 of Rodale book contracts stipulated that authors would be paid their fees in the market-value equivalent of amaranth if they failed to submit manuscripts on time.)

Rodale possessed more data about its ultimate customers than did publishers who sold through retail channels. Between the expanding roster of large-circulation magazines and the growing book business, the company was piling up names and addresses like never before. In the late 1980s, Rodale made a concerted effort to mine what it realized was a potential competitive advantage. "Up to that time you didn't know if a *Prevention* person also subscribed to *OG* and had bought books, too," said Pat Corpora. So the firm embarked upon an initiative in which staffers created a new computer application system—a mammoth list of 12 million active subscribers and 14 million inactive names. By categorizing customers by circulation and purchase history, Rodale realized it could target potential readers more efficiently and plan more effectively, by, for example, ordering larger print runs of books with greater confidence. "The ability to make in-house lists work is becoming the hallmark of a successful Rodale venture," Bob Teufel said in 1989.

The ability to mail efficiently became more important as the price of postage rose dramatically in the 1980s. In 1989, two-thirds of magazine revenue and more than 90 percent of book revenue derived from direct marketing sources. The book division sent out 2 million pieces of mail every two weeks. Consequently, an increase in postal rates would affect Rodale far more severely than it would many other publishers. In 1988, when postage rates rose 22 percent, it cost the company $8 million. Another 30 percent increase was slated for 1991. This led the company to look to some new alternatives, such as television. A *Prevention* television circulation campaign that ran on more than 100 stations in the first quarter of 1988 brought in 200,000 orders.

This also placed a heightened premium on the need to streamline operations. In the spring of 1989, Rodale struck an agreement to have St. Martin's Press market the trade titles published by Rodale and by Good Spirit Press, a new spiritual imprint that Bob had started. The company hired an outside firm, Neodata, to handle fulfillment for its newsletters and eliminated the 12-person

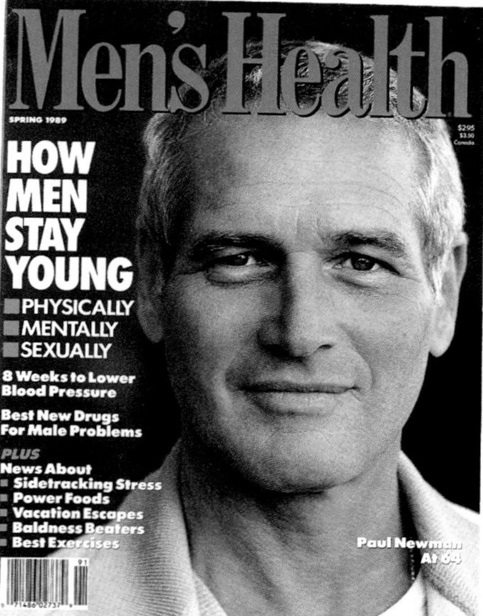

Celebrities peered out from the covers of the magazines.

second shift in Incoming Mail. Rodale remained an unusually introspective company, musing out loud about the reasons for, and the effect of, changes. The company explained in *WGOH* that it was reducing staff because it had bought an automated machine that could open and sort 10,000 envelopes per hour with one operator. And it noted that the reduction in incoming mail staff was more than offset by adding 18 people to Customer Communications.

Even as it grew in size, scope, and sophistication, corporate governance wasn't much of a priority. And while Bob Teufel noted that there was a board of directors at Rodale, "it's a board of one"; Rodale Press was still very much a family business. By the late 1980s, Bob, Ardie, and all four of their surviving children were involved with the enterprise at some level. And Bob trusted his executives, many of whom had been with him for two decades, to act in his interests as well as their own—to make a career at Rodale meant in large part buying into the company's—and hence Bob's—ethos. Few members of management smoked. CFO Paul Wessel was a marathoner, and many others were serious runners and bicyclists. In late 1988, Bob attended a corporate officers' meeting where they were discussing the possible purchase of a small magazine, *American Woodworker.* "They started talking about it, and it quickly became obvious that they'd already bought it," Bob recalled. He seemed nonplussed. But after all, he had set up a small discretionary fund so managers "could try small things without asking; take a few shots on their own; have some fun."

From a certain vantage point, Rodale in the late 1980s looked like many other media companies. In July 1988, *Bicycling* and *Runner's World* teamed up with Coors Light to sponsor biathlons. The March 1989 issue of *Men's Health* featured Paul Newman, and the April 1989 *OG* featured Meryl Streep, who was involved with an antipesticide campaign. This was a sign of transformation. "Without changing our basic stance one bit, we've become the mainstream," Bob Rodale wrote. "And that's made our prospective audience broader than ever. And to reach that point we didn't do anything other than stick to our philosophy." The little, willfully unorthodox company in out-of-the-way Emmaus had evolved into a big business. And the results were visible everywhere in 1989. *Men's Health* was thick with ads. On April 4, 1989, the incoming mail department brought in a

1989
Ardie Rodale writes *Climbing Toward the Light*.

March 2: The National Academy of Sciences calls for change in America's eating habits: more fruit, less fat.

March 24: The Exxon *Valdez* spills 240,000 barrels of oil into Alaska's Prince William Sound.

Exxon *Valdez*

Spring: *Prevention* holds its first All-American Walkers rally in Tampa, Florida.

June 4: China suppresses prodemocracy demonstrations in Beijing's Tiananmen Square.

November: Fall of the Berlin Wall

Bob traveled to China in 1990.

record $1.08 million in revenues. And the company continued to expand. The main building was in the midst of a large renovation, and plans were made for a new distribution center in Fogelsville, Pennsylvania, which would be more than twice as large as the existing distribution center.

But Rodale still cultivated a sense of difference. "Being distinctively different and socially responsible at the same time is not the easiest trick in the world," Mark Bricklin said. "Add economic viability and the agenda is even more challenging." While it had mainstream, large-circulation magazines and a large and growing book business, Rodale still devoted resources to efforts geared more toward improving people's lives than toward earning profits. The library staff, for example, produced a tiny newsletter, the *Vitamin A+ Sieve*. It was sent, free of charge, to 651 readers—mostly health workers fighting childhood blindness—in 87 countries. In Rodale's worldview, such a publication was just as central to its corporate mission as *Prevention* or *Men's Health*.

In its businesses, and in avowedly nonprofit ventures like the *Vitamin A+ Sieve,* Rodale was constantly seeking new frontiers. For Bob Rodale, doing so was part of a personal journey. While there was surely work to be done in disseminating the message of organic culture and regeneration in the United States, he saw the greatest opportunities—and needs—in the developing world. Traveling was a means of both spreading the message and regenerating his own spirit. "One of my main ways to actually be more alive is to walk fearlessly just about anywhere," he wrote in a 1990 *Prevention* column. "In the last few years I've walked in the 'dangerous' streets of Dakar, Senegal; Addis Ababa, Ethiopia; plus many small and large places in China, India, Russia, and other countries." On his trips, he was frequently accompanied by Anthony, who took photographs that illustrated Bob's articles.

In 1990, he went to China with a group of 37 sustainable-agriculture specialists. "I set myself the task of trying to take back to China some part of the gift of organic thinking that China had given to us many years ago." He visited Beijing Vegetable Research Center and reconnected with scientists who had brought amaranth to Rodale years before, and traveled to rural Heilonjiang province and to Nanjing in the south. A year after the Tiananmen Square uprising, he saw China at a crossroads. "Will it be able to regenerate its land so that a healthy agriculture can indeed feed an even larger population

December 20: The United States invades Panama to overthrow Manuel Noriega.

Prince Charles of England converts his 1,000-acre estate in Gloucestershire to organic agriculture.

The Seinfeld Chronicles premieres on NBC.

Cast of *The Seinfeld Chronicles*

Bob envisioned bringing the message of regeneration to the world.

in the 21st century?" he wondered. "Or will a continually deteriorating environment take away from China the capacity to use chemicals to produce more food? I plan to keep going back to find out."

In many ways, the most promising new frontier in 1990 was Russia. With the Communist Party beginning to release its grip and the Soviet Union slowly beginning to crack up, Bob saw Russia's vast and highly inefficient agricultural economy as a natural candidate for regeneration. In 1989, plans were made to launch *The New Farm* magazine in Russia with a local partner. And in September 1990, he planned a trip to Russia, along with Paul Wessel and Chuck McCullagh. They traveled to Moscow and Leningrad, toured farms, and met with farmers. In his phone calls to the States, Bob expressed great excitement at the progress made.

On the morning of September 20, he was preparing to return home. "He and the head of the Russian farmers' association and member of the Supreme Soviet cooked up the Rodale program to cure the country's agricultural and economic ills," said Paul Wessel. In the morning, Bob boarded a van that would take him to Moscow's airport. At 11:05, a city bus, which had swerved out of traffic to avoid a military truck, plowed head first into the van. Bob, seated in the front seat, was killed instantly. So were colleague Yevgenij Gringaut, the van's driver, and a woman who had worked as an interpreter.

Word of Bob's death began to circulate through the company in the midafternoon. "I was on the phone when John Griffin, the president in charge of magazines, and my daughters, Heidi and Maria, came into my office," Ardie recalled. "They said 'Hang up right away.' I knew it was something dead serious. I hung up and they told me he was killed." Griffin called a meeting to formally notify employees. Numbness and shock quickly set in, along with a sense of resolve. "One employee lit a fire in Bob's woodstove when he heard the news and lowered the flag," said Tom Stoneback. "He thought it was important to keep the spark alive." That day, Rep. Don Ritter, the congressman representing the Lehigh Valley, read a tribute to Bob into the *Congressional Record*. "He was the epitome of the 21st century man comfortable with the human uses of technology to enhance the spirit and the environment."

1990
February 11: Nelson Mandela is released from prison in South Africa.

February 13: An agreement is reached for a two-stage plan to reunite West Germany and East Germany.

Nelson Mandela

February 25: Smoking is banned on all U.S. domestic flights of less than six hours' duration.

April: *Men's Health* starts publishing bimonthly.

The Organic Foods Production Act (OFPA) of 1990 is adopted by Congress as part of the 1990 Farm Bill.

Bob Rodale, photographed in Moscow's Red Square by Anthony Rodale in 1988, saw Russia as a new frontier for the organic message.

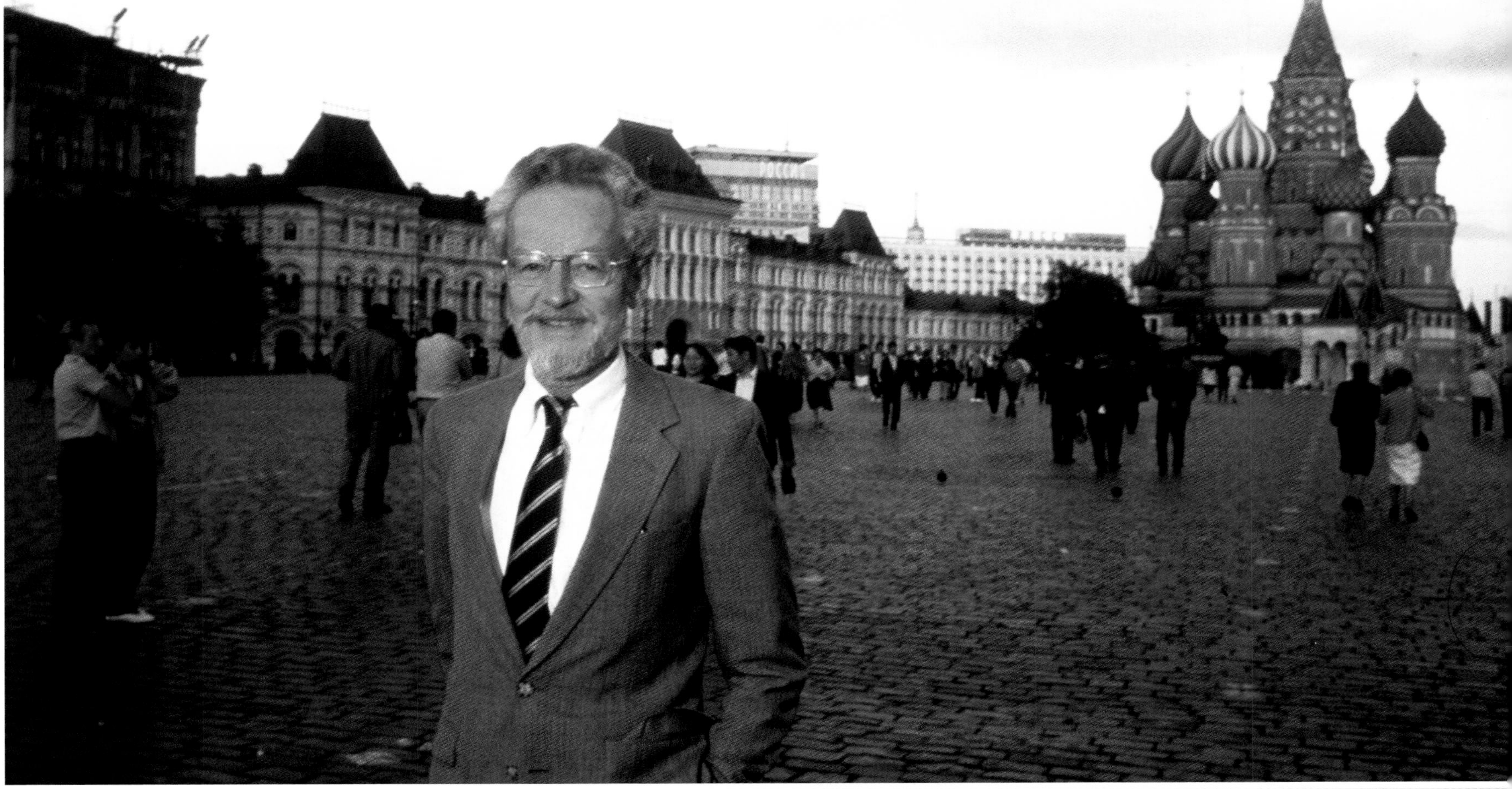

June 1: President Bush and Soviet leader Mikhail Gorbachev sign a treaty to end chemical weapon production.

August 2: Iraq invades Kuwait.

Iraq invades Kuwait

September 20: Bob Rodale dies in a car accident in Russia.

November 13: The first known Web page is written.

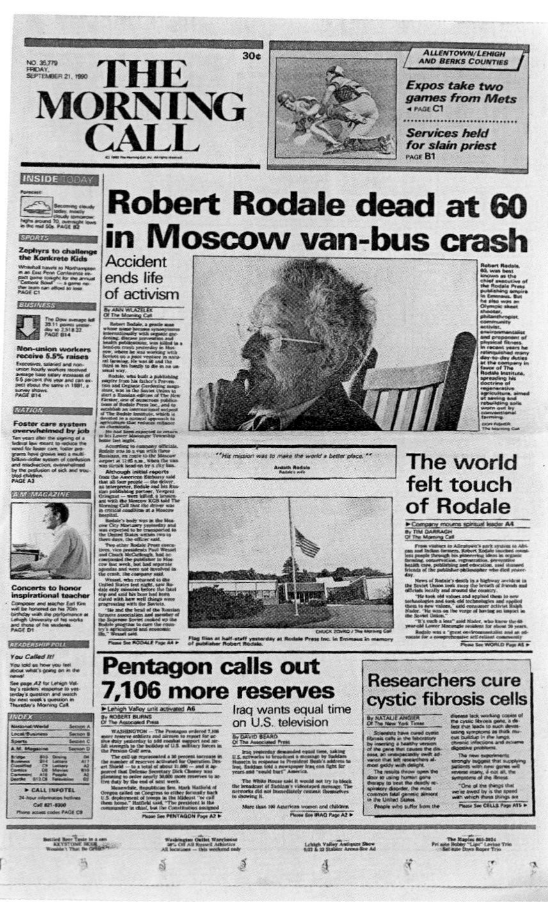
THE MORNING CALL

30¢

ALLENTOWN/LEHIGH AND BERKS COUNTIES

Expos take two games from Mets

Services held for slain priest

Robert Rodale dead at 60 in Moscow van-bus crash

Accident ends life of activism

The world felt touch of Rodale

Pentagon calls out 7,106 more reserves

Iraq wants equal time on U.S. television

Researchers cure cystic fibrosis cells

The Allentown newspaper reports the shocking news.

Bob's body was flown back to the United States on Saturday. And on the following Tuesday, September 25, a sunny fall day, hundreds of people gathered in a huge yellow-and-white tent at the old Rodale farm, in the backyard of the house where Bob had spent his teenage and adult years, and where he and Ardie had lived and raised their children. Many people walked or rode bicycles to the service to honor the spirit of the man who inspired them. Three tall, unearthed white pine trees—representing Bob, J.I., and David—stood behind his closed casket. In a service led by Rev. Al Robert, pastor of the Lutheran Church of the Holy Spirit, speakers—including his 10-year-old granddaughter, Shelbi Stoneback, and several longtime colleagues—recalled his life with joy. Chuck McCullagh read a poem he'd written on the airplane coming home from Russia. Bob was laid to rest alongside his father at the Northwood Cemetery in Emmaus. A plaque at the gravesite also commemorates the life of David Rodale. "Our friends were encouraged to walk over the farm after the service," Ardie wrote. "When the family returned from the cemetery, the fields were alive with people."

Alive with people. This simple three-word phrase neatly encapsulated the too-brief life, constant work, and expansive ethos of Bob Rodale—and of the company he and his father built, Rodale Press. As Rodale's guiding spirit for the previous two decades, he had helped bring professional management and vision, driven continuous growth through fidelity to inherited values, and displayed a willingness to push new frontiers—all in the name of inspiring people to improve their own health, fitness, and sense of well-being. Rodale Press in 1990 was a profitable company with revenues of nearly a quarter of a billion dollars, more than 17 times the total in 1971.

But Bob Rodale's legacy was far more vivid than a set of numbers on a balance sheet. His legacy could be seen in the buildings in and around Emmaus, in the velodrome he had built in Trexlertown, in the magazines that filled newsstands and books that filled mailboxes, and in the lives of farmers in Africa, Russia, and all over the United States. Perhaps the most important legacy he left was a committed staff and family, a wife and four children, who were prepared to carry on the work of Bob and J. I. Rodale into a third generation.

A citizen of the world, Bob Rodale, with his Great Pyrenees, Bandit, was deeply rooted in Emmaus.

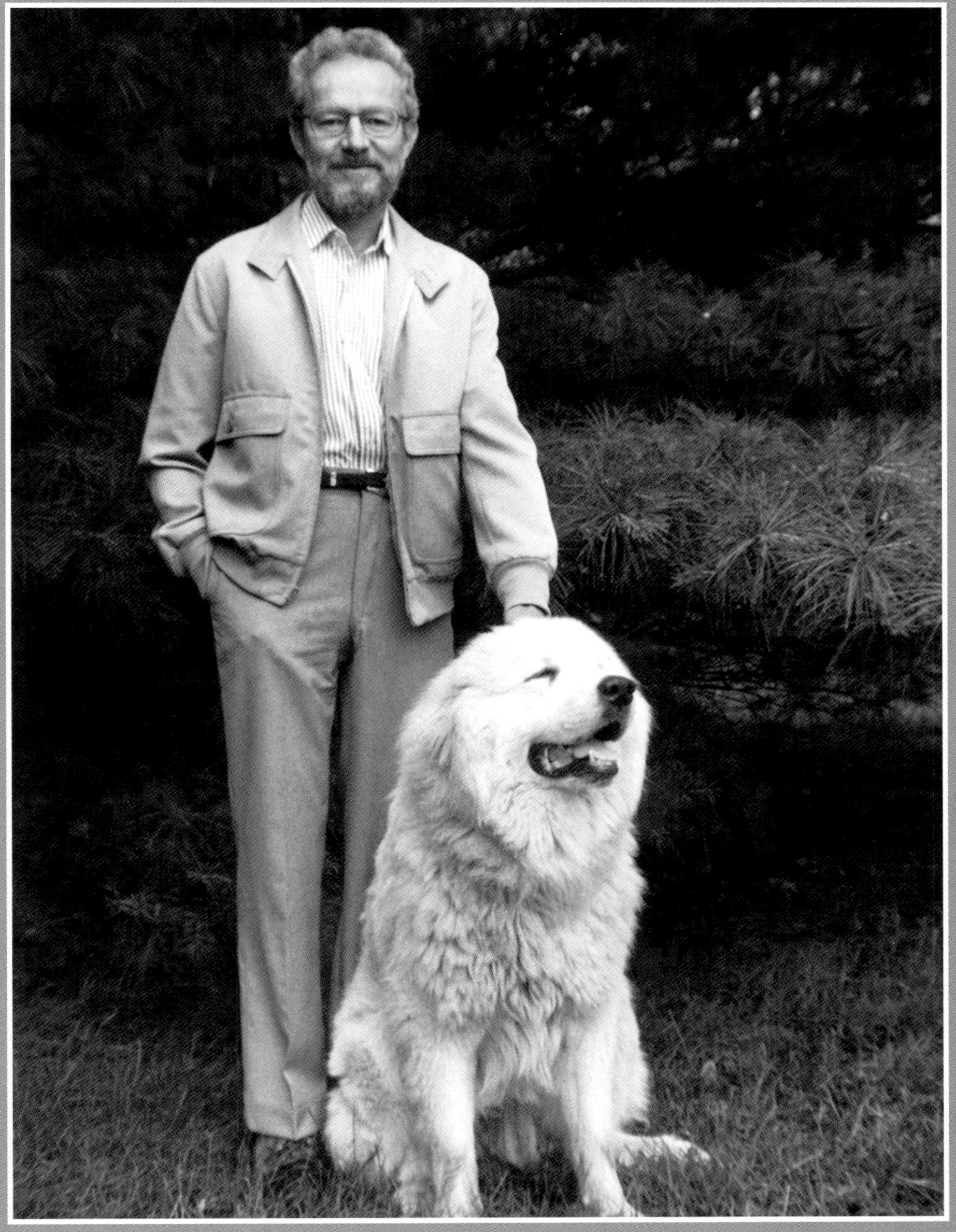

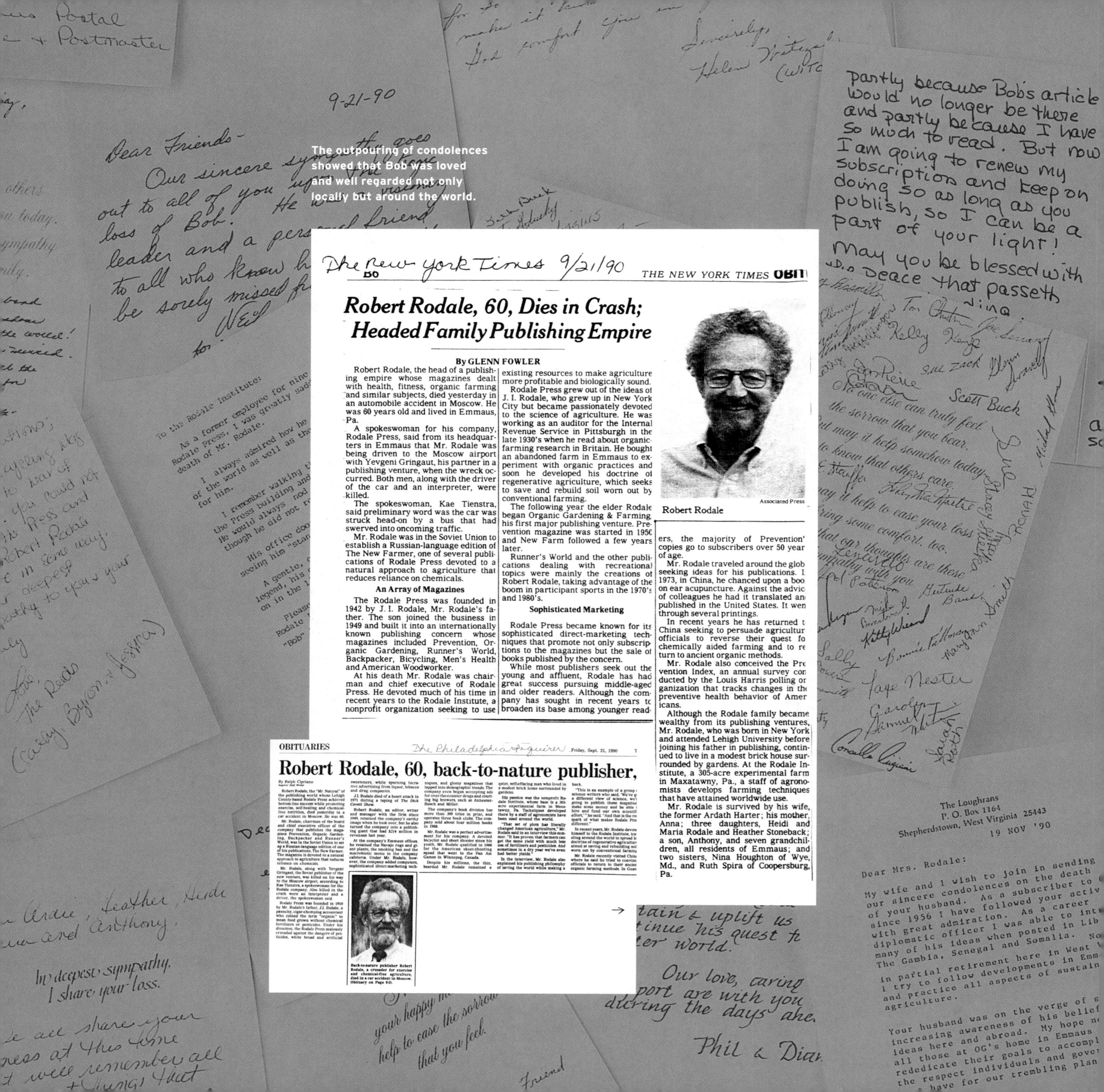

The outpouring of condolences showed that Bob was loved and well regarded not only locally but around the world.

The New York Times 9/21/90 — THE NEW YORK TIMES OBIT

Robert Rodale, 60, Dies in Crash; Headed Family Publishing Empire

By GLENN FOWLER

Robert Rodale, the head of a publishing empire whose magazines dealt with health, fitness, organic farming and similar subjects, died yesterday in an automobile accident in Moscow. He was 60 years old and lived in Emmaus, Pa.

A spokeswoman for his company, Rodale Press, said from its headquarters in Emmaus that Mr. Rodale was being driven to the Moscow airport with Yevgeni Gringaut, his partner in a publishing venture, when the wreck occurred. Both men, along with the driver of the car and an interpreter, were killed.

The spokeswoman, Kae Tienstra, said preliminary word was the car was struck head-on by a bus that had swerved into oncoming traffic.

Mr. Rodale was in the Soviet Union to establish a Russian-language edition of The New Farmer, one of several publications of Rodale Press devoted to a natural approach to agriculture that reduces reliance on chemicals.

An Array of Magazines

The Rodale Press was founded in 1942 by J. I. Rodale, Mr. Rodale's father. The son joined the business in 1949 and built it into an internationally known publishing concern whose magazines included Prevention, Organic Gardening, Runner's World, Backpacker, Bicycling, Men's Health and American Woodworker.

At his death Mr. Rodale was chairman and chief executive of Rodale Press. He devoted much of his time in recent years to the Rodale Institute, a nonprofit organization seeking to use existing resources to make agriculture more profitable and biologically sound.

Rodale Press grew out of the ideas of J. I. Rodale, who grew up in New York City but became passionately devoted to the science of agriculture. He was working as an auditor for the Internal Revenue Service in Pittsburgh in the late 1930's when he read about organic-farming research in Britain. He bought an abandoned farm in Emmaus to experiment with organic practices and soon he developed his doctrine of regenerative agriculture, which seeks to save and rebuild soil worn out by conventional farming.

The following year the elder Rodale began Organic Gardening & Farming, his first major publishing venture. Prevention magazine was started in 1950 and New Farm followed a few years later.

Runner's World and the other publications dealing with recreational topics were mainly the creations of Robert Rodale, taking advantage of the boom in participant sports in the 1970's and 1980's.

Sophisticated Marketing

Rodale Press became known for its sophisticated direct-marketing techniques that promote not only subscriptions to the magazines but the sale of books published by the concern.

While most publishers seek out the young and affluent, Rodale has had great success pursuing middle-aged and older readers. Although the company has sought in recent years to broaden its base among younger read-

Robert Rodale — Associated Press

ers, the majority of Prevention' copies go to subscribers over 50 year of age.

Mr. Rodale traveled around the glob seeking ideas for his publications. I 1973, in China, he chanced upon a boo on ear acupuncture. Against the advic of colleagues he had it translated an published in the United States. It wen through several printings.

In recent years he has returned t China seeking to persuade agricultur officials to reverse their quest fo chemically aided farming and to re turn to ancient organic methods.

Mr. Rodale also conceived the Pre vention Index, an annual survey con ducted by the Louis Harris polling or ganization that tracks changes in th preventive health behavior of Amer icans.

Although the Rodale family became wealthy from its publishing ventures, Mr. Rodale, who was born in New York and attended Lehigh University before joining his father in publishing, continued to live in a modest brick house surrounded by gardens. At the Rodale Institute, a 305-acre experimental farm in Maxatawny, Pa., a staff of agronomists develops farming techniques that have attained worldwide use.

Mr. Rodale is survived by his wife, the former Ardath Harter; his mother, Anna; three daughters, Heidi and Maria Rodale and Heather Stoneback; a son, Anthony, and seven grandchildren, all residents of Emmaus; and two sisters, Nina Houghton of Wye, Md., and Ruth Spira of Coopersburg, Pa.

OBITUARIES — The Philadelphia Inquirer — Friday, Sept. 21, 1990

Robert Rodale, 60, back-to-nature publisher,

By Ralph Cipriano
Inquirer Staff Writer

Robert Rodale, the "Mr. Natural" of the publishing world whose Lehigh County-based Rodale Press achieved bottom-line success while promoting exercise, self-healing and chemical-free nutrition, died yesterday in a car accident in Moscow. He was 60.

Mr. Rodale, chairman of the board and chief executive officer of the company that publishes the magazines Prevention, Organic Gardening, Backpacker and Runner's World, was in the Soviet Union to set up a Russian-language edition of one of his publications, The New Farmer. The magazine is devoted to a natural approach to agriculture that reduces reliance on chemicals.

Mr. Rodale, along with Yevgeni Gringaut, the Soviet publisher of the new venture, was killed on his way to the Moscow airport, according to Kae Tienstra, a spokeswoman for the Rodale company. Also killed in the crash were an interpreter and a driver, the spokeswoman said.

Rodale Press was founded in 1918 by Mr. Rodale's father, J.I. Rodale, a paunchy, cigar-chomping accountant who coined the term "organic" to mean food grown without chemical fertilizers or pesticides. Under his direction, the Rodale Press zealously crusaded against the dangers of pesticides, white bread and artificial sweeteners, while spurning lucrative advertising from liquor, tobacco and drug companies.

J.I. Rodale died of a heart attack in 1971 during a taping of *The Dick Cavett Show*.

Robert Rodale, an editor, writer and manager with the firm since 1949, retained the company's earthy image when he took over, but he also turned the company into a publishing giant that had $214 million in revenues last year.

At the company's Emmaus offices, he retained the Navajo rugs and giant plants, the smoking ban and the macrobiotic menu in the company cafeteria. Under Mr. Rodale, however, the company added computers, sophisticated direct-marketing techniques, and glossy magazines that tapped into demographic trends. The company even began acccepting ads for over-the-counter drugs and courting big brewers, such as Anheuser-Busch and Miller.

The company's book division has more than 300 titles in print, and operates three book clubs. The company sold about four million books in 1988.

Mr. Rodale was a perfect advertisement for his company. A devoted bicyclist and skeet shooter since his youth, Mr. Rodale qualified in 1966 for the American skeet-shooting squad that went to the Pan Am Games in Winnepeg, Canada.

Despite his millions, the thin, bearded Mr. Rodale remained a quiet, self-effacing man who lived in a modest brick home surrounded by gardens.

His passion was the nonprofit Rodale Institute, whose base is a 305-acre experimental farm in Maxatawny, Pa. Techniques developed there by a staff of agronomists have been used around the world.

"That set of plots has literally changed American agriculture," Mr. Rodale said in an interview this summer. "It has proven that farmers can get the same yield with much less use of fertilizers and pesticides. And sometimes in a dry year we've even had better yields."

In the interview, Mr. Rodale also explained his publishing philosophy of saving the world while making a buck.

"This is an example of a group science writers who said, 'We've g a different view of science, we' going to publish these magazine make some money and be able hire and fund our own scientif effort,'" he said. "And that is the re spark of what makes Rodale Pre different."

In recent years, Mr. Rodale devote himself to the Rodale Institute, tra eling around the world to spread h doctrine of regenerative agricultur aimed at saving and rebuilding soil worn out by conventional farming

Mr. Rodale recently visited Chin where he said he tried to convinc officials to return to their ancie organic farming methods. In Guat

Back-to-nature publisher Robert Rodale, a crusader for exercise and chemical-free agriculture, died in a car accident in Moscow. Obituary on Page 9-D.

11/27/90

Ardath -
I am not in the habit of
ng to strangers. But after
ing your memorial to
late husband, you are
ranger! I read with
of joy your tribute
r life together and
eaning of his transi

have a dear
ly became a
65 years of
picked up
nd's torc

Dear Staff,
How shocking to read in Organic Gardening
about Mr. Rodale's death. I was also beside
myself that I hadn't read or heard about it
sooner. Thanks so much for passing the news
along. It shows how lacking our news
media is for Mr. Rodale was not only a
very famous + respected person, but
his death ... Maybe I was
in the ... was announced

10/23/90

Sue Bitting — Ardella Fegley
Pat Roth — Kathy Washydupe
Rosie Onuschio — Sandy Gehman
Sally Drabick

Of the loss that you must bear.
We hope that you'll
be comforted
By knowing others care.

Sue Office Services Dept /
Rodale Press

Dear Ardie,
My deepest
Friday

93/157. 25 " 09 1990 r.
Moscow — Urgent

Dear Anna, Ardie, Hea
dear friends and colleag
Our hearts have wrung
have happened. There's n
On Friday we said far
the earth Helena and Gen
funeral of Yevgenij.
Now we are orphaned,
teachers. Bob has come t
desire to share his know
our country. We shall ne
cordiality and nobleness
Merciless decease has
allow the flame flared u
fade.
In this unbearably pa
and pray together with y

Yours
Vasiliy Se
Tatyana Ye
Helena Iva
Olga Marty
Lidiya Zot
Yuriy Naum
Olga Kalea
Svetlana S
Mariya Kat
Yuriy Polo
Alexander
Zoya Pikuli
Vasiliy Bel
Fjodor Sokh

IN MEMORIAM

Arnold & Porter
FAX: (202) 331-98-32
Att.: Mr. Jeffrey Burt
for Rodale Press Inc.

lost an extraordinary champion las
uto accident in Moscow, September

plant with its roots spreading deep
ly for the Press but also for its

In Memoriam

Mankind - indeed the earth that sustains
an extraordinary champion last month.

Robert David Ro

perished in an auto accident in Mosc
September 20th, 1990.

The Rodale Press trademark - a young green
its roots spreading deep into the soil - serve
symbol not only for the Press but also for its b
of the last thirty years.

The heart of the Press has always bee
Maxatawny, Pennsylvania, where in the 193
father, J.I., started to experiment with wa
worn out soil and to grow crops without ch
an idea ahead of its time.

Even in the early 1950s when Bob joined
which by then published Organic Gardenin
Prevention, few new - or cared - about su

It wasn't until the 1970s and 1980s th
healthier life took hold. Americans - and
the world - have caught up with the ide
Rodale. There is now hope that future
be lost in the name of progress.

Bob Rodale's life was dedicated to
and others in many lands - to pres
singular planet, to strive for healthi

Our friend and colleague Bob Rod
this earth, yet he will be a lasting le
manner he sought enrichment o
generations to come.

Be it resolved and proclaimed th
of the Magazine Publishers of A
their friend Robert David Rodale
and loving memory.

October

Donald D. Kummerfeld
President
Magazine Publishers of America

RODALE PRESS

October 1,

Dear Vasily, Tatyana, Helena, Olga, Li
Svetlana, Maria and the Families
and Gennadij:

We cry with you as we share the g
Bob Rodale and three of your wonderful
Helena, and Gennadij. ALL THREE were
at our Service of Remembrance here on
2,000 people came to express their so
up in love. I pray that you felt the
love - for it was very strong. The s
a tent in the back of our house looki
and the fields. After the service, p
walk over the farm and feel the peace
and touched our hearts. There were m

We must continue the dreams and
together on this special venture betw
and you in Russia. We want to work w
see this dream become a reality.

I wrap my arms around you and pr
in strength and love for one another

Ardath R

Rodale Press, Inc., 33 East Minor Street, Emmaus, PA 18049
215-967-5171 Telex #847338

United States of America
Congressional Record
PROCEEDINGS AND DEBATES OF THE 101st CONGRESS, SECOND SESSION
Vol. 136 WASHINGTON, FRIDAY, OCTOBER 19, 1990 No. 142

To Ardie
your friend

House of Representatives

TRIBUTE TO ROBERT RODALE

HON. DON RITTER

OF PENNSYLVANIA
IN THE HOUSE OF REPRESENTATIVES
Friday, October 19, 1990

Mr. Ritter. Mr. Speaker, I rise today sadly to pay tribute to a gentle man, to my good friend and American pioneer, Robert Rodale, Chairman and Chief Executive Officer of Rodale Press, Inc., Emmaus, Pennsylvania, who passed away 21 September 1990, at age 60.

Tragically, it was in the USSR where a freak automobile accident took place, killing Bob Rodale and his Russian colleagues instantly, when an oncoming bus veered into the path of their van as they were headed to the Moscow airport and back to the USA for Bob.

If there ever was a friend to the world, it was Bob Rodale. Through his publishing empire—Prevention, Organic Gardening, Runner's World, Men's Health, Backpacker, Bicycling and American Woodworker magazines along with books and newsletters—he touched countless people with his groundbreaking ideas in organic farming, conservation, regeneration, preventive health care, and education.

Bob was an environmentalist in the best sense of the word. His was an environmentalism that people could see, feel, touch, understand. His was an environmentalism that promoted the doable, the practical, the sensible. The Lehigh Valley of Pennsylvania, the nation and the world have benefited from Bob Rodale's brand of environmentalism.

In 1949, he began working for the company, founded by his father, J.I. Rodale, but his passion in recent years was the nonprofit Rodale Institute, whose base is a 305-acre experimental farm in Maxatawny, Berks County, Pennsylvania. "That set of plots has literally changed American agriculture," he said in an interview this summer. "It has proven that farmers can get the same yield with much less use of fertilizers and pesticides. And sometimes in a dry year we even had better yields." And today, it is changing agriculture worldwide.

Typical of the Rodale approach is a new project in Guatemala "to basically re-create the lost agriculture of the Mayan culture". Ignoring techniques used in developed nations and being pushed in the African bush, Rodale showed the farmers in Tanzania how to better their lots without using the expensive chemicals and agricultural equipment being peddled by others — items the country could not afford. One day Tanzania's president mentioned to Bob his own communications problems. Later Bob gave the leader a computer system needed for the task. In China, he tried to convince officials to take advantage of some of the positive aspects of their ancient organic farming methods. His latest project, the Russian-language edition of The New Farmer will begin this Fall.

Indeed his joint venture in the Soviet

Ro
re de
the w
rt Ro
male a
Spe
Rodale
his read
their
concern
e world.
Campbell

Family
We are from
but have st
with you fo
the soil.
We consider your
present loss to be
incalculable, personally
and now world-wide.
May God cherish
you and your

May memories
of the happiness
you shared
with your loved one
help to lighten your sorro

him, have been instrumental
in helping many people learn
how to live better lives with
whatever they have at hand.
God's blessing surely rests on
all of you as you continue the
work so nobly begun.
With much

and hoping you will know
This brings you
deeper sympathy
than these few words
can show.

Harold and Pearl Ber

Ardath Rodale stepped in to lead Rodale and ensure continuity after the sudden death of her husband.

CHAPTER 8

1991 TO 2000

A Company in Transition

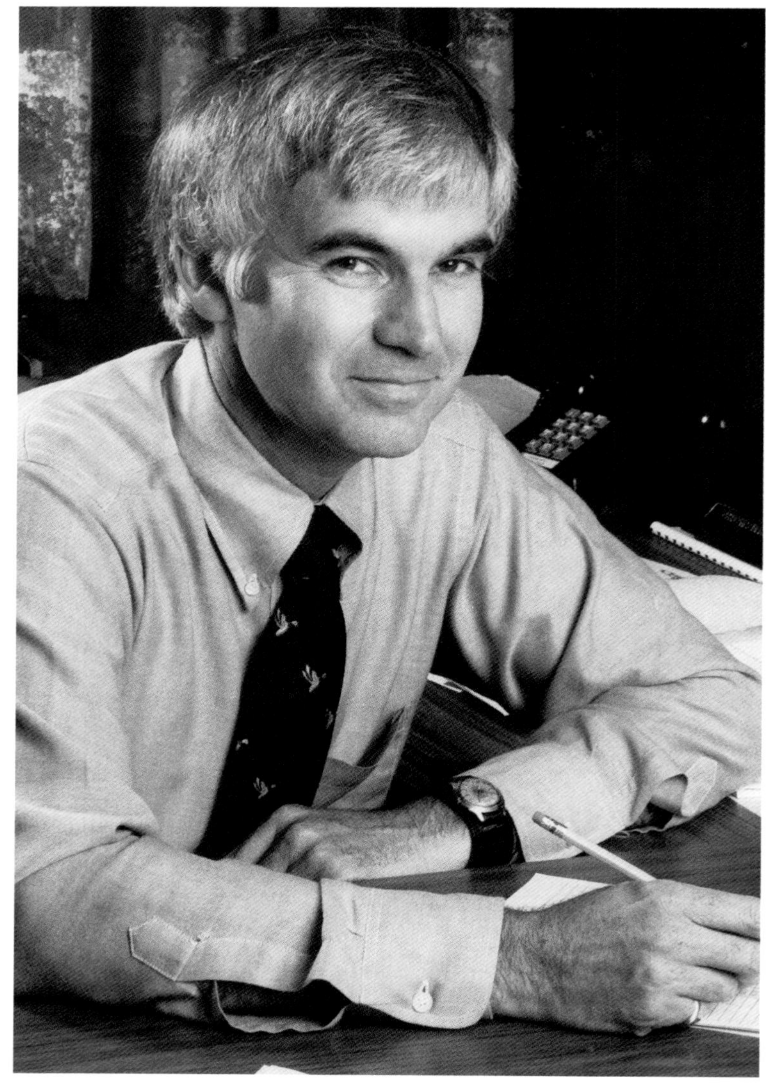

Robert Teufel continued as president of Rodale until the end of the decade.

IN THE FALL OF 1990, Rodale Press was once again jolted by the death of its visionary chief executive officer. And yet the transition Rodale Press had to negotiate after Bob Rodale's death was different from the one it had endured nearly 20 years before. Rodale was a far larger company now, and its various divisions were run by experienced executives accustomed to following budgets and business plans. And because Ardie and Bob's four children all played integral roles in Rodale enterprises, the transition would be characterized by continuity rather than abrupt change.

The same could not be said of the media industry in the 1990s. The advent of the Internet, an unprecedented economic boom, industry consolidation, and a general expansion of traditional media created challenges that simultaneously threatened traditional media businesses and provided them with a wide array of new platforms and opportunities. As the decade unfolded, Rodale would grow by broadening the audience for its traditional health and organic messages, investing significantly in the book business, pushing carefully into international markets, and taking tentative steps onto the Internet.

Bob Rodale's will had stipulated that Ardie would succeed him as chief executive officer. "You'll have to trust Ardie. I do. I've worked with Ardie all my life. She knows the company," he had told Rodale president Bob Teufel. Indeed, Ardie had spent virtually her entire adult life working at Rodale in various capacities. And while the four members of the third generation were left an equal stake in the company, Bob had also stipulated that Maria Rodale, then 28 years old, would ultimately succeed Ardie and retain effective voting control of the company's stock, thereby maintaining family ownership and control of the company.

A woman running a large company was rare in 1990, even for a progressive company like Rodale. But it was a role Ardie embraced wholeheartedly, despite her grief at suddenly losing her husband of nearly 40 years. She spent her first month, at the advice of Teufel, visiting department heads and vice presidents in their offices simply to listen to their visions and gain their confidence. As significantly, she assumed the role that J.I. and Bob had long carried out—as the company's spiritual and cultural leader. She began to write a column sharing her thoughts and ideas with employees in *What's Going On Here? (WGOH)*. And she carried on J.I. and Bob's tradition of conveying Rodale's culture directly to readers by writing a column in *Prevention*.

In the spring of 1990, the company had been reorganized into two operating divisions: the book division, run by Pat Corpora, and magazines, led once again by John Griffin, who had left

Ardie wrote columns in *WGOH* and *Prevention* magazine to share her vision.

reflections

WALKING IN THE SUN

Ardath Rodale

EACH MORNING, AS I TAKE MY EARLY-morning walk, I step into the sun. I am sure that I hear you saying, "But sometimes the sky is filled with heavy clouds." To me, the sunshine is in my mind and heart. I am a winner over cancer. The experience has taught me that each day is a special gift to be filled with joy and appreciation and love. To be healthy, I have learned to turn away from the shadow and face the sun. Perhaps you, too, have been faced with a challenge that has changed your life.

Come with me as we open the door to take that morning walk. We are filled with anticipation of what we might find that's new. To hear the music of birds urges us to join their chorus. Their cheerfulness fills us with energy as we notice their busy activity, gathering food and building nests.

To smell the aroma from the myriad varieties of bright flowers wakes us to the anticipation of the many facets of life that we might have the opportunity to face. Through each experience we have the chance to grow in understanding and love.

The moist, damp earth, after the rain from the night before, causes us to expand our lungs with fond remembrances as we recall other experiences of walking in the woods or camping, or walking by a cool, clear, rippling stream.

We notice the intricate spider webs that were not there yesterday, and we marvel at their perfection as they glisten in the sun. Do you know that some of them look to me as if they were white feathers blown by the wind and caught by the tips of some shrubs just as they were beginning to bloom?

There is so much more to discover now as we walk side by side. We value the uniqueness of each other. Each of us is one of a kind—like snowflakes. As we have the opportunity to share our thoughts, we develop a kinship of closeness. We have the chance to reach out and touch.

As we come back, we return with gratitude for the privilege it is to be alive in this beautiful world. Thank you for being with me on this brief walk. We return now to the companionship of our own thoughts as we proceed to continue the day in the larger community of our families and workday world. Our challenge each day is to share the healing touch of all this glory of living. It all becomes possible when we open our hearts to let the sun shine in! ■

Ardath Rodale is the Chairman of the Board and CEO of Rodale Press, and is author of the book Climbing Toward the Light *(Rodale Press, 1989).*

144 PREVENTION SEPTEMBER 1995

Message From Ardie ~ Solar Magic

In the corner of my sunroom on a stump of a tree rests a beautiful, simple sculpture—a set of solar chimes. On a sunny afternoon, the chimes peal softly, reminding me of angel voices singing praise for the joy of being alive. When a cloud passes over the sun, the music is silenced. This suggests to me that in our busy schedules we need to pause and look around us at the many gifts of nature and friendships we are privileged to enjoy.

My husband came home one day all excited. He had a special gift for me—a solar music box that played "Over The Rainbow." The little green box was activated by a strong light bulb or by the warm sun's rays. Now, when I need a lift or a way to delight a child, that magical music is there.

The power of the sun is all around us. Many people are affected by the lack of it when the winter months are upon us. They feel decreased energy, disturbed concentration, sluggishness, a tendency to overeat, and sometimes withdraw socially. Minds appear to be drawn within—almost like being wrapped in a cocoon while waiting for the dark days to vanish.

Light therapy and vitamin D supplements can ease these symptoms. By strengthening our inner thoughts with light, we are better able to cope with nature. The power of humor can be a big "lifter upper." We can be innovative and look for creative ways to raise our spirits.

The sun will appear again, and that is the time we need to reach out and bring it into the pockets of our hearts. This reminds me of a wonderful metal sculpture at the office. A smiling child holds his cut-out heart in his hand as he reaches out to share his warmth. By reaching out to others, we, too, can share *our* solar magic even on dreary days!

Today as I sit in my sunroom in absolute silence, I ask, "What is breathing beside me?" My chuckle fills the air! This past holiday season, my son and his family gave me a gift that was chosen by their 4-year-old daughter. Being a kindred spirit, she knew I would love it. It is a copper butterfly sitting on a rock. As the sun touches the sensor, the wings flap slowly making it sound as if the butterfly is breathing in and out. I breathe deeply in harmony with those tiny wings. The butterfly—symbol of change and hope—takes flight into my silent self and fills me with peace. Then, glancing out the window, I realize that the sun also has kissed the earth's cocoon and started the metamorphosis of winter into spring.

1991
February 4: The Baseball Hall of Fame votes to ban Pete Rose.

Summer: *Doctors Book of Home Remedies* sells 2 millionth copy.

November 6: The FDA requires a more detailed listing of contents on all food labels.

***Novii Fermer* begins publication in Russia.**

***Prevention* has a monthly circulation of more than 3.2 million.**

Maria Rodale appointed creative director.

Rodale opens child-care center at for the children of employees.

Rodale buys a majority interest in Yankee Press.

Rodale acquires Leman Publications, publisher of *Quiltmaker* magazine.

Rodale's main building expanded again—this time with a second story for editorial offices.

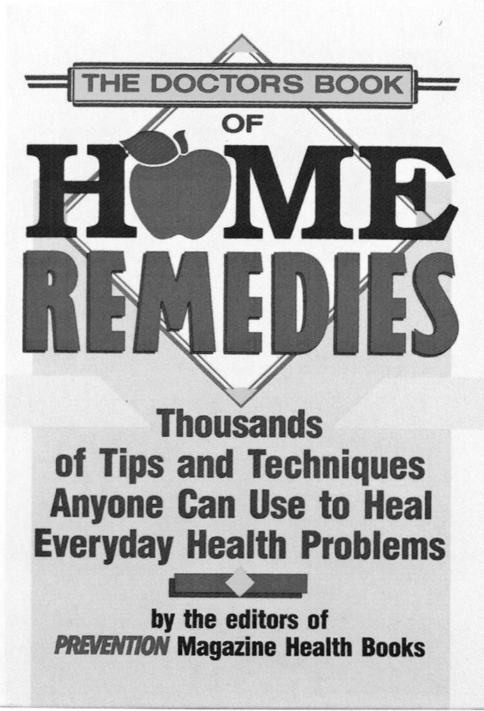

The Doctors Book of Home Remedies became the company's all-time bestseller in 1991.

Rodale in 1987 but returned. The 1990 *Ad Age* list of the top 300 magazines in gross revenues included four Rodale publications: *Prevention* (52), *OG* (153), *Bicycling* (174), and *Runner's World* (177). All the executives knew their mandate was to carry out Bob Rodale's mission to use Rodale's resources to champion the ideals he and J.I. had cherished.

In the fall of 1990, a crew began knocking down the old editorial wing of the main building to make way for a wider, two-story building. Typical for a Rodale construction project, once again overseen by Ardie, the new wing used oak and cherry wood from nearby South Mountain. Also in 1990, a new company-wide recycling plan enabled Rodale to recycle between 70 and 90 percent of its waste and earned the company $67,000 selling used paper, cardboard, glass, aluminum, and film. Bob's larger ambitions continued to come to fruition, too. Mid-January 1991 saw the publication of the first issue of the Russian language *Novii Fermer* (*New Farmer*) magazine, which had been Bob's pet project. George DeVault moved to Moscow to serve as its editor.

After pursuing different paths, each of Bob and Ardie's surviving four children had found professional homes at Rodale Press in the 1980s. Each would assume more responsibility in the 1990s. In the fall of 1991, with Heather Rodale managing leadership development and perpetuating Rodale's distinctive corporate culture, Heidi Rodale led the effort to open a child-care center for the children of employees in Emmaus, managed Rodale's Brand Awareness project, and developed the "You Can, I Did" corporate advertising campaign. Maria Rodale was appointed creative director, overseeing the production of direct mail and subscription promotions for all Rodale books and magazines. And Anthony Rodale continued to spearhead the globally minded agricultural research that Bob had championed through the Rodale Institute.

The company entered the 1990s in an expansive mode, in large part due to the success of *The Doctors Book of Home Remedies,* first published in 1990. A television commercial shot by Bill Gottlieb that aired nationally on network affiliates and cable generated 300,000 orders by April 1991, and by the summer of 1991, with sales of 2 million copies, *The Doctors Book* surpassed *Rodale's Practical Encyclopedia of Natural Healing,* first published in 1976, as the company's all-time bestseller.

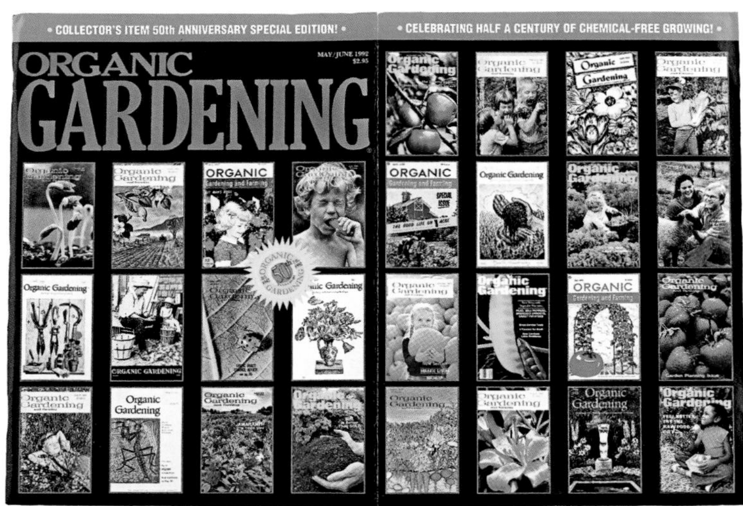

Organic Gardening magazine celebrated its 50th anniversary in May 1992.

The success of *The Doctors' Book* helped turn the book division into an engine of growth. The long-standing book clubs were also revitalized. In the first two weeks of 1992, more than 900,000 books were sold through mail order, more than were sold for all of 1984. As it had from its origins in the 1930s, Rodale's book business continued to rely almost entirely on direct marketing. And the standards of success weren't necessarily reviews in the Sunday *New York Times* or sales at the ever-expanding chain Barnes & Noble, but the response ratios to direct marketing mailings.

The Rodale magazines were contributing to the company's success as well. By 1992, *Prevention* had 3.2 million subscribers and was still remarkably profitable, although its audience was aging. *Runner's World* and *Backpacker* reported rising numbers of ad pages. Even Rodale's first magazine, *Organic Gardening,* which had lost money for years, was regenerated. Magazines face a tension between catering to a core niche audience and reaching out to the mainstream, and a change in trajectory always runs the risk of alienating the existing audience, which is precisely what happened to *OG* in the 1980s. "To attract a wider base of advertising, *OG* had become more of a general-interest magazine, talking about food, home, and environment. It was trying to appear chic to a trendy New York market, only New York wasn't buying it," as *WGOH* put it. And so *OG* returned to its roots. In a rare move, Rodale in 1989 reduced the rate base from 1 million to 600,000 readers. "We did it by raising the price 133 percent per copy over two years to weed out the readers who weren't really interested in the magazine," said publisher Barbara Newton. Frequency was reduced to nine times a year and promotions were cut. In the process, Rodale learned how committed readers were to *OG*. Circulation stabilized at 700,000, and traditional advertisers such as Burpee seed company returned. Mike McGrath, a six-year veteran of Rodale, became the magazine's new editor.

By 1992, company-wide sales had risen to $350 million, up 32 percent from 1990. But Rodale's magazine business needed a third pillar. *Men's Health* would fit the bill. Magazines like *Prevention* and *OG,* which had been years, even decades, ahead of their time, struggled initially to find both readers and advertisers. But *Men's Health* seemed to connect with its audience almost

1992
April 8: *Punch* magazine publishes its final issue.

Spring: Rodale begins to use recycled paper in some of its magazines.

May 22: Johnny Carson hosts *The Tonight Show* for the last time.

July 25: Summer Olympic Games begin in Barcelona, Spain.

***Rodale's Scuba Diving* begins publication.**

The Clean Air Act is revised to implement stricter limits on toxic air emissions.

Whole Foods Market acquires Bread & Circus.

Rodale has total sales of $289 million.

Rodale publishes *Young Executive* and *Healthy Cooking* as specials.

Bob Teufel named to a two-year term as chairman of the board of the Magazine Publishers of America.

In the span of a few years, Rodale had built *Men's Health* into a blockbuster magazine.

immediately. Baby-boomer males were finding their bodies and appearances changing at the same time they were entering their peak earning periods. As a result, *Men's Health* would become a commercial and cultural phenomenon.

Having grown rapidly from its origins as a newsletter and special magazine in the 1980s, *Men's Health* went quarterly in spring 1989, bimonthly in summer 1991, and then 10 times annually in 1993. In the second half of 1991, *Men's Health* was the fastest-growing consumer title audited by the Audit Bureau of Circulation, pushing Rodale more firmly into the world of mainstream glossy magazines. The goal was "to firmly establish the magazine as an equal player in the mainstream men's field, which includes *GQ*, *Esquire, Playboy, Rolling Stone,* and *Sports Illustrated,*" according to the sales plan in December 1991. "In short, we have the opportunity to be an *important magazine.*"

Rodale invested in *Men's Health* through aggressive marketing and by bringing in new talent. Joseph Heroun, who worked on the redesigns of *Sports Illustrated* and *Mirabella,* was brought in as design director. And with its mix of editorial focusing on issues such as health, sex, and fitness—a set of topics touched on only glancingly by most men's magazines—*Men's Health* plainly struck a chord. A direct mail subscription package in December 1992 received a record 7.28 percent gross response on 4.4 million pieces. By 1993, having increased the rate base four times in three years, circulation was up to 650,000. By the end of 1993, the rate base had soared to 1 million.

Rodale had generally taken a cautious approach toward acquisitions and had found success in the past two decades with *Bicycling, Runner's World,* and *American Woodworker.* In the early 1990s the company branded itself as "America's Leading You Can Do It" magazine publisher and began to search for appropriate properties to add to its stable. In 1991, Rodale bought a majority interest in Yankee Press, a Camden, Maine–based publisher best known as the distributor of the *Old Farmer's Almanac,* and Colorado-based Leman Publications, which published *Quilter's Newsletter, Quiltmaker* magazine, and a mail-order catalog. In both instances, in a departure from prior practice, Rodale let the offices and most of the employees of the acquired magazines remain where they were rather than move to Emmaus.

In search of the next potential *Men's Health,* the company continued its specials program. In the first half of 1992, it tested *Young Executive* and *Healthy Cooking.* And in May 1992 it bought *Scuba Diving Magazine,* with an initial circulation of 125,000 and the goal of becoming a monthly by 1994. The magazine's editorial offices were based in Savannah, Georgia.

On the international front, one of the least established and stable markets in Europe—Russia—was one of Rodale's first destinations for expansion in both magazines and books. After introducing *Novii Fermer* in 1991, Rodale translated Dave Barry's *Guide to Marriage and/or Sex* into Russian; it sold 150,000 copies in a week. The experience pointed to international opportunities.

The effort to expand internationally was fraught with challenges, though, in large part because the experience Rodale had selling advertising and books through direct marketing in the U.S. market wasn't easily transferred. In the 1980s, Rodale had invested significant sums to build a robust database containing 23 million names of customers. Overseas, it had virtually no such data. The company thus developed a multipronged strategy for entering foreign markets. Generally, in English-speaking countries, Rodale chose to buy or establish wholly owned properties. In non–English-speaking developed countries, it tended to enter joint ventures. And in unestablished foreign markets, it would license editorial material to other companies, letting them publish and market it themselves.

In books, the international push was led by *The Doctors Book,* which, after launching in 1992 in the United Kingdom, was translated into Spanish, Finnish, French, and Portuguese by the end of 1993. Rodale also saw the great potential of bringing the health message to the 25 million–strong (and growing) Hispanic market in the United States. When the company sold the Mexican trade rights to *The Doctors Book,* it negotiated for the use of the translation at home and in early 1993 pitched a Spanish-language edition of *The Doctors Book* through the mail.

Runner's World led the magazine division overseas. Just three years after Nelson Mandela's release from prison spelled the end of Apartheid in South Africa, Rodale launched *Runner's World* there in 1993 in conjunction with the Comrades Marathon, a 55-mile race from Pietermaritzburg to Durban. *Runner's World* editor Amby Burfoot, the 1968 Boston Marathon champion, finished the race in under 11 hours.

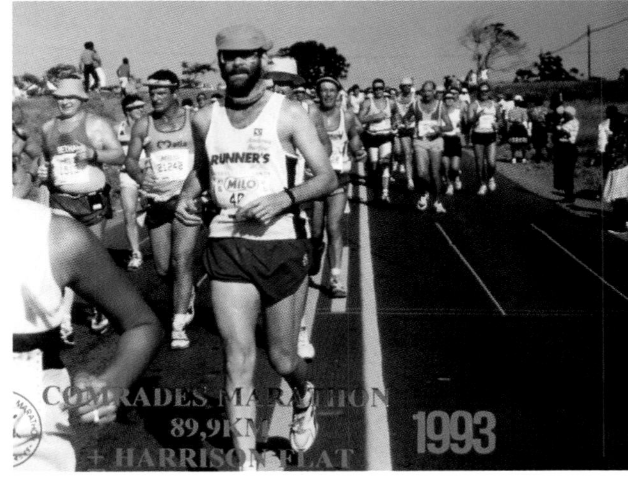

Twenty-five years after winning the 1968 Boston Marathon, *Runner's World*'s Amby Burfoot participated in the famous Comrades Marathon in Durban, South Africa.

1993
January: Bob Rodale posthumously receives the Magazine Publishers Association Henry Johnson Fisher Award.

March 5: Canadian sprinter Ben Johnson is banned from international competition for life after testing positive for banned substances for the second time.

Ben Johnson

April 22: Version 1.0 of the Mosaic Web browser is released.

July: *Heart & Soul* debuts.

Direct sales of *The Doctors Book of Home Remedies* introduced in the U.K. and France.

***Runner's World* launches in South Africa.**

Rodale purchases *Runners* magazine and converts it into *Runner's World UK*.

***Men's Health* rate base reaches 1 million.**

Men's Health, in Mexico

Next came Europe. Rodale purchased Great Britain's *Runners* magazine and converted it into *Runner's World UK* in 1993 and in 1994 struck a licensing agreement with Dutch publishing company Weekbladpers, BV, under which the Dutch magazine *Runner* would become *Runner's World. Runner's World* was followed by the company's health magazines. By 1993, *Men's Health* was licensed in Mexico, where it was known as *Hombre Saludable,* and *Prevention* was licensed in South Korea (as *Health 365*) and in South America (as *Prevención*).

The company was gaining international recognition. In late 1992, Bob Teufel was named to a two-year term as chairman of the board of the Magazine Publishers of America, succeeding Reg Brack, chairman and CEO of Time Inc. And in January 1993, Bob Rodale received, posthumously, the MPA's highest honor, the 1993 Henry Johnson Fisher Award. When Ardie accepted the award at a black-tie dinner at the Waldorf-Astoria in New York, it represented a bittersweet triumph. By seeking and relentlessly pursuing its own path, Rodale had evolved to become part of the publishing establishment. It was a status that J. I. Rodale wished for but likely never would have imagined. After all, the company had always prided itself on its independence. And in its values and its goals, its location and its corporate culture, Rodale had long seen itself as being apart from the New York–centric publishing world. But as it sought to appeal to new markets, the company began to acquire a greater appreciation for the usefulness of working with other companies—abroad and at home.

A new corporate ad campaign emphasized the Rodale message of living an active, healthy lifestyle.

In 1993, by which time *The Doctors Book* had sold more than 10 million copies, Rodale published *The Doctors Book II,* which contained more than 100 new conditions and symptoms and more than 1,000 new remedies. Although it didn't match the success of the original, its sales created enough revenue that 1994 proved to be a huge year for the company. Books were the new cash cow, with almost as much in sales as the rest of the company in 1990.

You can!

"I did!"

Rodale Press helps you grow

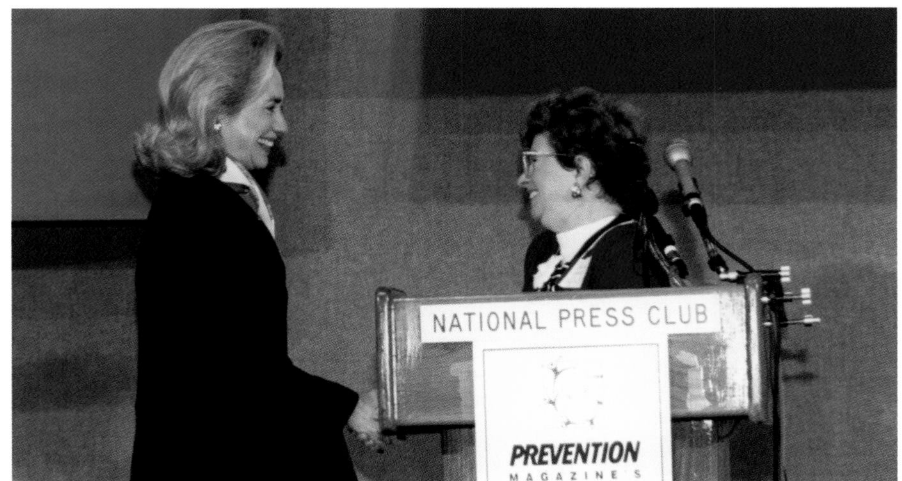

Ardie welcomes keynote speaker Hillary Clinton at the introduction of *Prevention*'s Children's Health Index.

Rodale's corporate culture and message was constantly evolving, while remaining tethered to core values. In the 1990s that message centered around a vigorous, healthy lifestyle more oriented toward men in their active years than it had been in the past. In the fall of 1993, Rodale introduced a new corporate ad campaign. The ads featured the slogans "You Can!" and "I Did!" One ad showed a *Men's Health* reader seated atop a horse. Inspired by the magazine, he had decided to take a working vacation at a cattle ranch in Utah.

In 1994, Rodale adopted a new mission statement that called for "gathering, rethinking, and utilizing information on health, fitness, and home and garden to enable Rodale customers to lead more self-reliant, vital lives." The language may have been slightly different, but the impulse was essentially that which had informed J.I. and Bob's efforts: showing people how to use the power of their minds and bodies to improve their lives, the environment, and the world. "While we realize we must be profitable to exist, we don't exist just to be profitable," read one line of the mission statement. As Ardie put it in an interview in *USA Today,* "You don't have a job here but a way of life."

A series of events in 1994 and 1995 bore witness to the company's commitment to its past and its role in the broader culture. In April 1994 a full-length documentary about Bob Rodale, *A World of Sense,* was completed by Burt Fox, who had worked for Rodale's video unit in the 1970s. In 1995, in a realization of one of Bob Rodale's more ambitious visions, the trials for the U.S. Olympic bicycling team were held at the Trexlertown velodrome. That fall, First Lady Hillary Rodham Clinton gave the keynote address as *Prevention*'s Children's Health Index was formally introduced at an event jointly sponsored by *Prevention* and the American Academy of Pediatrics. As well, several dozen government officials, farmers, and scientists from across the nation gathered at the experimental farm for the opening of the Rodale Institute's Composting Research and Education Center.

But even as Rodale was making its impact on the world, it remained deeply rooted to its history and to its home base. The company and the Rodale family had supported the creation of the Rodale Aquatic Center at nearby Cedar Crest College. Heidi Rodale helped lead efforts to raise funds, and the Rodale Family Foundation donated $1 million to help build the complex.

RODALE PRESS

Mission

Rodale Press is a publishing company which produces and sells magazines and books profitably by gathering, rethinking, and utilizing information on health, fitness, and home and garden to enable Rodale customers to lead more self-reliant, vital lives.

Operating Values

- Rodale Press cares about our family of co-workers by encouraging a healthy lifestyle, being sensitive to personal needs, and showing people how to use the power of their minds and bodies to make their lives better.
- We are committed to constant improvement of our products, operations, and ourselves.
- We are committed to a better world through environmental leadership in business and society.
- We are committed to an internal culture of cooperation, courtesy, honesty, and respect.
- While we realize we must be profitable to exist, we don't exist just to be profitable.

The Rodale Press mission statement, 1994

1994
April: *A World of Sense*, a documentary film about Bob Rodale, is released.

May 9: Nelson Mandela is inaugurated as South Africa's first black president.

InStyle magazine debuts.

'Flavr Savr', a red tomato and the first genetically altered whole food to be approved for sale by the U.S. Food and Drug Administration, hits the market.

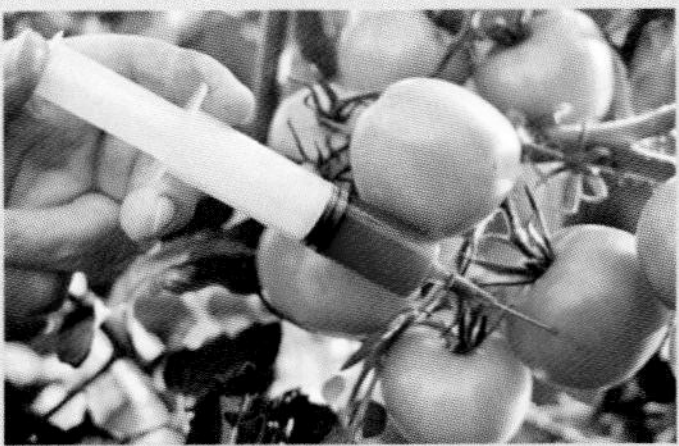

Tomato syringe

***Men's Health Latin America* becomes the magazine's first overseas edition.**

Rodale strikes a licensing agreement to turn Dutch magazine *Runner* into *Runner's World*.

The South Mountain Center was built in 1995. The three-story building featured a large skylight that created a cylinder of light through the center of the structure. A kiva, a traditional Pueblo Indian ceremonial space, was added as a refuge for reflection.

(It opened in 2002.) As part of its effort to build the Rodale active sports magazines, Rodale Press in 1994 bought *Fitness Swimmer* and Heidi Rodale was named publisher.

Rodale was now a large and far-flung company. By the end of 1995, it had business partners in Germany and Russia, licensees all over the world, the organic farm, offices throughout the United States, and a series of joint ventures. Given the size of the company and the number of employees, and with ownership now distributed among two generations and several Rodale family members, it became clear that it needed stronger governance. In the spring of 1995 the board of directors, which included Ardie and her four surviving children, Bob Teufel, John Griffin, Pat Corpora, and Dave Widenmyer, adopted new governance procedures. Committees on finance, strategic planning, and human resources were established, composed of senior executives and family members, who would rotate through them.

Planning was also under way for a large new building in Emmaus, on 10th Street. Originally intended to house the burgeoning book division, the South Mountain Center was located across town, about a mile from the main building on East Minor Street. With a capacity of 360 people, it was designed by architect William McDonough to allow a maximum of natural light and had an energy-efficient cooling system that included an 80,000-gallon tank filled with ice that cooled water at night. At Ardie's suggestion, the architect placed a kiva, a quiet room pierced by light from a skylight window and reserved for quiet contemplation, as the building's centerpiece.

Advances in information technology were beginning to course through the media. As the 1990s unfolded, the Internet gained more of a user base. Online businesses were growing and gaining scale. America Online aggressively signed up millions of customers for dial-up Internet access, and the July 1995 initial public offering of browser inventor Netscape represented a watershed. As the Internet evolved from the playground of the technologically savvy into a new mass medium, it became clear that it would affect magazines and books. But despite the grand scenarios described by management consultants and technology gurus, nobody was clear precisely how it would do so.

1995
July: Amazon.com Web site starts offering books for sale to the public.

July 17: The NASDAQ stock index closes above the 1,000 mark for the first time.

August 9: Internet browser company Netscape holds successful initial public offering.

Fall: Conference at Rodale Institute opens the Composting Research and Education Center.

Chef Alice Waters forms an alliance with a middle school in Berkeley, California, to turn its playground into an organic garden and outdoor classroom.

First fatality from mad cow disease occurs in Britain.

Rodale launches *Fitness Swimmer*.

First Lady Hillary Rodham Clinton delivers keynote address at the introduction of *Prevention*'s Children's Health Index.

***Men's Health* launches in the U.K.**

AMERICA'S LEADING HEALTH MAGAZINE
PREVENTION
Give Yourself A
NATURAL
TUMMY
TUCK
New Tools To
BEAT BREAST
CANCER
Sleep
Tight Tonight
BEYOND
CHOLESTEROL
Biggest Breakthrough
Since Antioxidants!

Prevention grew to be the 11th largest magazine in the United States in 1994.

Rodale first embraced the Internet as a means of selling subscriptions. As early as 1992, *Prevention* was one of nearly 400 titles offered for sale by Publishers Clearing House on the Prodigy network. Magazines such as *Bicycling* began to provide some content to AOL, which in 1994 set up an *American Woodworker* chat room. The next step was to launch Web sites for the individual magazines. The Web site www.runnersworld.com launched on January 1, 1996. The following month, Rodale signed a deal that would make information from *Men's Health, Prevention, Heart & Soul,* and Rodale health books available on the Health and Fitness section of AT&T's online service. Cybertree, Rodale's new intranet, was built in 1996. It was clear that people were using the Internet to access information and to communicate. By February 1997, *Bicycling*'s AOL site had notched its 3 millionth visitor, but it was still unclear how to connect with those potential customers. Online advertising was very slow to develop, and media companies had little success in selling subscriptions to online publications. As a result, Rodale took a measured approach to its Internet investments, even as a tide of enthusiasm surrounding the new medium grew.

Meanwhile, the company's core businesses continued to thrive. *Prevention* in the second half of 1994 leapfrogged *Sports Illustrated, Playboy,* and *People,* to become the nation's 11th largest magazine, with 3.427 million in circulation. *Men's Health* hired Marvin Traub, the former head of Bloomingdale's, as an advertising consultant, and he helped lasso Ralph Lauren as an advertiser. When other major companies followed the example of the well-known trendsetter, *Men's Health* surpassed *Prevention* as the company's most profitable periodical.

How could Rodale continue to grow? For books, the answer was to start thinking about transforming the way the business ran. In 1996 the book division was still almost entirely dependent on through-the-mail sales. Editors would compile 150-word descriptions of book ideas, ask readers to rate them on surveys, and devise and test promotions. Every year nearly 200 million pieces of direct mail were sent out. The system worked great when the company picked a winner, but in Emmaus, executives began to think about how they could transform their product-driven business into a customer-driven business. They began to think about establishing strategies to sell

1996
January 1: The Web site www.runnersworld.com is launched.

April 6: Major League Soccer debuts.

July 5: Dolly the sheep, the first mammal to be successfully cloned from an adult cell, is born.

***Men's Health* begins publishing in Germany.**

Dolly, the sheep

July 19: 1996 Summer Olympics open in Atlanta, Georgia.

U.S. Olympic bicycling team conducts Olympic trials at the Trexlertown velodrome.

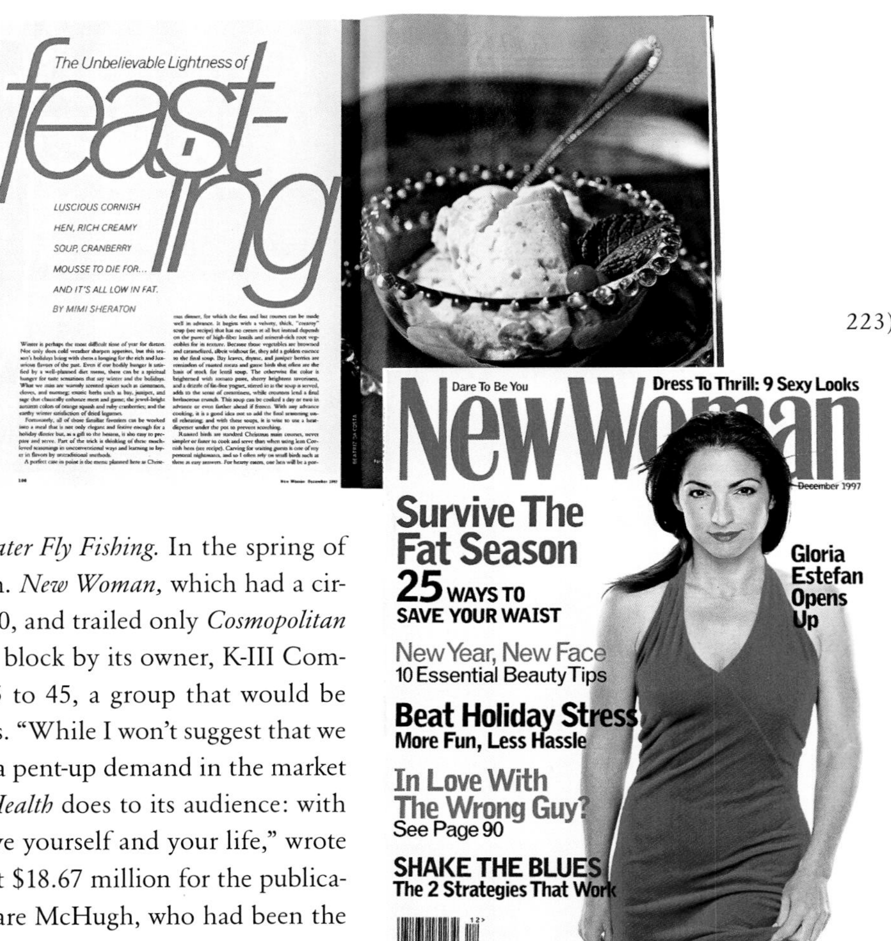

Rodale bought *New Woman* in 1997 in an effort to reach younger women.

Rodale books on the Web, to do more with Spanish-language books, and to become a leader in publishing trade health books (sold primarily through bookstores, not through the mail).

For magazines, the short-term response was to buy growth. In 1997, Rodale bought Abenaki Publishers, which owned small-circulation titles such as *American Angler* and *Saltwater Fly Fishing.* In the spring of 1997, Rodale formed a task force to examine a far larger acquisition. *New Woman,* which had a circulation of 1 million and monthly newsstand sales of about 400,000, and trailed only *Cosmopolitan* and *Glamour* in the women's magazine field, had been put on the block by its owner, K-III Communications. Rodale didn't have a magazine for women ages 25 to 45, a group that would be expected to respond to the company's message on health and fitness. "While I won't suggest that we try to re-create *Men's Health* with a female persona, I think there is a pent-up demand in the market for a women's magazine that speaks to its readers the way *Men's Health* does to its audience: with confidence, humor, and simple, practical advice on how to improve yourself and your life," wrote one executive at the time. In June 1997, Rodale agreed to pay about $18.67 million for the publication, by far the largest sum Rodale had paid for an acquisition. Clare McHugh, who had been the editor of the U.S. edition of *Maxim,* was named editor in chief of *New Woman.*

A similar impulse to get younger and a little glossier fed the next round of regeneration at *Prevention.* In the summer of 1997, Anne Alexander, a former editor at *Self, Vogue,* and *Natural Health,* was named editor when Mark Bricklin was promoted to head New Initiatives, which included Rodale's new media and Internet efforts. Research had shown that 75 percent of *Prevention*'s readership were women in their 50s and 60s, and the magazine wanted to attract a new audience. Alexander reengineered the news section, renamed some columns, and instituted a column on caring for parents. *OG* also got a new editor in late 1997, when Nancy Beaubaire, a former editor at *Country Living Gardener,* signed on at the end of the year.

Toward the end of the '90s, Maria Rodale began to assume more corporate responsibilites. She was named vice chairman in 1998.

Meanwhile, *Men's Health* continued to expand, launching overseas in Germany, Latin America, South Africa, Australia, and Russia. Paced by this growth, Rodale's magazine business had changed significantly. Between 1991 and 1997, among the magazine companies examined by Publisher's Information Bureau, Rodale saw the greatest growth in advertising revenues: 192 percent. For virtually all of its existence, Rodale had derived more revenues from circulation than from advertising. But in the 1990s, with the growth of *Men's Health,* that began to change. In 1997, advertising revenues for the first time topped 50 percent of the division's revenues.

Rodale was approaching a crossroads. Now a big company, with 1,500 people and $500 million in sales, it faced some big choices. As John Griffin put it at the time, "The biggest challenge that we face at Rodale without question is that we don't have good ideas for magazines, we've got a hundred good ideas." But the company didn't have the human and financial resources to back 100 good ideas. If Rodale were to continue to grow–and grow profitably–in an ever-expanding media world, it would have to narrow its focus. Ardie was approaching 70, Bob Teufel, who had been with the company since 1961, was nearing retirement, and Maria Rodale was assuming a more prominent role. For once, Rodale and the Rodales would have the opportunity to plan for a generational transition. In 1997, the family adopted a purpose statement, which read in part: "By the year 2000 we will have successfully defined the strategic direction of the company to continue our global growth through the 21st century."

Rodale took this opportunity to take a hard look at the company, its products, its brands, and its place in the evolving media world. "Now is the time for the Rodale family to take a fresh look at all aspects of the company," as Pat Corpora put it. Top executives, board members, and employees broke into teams to examine broad themes such as strategic renewal and competitor and customer awareness. Corpora interviewed executives at other companies to learn more about organizational structure. Consultants interviewed other editors and consumers. They found that customers didn't see Rodale as a strong brand, and that while the quality of content was given high marks, the design of its magazines and books was less impressive.

1997
January 23: Madeleine Albright becomes the first female Secretary of State.

August: Rodale acquires *New Woman.*

The USDA's proposed organic guidelines are released. The public balks at the inclusion of sewage sludge, irradiation, and genetically modified organisms in the regulations and soundly rejects the proposal.

The Kyoto Protocol, an agreement intended to set legally binding limits on man-made emissions in 38 industrialized nations, is put forth.

USDA organic symbol

Rodale acquires Abenaki, publisher of *American Angler, Saltwater Fly Fishing,* and other fishing magazines.

Rodale forms partnership with Interweave Press to publish herbal magazines.

Maxim magazine debuts.

Jane magazine debuts.

Many of the properties were obviously core strategic holdings: *OG, Prevention, Men's Health, New Woman,* and all the lines of health-related books. Spanish-language health was nearing critical mass. In sports and fitness, *Runner's World, Backpacker,* and *Bicycling* were all both profitable and significant. But the analysis left out African American health (i.e., *Heart & Soul*), cooking, niche magazines such as *Scuba Diving* and *Fitness Swimmer,* along with the fishing publications—all seen as too small. Woodworking and quilting, while profitable, had limited growth potential.

In February 1998, Rodale announced a new strategic plan. "By 2008, Rodale Press will be the world's leading independent source of ideas, advice, and motivation for healthy active living." Going forward, the company would grow through building its brands and customer relationships, improving financial discipline, and increasing its international businesses. Several units would be sold: Leman Publications, *American Woodworker,* and the woodworking, Yankee, sewing, and quilting book lines. To minimize the effect on employees of those units, Rodale imposed a temporary hiring freeze.

The announcement represented an important inflection point. In the previous eight years, the business had grown in so many directions that rationalization was overdue. The company was also taking the opportunity to rebrand, recharge, and refocus its vision for the coming decades. The announcements marked Maria Rodale's ascent to vice chairman and the emerging public face of the company. As part of the strategic review, Rodale also decided to drop the word "Press" from the company name to reflect a focus that included new media. "We need to think of ourselves not as a book division and a magazine division, not as a publisher, but as a company of strong brands that can help people have healthy active lives," Maria said. The trefoil logo would also change.

The company moved quickly to implement the new strategic plan. It sold *Heart & Soul* back to its joint venture partner in 1998 and started the process of selling several other lines of business. Management refined the strategic plan and worked to include employees in the transformation. In the summer of 1998, Rodale held a town meeting in the Phoenix Room of the new

Rodale dropped "Press" from its name and modernized the logo.

1998

January 1: Smoking is banned in all California bars and restaurants.

March: *ESPN: The Magazine* debuts.

May 6: Apple Computer unveils the iMac.

September 7: Google Inc. is founded.

October 29: Space shuttle *Discovery* blasts off with 77-year-old John Glenn on board, making him the oldest person to go into space.

Rodale creates a 10-year plan called Project 2008, headed by Maria Rodale.

***Organic Gardening* magazine is redesigned.**

John Glenn

Rodale Press receives Pennsylvania governor Tom Ridge's Excellence Award for increasing export sales of *Men's Health.*

***MH International* launches editions in the Netherlands and Scandinavia.**

***Men's Health* marks its 10th anniversary.**

ORGANIC GARDENING

Experimental Farm

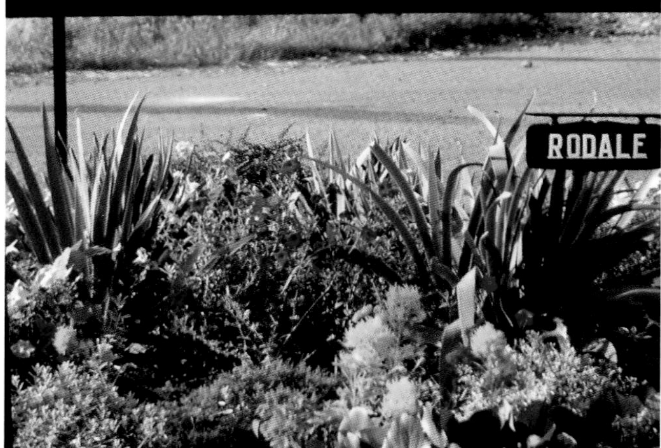

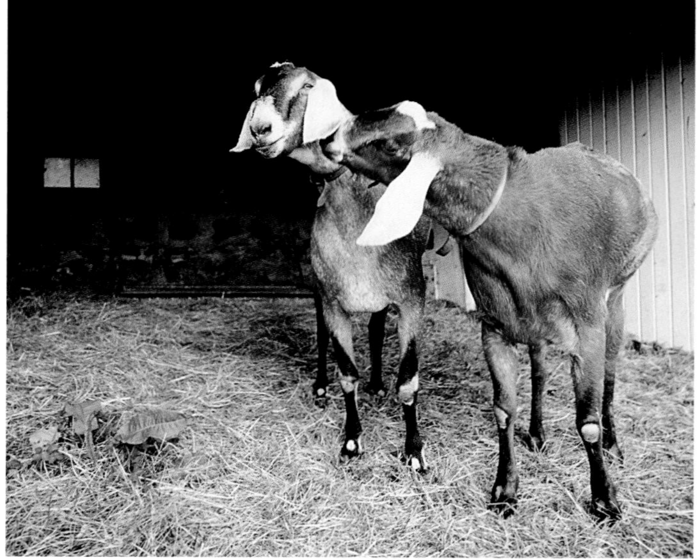

The original Organic Gardening Experimental Farm remains the site of several Rodale-family homes and is still an active organic farm, producing food for the Rodale family and company food service. The Rodale day care holds a summer camp on the grounds for school-age children.

Rodale Institute is a nonprofit research and education organization that focuses on regenerative agriculture and its impact on health and the environment. Located on 333 acres near Kutztown, Pennsylvania, the Institute has a working certified organic farm that hosts the longest running research trial in the United States comparing conventional and organic farming methods. The Institute has trained farmers throughout the country and abroad and hosts nearly 25,000 visitors a year. Most recently, Rodale Institute launched a new Web site at www.rodaleinstitute.com, which features a free Transition to Organics online course and provides information and expertise for farmers, policymakers, and consumers about how regenerative agriculture can help solve global warming, improve nutrition, and prevent worldwide famine.

Colloquially still referred to as the New Farm by old-timers, the Institute also hosts the Rodale company picnic each year in June.

FASTEST PERENNIALS EVER • BEST VEGETABLES FOR YOUR REGION

ORGANIC GARDENING

ROSES
Easy & Beautiful...Naturally

Chef's Secrets for a Healthy Classic
12 Must-Have Tools
Let Nature Guide Your Designs

ORGANIC ELEGANCE

SMART DESIGN AND WELL-TIMED CARE ARE KEYS TO THIS EDIBLE LANDSCAPE'S SUCCESS. *by* Dayna Lane

A FORTUNATE GARDENER IS ONE who's given the chance to start a garden with a design based on sound organic principles. Although most of us inherit already-established landscapes, organic-landscape designer Rosalind Creasy is one of the lucky gardeners who has the chance to create organic gardens from the ground up.

In 1992, Creasy was asked by Marva and John Warnock of Los Altos, California, to design a landscape that would integrate edibles with ornamentals in the lot next to their home. (I was hired to be the head gardener, a position that I held until 1996). While Creasy designed the garden for the Warnocks, she kept organic principles in mind and addressed both the ongoing need for water conservation in California's semiarid climate and the Warnock's desire to entertain—formally and informally—outdoors. She also had to design the garden around

Marva Warnock and head gardener Maureen Gough-Decombe relax in the Warnock garden, which includes a greenhouse (left).

OG MARCH/APRIL 1999 23

Organic Gardening changed to a larger-format magazine in 1998.

headquarters, led by Ardie, Maria, Bob Teufel, and Pat Corpora, to discuss Rodale's goals for the coming decade. By 2008, they said, 25 percent of revenues would come from non-print sources, the next big brand and market/audience would be defined and captured, and 25 percent of revenues would derive from international products and sales.

Implementing the new strategy meant reorganizing existing business lines. In the fall of 1998, the book division was divided into four groups: Trade, Healthy Living, Active Living, and International, each with its own publisher. Since Organic Living had been designated as a unit that would drive growth, Rodale decided to integrate *OG*, gardening books, and the organic gardening Web site into a single multimedia unit. *OG* still had a sense of activism at its core. When the U.S. Department of Agriculture in December 1997 proposed rules for a federal organic certification program, which would have permitted genetically engineered products and products treated with sewage sludge to be certified as organic, *OG* helped lead a drive to convince Agriculture Secretary Dan Glickman to revise them. But with the continuing evolution and growth of organic agriculture and products, it was becoming as much of a lifestyle as a mission. In the fall of 1998, *OG* was redesigned with a broadened editorial focus, enlarged from a digest to a full-size magazine, and filled with more color photography. "I feel like I have a family treasure in my hands," said editor Nancy Beaubaire. "We're branching out, not uprooting ourselves."

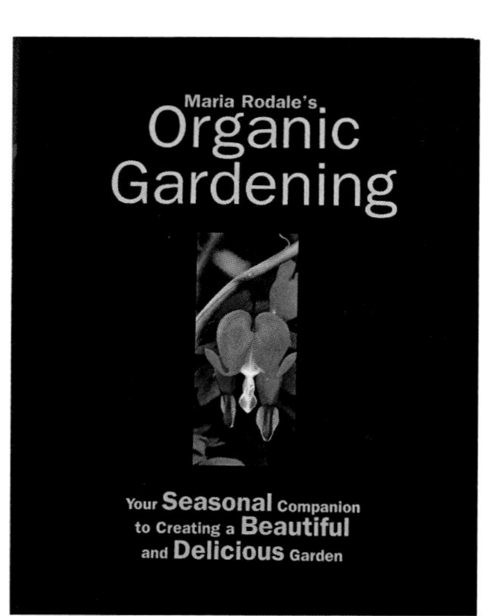

Maria Rodale set forth her philosophies in her book *Maria Rodale's Organic Gardening.*

The redesigned *OG* was the cornerstone of the new Organic Living division, formed in January 1999 and led by Maria Rodale. She published a book, entitled *Maria Rodale's Organic Gardening,* which included some 600 color photos, many of which she took. In September 1, Oprah Winfrey taped two segments with Maria in her garden for Oprah's "Remembering Your Spirit" series. And Maria began planning a new magazine, tentatively named *Organic Living.* In January 1999, a new organicgardening.com Web site was launched to sell subscriptions, promote books, post content from the magazine, and have interactive features such as answering questions submitted by readers.

1999
January: New organicgardening.com Web site is launched to sell subscriptions and promote books.

***Men's Health* launches in Finland and France.**

May 3: The Dow Jones Industrial Average closes above 11,000 for the first time, at 11,014.70.

July 25: Lance Armstrong, having recovered from metastatic testicular cancer, wins the Tour de France.

Field trials at the Rodale Institute in Maxatawny, Pennsylvania, reveal that organic soybean and corn fields soak up greenhouse gases.

August: *Talk* magazine debuts.

Lance Armstrong

Biotech giant Monsanto decides to produce seeds genetically engineered to produce infertile offspring. Public outcry persuades Monsanto to abandon the pursuit.

Studies conducted at Cornell University reveal that monarch butterflies feeding on milkweed dusted with pollen from genetically engineered corn die within four days.

Runner's World expanded internationally into eight countries, including Australia, South Africa, and Germany.

The goal of having one-quarter of revenues derive from international businesses may have seemed ambitious, but the experience of the 1990s surely made Rodale confident. *Runner's World* by 1998 had eight overseas editions: company-owned ones in Australia and the United Kingdom, joint ventures in Germany and South Africa, and licensees in Sweden, the Netherlands, Belgium, and Austria. Together, they had a combined circulation of 600,000, greater than *Runner World*'s U.S. circulation of 480,000. And by 1998, *Men's Health,* which had quickly grown to become the company's single most valuable asset, had 12 international editions. As had always been the case, Rodale sought to develop systems for managing complexities. David Zinczenko, the then-28-year-old executive editor for *Men's Health* International, oversaw the content of all editions and worked closely with editors overseas. Rodale would prescribe universal stories to form the foundation of the foreign editions and review copy well in advance of ship dates. In September 1998, when *Men's Health* marked its 10th anniversary with a party at New York's trendy Lot 61 nightclub, its U.S. circulation was 1.585 million, larger than those of *GQ* and *Esquire* combined.

The reorganization was in many ways bold and far-reaching, but it didn't fundamentally alter the book business. And it didn't solve the challenge that Rodale and other publishing companies faced in the late 1990s. The expansion of media meant broader platforms on which to launch new ideas. J.I. and Bob had really only had magazines, and secondarily books, with only occasional and not sustained forays into television and radio. But now things were different. On the one hand, the message from the business press, consulting companies, and technology services providers was that print in all its forms—the dead-tree business—would soon be left behind by the Internet, which offered greater reach and more efficient distribution. The migration of news and other content to the Web and the advent of e-books threatened to undermine the business models of businesses ranging from the *New York Times* to Simon & Schuster. On the other hand, print companies seemed uniquely positioned to work in the Internet space. Rodale had entertained the idea of buying an Internet company as part of its strategic thinking. But instead it chose a host of smaller investments and initiatives, inside and outside of the company. A new e-commerce site launched

"Rodale Inc." replaces "Rodale Press Inc." as corporate name.

Rodale Inc. named one of *Fortune* magazine's "100 Best Companies to Work for in America."

John Haberern celebrates 40 years with Rodale.

A portion of the Trexlertown Trap and Skeet Club is designated as the Bob Rodale Skeet Fields.

***Maria Rodale's Organic Gardening* is published.**

Maria Rodale is named president of Rodale's Organic Living division.

***Prevention* drops to the 16th-largest magazine in the country.**

Ardie Rodale named one of 1999's Leading Women Entrepreneurs of the World.

Rodale sells *New Woman*.

The Rodale store Web site was launched in 1998.

RODALESTORE
RODALESTORE.COM

for Rodale Books in November 1998 had one main store featuring all Rodale's in-print books and six branded storefronts. By 1999 the company was selling 20,000 magazine subscriptions per month over the Internet. Like many other media companies, Rodale also invested in new media companies. Pat Corpora was named to head a new unit, Rodale Interactive Initiatives. By 1999, Rodale had taken equity stakes in companies such as women.com, petsmart.com, and mothernature.com, which sold vitamins online. Under the leadership of Mike LaFavore, it was planning to develop internal Web-based products that pivoted off existing Rodale lines of business: manslife.com and naturemd.com, for example.

The Internet and its associated technologies seemed to offer limitless long-term opportunities, even if revenues were slow to materialize at first. But amid all the optimism, there was the potential to lose focus. And in 1999, several forces that had long been gathering strength came to a head. Even before the stock market and economy began to taper off in 2000, conditions grew difficult in the magazine and book industries. And it turned out that the greatest competition for print media in the late 1990s wouldn't be the Internet, but other print media. Fed by a continually rising economy and stock market, magazines were launched at a feverish pace: more than 1,000 in 1998 and another 866 in 1999. Many were niche publications, but some were large-scale publications that directly challenged Rodale properties. The growth of *ESPN: The Magazine* and *Maxim* hurt *Men's Health,* for example. *New Woman* continued to struggle in the crowded women's field. Rodale as a company was more dependent on advertising than it had been at any point in the past, and the market was growing crowded.

That left tremendous pressure on subscriptions as a source of revenue. But Rodale and other magazine companies faced problems in this area, too. Third-party sweepstakes companies such as Publishers Clearing House had long been a significant source of new business for Rodale magazines, especially *Prevention, New Woman,* and *OG.* In 1999, a series of state and federal investigations into the sales practices of sweepstakes companies led to changes in the business and cut deeply into sales. *Prevention* alone lost hundreds of thousands of subscriptions. Meanwhile, magazine distribution was

2000
January 10: America Online announces an agreement to buy Time Warner for $162 billion.

February 29: Anna Andrews Rodale dies, at age 95.

March 10: NASDAQ stock index peaks at 5,048.62.

Toyota releases the Toyota Prius, the first hybrid four-door sedan available in the United States.

A study released by researchers at Stanford University and the Universities of Minnesota and South Carolina finds that exercise in the garden compares favorably to other types of recreation generally considered more vigorous.

Toyota Prius

Spring: Robert Teufel retires after 39 years at Rodale.

April: Steven Pleshette Murphy joins Rodale as president and chief operating officer.

Hain Food Group merges with Celestial Seasonings.

April: *O, The Oprah Magazine* is launched.

continuing to change in ways that were unfavorable to publishers. Wal-Mart emerged as the single largest purchaser of magazines in the country, and with the consolidation of both wholesalers and retail outlets, magazine publishers suddenly found themselves dealing with just a few wholesale customers, rather than hundreds. As they demanded lower prices, this shift in dynamic also cut into profit margins.

For Rodale, this combination of a tougher advertising climate, falling subscriptions, and narrower magazines spelled trouble in the magazine business. Meanwhile, the book division, lacking a blockbuster, fell short of budget and experienced weakness in virtually every segment. As a result, the company's sales fell sharply in 1999.

Suddenly, Rodale found itself with a bloated cost structure and some significant drags on its business. The company reacted swiftly. In 2000, *New Woman* was closed. And as the restructuring planned in 1998 continued, Rodale experienced the first large-scale layoffs in the company's history. It was a difficult and occasionally dispiriting time. But even amid the challenge, the company was looking to regenerate. In January 2000 it relaunched its public Web site. And in the spring of 2000, when Bob Teufel, who had been with the company for 39 years, retired, Rodale looked outside for a new president. In April 2000, Steven Pleshette Murphy joined Rodale from Disney Publishing as president and chief operating officer.

By the spring of 2000, then, Rodale was in the midst of yet another transition. And like the previous ones, this transition would depend more on continuities than on sharp shifts in direction. At the close of the 20th century, the one J. I. Rodale had so fervently wished to witness in its entirety, Rodale Inc. employed 1,300 people. It was one of the largest family businesses in the United States. *Prevention* had a circulation of 3 million, and *Men's Health* had a circulation of 1.25 million. The company sold more than 20 million books. And Rodale had relationships with literally tens of millions of customers throughout the world. After a turbulent decade, the company had established the leaders, the core businesses, and the vision that would propel it into the 21st century.

Changes to the way magazine subscriptions were sold through third-party companies like Publishers Clearing House caused a sharp drop in subscription sales for *Prevention* and other magazines.

April: *Real Simple* debuts.

April 23: *Dr. Shapiro's Picture Perfect Weight Loss* becomes the first Rodale book to land on the *New York Times* bestseller list.

May: *Men's Health* launches in Italy.

August: *MH-18* debuts as a special.

Sydney Opera House

September 15: The 2000 Summer Olympics open in Sydney, Australia.

October: Rodale unveils new strategic plan: The Power to Grow.

November: Rodale and Integrative Medicine Communications create strategic partnership to deliver health education and outreach programs.

ANNA RODALE

FEBRUARY 9, 1905 to FEBRUARY 29, 2000

Anna was fearless, honest, supportive, and demanding. She was a woman of vision and accomplishment and a force for change—a true organic pioneer.

"We were daring. There was never anything conservative. Creating was the most important thing. Without it, you are nothing."—Anna Rodale

"We made many sacrifices when we were young, but it was a wonderful life, and fun. J.I. was always preparing for the future. He made each moment count. When you live to do creative thinking, it cannot be turned off until you stop breathing."—Anna Rodale

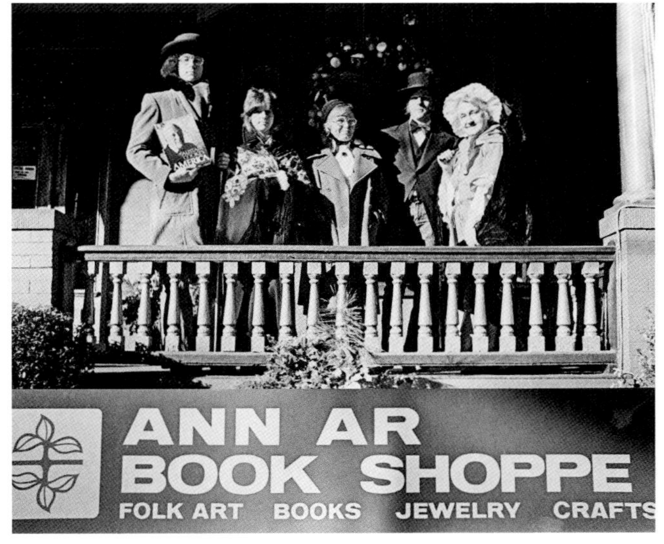

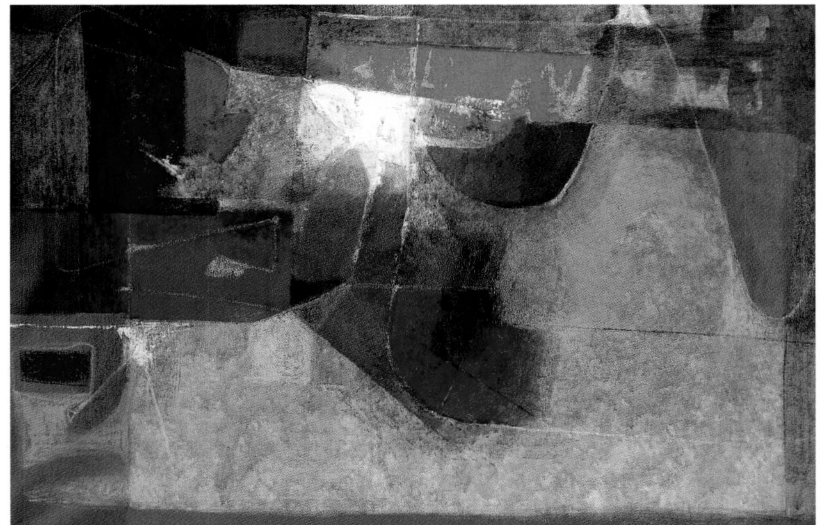

PHOTOGRAPH: ANTHONY RODALE

Paintings by Anna Rodale

A Retrospective Exhibition

CHAPTER 9

2001 TO 2008

Growing into a Whole Life

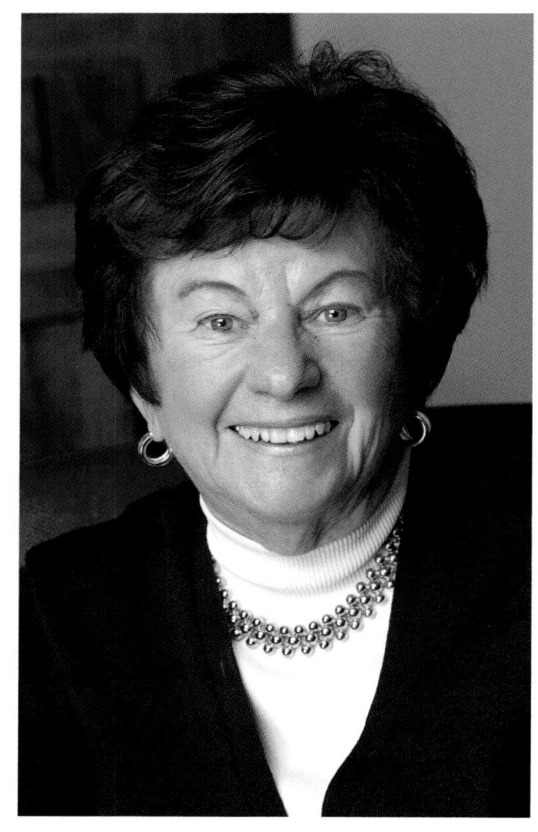

Ardie Rodale

FOR THE ECONOMY at large and the media industry, the long-running 1990s boom ended in 2000. For Rodale, it came to an end somewhat earlier. In 1999, stung by large losses in *Prevention* subscriptions, a weakening advertising market, and disappointing book sales, the company's revenues fell 46 percent. Once again, as it had throughout its history, Rodale faced a series of disruptions that would spur it to regenerate–and to grow. Rodale had always been led by individuals who had made the company their life's work–first J. I. Rodale, then Bob Rodale, who started working at the company as a teenager. Bob was succeeded as CEO by Bob Teufel, who joined the company out of college in 1961, and as chairman by Ardie. Through her columns in *WGOH* and *Prevention* magazine, her books, and her public appearances, Ardie, a remarkably energetic grandmother of 11, continued to act as Rodale's public face.

In 2000, Rodale ranked 34th on *Working Woman* magazine's annual list of Top 500 Women-Owned Businesses, with more revenues than Martha Stewart Living Omnimedia and Oprah Winfrey's Harpo Entertainment Group. Maria Rodale, named vice chairman in 1998, was emerging as the third-generation leader.

But in early 2000, when Bob Teufel retired, Rodale decided to look outside the company for senior executive leadership. The company found it in Steven Pleshette Murphy, who was formally introduced to Rodale at a monthly managers' meeting in February 2000. Murphy, had been a division president at Simon & Schuster in the 1980s and spent much of the 1990s as president of EMI/Angel Records before becoming executive vice president and managing director of Disney Publishing Worldwide in 1998. Dynamic and articulate, Murphy was mindful of the fact that he was entering a unique corporate culture that had been built over the course of several decades. "I want to help create a Rodale story, a clear narrative we can all live with and believe in," he said. "If we can crack the code of user behavior for the new technologies and figure out how best to satisfy people's needs, we will succeed."

Murphy had a mandate to direct change, something that was simultaneously uncomfortable and yet part of the company's DNA. "Our whole existence is based on change—showing people how they can change their lives and the world around them for the better," as Maria Rodale put it. "But, on the other hand, there are certain things about Rodale that we will never change." After all, the themes that lay at the core of the business—the involvement of the Rodale family, its connection to Emmaus, the importance of spreading the health and organic message, inspiring and enabling people to improve their lives and the world around them—remained the same in 2000 as they had in 1950. And they would continue to inform Rodale's culture as it entered the 21st century.

The task facing the management team in spring 2000 was threefold. After rapid growth in the 1990s and a sharp contraction in 1999, the company needed to return to desired levels of profitability. At the same time, Rodale had to figure out how to recapture growth and enter new markets by revitalizing its magazine and book publishing operations. For the long term, the company had to think about how it would thrive and prosper in a rapidly changing media environment.

Maria Rodale

Steven Pleshette Murphy

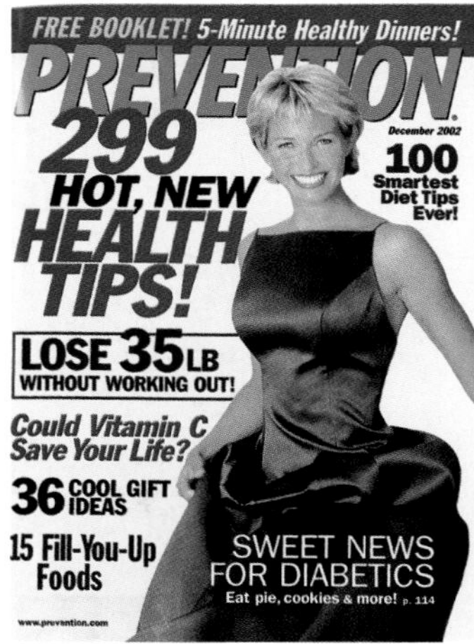

In 2000, Rodale enjoyed strong core audiences of older women—in *Prevention*—and younger men—in *Men's Health, Bicycling,* and *Runner's World*. But the company needed to reach beyond those groups to grow.

Through subscriptions, book sales, and Web sites, Rodale reached some 25 million customers. The company's core products enjoyed significant penetration among certain demographic groups. Rodale was strong among older women—the core audience of *Prevention*—and among younger men—the core audience of *Men's Health, Runner's World,* and *Bicycling*. To grow, the company would have to deepen relationships with the core audiences while targeting new demographics—older men and younger women, for example. In the first decade of the new century, Rodale would regenerate and thrive by adopting a broader vision and crafting a new strategy that combined the traditional value of editorial excellence with new efforts to connect with and understand customers, extend product lines, capitalize on Rodale's brand, and push into new media.

To align resources with the company's objectives, Rodale created a new organizational structure. The reorganization, the biggest in the company's history, was announced in September 2000. It was the cause of great concern, since it meant both a significant change in the way business was conducted and the loss of a certain number of jobs. On October 11, 1,000 employees of Rodale rode a bus caravan to the Zoellner Arts Center at Lehigh University to learn about the changes. Ardie led the meeting. "I feel as if we are experiencing a rebirth," she said. "It is an exciting new adventure that will encourage possibility thinking, growth of creativity, and a stronger sense of community and love."

Steve Murphy encouraged employees to reimagine their customers and the business, to view Rodale not simply as a publisher of books and magazines. Every day, borders were being broken within the media, and Rodale's potential for growth had always been in creating synergies among books, magazines, and other media. "We are in the business of building communities of people who are drawn to our editorial voice, who get value from it, and who want a relationship with that voice," he said.

In order to deploy resources more efficiently and effectively, Rodale reorganized its businesses not by format, such as books and magazines, but by customer and brand groups. By working as part of larger groups, the once-discrete magazine and book lines could combine and consolidate marketing and make better use of all resources, from the database to advertising relationships.

Bob Rodale was named the Person of the Century in the Lehigh Valley by *The Morning Call* for his efforts to encourage people locally and around the world to lead healthy lives.

THE MORNING CALL

SATURDAY, JANUARY 1, 2000 50¢

the Person *of the* Century

The Morning Call set out to put together a puzzle with pieces strewn over the course of 100 years: What 20th century local figure had the most impact, effected change and had influence that will endure? We considered the thoughtful nominations of hundreds of readers, pored over the lessons of the past and stretched our imaginations into the future.

Now, as the calendar pages turn, we present our choice for Person of the Century and recognize others who have reached the pinnacle in 20 fields.

VIKKI HALL-WEBSTER / The Morning Call

Robert Rodale

While other people shaped their times, Lehigh Valley visionary Robert Rodale transcended his. His work in agriculture, the environment and healthful living continues to reach millions around the world.

page A3

Organic Style magazine set out to show that "organic" and "stylish" were not opposing concepts and at the same time bring in a younger audience.

Murphy described the new organizational structure and introduced the concept of planning for the future, called Horizons: Horizon 1 was defined as building the core business and improving profits; Horizon 2 involved building extension businesses from the core; and Horizon 3 was creating new brands, businesses, and formats. And while there would be significant changes in Emmaus and New York, Murphy and the Rodales stressed the theme of continuity. "We are building on—not away from—the core values that attracted each of us to this company," Steve Murphy said. "Rodale's values will be as much a part of our future as they have been of our past."

At the time, efforts to extend brands to new, underserved demographics were already underway. In August 2000, for example, Rodale launched *MH-18,* an extension of *Men's Health* for teenagers. A second magazine in the works, *Organic Style,* represented an effort to bring the message of *Organic Gardening* to a larger, younger audience and to tap into the growing acceptance of organic foods and materials. Test issues were created in 2000 and plans were made for a formal launch in 2001.

For six decades, Rodale had been pushing for its message to become part of the mainstream. And in the 1990s, especially with *Men's Health,* it was clear that it had. Rodale's magazines attracted large numbers of subscribers and, increasingly, the kinds of upscale advertisers that all magazines cherished. The company had always had success with direct sales of books and experienced occasional blockbusters such as *The Doctors Book of Home Remedies,* which had sold some 15 million copies by 2000. But Rodale didn't have an equivalent presence in trade books—the type sold through bookstores.

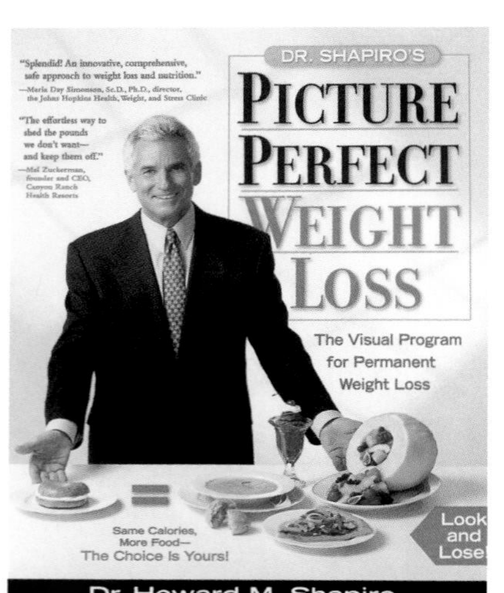

Picture Perfect Weight Loss **was Rodale's first book to appear on the *New York Times* bestseller list.**

In spring 2000, however, Rodale finally broke through. In 1999, the company had acquired the rights to publish *Dr. Shapiro's Picture Perfect Weight Loss,* a diet book by Dr. Howard Shapiro. A commonsense guide to weight loss, it called attention to the different levels of calories and fats in foods by pairing them side by side in photos. Other publishers had rejected the book because it was a four-color volume, and hence would be more expensive to produce. "We pushed this book through our pipeline in about a year, knowing that it had the potential to be a break-

2001
January 18: Rodale named one of 100 best companies to work for by *Fortune*.

January 20: George W. Bush sworn in as 43rd president.

February 15: Rodale announces exclusive multimedia partnership with Dr. Andrew Weil.

March: Rodale child-care center opens for families of employees.

June 27: Rodale is 32nd on *Working Woman*'s list of top 500 women-owned businesses.

June: The National Academy of Sciences reports that global warming is on the rise, primarily due to human activity.

September 10: Rodale's child-care center opens to the public.

In 2001, Rodale opened its new child-care-center building for children of Rodale employees at the base of South Mountain, just steps away from the South Mountain Center.

through bestseller for us," said Susan Massey, publisher of trade books at that time.

Picture Perfect Weight Loss was a big hit at bookstores. And on April 23, 2000, it became the first Rodale book to appear on a *New York Times* bestseller list, placing fourth on the Miscellaneous and How-To list. Seeing the opportunity to create a new trade-oriented brand, in summer 2000 Rodale inked a three-book deal with Dr. Shapiro for a new trade paperback, a hardcover, and a cookbook.

The company was also seeking larger markets for its magazines at home and overseas. In 1994, Rodale Books had launched its first Spanish-language book, a translation of the *Doctors Book of Home Remedies.* In early 2000, *Prevention en Español* was launched. Later that year, a deal was struck for a Philippine version of *Prevention,* the fourth foreign edition. *Men's Health* continued its rapid expansion abroad by launching an Italian edition in spring 2000. And when the Spanish and Portuguese editions debuted in early 2001, they became the 24th and 25th editions, respectively, making *Men's Health* the largest men's lifestyle magazine in the world.

As a result of the restructuring, there was a significant turnover in employees, with many new executives joining from outside the company and many long-standing Rodale employees promoted. David Zinczenko, who had initiated nine successful international launches of *Men's Health,* was named editor in chief of the magazine.

True to its roots, Rodale continued to invest in Emmaus. In March 2001, a new 6,400-square-foot child-care center with room for 160 children was built at 420 South 10th Street in Emmaus. As with all Rodale projects, the center featured environmentally friendly benefits such as natural linoleum flooring and play equipment made from recycled plastic. "The center gives the children a bright, open environment in which to thrive and grow," said Ardie. On September 10, 2001, Ardie announced it would be open to the public at large.

The growing sense of optimism and recovery at Rodale suffered a significant blow on September 11, 2001. Rodale's New York offices, on Third Avenue in midtown Manhattan, were some

September 11: Terrorists attack the World Trade Center in New York City and the Pentagon in Washington, D.C. A third attempt ends in a field in Pennsylvania.

October: Rodale publishes *From the Ashes: A Spiritual Response to the Attack on America.*

Fall: *Organic Style* launches and is named one of the best new magazines of 2001 by *Library Journal.*

November: Rodale and BeliefNet create a multimedia joint venture.

Sales of organic foods soar by as much as 20 percent in France and Germany; local production of organics can't meet the growing demand.

Organic food in European market

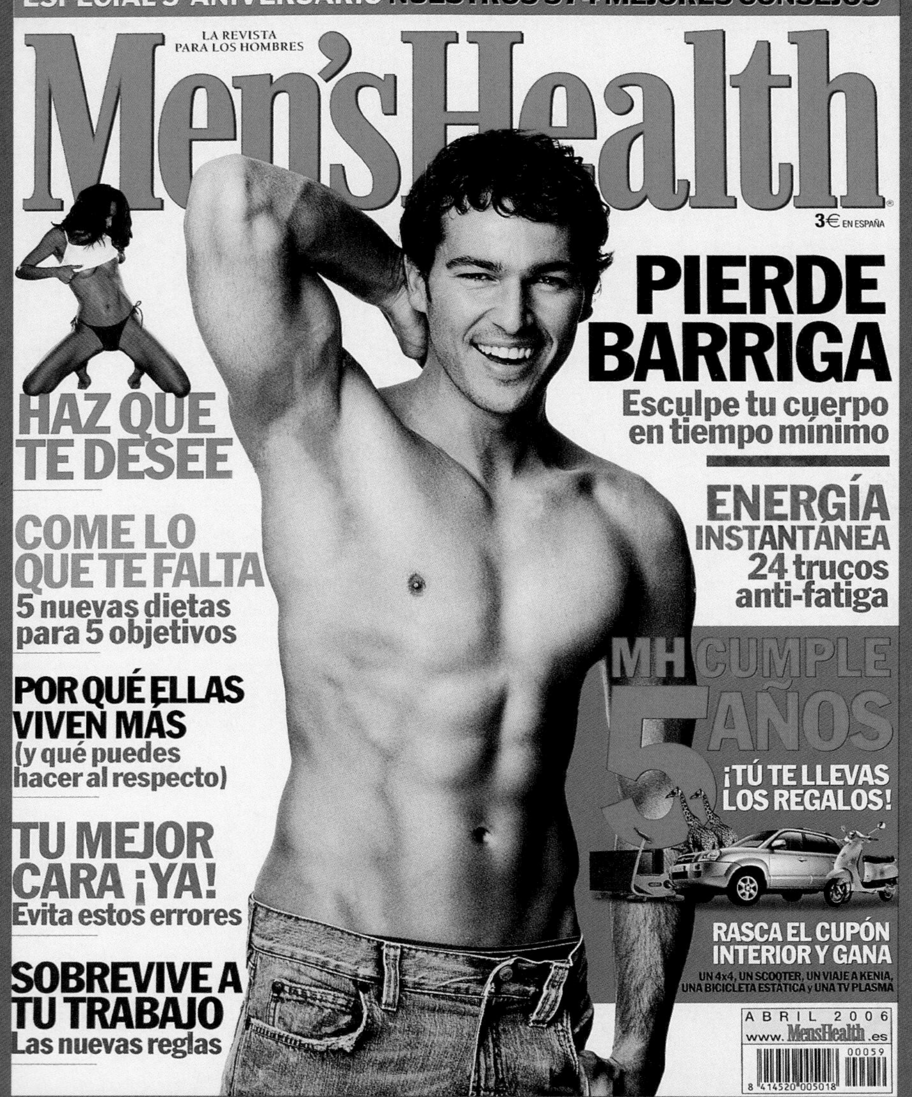

ESPECIAL 5°ANIVERSARIO NUESTROS 574 MEJORES CONSEJOS
LA REVISTA PARA LOS HOMBRES
Men'sHealth
3€ EN ESPAÑA
PIERDE BARRIGA
Esculpe tu cuerpo en tiempo mínimo
ENERGÍA INSTANTÁNEA
24 trucos anti-fatiga
HAZ QUE TE DESEE
COME LO QUE TE FALTA
5 nuevas dietas para 5 objetivos
POR QUÉ ELLAS VIVEN MÁS
(y qué puedes hacer al respecto)
TU MEJOR CARA ¡YA!
Evita estos errores
SOBREVIVE A TU TRABAJO
Las nuevas reglas
MH CUMPLE 5 AÑOS
¡TÚ TE LLEVAS LOS REGALOS!
RASCA EL CUPÓN INTERIOR Y GANA
UN 4x4, UN SCOOTER, UN VIAJE A KENIA, UNA BICICLETA ESTÁTICA y UNA TV PLASMA
ABRIL 2006
www.MensHealth.es

The World's Largest Men's Magazine
Change Your Lifestyle!
남자들이 멋있는 이유
내가 멋있게 변하는 이유
Men'sHealth
최고의 남자誌 맨즈헬스 한국판
Get a Star's body
전세계 스타들처럼
당신도 몸을 만들어라
12명
톰 크루즈, 브레드 피트
매트 데이먼, 윌 스미스
톰 행크스, 어셔
크리스천 베일
데니스 퀘이드
배용준, 권상우
천정명, 이서진
Fight Fat!
올리브오일은
지방을
감소시킨다
쇠고기를 꾸준히
먹으면 다이어트
효과가 있다
| 남자를 위한 모든 것 |
피트니스, 스포츠, 남성상식, 영양
섹스와 남녀관계, 패션과 스타일
그루밍, 문화, 엔터테인먼트, 자동차
하이테크, 디자인, 레저, 여행
스트레스, 커리어 관리
MARCH 2006
MensHealth
ISSN 1739-9548
www.e-menshealth.co.kr
Start Now!
For Your Best Year
올해를 당신 인생에서
최고의 해로 만드는 방법
sex on the brain
머리가 좋아야 섹스도 잘한다
생활 속에서 챙기는
2분 건강법 26가지
한국 여자들이
좋아하는
나쁜남자의 특성
스트레스 따돌리기
음식으로 두뇌 회전
속도가 더 빨라진다
성공한 쿨가이들의
스타일 감각 발견
라이프스타일에 맞는
첫 차 고르는 법
2006.3
전세계 남자들의 공통 관심, 유용한 정보
NEW
창간호

***Men's Health* continued to expand into international markets, here showing Spain and Korea's editions.**

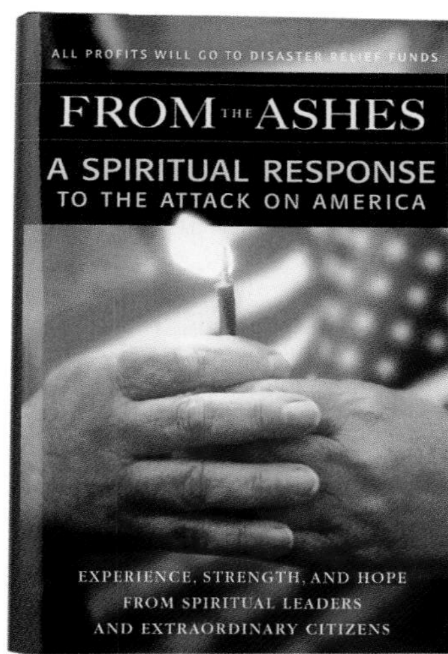

In the spirit of helping to heal the nation, Rodale published *From the Ashes* and donated the profits to a firefighters' scholarship fund.

distance from Ground Zero, and Emmaus was many miles removed from Washington and from Shanksville, Pennsylvania, where one of the hijacked planes crashed. But the attacks nevertheless hit close to home. On September 11, the 112 people working in the company's midtown New York offices were evacuated by the early afternoon. Dennis Mojica, a fireman who was the fiancé of Maria Barreto, one of Rodale's New York employees, died fighting the fire at the World Trade Center.

Rodale employees pitched in to help in the relief effort. A member of the Marketing Services Group drove from Emmaus to the city each day following the attacks to deliver donated supplies. Rodale tried to help heal the nation's wounds in other ways. In 31 days, Rodale produced a book, *From the Ashes: A Spiritual Response to the Attack on America,* in conjunction with BeliefNet. It included contributions from a diverse set of writers, ranging from Fred Rogers to Nobel Prize Laureate Desmond Tutu. All profits from the book were donated to the NYC Bravest Scholarship Fund.

A difficult year for the economy at large and for the media industry, 2001 was a year of transition for Rodale. As the nation endured its first recession in nearly a decade, more than 100 magazines closed, among them *Working Woman* and *Mademoiselle.* But Rodale returned to profitability, in part by identifying some $40 million in cost savings. *Organic Style* was named one of the best new magazines of 2001 by *Library Journal,* and the company had some modest successes in books, such as *The Peanut Butter Diet.* More important, Rodale had mapped out a new course and brought in several new leaders. In January 2002, Steve Murphy was promoted to president and chief executive officer, while Ardie retained the title of chairman. "Steve's broadened role reflects not just his accomplishments to date but also our family's belief that his stewardship and vision make him the ideal executive to lead the company forward in a way that preserves the great legacy of Rodale," said Ardie.

During the dot-com era, many media companies had rushed headlong into new media, striking alliances; merging, as Time Warner did with AOL; and investing huge sums in businesses that turned out poorly. After the bursting of the tech bubble, many assumptions, business models, and modes of operating that were accepted as gospel in the 1990s were suddenly rethought. But

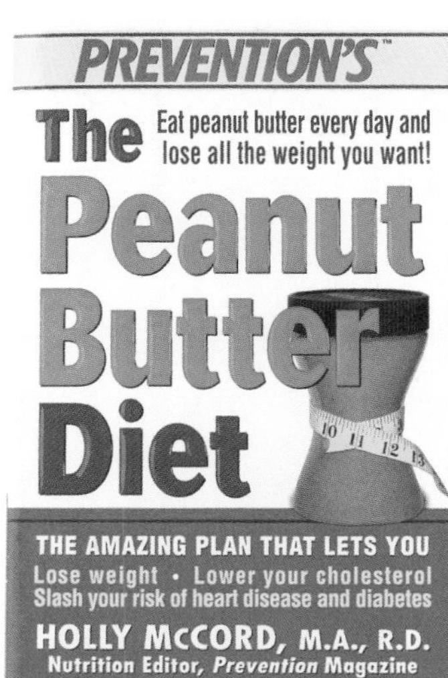

***The Peanut Butter Diet* was a bright spot in 2001.**

Ardie stays in touch with the employees. Here she is having one of her regular talks with children at the Rodale child-care summer camp at the farm.

Ardie's perseverance facing her challenges inspire many who know her.

Rodale had never strayed far from its moorings—financially, ethically, or philosophically. "Rodale is a company that has always been ahead of its time in commitment to health and the environment," Ardie said. "I feel that part of our uniqueness is due to listening to our own inner voice."

Listening to an inner voice can also mean being sensitive to change. The evolution of the larger culture over time didn't simply result in the mainstream embracing Rodale; it resulted in Rodale embracing the mainstream to a greater degree. As the company matured, expanded, and found greater acceptance, its attitude became more flexible and open. The approach could be seen in the pages of the magazines, but also in the actions and speech of executives. And it was apparent in Ardie Rodale's successful battles against cancer, in which she relied on integrative health, nutrition, positive thinking, *and* traditional medicine. Her battles were both an inspiration to fellow employees and a learning experience. Rather than seeing itself as antagonistic to the medical establishment, as J.I. and Bob frequently had in the 1950s and 1960s, Rodale explicitly viewed the *Prevention* ethos and the Rodale culture as forces that could work in concert with the medical establishment.

Ardie led by example, by deed, and by word. In 2002, she published *Reflections: Finding Love, Hope, and Joy in Everyday Life,* a new book of more than 50 essays that had appeared in *Prevention s*ince 1996. She and other members of the family also worked tirelessly to build Bob's legacy. On August 25, the Rodale Aquatic Center for Civic Health at Cedar Crest College in Allentown, Pennsylvania, was dedicated. "Sometimes dreams take a very long time to materialize, and there were times when we wondered whether the center would ever be built," said Ardie. The complex featured two pools—an eight-lane fitness/competitive pool and a 25- by 40-foot warm-water exercise and therapy pool.

Increasingly, Maria Rodale was stepping to the fore as the leader of the third generation of the family and the company. At the spring 2002 all-employee meeting, she outlined the company's new direction. "What do our customers need from us now? What's the next step in our evolution? Healing is the answer. Because of everything we have learned at Rodale up to this point, we can now truly help people heal in a meaningful way."

The Rodale Aquatic Center, dedicated in 2002, had been a long-standing dream of Bob Rodale's.

In 2002, after having stabilized the businesses, Rodale invested in efforts to redesign and regenerate its core magazines. *Runner's World* underwent a redesign and received the ultimate stamp of acceptance. In August 2002, managing editor Bob Wischnia and footwear editor Paul Carrozza were invited to run with President Bush and White House staff in a 3-mile fitness race at Fort McNair military park, after which Bush, an enthusiastic and competitive runner, sat for an interview. *Bicycling* likewise underwent a redesign and an editorial overhaul that focused more on storytelling. The phenomenal success of Lance Armstrong, who, beginning in 1999, would go on to win seven straight Tour de France victories after his recovery from testicular cancer, was a boon for *Bicycling*. *Prevention*'s circulation rose again, from 3.1 million to 3.2 million in January 2003, surpassing *Sports Illustrated*. In 2002, Rodale's magazine titles were up 15.4 percent in ad dollars for the year, compared with 4.8 percent for the industry.

In fall 2002, *Best Life*, an extension of *Men's Health* aimed at older, more affluent readers—a sort of men's magazine for baby boomers—was launched as a special, with a circulation of 500,000. Designed by Joseph Heroun, who had been so influential in *Men's Health*'s success, it featured the actor Stanley Tucci on the cover. The idea came from the editors of *Men's Health*'s German edition, who had published four issues of the special geared toward their own upper demographic.

Books did well in 2002, too, with three on the *New York Times* bestseller list: Jorge Cruise's *8 Minutes in the Morning*, *Dr. Shapiro's Picture Perfect Weight Loss 30 Day Plan*, and *Pilates for Every Body*, by Denise Austin. Through direct response, *Pilates for Every Body*, *Joey Green's Amazing Kitchen Cures*, and *Betty Crocker's Healthy Home Cooking* were among the company's top-performing titles. But Rodale Books was pushing beyond the health message, extending further into trade sales.

The books business was evolving into a hybrid of a direct-marketing, health-and-fitness-oriented publisher and a traditional trade publisher. The goal of the book division was to encourage agents and writers to approach Rodale, and to become more involved in the broader literary marketplace, all while maintaining a publishing program in keeping with the company's history, ethos, and customer base.

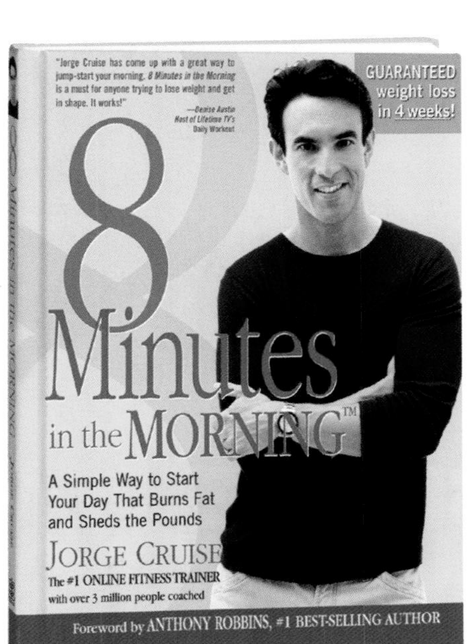

One of the first Rodale titles on the *New York Times* bestseller list

2002
National Organic Standards are implemented.

January: Enron declares bankruptcy.

January 14: Steve Murphy is promoted to chief executive officer.

February: Queen Elizabeth II marks her 50th year on the throne of Great Britain.

Organic produce

July: Balloonist Steve Fossett completes circumnavigation of the earth in a balloon in 14 days.

August 25: The Rodale Aquatic Center for Civic Health at Cedar Crest College in Allentown, Pennsylvania, is dedicated.

September 17: Rodale announces the creation of Rodale Books International, based in London.

September: Institute of Medicine suggests that people exercise at least 1 hour per day, ½ hour more than previously suggested.

November: *Best Life* launches as a special.

***Scuba Diving* acquires the trademark and list of *Skin Diver* from Primedia.**

WHAT MATTERS TO MEN
BEST LIFE
8 LAWS OF BUILDING WEALTH
Strategies That Work Now
Your Ultimate Checkup:
An Essential Checklist
6 SECRETS OF STAYING YOUNG
The Erotic Marriage
Real Couples Reveal What Works for Them
SIMPLE LUXURY
8 Things a Man Needs To Live the Best Life
The Best List
9 Products, Places, and Ideas That Will Enrich Your Life!
PLUS
How Strong Is Your Faith? By David Mamet
The Hero Dads of Houma, Louisiana
ACTOR JOSH LUCAS: "I'm finding my own sense of confidence"

WH BOOK BONUS! The Perfect Body Diet
IT'S GOOD TO BE YOU™
Women'sHealth
YOUR FITTEST YEAR
STARTS NOW!
ALL-NEW WORKOUTS! INSTANT RESULTS!
NO-FUSS PARTY FOODS
TAKE OUR QUIZ AND
THINK SMARTER!
BEST CARDIO MOVES FOR YOUR BUTT
ONLINE BONANZA
31 DAYS OF FREE STUFF!
26 WAYS TO LOSE FAT FAST
Get Away & Get It On!
p.52
DEAR DIARY
REAL WOMEN—REAL SEX SECRETS!
womenshealthmag.com

Best Life, launched as a special in 2002, evolved into a bimonthly magazine by 2004. *Women's Health* launched in fall 2005 and took off right away, attracting an enthusiastic audience of readers and advertisers.

***The South Beach Diet* was on the *New York Times* bestseller list for more than a year.**

But Rodale didn't have to stray very far from its origins to find big hits in books. Among baby boomers there was a growing interest—bordering on obsession—with the relationship between food, diet, and health. In the late 1990s, the Atkins diet craze—in limiting carbohydrates and emphasizing proteins—had taken the nation by storm. *Dr. Atkins' Diet Revolution,* first published in 1972, spawned several best-selling books, an industry of prepared food, and a revival of steakhouses.

Dr. Arthur Agatston, a cardiologist in Miami, viewed the rise of the protein-heavy diets with alarm. He was concerned about obese and prediabetic patients and didn't believe that simply dispensing with all carbohydrates and loading up on potentially saturated fats in meat and fried foods was a healthy alternative. In 1996, he devised a 10-page pamphlet, *Modified Carbohydrate Diet,* aimed at helping patients ward off stroke and heart disease. The idea was to cut out processed carbohydrates like white flour and white sugar. For two weeks, people should avoid bread, pasta, rice, sugars, fruit, and alcohol and focus on meat, eggs, nuts, good fats like olive oil, and vegetables. After two weeks, the patients could add back whole-grains foods, some fruits, and moderate amounts of wine. In 1999, Agatston did a series based on the diet on local television. After that, things moved relatively quickly.

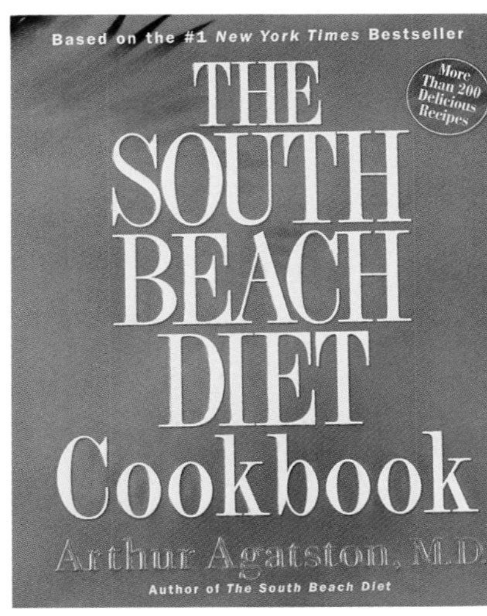

Rodale sensed it had something big in *The South Beach Diet,* and it pursued an innovative marketing strategy. Most diet books were published in January, the better to attract readers who had gained weight during the holiday season. But Rodale decided to publish *The South Beach Diet* in April 2003, when there would be less competition. By February 2003, when the first printing of 50,000 copies was at the printer, 1,500 copies had been sent to publications and another 500 copies were distributed to influential celebrities, including CNN's Larry King and former president Bill Clinton. *Prevention* serialized the book in an 11-page excerpt and sent out a South Beach edition of its e-mail newsletter. Rodale hired Waterfront Media, Inc., which creates content based on books. The firm built a Web site, www.southbeachdiet.com, where people could get customized eating plans, and it did interactive marketing. It attracted tens of thousands of paid subscribers.

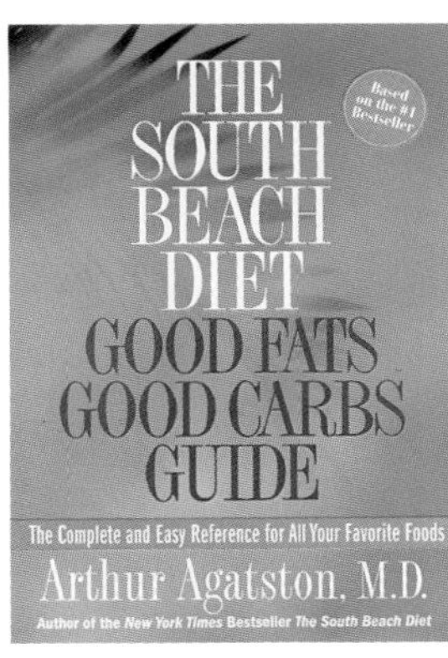

2003
U.S. organic food and nonfood sales reach $10.8 billion. Organic food sales now represent approximately 2 percent of all U.S. food sales.

March: The United States attacks Iraq.

May: *The South Beach Diet* is the number-one *New York Times* bestseller.

Organic produce

June: David Willey named editor in chief of *Runner's World*.

June: *Men's Health* launches in Singapore.

October: Rodale helps ABC produce the childhood obesity special *Fat like Me: How to Win the Weight War*.

Fall: *Runner's World* launches in Finland.

Rodale receives Organic Trade Association's Organic Leadership Award.

Whole Foods Market is the first major supermarket chain to require organic certification for its stores (140 of them). The natural-foods retailer posts annual sales of $2.7 billion.

November: *Organic Style*'s "Green Is the New Black" advertising campaign starts.

Published in April 2003, *The South Beach Diet* became Rodale's first number-one *New York Times* bestseller in May. In June, *New York* magazine reported that President Clinton had been on the diet and lost weight. By July, some 1 million copies were in print, and it became the first Rodale book to sell 1 million copies through the trade channel. *The South Beach Diet* spent more than 58 weeks on the *New York Times* bestseller list, including 26 at number one, and became a self-sustaining media phenomenon. On the same night in August, by which time *The South Beach Diet* had already sold 1.7 million copies, both NBC's *Dateline* and ABC's *20/20* featured reports on the diet. "The planets have lined up," said Steve Murphy.

My Prison Without Bars followed *The South Beach Diet* to the top of the *New York Times* bestseller list.

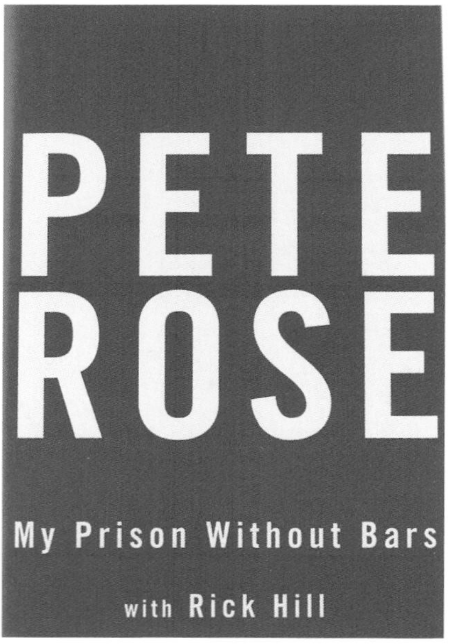

Rodale quickly set about extending the brand into new markets and through new products. *The South Beach Diet* was licensed for translation into 20 foreign editions. And as it remained atop the bestseller lists, plans were made for follow-up books. In January 2004 came *The South Beach Diet Good Fats/Good Carbs Guide* and a Spanish edition of the original book. *The South Beach Diet Cookbook* debuted in April 2004. But South Beach wasn't simply a marketing phenomenon. In a company-wide survey in July 2004, 80 employees said they were on the diet. The Energy Center developed an ab-flattening South Beach workout, and Rodale's cafeterias added South Beach Diet entrées and snacks.

South Beach was followed by another blockbuster book: the autobiography of baseball legend Pete Rose. *My Prison Without Bars,* which had a first printing of 500,000 copies, was excerpted in *Sports Illustrated* and featured on ABC's *Primetime* news magazine show. On January 25, 2004, it topped the *New York Times* hardcover nonfiction bestseller list; the same day, *The South Beach Diet* was the best-selling advice hardcover.

Powered by the success of *The South Beach Diet,* the second-best-selling nonfiction book of 2003, Rodale grew rapidly. In 2003, it added more than 4 million new people in key, targeted demographics to its 25 million–person database. As part of the constant regeneration, *Prevention* was redesigned in January 2004 under vice president/editorial director Rosemary Ellis, who was appointed in May 2003. In January 2004, *Prevention* raised its rate base by

Rodale's all-time company bestsellers from direct mail and trade sales

***Prevention* magazine was redesigned in April 2007 to appeal to a younger audience.**

100,000, to 3.3 million—its largest ever—making it the 12th-largest magazine in the nation.

At an all-employee meeting on March 9, 2004, Rodale's leadership discussed the best year in the company's history. "Rodale is not just the sum of its parts," said Murphy. "It is each of our great and motivated teams pursuing their own goals while working more and more in concert as a company ... as a true whole." The meeting was dedicated to the customers—39 million people who purchased a Rodale product in 2003. The figure was, in some ways, staggering. And keeping track of the spending and purchasing habits of that many people would seem to be a fool's errand. But Murphy argued that to grow further, Rodale would have to gain a better understanding of who its customers were, where they lived, and how they interacted with the company.

J. I. Rodale, with his wide-ranging correspondence, had found that his audiences had frequently defied geographic and demographic assumptions: There were progressive organic farmers in Alabama in the 1940s and health-food devotees in Cleveland in the 1950s. In the age of the Internet and easy travel, the maxim that geography was no longer destiny was doubly true. There were scuba-diving enthusiasts in Minnesota and organic gardeners in Manhattan. And so the challenge for a company with a heritage in direct marketing was to figure out how to reach potential customers effectively and, once the relationship had been formed, how to cultivate it. Rodale's direct marketing team in 2003 started a project to make direct marketing more focused and personalized and to figure out how to turn onetime book buyers into multiple-product customers. They set out to analyze the transaction history and demographic information of Rodale's existing customers to assign each a lifetime value, a calculated prediction of whether a customer is likely to have a positive or negative impact on profitability over his or her entire relationship with Rodale.

Rodale had always subscribed to the concept of thinking globally and acting locally. But increasingly Rodale had the reach and resources to think globally and act globally. The company

2004
January: *Prevention* redesign is launched.

January 25: *The South Beach Diet* and Pete Rose's *My Prison Without Bars* are number one on the New York Times advice hardcover and nonfiction hardcover lists, respectively.

March: *Organic Style* increases frequency to 10 times per year.

April 28: Rodale has three books on the *New York Times* bestseller lists: *The South Beach Diet*, *The South Beach Diet Cookbook*, and *The Imus Ranch*.

May 7: *Men's Health* wins a National Magazine Award in the Personal Service category for a package on heart health.

June 2: Maria Rodale receives the Rachel Carson Award at the National Audubon Society's Women in Conservation Awards luncheon.

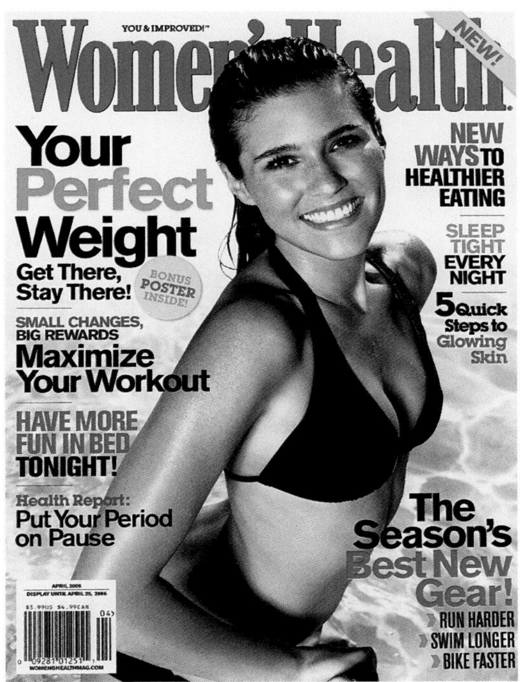

Women's Health magazine garnered attention from young women, an audience Rodale had targeted.

decided that, as Murphy put it, "moving forward, all new product development will be done with an eye toward global potential." *Men's Health,* with 17 million readers among its 31 editions, continued to lead Rodale into overseas markets.

In spring 2004, Rodale was finding validation in the marketplace. In May, *Best Life* debuted with a 200,000 rate base. And in August, *Men's Health* launched in the world's largest potential consumer market: China. *The South Beach Diet Cookbook,* released in April with an initial print run of 1.5 million—the largest in cookbook history—topped the *New York Times* Hardcover Advice, How-To and Miscellaneous list on May 2. *The South Beach Diet* placed second, marking its 54th week on the list—7 million copies in 24 printings. And *The South Beach Diet Good Fats/Good Carbs Guide,* published in January 2004, had 3 million copies in print.

The company was also finding validation among its peers. In May, in a first for a Rodale publication, *Men's Health* won a National Magazine Award (NMA) in the Personal Service category, for the magazine's July 2003 36-page feature package on heart health, "Your Heart Will Stop." *Bicycling* was also a 2004 NMA finalist in the General Excellence category for magazines with circulations of 250,000 to 500,000.

Midway through the first decade of the 21st century, Rodale had clearly regenerated and resumed a trajectory of growth. Amid a difficult time for the industry, Rodale's magazines thrived. In both 2004 and 2005, Rodale notched the highest percentage growth in advertising dollars among major magazine companies. In 2005, as part of the continuing effort to reach the demographic of young women, Rodale launched *Women's Health.* The magazine caught on very quickly. *Women's Health,* launched in October 2005, was a significant success. With Rodale's trademark blend of a positive message, solidly reported stories, and a focus on personal improvement, it showed an ability to connect to readers in a crowded and highly competitive market. The circulation rate base, which started at 400,000, rose to 600,000 in July 2006 and to 750,000 in January 2007. It attracted a devoted and growing audience of readers and advertisers.

Organic Style was shut down in September 2005. It was considered ahead of its time by

***Men's Health* launches in China.**

September: *Best Life* launches as bimonthly.

October 29: Rodale issues free recommendations on preventive health measures for avoiding the flu.

November: Rodale forms Marketing Solutions Group to work with outside marketers.

Datamonitor predicts that the U.S. market for organic/natural foods and beverages will hit $30.7 billion in 2007 and that the world market will hit $46.7 billion the same year.

Curves International hires Rodale Custom Publishing to launch *diane* magazine.

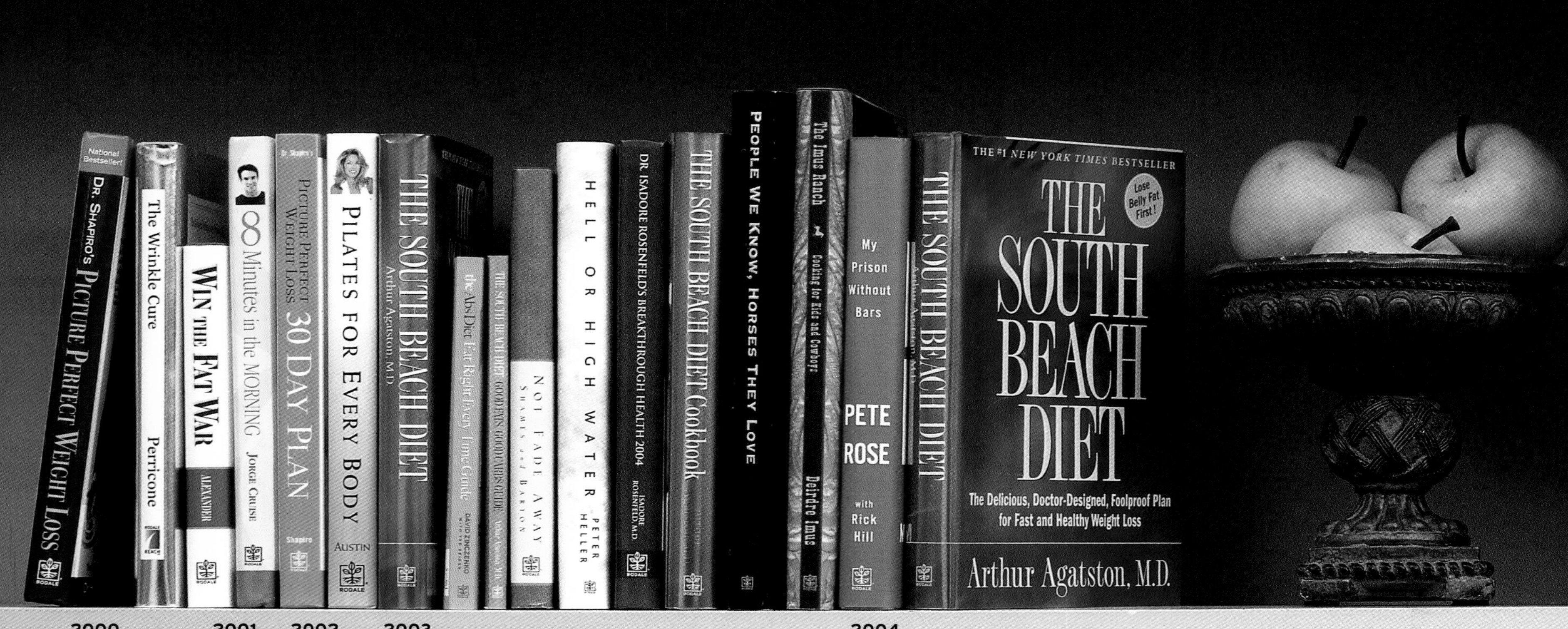

2006

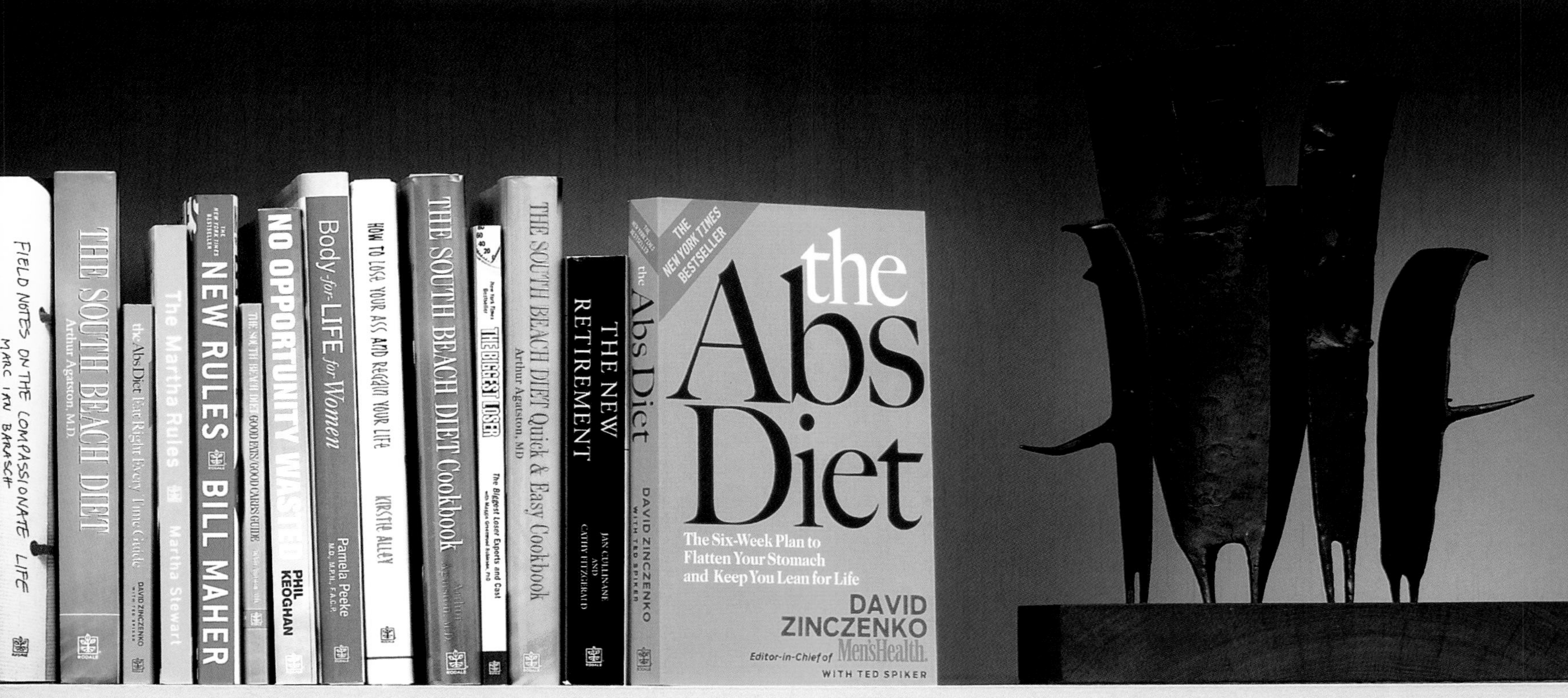

2005

Rodale's trade bestsellers, shown grouped by year

2007

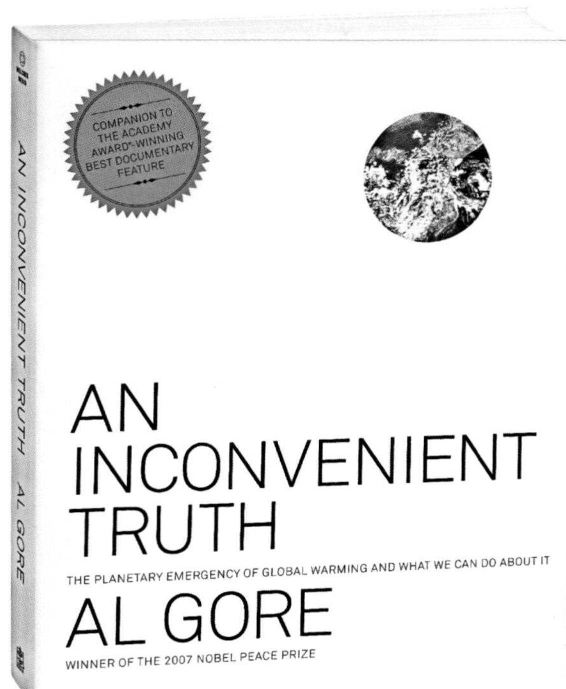

***An Inconvenient Truth,* by Al Gore, became a number one *New York Times* bestseller and remained on the list for nearly a year.**

many, and the brand name was sold in 2007. It is now an online store specializing in organic merchandise and flowers. Rodale still owns a small percentage of the company.

Trade books continued to expand with high-profile volumes such as Martha Stewart's *The Martha Rules,* a companion book to the reality television show *The Biggest Loser,* and, in spring 2006, *An Inconvenient Truth,* a book on global warming by former vice president Al Gore.

The company expanded its presence in New York, taking new space at its midtown Manhattan headquarters and placing the company name on the building. The environmentally friendly remodeling was done in keeping with Rodale's ethos. A glass-encased yoga space is situated at the heart of the offices.

And it continued to find new markets for well-established titles. In 2005, editions of *Men's Health* were launched in Romania, Ukraine, and the Philippines, while *Prevention* debuted in Greece and *Prevention en Español* was relaunched. By the end of 2005, Rodale boasted 55 international editions in 48 countries, including 34 international editions of *Men's Health,* 9 editions of *Runner's World,* and 4 editions of *Prevention.* In early 2006, *Men's Health* and *Prevention* were launched in India, and *Men's Health* debuted in Brazil and South Korea. That year, the company's global trade-book operation sold 8.6 million volumes in 33 languages. Leading the charge was *The South Beach Diet* series, with more than 19 million copies in 31 languages having been published, and *The Abs Diet,* first published in 2004, with 18 international editions. Regardless of the language in which they are written or the office in which they are edited, Rodale's publications bear the firm's hallmarks. "The adherence to quality and to the Rodale editorial point of view is seamless, whether it's Emmaus or New Delhi, Milan or Beijing," said Steve Murphy.

That mentality extends across media platforms as well. Rodale today understands that magazines and books are only part of the story—part of the opportunity for disseminating ideas

2005
The Organic Trade Association, formerly known as the Organic Foods Production Association of North America, has grown to nearly 1,500 members and celebrates its 20th anniversary.

With sales increasing more than 27 percent annually, organic dairy farmers are having difficulty keeping up with the demand for organic milk.

January: Rodale agrees to publish tennis star Martina Navratilova's diet and fitness book, *The Shape of Your Life,* scheduled for winter 2006 publication.

Organic dairy farmer

January 18: Rodale acquires comedian Bill Maher's *New Rules*.

March: *Men's Health* launches in Romania.

April 18: *Prevention* launches line of premium vitamins and supplements under license with Windmill Health Products.

Rodale leased offices for its expanding New York staff in 1993 and put its name on the building in 2007.

May 22: *Backpacker* partners with New York City Department of Parks and Recreation to stage the *Backpacker* Gear Expo in Manhattan's Union Square Park.

June: Martha Stewart agrees to publish *The Martha Rules* with Rodale.

August: Hurricane Katrina hits New Orleans and surrounding areas.

September: *Organic Style* ceases publication.

October: Rodale launches *Women's Health*.

As of early 2008, Rodale magazines sported these international editions.

Men'sHealth

- Australia
- Brazil
- China
- Croatia
- Germany
- Greece
- India
- Indonesia
- Italy
- Kazakhstan
- Argentina
- Central America
- Chile
- Colombia
- Ecuador
- Mexico
- Peru
- Puerto Rico
- U.S. Hispanic
- Venezuela
- Malaysia
- The Netherlands
- Philippines
- Poland
- Portugal
- Romania
- Russia
- Serbia
- Singapore
- Slovenia
- South Africa
- South Korea
- Spain
- Thailand
- Turkey
- Ukraine
- United Kingdom
- United States

RUNNER'S WORLD

- Australia
- New Zealand
- Belgium
- France
- Germany
- Italy
- Mexico
- The Netherlands
- South Africa
- Spain
- Sweden
- United Kingdom
- United States

Prevention

- Greece
- India
- Argentina
- Central America
- Chile
- Colombia
- Ecuador
- Mexico
- Peru
- Puerto Rico
- U.S. Hispanic
- Venezuela
- Poland
- Romania
- Ukraine
- United States

BESTLIFE

- Germany
- The Netherlands
- Portugal
- South Africa
- Spain
- United States

Bicycling

- South Africa
- United States

- Australia
- Argentina
- Central America
- Chile
- Colombia
- Ecuador
- Mexico
- Peru
- Puerto Rico
- U.S. Hispanic
- Venezuela
- United States

www.menshealth.com

www.prevention.com

www.runnersworld.com

www.womenshealthmag.com

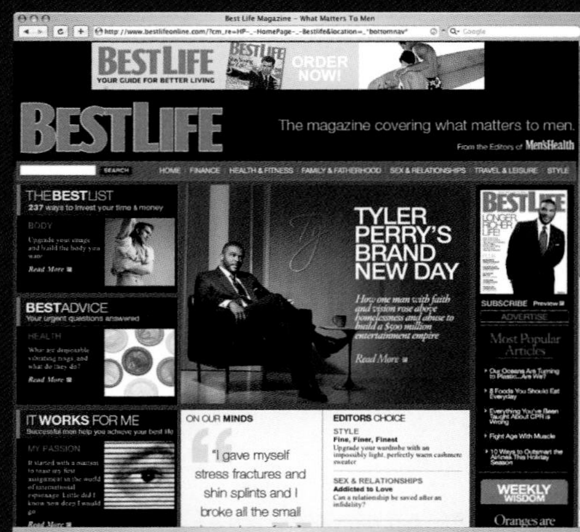

www.bestlifeonline.com

www.bicycling.com

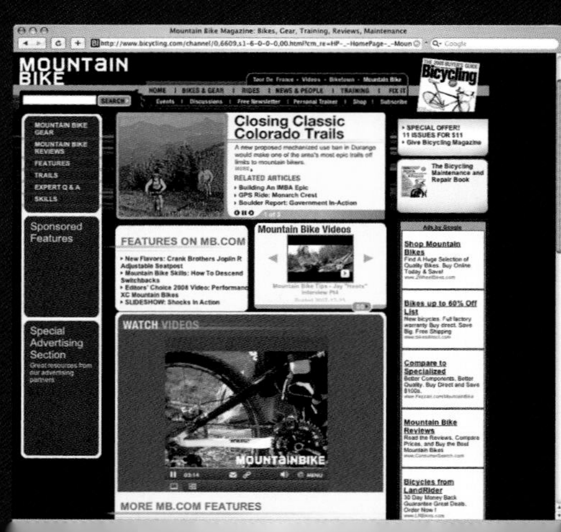

As ephemeral as books are permanent, the Rodale magazine Web sites contribute another vehicle for delivering the Rodale message to the public. In addition to www.rodale.com and the sites shown here, Rodale also has these sites:

www.runningtimes.com
www.iyogalife.com
www.biggestloserclub.com
www.thebestlife.com
www.sugarsolutiononline.com
www.absdiet.com
www.frenchwomendontgetfat.com
www.rodalecustompub.com
www.rodalestore.com

and information that improve people's lives. The company has a long history of dealing directly with customers, through book sales and magazine circulation efforts. But Rodale places a greater premium on customers. Increasingly, Rodale's strategy calls for using technology and information it gathers about consumers to offer related—and relevant—products and services.

As part of this strategy, the company makes efforts to view a great idea not just as a great book, or a great magazine article, but as great multimedia products. Because its well-established core brands—*Men's Health, Women's Health, Prevention,* and *Runner's World*—have earned the trust of consumers, Rodale has the opportunity to reach them in new ways. In 2005, for example, *Prevention* created the Prevention Fitness Systems—a collection of videos. Promoted in the magazine, the long-form DVDs have quickly become one of the top sellers at retail in the United States, selling at outlets like Target, Wal-Mart, and Sam's Clubs, with projected sales of 800,000 videos in 2006. The *Abs Diet* has similarly emerged as a franchise of *Men's Health.* The program outlined in the best-selling book series has become the house diet of the magazine. It is promoted and discussed in the pages of *Men's Health*, in a line of videos, and in a premium online subscription service.

In recent years, Rodale has also made significant efforts to turn its brands into meaningful online brands. Rodale is strongest in two areas where consumers have shown a desire to engage online: health and well-being. But rather than merely put its magazines online, Rodale has made efforts to put its brands online. Beyond offering content similar to what might be seen in magazines, Rodale's Web sites offer a high degree of interactivity, rich media, and premium subscription-based service. After publishing a series of books associated with the NBC reality television show *The Biggest Loser,* Rodale created an online Biggest Loser diet and fitness program that has attracted more than 100,000 subscribers.

The ability to create these synergies and to leverage the large and successful investments Rodale has made in building communities of readers gives management the confidence that brand extensions will continue to fuel growth. The company has the capacity, the talent, and the vision to think big.

2006
January: Nancy Pelosi is sworn in as first woman Speaker of the House.

February: The XX Olympic Winter Games open in Turin, Italy.

February 8: *The Journal of the American Medical Association* releases results of an 8-year-long study that finds a low-fat diet doesn't lower risk of heart disease, cancer, and stroke.

Spring: *Bicycling* magazine takes BikeTown to Botswana.

May: *Backpacker* wins the National Magazine Award in the magazine section category.

Rodale is named one of *Working Mother*'s 100 Best companies for working mothers for the first time.

August: Pluto is demoted from its status as a planet. It is now a "dwarf planet."

Fall: Advertising Age names Rodale the Magazine Publisher of the year.

***Men's Health* and *Prevention* launch in India.**

The Rodale Pleasant Park Community Garden in New York City's East Harlem was once an abandoned area but now proudly supports lush community gardens.

Indeed, the company that traces its origins to a few ideas in J. I. Rodale's prodigious mind and scraps of paper on his dining room table had grown into a large institution publishing nine national magazines and more than 100 books yearly, reaching more than 29 million customers, employing more than 1,000 staff located in offices in Emmaus, New York, Chicago, Detroit, Los Angeles, and San Francisco, and boasting annual sales of more than $600 million. "We're very strong today," said Murphy. "We have established a new level of financial security and success, which is the foundation one needs to allow one to be creative."

In many ways, Rodale is a changed company, with an expanded scope of operations and a large number of new faces. "I've found it to be inspiring," said Maria Rodale. "The new people who have come in had a hunger for our mission, and it fulfilled a longing for many of them to have a job that they could work at but that also has meaning."

Despite all the growth and accolades, despite the rise of operations that spanned globe and the burgeoning trade publishing business, Rodale remains at its core the same company it has always been in some fundamental ways. The company and its products are bound together by common threads and ideals: health and active living, authenticity and credibility, practicality, inspiration, and leadership, empowering individuals to change their lives and the world in which they live. Rodale is intent on enabling people all over the world, with all kinds of interests and capabilities, to live their whole lives. "Living your whole life is about putting the pieces together so you can always be and feel like your whole self–no matter where you are or what you're doing," as Ardie puts it. And the company is still intent on producing high-quality editorial products. As of spring 2008, five Rodale magazines received a collective 16 nominations for National Magazine Awards.

True to its roots, the company remains an energetic promoter of J. I. Rodale's first obsession: the organic message. In 2005, the Rodale family and *Organic Gardening* magazine donated $250,000 to support an organic garden in East Harlem, where Mexican immigrants are growing produce on a previously abandoned lot. In 2003, the Rodale family received the Organic Trade Association's Organic Leadership Award. In spring 2004, Maria Rodale was honored by the

The home of J. I. and Anna Rodale has been remodeled and preserved for generations to come.

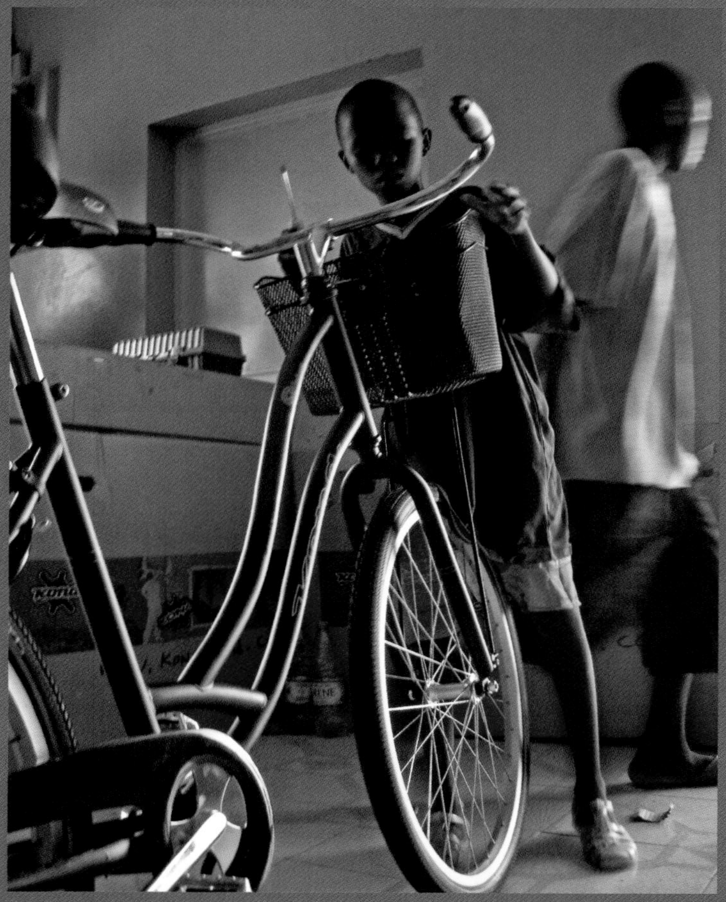

Bicycling magazine partnered with Kona Bicycle and other corporate sponsors to expand its popular BikeTown program to Botswana, Senegal, and Namibia in 2006 and 2007. The Rodale Institute and Anthony Rodale (*at right*) participated in Senegal's program.

In bottom left photo, the BikeTown Namibia team, from left: Steve Madden, Anne Thompson, Sean Leslie, Michelle Gault, Joey Parr, Beryl Mohr, Brad Shroeder, Victor Nakalenga, David Brienza, and Erich Afrikaner

Audubon Society with its inaugural Women in Conservation Award for both her own efforts and also those of Rodale Inc. to further environmental conservation and education. (In 1998, Bob had been recognized by Audubon as one of 100 people who had shaped the environmental movement.) And the Rodale Institute continues to make contributions to science, to public policy, and to the greater awareness of organic ideas.

Rodale also remains committed to continuing the work of improving people's ability to manage and improve their own health. In fall 2003, Rodale sponsored a company-wide initiative to address the issue of childhood obesity. The company collaborated with *ABC News* on a one-hour special, and each of Rodale's nine magazine titles ran articles on childhood obesity in their November issues. And in October 2004, when the United States suffered a flu-vaccine shortage, Rodale's editors published a host of preventive measures on its Web site for free. "What does Rodale stand for?" asks Heidi Rodale. "Empowering people, and giving them information they can use to make their lives better."

The company also remains true to its deep roots by maintaining a commitment to having its people, products, and services do larger work in the world. Starting in 2006, working with the Bristol-Myers Squibb Foundation and the Kona Bicycle Company, *Bicycling* took its highly regarded BikeTown USA program to Botswana, Namibia, and Senegal. The program, BikeTown Africa, provides specially designed bikes to health-care workers who help in the delivery of home-health aids and services to patients with HIV and AIDS.

A global presence and a global corporate citizen, Rodale nonetheless remains firmly rooted in the soil in and around Emmaus, Pennsylvania, as it has for more than 60 years. The corporate nerve center remains in the small town to which J. I. and Joseph Rodale relocated their struggling manufacturing company in 1930. From the new building on South Mountain to the older headquarters on East Minor Street, from the former silk mill on North Street that now houses *Bicycling* and *Runner's World* to the velodrome in Trexlertown, from the old organic farm at the corner of Minesite Road and Cedar Crest Boulevard to the Rodale Institute in

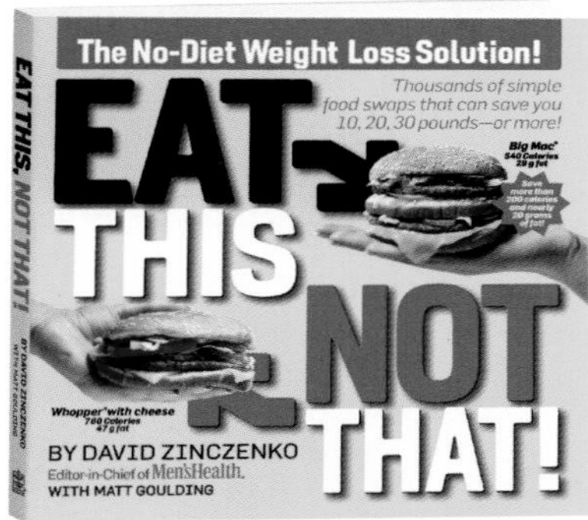

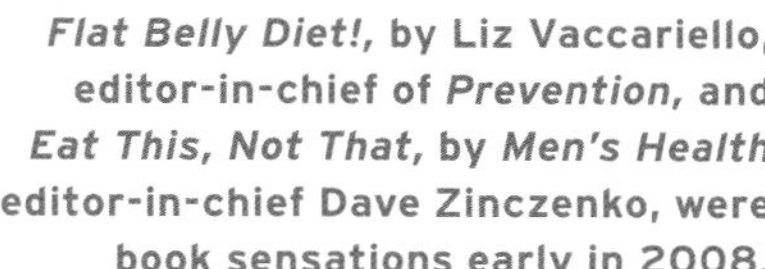

Flat Belly Diet!, by Liz Vaccariello, editor-in-chief of *Prevention*, and *Eat This, Not That*, by *Men's Health* editor-in-chief Dave Zinczenko, were book sensations early in 2008.

Maxatawny, Rodale has planted deep roots and built strong limbs throughout its home community.

The ideas and visions that took root in this fertile ground have proven so powerful that they have echoed and been amplified throughout the world. "The forest has grown up, and Rodale has become the grandfather tree," said Anthony. "Our intent was to make a major change in society, and in a sense Rodale has been integrated and accepted now as a player in society." To a degree that J. I. and Robert Rodale could not have anticipated, the organic message, the appeal of preventive medicine, and the imperative to improve personal fitness have become mainstream ideas, large industries, and integral parts of modern life.

Rodale sees as its mission not simply to make profits and entertain, amuse, and divert—although Rodale does all those things and does them well. Rather, it is the rare company that sees as one of its core missions to empower and inspire, to enable personal growth and development, and to help people build up and regenerate their minds, bodies, spirits, homes, and communities and the world. "We're not just publishing," said Ardie, who stepped down as chairman and took on the role of Chief Inspiration Officer in June 2007. "We're trying to make the world a better place, a healthier place." That ethos carries over to the way the company regards its role as an employer. Whether it is offering healthy food in the cafeteria, sponsoring wellness programs, or maintaining a family-friendly environment, the company seeks to enrich and improve the lives of the talented people who make Rodale Inc. thrive. In 2006, Rodale was named one of *Working Mother*'s 100 Best Companies for working mothers.

Dave Zinczenko was named Editor of the Year by *Adweek* magazine in spring 2008.

And in the fall of 2006, in a validation of the company's strategy, *Advertising Age* named Rodale the Magazine Publishing Company of the Year. The company had "transformed itself into a responsive, nimble-on-its-feet mainstream force," *Ad Age* concluded. "With its emphasis on health, fitness, and organic, Rodale is perfectly positioned."

Rodale's challenge today is to continue to push the established businesses into new directions. "We have to have the courage to look where our customers and our advertisers are

2007
May: *Backpacker* is sold to Active Interest Media in Boulder, Colorado.

June: Ardie Rodale steps down as chairman and takes on title of Chief Inspriation Officer. Maria Rodale steps up to be chairman of the board.

July: Ardie publishes her fourth book, *Everyday Miracles: Reflections on Living an Extraordinary Life.*

Fall: The Rodale Institute and *Bicycling* magazine take BikeTown to Senegal.

October: Marion Jones, winner of three gold medals at the 2000 Olympic Games, admits to taking steroids.

October: Al Gore and the UN's Intergovernmental Panel on Climate Change win the 2007 Nobel Peace Prize for their work on global warming.

Al Gore

October: *Prevention* is named to *Advertising Age*'s "A-List," ranking no. 6 out of 10.

***Men's Health* is ranked no. 1 on the "Media Brand Leaders Hot List" of *Adweek, Brandweek,* and *Mediaweek*.**

At the close of 2007, *Prevention* ranks as the 9th largest magazine in the nation.

Mary Ann Bekkendahl, Ardie Rodale, Steve Murphy, and Maria Rodale rejoice in the news that *Advertising Age* named Rodale the Magazine Publishing Company of the year in 2006.

moving—the online arena—and to ensure we can continue the mission in the new environment," said Steve Murphy. And it must continue to forge new paths. "Our main job is still to be on the forefront in health, wellness, and the environment," said Maria Rodale. "But we have to be able to step outside again, to keep our fingers on the pulse of what is going on that is new and radical and different."

As it looks to the future, Rodale will continue to be guided by the principles, experience, and example of the Rodale family. "Our father taught us the mission of Rodale," said Heather Rodale. "And because we live and breathe it, we're the caretakers. It's our job to hold management accountable for the mission." But the company has evolved beyond the impromptu and comparatively informal style favored by J. I. and Robert Rodale. The company has a board of directors that includes two non-family members. And in recent years, Rodale has started an intensive effort to educate the 11 members of the fourth generation of Rodales about the business. "We take the education process very seriously," said Heather. "We want them to learn how to be responsible owners." Going forward, it's no guarantee that members of the family will occupy senior management positions. But the Rodales are intent on managing the company as an entity that will continue to be inextricably linked with the vision laid down by J.I. and Robert. "A private family business has the strategic luxury of making decisions for the long-term good," said Maria, who succeeded her mother as chairman of the Board of Directors in June 2007.

In its seventh decade, and under its third generation of family leadership, Rodale is neither complacent nor comfortable with power. Despite all the success and growth, the company has never succumbed to a sense of entitlement. And in the millions of magazines and books that it publishes every year, the exuberance and creative spirit of J. I. Rodale, the determination and humility of Bob Rodale, the spirit and strength of Ardie Rodale—and the promise of a bright future—shine through. As Maria Rodale puts it: "Our goal is to reach as many people as possible with our message and to change the world for the better."

2008
March: Dave Zinczenko is named Editor of the Year by *Adweek*, *Brandweek*, and *Mediaweek*.

***Adweek*, *Brandweek*, and *Mediaweek* name three Rodale magazine titles to the "10 under 50" hot list of titles with less than $50 million in advertising revenues: *Women's Health* at no. 1, *Best Life* at no. 2, and *Bicycling* at no. 10.**

"One of these fine days, the public is going to wake up and will pay for eggs, meats, vegetables, etc., according to how they were produced."

J. I. Rodale, in *Organic Farming and Gardening*, May 1942

ACKNOWLEDGMENTS

THIS BOOK HAS BEEN AT LEAST FIVE YEARS in the making and the team of people who came together to create it has evolved over the years.

We would like to thank the people who made significant contributions, helping to get the book off the ground: Eric Baker, Tami Booth Corwin, Charlie Gerras, Cindy Goldstein, Brenda Miller, Jackie Ney, Chris Potash, and David Rodale.

A core team of people carried out the project, meeting weekly, edging ever closer to the goal. Our sincere thanks to Nancy N. Bailey, Andy Carpenter, Robin Hepler, Mark Kintzel, Darlene Schneck, and Anthony Serge.

Other people contributed in ways that were most helpful to the process and we appreciate their input. Thanks to Marshall Ackerman, Tom Aczel, Beth Bazar, Nanette Bendyna, Keith Biery, Pat Brown, Amby Burfoot, Mia Carbonell, Budd Coates, Jonathon Collani, Sara Cox, Ellen Destasio, Lynn Donches, Duane Elsasser, Diana Erney, Dolores Evangelista, Jim Federico, Eileen Fehr, Carol Hupping Fisher, Jim Gallucci, Jennifer Giandomenico, John Haberern, Faith Hague, Bob Juliano, Jen Keiser, Chris Krogermeier, Steve Madden, Caroline McCall, Lisa McGilvray, Erin McGuigan, Nadea Mina, Steve Murphy, Scott Meyer, Brooke Myers, Christa Neu, Tom Ney, Alexander Norelli, Josephine Parr, Anita Patterson, Cindy Ratzlaff, Eric Rineheimer, Joshua Rodriguez, Staci Sander, Sue Signorello, Ann Snyder, and Kathy Wieand.

Our deepest gratitude goes to writer Daniel Gross, who traveled back and forth from New York innumerable times to do research in the Rodale archives, digging through old records, letters, file folders, and so on, to ferret out Rodale history milestones and turned those pieces into a coherent story.

And, finally, we thank the Rodale family who provided photographs and stories and read and reread versions of the manuscript and pages.

PHOTO CREDITS

© Nick Cardillicchio: 266 (David Zinczenko)
© Dennis Chalkin: 108
Courtesy of the Comrades Marathon Association: 217 (Amby Burfoot)
© Corbis: 18 (prohibition), 23 (James Joyce), 50 (soldiers), 102 (Richard Nixon & Nikita Krushchev), 105 (Richard Nixon & John Kennedy), 128 (Thurgood Marshall), 136 (Neil Armstrong), 167 (peace accords).
© Ansa/Corbis: 36 (William Faulkner)
© Bettmann/Corbis: x, 4 (Horatio Alger), 6 (Andrew Carnegie), 7 (subway), 8–9, 12, 16 (Herbert Swope), 17 (Nicholas II), 20 (Babe Ruth), 21 (F. Scott Fitzgerald), 22 (Rudolph Valentino), 28 (Cole Porter), 31 (Charles Lindbergh), 33 (newspaper), 34 (Sinclair Lewis), 38 (Apollo Theater, Shirley Temple), 39 (George Gershwin), 41 (Hindenburg), 44 (Howard Hughes), 50 (John Steinbeck), 56 (Pearl Harbor), 64 (D-Day), 66 (surrender), 69 (Winston Churchill, *It's A Wonderful Life*), 70 (Jackie Robinson), 77 (soldiers), 82 (J.D. Salinger), 88 (Jonas Salk, Edmund Hillary & Tenzing Norgay), 93 (Roger Bannister), 95 (Emmett Till), 96 (Elvis Presley), 99 (Sputnik), 106 (Yuri Gagarin), 111 (Rachel Carson), 112 (newspapers), 115 (Jean Paul Sartre), 126 (Michael DeBakey, arch), 132 (soldiers), 151 (Richard Nixon & Mao Tse-Tung), 155 (Spiro Agnew), 156 (Patricia Hearst), 161 (*Saturday Night Live* cast), 162 (John Sculley, Steve Jobs & Steve Wozniak; Bill Rodgers), 165 (Elvis Presley), 166 (Love Canal), 168 (Three Mile Island), 169 (demonstrators), 170 (Mount St. Helens), 171 (Ronald Reagan), 177 (Walter Cronkite), 178 (memorial), 180 (*MASH* cast), 181 (Sally Ride), 202 (Exxon *Valdez*), 217 (Ben Johnson)
© Geoffrey Clements/Corbis: 15 (*Water Lilies*)
© Ashley Cooper/Corbis: 243 (organic produce)
© Envision/Corbis: 224 (USDA organic)
© Najlah Feanny/Corbis: 249 (grocery store)
© Christopher Felver/Corbis: 163 (Saul Bellow)
© Owen Franken/Corbis: 164 (gas shortage)
© Robert Holmes/Corbis: 171 (Whole Foods Market)
© E.O. Hoppé/Corbis: 10 (Rudyard Kipling)
© Hulton-Deutsch Collection/Corbis: 5 (airship), 11 (Ernest Shackleton), 29 (John Scopes), 40 (Jesse Owens), 100 (people), 112 (Martin Luther King Jr.), 160 (Arthur Ashe)
© Phil Klein/Corbis: 247 (strawberries)
© Dan Lamont/Corbis: 256 (cows)
© James Leynse/Corbis: 153 (cigarette pack)
© The Mariners' Museum/Corbis: 13 (*Titanic*)
© Wally McNamee/Corbis: 198 (ice skaters, C. Everett Koop)
© Gail Mooney/Corbis: 103 (Guggenheim)
© Michael Ochs Archives/Corbis: 122 (Malcolm X)
© Neal Preston/Corbis: 190 (Farm Aid)
© Roger Ressmeyer/Corbis: 100 (NASA), 179 (Alice Walker), 186 (computer)
© Reuters/Corbis: 84 (Anne Frank), 170 (Lech Walesa), 193 (Greg Lemond), 222 (sheep), 233 (Sydney Opera House), 266 (Al Gore)
© Sunset Boulevard/Corbis: 60 (*Casablanca*)
© Swim Ink/Corbis: 16 (Vladimir Lenin)
© Sygma/Corbis : 225 (John Glenn)
© David Turnley/Corbis: 203 (*Seinfeld* cast)
© Peter Turnley/Corbis: 190 (Mikhail Gorbachev)
© Underwood & Underwood/Corbis: 20 (suffragettes), 56 (Orson Welles)
© Stuart Westmorland/Corbis: 192 (Statue of Liberty)
© Oscar White/Corbis: 37 (Franklin Roosevelt)
© William Whitehurst/Corbis: 194 (label)
© Doug Wilson/Corbis: 160 (Bill Gates & Paul Allen)
© Steve Allen/Brand X Pictures/Corbis: 219 (tomatoes)
© Sergey Chirikov/EPA/Corbis: 132 (musical)
© NASA/Roger Ressmeyer/Corbis: 111 (John Glenn)
© Eric Gaillard/Reuters/Corbis: 230 (Lance Armstrong)
© John Hillery/Reuters/Corbis: 232 (Prius)
© Micah Walter/Reuters/Corbis: 154 (protestors)
© Olivia Baumgartner/Sygma/Corbis: 165 (child)
© Hans Gedda/Sygma/Corbis: 204 (Nelson Mandela)
© JP Laffont/Sygma/Corbis: 156 (Richard Nixon)
© Jacques Langevin/Sygma/Corbis: 205 (soldiers)
© Universal/TempSport/Corbis: 153 (Eddy Merckx)
© Mystic Stamp Company/Handout/Reuters/Corbis: 17 (stamp)
Courtesy of the Emmaus Historical Society: 178 (downtown Emmaus)
© Time & Life Pictures/Getty Images: 40 (*Life* magazine)
© Image Club: 258 (flags), 259 (flags)
© Christopher Hudson/Istockphoto: 258–259 (map)
Courtesy of Seong Kwon Photography/Suben-Dougherty Partnership, Architects: 257 (building interiors)
Courtesy of Michael Linke: 264 *(bottom right)*
© Dana Meilijson: 239 (Steve Murphy)
© Don Fisher/*The Morning Call*: 174

Courtesy of Amy Gavaris/New York Restoration Project: 262
© Susan Pollack: vii (Heidi Rodale), 224 (Maria Rodale)
Courtesy of Anthony Rodale: 264 *(center left)*
Courtesy of the Rodale Family Archives: vi (sculpture unveiling), 2, 3, 4 (Cohen family), 5 (contract), 6 (tickets), 7 (Michael Cohen), 10 (gentlemen), 11 (Cohen sisters), 13 (Jerome Cohen, grades), 14, 15 (Jerome Cohen), 17 (Jerome Cohen, letter), 18 (Jerome Cohen), 19, 21 (Jerome Cohen, newspaper clipping), 22 (Joe & Esther Rodale, car), 23 (pamphlet), 24, 26, 27, 28 (Andrews family), 29 (Anna Andrews), 30, 31 (J.I. & Anna Rodale, traffic plan), 32, 33 (farm), 34 (J.I. & Joseph Rodale, letterhead), 35, 36 (J.I. Rodale), 37 (magazine cover), 39 (J.I. & Anna Rodale), 41 (Rodale family), 42, 43, 45, 46, 49, 52, 54 (Albert Howard), 55 (farmhouse), 56 (farm), 57, 58, 63, 64 (cows), 65, 68, 69 (J.I. Rodale & Gloria Swanson), 71, 72 (story classic), 73 (Robert Rodale), 74, 77 (J.I. & Robert Rodale), 78, 81, 82 (Bob & Ardie Rodale), 84 (J.I. Rodale), 85, 86, 87, 88 (J.I. Rodale), 89, 94, 96 (J.I. Rodale), 97, 98, 100 (building), 102 (Bob Rodale), 103 (J.I. & Anna Rodale), 107, 114, 118, 119, 120 (tickets), 121, 122 (documents), 123, 125, 130, 131, 132 (certificate, ID card), 133 (team), 138, 139, 143, 144, 145, 146, 147, 148, 151 (Bob & Anna Rodale), 152, 153 (Ardie Rodale), 154 (newsletters), 155 (*Annual Report*), 157 (farm), 158, 173, 176, 179 (farm), 181 (op-ed), 185, 186 (Rodale family), 193 (David Rodale), 203 (Bob Rodale), 204 (Bob Rodale), 205 (Bob Rodale), 207, 208, 209, 210, 219 (Hillary Clinton & Ardie Rodale), 234, 235, 241
The Evening & Sunday Bulletin/Courtesy of the Rodale Family Archives: 198 (staff)
Paul George/Courtesy of the Rodale Family Archives: 269
© Rodale Images: 141 (Ruth Stout), 150, 159, 160 (velodrome, Bob Rodale), 161 (bike race), 163 (fish ponds, Energy Cycle, food dehydrator, solar greenhouse), 164 (amaranth), 165 (building, *Sieve*), 166 (executives, test kitchen), 171 (photo lab, Rodale Resources), 182, 183, 184 (Bob Rodale), 188, 189, 191 (*Vitamin A+*), 194 (booklet, newsletter), 195 (executives), 196, 197, 200, 212, 213 (*Solar Magic*), 225 (logos), 226 (sign), 231, 232 (logo), 247 (book cover), 248, 252, 253 (*diane* cover), 256 (book cover), 260, 266 (book covers)
© James Gallucci/Rodale Images: 99 (*Health Finder* cover), 124 (*Skeet Shooting Review* cover)
© Robert Gerheart/Rodale Images: 171 (Food Center)
© John P. Hamel/Rodale Images: 238
© Mark Kintzel/Rodale Images: 246 (Ardie Rodale & children)
© Thomas MacDonald/Rodale Images: 37 (magazine interior), 40 (Verb Finder), 44 (book cover), 47, 48 (book cover), 51 (*This is Upton Sinclair, The Flivver King*), 61, 62, 66 (*Pay Dirt*), 70 (book cover), 72 (*The Healthy Hunzas*), 73 (story classics), 75 (*The Organic Farmer*), 76, 80, 83, 90, 91, 92 (book interior), 95 (magazine cover, book cover), 99 (*Health Builder* cover), 104, 105 (*Compost Science*), 106 (book interior), 111 (book cover), 112 (*Health Bulletin*), 115 (magazine cover), 116 (magazine cover), 117, 124 (*Skeet Shooting Review* interior), 126 (magazine interior), 127 (FDA), 128 (magazine cover), 134, 135, 136 (book covers), 140, 141 (magazine cover), 142, 155 (book cover), 156 (book covers), 157 (book cover), 162 (book covers), 167 (magazine cover & interior), 168 (magazine cover), 169 (magazine cover), 170 (magazine & book covers), 172, 177 (magazine covers), 180 (magazine covers & interior), 181 (*The Cornucopia Project*), 184 (magazine cover), 187, 190 (magazine covers), 191 (magazine covers), 192 (magazine covers), 193 (book cover), 195 (magazine covers), 199, 202 (magazine covers), 206, 213 (*Reflections*, magazine covers), 214 (book cover), 215, 216, 218, 219 (poster), 221, 222 (magazine cover), 223, 230 (book cover, magazine cover & interior), 233 (magazine cover), 239 (Maria Rodale), 240, 242, 244, 245, 249 (book covers), 250, 253 (*Women's Health* cover), 257 (building exterior), 261
© Mitch Mandel/Rodale Images: 38 (*Fact Digest*), 48 (book interior), 51 (*My Cousin Mark Twain*), 54 (book cover), 55 (book covers), 59, 60 (*War Digest*), 67, 92 (book cover), 93 (magazine cover & interior, book cover), 95 (magazine interior), 101, 105 (book cover), 110, 113, 115 (magazine interior), 116 (magazine interior), 120 (posters, script), 127 (diet control), 129, 137, 236, 251, 254–255
© Christa Neu/Rodale Images: vi–vii (farm scene), 201, 214 (building), 220 (building exterior, sign, kiva interior), 226 (tractor, garden, flowers, farm), 227 (chickens, flowers), 243 (child-care center), 247 (Aquatic Center), 263 (red door)
© Lori Stahl/Rodale Images: 136 (Fitness House), 180 (Energy Center), 220 (kiva skylight, kiva exterior), 226 (goats), 227 (geese, arbor, hat & glove, sculpture), 228, 229, 263 (library interior)
Courtesy of Bradley Schroeder: 264 *(top left)*
Courtesy of James Startt: 264 *(center right)*
© Brenda Veldtman: 264 *(top right, bottom left)*
© Andrew Walker: 267
Wikimedia Commons: 29 (*The Great Gatsby*), 75 (*1984*), 133 (catalog)
Tiziano Garuti/Wikimedia Commons: 164 (computer)
© Darren Modricker/Willow Street Pictures, Inc.: 246 (Ardie Rodale)

INDEX

Underscored page references indicate time line entries. **Boldface** references indicate photographs and photo captions.